Scott S Zabower
October 1983

SUCCESSFUL RESTAURANT OPERATION

distributed by

the culinary institute of america

bookstore CIA

SUCCESSFUL RESTAURANT OPERATION

T. F. Chiffriller, Jr.

CBI Publishing Company, Inc.
51 Sleeper Street
Boston, Massachusetts 02210

Production Editor: Kathy Savago
Text designer: Trisha Hanlon
Cover designer: Bruce Kennett
Compositor: Modern Graphics

Library of Congress Cataloging in Publication Data

Chiffriller, Thomas F.
    Successful restaurant operation.

    Includes index.
    1. Restaurants, lunch rooms, etc.   I. Title.
TX911.2.C46   647'.95'068   81-10093
ISBN 0-8436-2221-0   AACR2

Printing (last digit): 9 8 7 6 5 4 3 2 1

Printed in the United States of America.

To my father

Contents

Preface

I had two reasons for writing this book. First, there was at that time no book devoted entirely to the small restaurant operator. Second, the inexperienced person who wants to open a restaurant has no idea where to turn to get started. I hope that this book has solved both these problems.

Many books have been written about restaurant operations. The better ones deal primarily with the medium-size or large restaurant. A few books are devoted to the smaller operator, but these are incomplete and lack detail, and, therefore, of little practical value. The beginner needs an accurate map to follow every step of the way. Systems that work well for the large operator can be too cumbersome and involved for the small restaurant owner.

Fortunately for the eating-out public, there are still individuals with imagination and initiative who feel they are capable of running a fine restaurant. Such people place excellent service and quality food above all else. Their satisfaction is derived from pleasing others. This book is intended to give such individuals an insight into the small restaurant business and to provide them with the information they will need to get started.

The restaurant business is demanding. It requires your money, your time, and all the effort and attention you can give it. In the end, it may change your social life, your marriage, and your health, but in return, it can give you a deep satisfaction, new friends, financial rewards, and a prestige which can more than offset the setbacks which may occur.

One of my goals is to have the reader understand the need for an efficient operation. The money required to start a restaurant is not easily obtained. To lose it all, because of poor financial management, would be a disaster to a small owner. Good planning can never be overemphasized.

The restaurant business is an indispensable part of our society. Restaurants are used for business meetings, celebrations, entertaining and as places in which to relax. True, such events take place in restaurants of all sizes, but somehow they seem more meaningful in the small, intimate places. That may be one reason people expect more from the smaller restaurant than the large, impersonal one. There is an unquestionable need for the small restaurant and the individual attention it provides.

To be successful today one must be both good and different. The average, run-of-the-mill operation will not survive. There is no incentive for the diner to seek you out, if you do not provide something unique. This is one reason I have stressed quality throughout this book. It is not necessary to have French food, for example, but it is necessary to have the highest standards for the food and service you do provide.

The material presented in the following chapters is based primarily on my own experience and that of other operators. It is meant to provide insight and solid background material to aid you in making the myriad decisions that will be required in your new venture. The factual information (as opposed to opinion) is backed up by formal sources.

Finally, I want to acknowledge, with grateful thanks, the help I received from my family and friends. Without their help and support, I probably would not have been suc-

cessful enough to write this book. I especially thank Nancy, who willingly jumped into a world she knew nothing about. My daughter Kathy must also be singled out in this regard. Thanks to my friends, Vernon, Harold, Bob, Peggy, Dorothy, and Douglas whose help and encouragement were priceless.

Good luck to you, in your new venture.

It is not a crime to be idealistic
but it is a sin to die old and poor.

Author unknown

SUCCESSFUL
RESTAURANT
OPERATION

Chapter One

Personal Problems Facing the New Restaurateur

The first challenge to be faced when entering any sort of small business is obtaining proper financing. In addition, there are problems of a universal nature, such as hiring personnel and finding a suitable location. These are real things which can be met head-on and settled. But what of the personal problems encountered in a new business, especially the restaurant business? They can be categorized as:

1. Developing personality,
2. Getting along with and understanding others,
3. Making decisions,
4. Developing physical and mental stamina,
5. Coping with personal and social needs.

None of the five is unique to the restaurant business, but each must be handled in a special fashion by the new restaurateur.

Developing Personality

What is personality and why is it important? To answer these questions, we should first define the term.

> *Personality is the distinctive quality of an individual that motivates his or her behavior, temperament, emotions, and character.*

We often speak of the quality of other people's personality. "He is so dull," or "she just bubbles with enthusiasm" for example. We are referring to the way others project themselves—the impression they make on us.

Developing a pleasant personality is a real challenge for someone who has not had such an opportunity before entering the restaurant business. You can read any number of books on the development of a satisfactory personality, but only you are capable of improving your own personality. You must be sincere, or you may do more harm than good. Most people dislike hypocrites. You must be calm when the unusual occurs, you must be friendly and pleasant when you would rather not be. Finally, you must be able to stick with it when it would be easier to give up.

The key to success in business is you and your personality.

Getting Along with and Understanding Others

I am a strong believer in principles. Everyone should have them. Set your goals, stick by them, and don't vacillate from one occasion to another. Vacillation confuses people, especially employees, and they are uncertain how to respond. Learn to get along with people within the framework of your ideals. There will be times when a guest may present an opposite point of view from yours. The test is the way you handle it. Do you argue, ridicule, or merely change the subject? By choosing the latter, you have not really lost face or changed your thinking, you have just sidestepped the subject. That's getting along. There will come a time when one of your principles will be directly challenged. When this happens, put your foot down and face up to it. Don't compromise.

Understanding others is important in helping you get along. Put people in categories. Treat those in particular categories in certain ways. Most of your guests will be fine, down-to-earth people who will not need analyzing. You will only have problems with those who do not fit your categories.

By understanding others, you will gain insight into how to get along with them. This is an important aspect of keeping satisfied customers.

Making Decisions

If making decisions is not one of your strong points, it is certainly an ability worth developing. To be able to make a decision when one is needed is an admirable trait. In our everyday life, we are seldom called upon to make important decisions. In the restaurant business, you may be called upon to make them in rapid succession. Most of your decisions will involve employees. Employees want someone else to make decisions. They seldom volunteer for this responsibility. Be capable of making quick and correct decisions. Don't flounder or stutter. When a decision must be made, stay calm, analyze the facts, and give an answer to those who need it. Don't sidetrack an issue. You'll be respected for your decision-making ability.

Developing Physical and Mental Stamina

The restaurant business is not unique in demanding a great deal of time and effort from its owners. The amount of time involved, especially in the early stages, can be enormous. With all my previous food service experience, I had no idea of the number of hours I would be working in my own business. Eighteen-hour days were not unusual. You too will discover countless tasks you had not anticipated. In addition to the physical stress, there is the mental pressure. Decisions must be made constantly. Where does this go? How should I do it? Where is the money coming from? Why didn't they deliver the rolls? Are the candles lit? *You* are the central feeding station for problems. No wonder the restaurant business is plagued by so much mediocrity. It is far simpler to tell someone to do it any old way, just so you have one less decision to make.

Much of the initial stress will disappear after a month or so. Both you and your employees learn their basic job functions and settle into them. Many problems iron themselves out with time.

Once the early problems are put to rest, you can look forward to revising some of the concepts that are not working out as you had planned. After that you can start creating new ideas to keep more customers coming.

So you see, it's never dull. If you do not have the physical stamina, you can always hire someone to do the work, but the mental energy must be all yours. After all, would you want someone else making the decisions?

Coping with Personal and Social Needs

If you are single, you can devote all of your time to the restaurant without feeling the guilt of neglecting a family. Unfortunately, you will find friends and social life slipping away. Your life style will be completely changed, at least for a while. You become devoted to the new venture. Friends and family often find this withdrawal difficult to understand, and this creates personal difficulties.

If you are married when you enter the small restaurant business, it is important that your spouse have a part in the operation. Otherwise, one partner becomes like the single person mentioned before and the other is left out. There is no assurance, of course, that the two of you can work together in harmony. Only you can make a realistic appraisal of your personal situation. The stress of opening a small business is very strong. It will take two understanding people to keep the marriage together.

In the beginning, a common problem to both the single and married is an almost complete lack of income—no weekly paychecks. Until you are successful, the only money available to you is the amount you can eke out of the business. This too exerts a tremendous amount of pressure on your personal and social life. Until the business matures, it will probably be quite a while before you can enjoy life as you did before.

If after reading all this you are getting a little apprehensive, don't be surprised. Many persons contemplating entry into their own business are not aware of the limitations imposed on them by such a venture. If you are not willing to work harder than you ever did before, survive on a limited income, get along with others, develop a pleasant personality, and forego your usual social life, you should think again before starting your own business. Perhaps you are one of the lucky ones who will step into a going, successful business or become an instant hit. However, most will not be so fortunate and their life style will change drastically. If you feel the eventual rewards, and there are many, outweigh the initial limitations, then go to it.

Chapter Two

What You Need to Know About Financing and Money Management and Didn't Know Who to Ask

Capital is the money needed to purchase and operate a business. This chapter will help you locate sources of capital and give you a firm understanding of the information required when approaching them.

Regardless of your talent, industry, or ability to be a success, you cannot start a business without capital. In addition to the purchase price of the business and fixed expenses thereafter, you need money to purchase equipment, food, supplies, and liquor. Most potential entrepreneurs do not have the cash or credit for all these expenditures.

Bear in mind that your past business experience will be the key to obtaining a loan. If you have experience in the field of your proposed venture, the loan will be significantly easier to obtain. On the other hand, the loan will be appreciatively more difficult to obtain when the venture is out of your field. This should not discourage you. Every day there are people who enter new businesses with little experience. Because of sound, prac-

tical business sense and experience, these people are successful. The way you present your background and expertise may be the key to obtaining the loan.

This chapter deals with raising capital to get started. However, it is important to note that all the sources mentioned can be used later if you need additional capital for one reason or the other. At that time you will also have internal financing, a source which is not available at the outset. Furthermore, you will have developed a good credit rating, which will make additional borrowing much easier. Internal financing and a good credit rating are two good reasons to start out on a firm basis.

What you are looking for, then, is the money to purchase either a going business or the potential location for a business, and the necessary funds needed to remodel, and possibly refurbish, an existing property or location in a suitable manner. You also need additional funds for the purchase of food, liquor and supplies, payroll, and any number of initial expenses that may arise. A good rule of thumb is to have enough money to cover a minimum of two months projected operating expenses because you never know how well things will go when you first open.

There are two basic forms of capital. One is *equity capital* and the other *debt capital*. Equity capital is that which you provide and stand to lose yourself. Debt capital is borrowed and must be paid back to the lender. There is almost always a charge for the second type of capital. Equity capital is of particular interest to anyone providing debt capital, because the lender wants to know what you stand to lose. Naturally, the more of your own funds you invest, the more confident lenders will be.

Sources of Equity Capital

Life Savings. You have probably been thinking about owning a business for some time. During this time you have been building up your savings in the form of bank savings, securities, or real estate. This will be your primary source of equity capital.

Life Insurance. Most people have (and are not always aware of) life insurance cash value. Except for term insurance, life insurance builds up loan values. This loan or cash value is available to you to borrow, at a low interest rate, whenever you need it. The larger and older the policy, the more cash value available. Call your insurance company to determine just how much is available to you.

Home Mortgage. If you have a mortgage on your home or any other property, it may pay you to refinance. This method will be advantageous if you have been paying off the first

mortgage for some time, or if the property has substantially appreciated in value. Refinancing will provide you with additional funds, but your mortgage payments will then be higher due to interest rates and a larger principal. If this higher monthly payment is a financial problem, it may not be advisable to refinance. A careful financial analysis will help you with this decision.

Personal Friends and Family. Borrowing from friends or relatives seems to bring about ill will and strained relationships. However, if all else fails, and they are willing, you may not be in a position to refuse. Parents and close friends are often willing to lend money without expecting a return because of their confidence in you and your ability.

Equity capital obtained in any of the above arrangements will be your personal contribution to the business. You will be personally responsible for repayment, if repayment is required.

Sources of Debt Capital

Banks. The best sources of debt capital are banks, but banks have a reputation for being conservative investors because of their need to protect their depositors. Because of this, a convincing argument concerning your ability, along with a complete picture of your financial condition, is necessary. You must have all the possible information that the bank will require available. This includes a financial statement of your net worth, a *pro forma* statement for the restaurant, your resume, and any other information you deem necessary or helpful. Do not be afraid of providing too much information. Just be sure it is relevant and not a lot of frosting. Loan committees look at your application purely from a business point of view. They may not be able to see the potential you see, because they are not restaurant people. You have to make them aware of this potential.

If you are not successful in obtaining a bank loan on your own financial merits, consider a *co-signer*. A co-signer will sign for a loan with you and guarantee repayment if you should default. Co-signers are not easy people to find because of the responsibility they incur. However, if you are able to come up with such a person, ask the bank to reconsider its decision with this new arrangement. If a bank refuses your application for a loan, ask them for the reasons. They will very often be happy to tell you. Such information may be useful when applying at other loan sources.

Present Owner. When selling a business or a property, the owner will often be happy to finance the sale. It will be done in much the same manner as a mortgage (*i.e.*, amortization of principal, plus interest). By providing such an arrangement, the owner has the sale and you have a large portion of your financing. In most cases, the owner will want no more than 30 percent down payment and the balance in periodic installments. Any such arrangement must be carefully worked out with your attorney. This type of financing works best when purchasing a complete business. If only the real estate is purchased in this way, additional money will be needed to convert the property into a restaurant. Such additional money may be difficult to obtain and will carry a high rate of interest (see section on chattel loans, p. 10).

Small Business Administration (SBA). This is an agency of the federal government set up to assist small businesses. My own experience with them has been very disappointing, probably due to my overly high expectations. Applying to the SBA is likely to be one of your most frustrating attempts to obtain funding. To begin with, the SBA seldom lends money directly. Except under *The Economic Opportunity Loan Program*, the SBA will not make a direct loan unless you are unable to get one through a private lender. The SBA's primary function is to guarantee loans, much like a co-signer.

There are three ways in which the SBA may be of value for your capital requirements. They may act as a guarantor for a loan obtained through a local bank, participate with a local bank in lending the money needed, or lend the needed money directly to you.

Regardless of which method is used, the first step is an attempt on your part to obtain a private loan from a bank. Only if the bank refuses your request can you apply directly to the SBA. When making application to the SBA you will need a letter from this bank (and another, if you are in a city with a population of over 200,000) stating the amount of the loan and the maturity. Give this information, along with a statement of your net worth, a *pro forma*, and your resume to the regional office. Be prepared to wait six to eight weeks for a decision. This is definitely a negative aspect of SBA financing. It can be quite disheartening if you are turned down.

The chance of obtaining a direct loan from the SBA is almost nonexistent. However, if you want to take the chance and can stand the wait, the advantages of lower interest rates, longer maturities, and more liberal collateral requirements will make it worthwhile.

To be eligible, you must be a small business, be of good character, have a certain amount of your own capital in the business, be able to prove you are capable of operating a business successfully, and demonstrate that the business will generate enough income to pay off the loan.

A better approach would be to find a bank who would consider your loan under the *Loan Guarantee Plan*. In any case, do not sit idly by waiting for the SBA to come through. Try other means of obtaining financing while you are waiting.

Finance Companies. There are finance companies willing to make loans to new business undertakings. Because they are willing to take risks more conservative investors would not take, their interest rates will be considerably higher and maturities will be shorter. Be careful not to lock yourself into terms you will have difficulty in meeting later on. Finance companies are satisfactory for small loans, but not advisable for large ones or those of long maturities. If you are so desperate as to have to consider a loan company for most of your financing, it would be a good idea to reevaluate your decision to enter business at this time. No matter which way you go, consult with your lawyer regarding the agreement.

Insurance Companies. Some insurance companies lend so-called venture capital. It is not easy money to obtain. However, this source is worth looking into.

Small Business Investment Companies (SBICs). Although these companies are licensed by the SBA, they operate independently of the government. Obtain names through your local SBA.

Other Agencies. The Office of Housing and Urban Development (HUD) is a federal agency that makes loans to restore and rehabilitate homes, buildings, and entire areas. It does not make loans for businesses. However, you as an individual may have a building you would like to restore. The intended use of the building will not limit your obtaining a loan to restore it, although local codes may. There are a number of requirements for HUD loans, and I would not begin to offer any encouragement with this type of loan. If the situation is appropriate, try it.

Another remote source is a national or local historical society. Either may want to see a particular building restored and be willing to lend, or even grant, money toward this end. If you can meet their restrictions or needs, give them a try.

Venture Capital Companies or Individuals. Venture capitalists are individuals or entities who are willing to invest in high risk situations, such as new restaurants, with the expectation of better than average return on their money. In return for this capital investment, venture capitalists will require a large percentage of ownership. You should understand that with this type of loan you are taking on a partner who will share in your profits and probably offer advice from time to time. If such limitations are not what you want, do not consider obtaining money from a venture capitalist. Contact the SBA and the local Chamber of Commerce for names.

Figure 2–1.

Precautions for Obtaining Loans

1. Do not finalize any loan without first showing it to your attorney or accountant.
2. Be sure you can prepay a loan. Be sure it can be prepaid without penalty.

3. If you get into a participation loan, be sure the terms are carefully spelled out. Also, be sure you can get out of the loan under certain conditions.

4. If you obtain a construction loan, be sure you do not pay interest on the commitment. You only want to pay on the money as you use it.

5. Shop around for the very best terms.

6. Remember, a discounted or prepaid loan carries a higher rate of interest than is indicated because you are getting less money to begin with.

7. Try to get a loan commitment before you negotiate for the business. That way you will know how far you can commit yourself.

8. Get all loan commitments in writing. Do not trust oral commitments.

Loans Are Not Always What They Appear to Be

Discounted loans are more expensive than straight loans. A discounted loan is one that provides the principal after the interest has been paid (in advance).

Illustration

Discounted

Principal $50,000, Interest rate 9%

$50,000 × .09 = $4,500
$50,000 − $4,500 = $45,500

(amount you receive)

You are really paying 9.89% interest
$4,500 ÷ $45,500 = 9.89%

Simple Interest

You still pay $4,500 interest, but it is paid over the life of the loan. You receive $50,000 initially.

Other Financing Arrangements

Until now, we have been concerned with the raising of major capital. There are areas of financing, although not large, which may still be of aid. These concern leasing, extended terms, and discounts. The areas to be covered are:

1. Financing or leasing equipment,
2. Borrowing equipment,
3. Purchasing of equipment by a second party,
4. Obtaining a credit line with purveyors.

If you are buying new equipment, you will most likely be buying it from a kitchen supply house. These houses are usually quite willing to provide financing, or to arrange it with a local bank or some large equipment company. The terms will be fair because the equipment itself will be used as collateral. Similar arrangements can usually be made for furnishings. The advantage of this method of financing is the small monthly payment instead of a large, initial lump sum.

Leasing is another method of obtaining needed equipment and furnishings without a large initial outlay. An advantage of this method is that you may eventually purchase the item if you so desire. If not, you may continue leasing. In many cases, repair service is included with the lease arrangement. In addition to the interest charge, the cost to you will be for wear and tear (depreciation), dealer profit, and service. At the end of the lease you may have the option to purchase the item for a nominal amount. In most cases, this will be worth your while. Many restaurants lease even when they can afford to purchase, because they prefer the fixed charge each month.

Often, companies that sell such products as coffee, ice cream, and detergents will furnish equipment for your use while you use their product. In some cases the equipment will be an outright loan. In others, a small rental charge will be worked into the cost of the product you use. The only way you will be able to find out who loans equipment is to ask the companies you plan to deal with. However, do not let these deals influence you to use a poorer quality product.

Purveyors are sometimes able to obtain equipment for you at a very low cost, because they buy in large quantities for their own use. An example might be a coffee maker or, perhaps, a freezer. The purveyor would order and pay for the equipment in its name and have it delivered to you, and then bill you the cost. One disadvantage might be that you must pay cash. If the savings were great enough (and they probably will be) you could borrow the money on a note. This way you would have only monthly payments to make.

One of the most important aspects of financing is establishing your line of credit. When you start out in business with no past experience or history it is extremely difficult to establish credit. Nowadays, with money as tight as it is and business failures so prevalent, companies are reluctant to take chances with new operations. Even if you are fortunate enough to be taking over a successful restaurant, you will find this to be a problem. It is, therefore, essential to establish credit terms for your day-to-day operations. This is an aspect of business financing that is often overlooked.

Companies will frequently require cash on delivery from newly established businesses. After you develop some credit standing, they will bill you. These bills may be due upon receipt or in ten days from when received. If this is the best arrangement you can get, you will have to live with it. However, it would be far better if you could visit the companies with which you plan to do busi-

ness and establish satisfactory terms from the beginning. Try for monthly billing. This is the most advantageous to you because it gives you until the tenth of the following month to pay.

A word of advice. Pay your bills when, or before, they come due. This way, you establish your business as reliable and your credit rating will be established much more quickly. There is no substitute for a good credit rating in business.

That about sums up the methods available to you in obtaining money, financing, or credit. Granted, some of the ideas mentioned may not be immediately helpful, but when you need those extra few dollars, any source is worth a try. No matter what you borrow, how much, or from whom, it must be paid back. Therefore, it now becomes a part of your business as a financial obligation. This must be considered when ascertaining the initial amount required to enter business. If you do not feel you can meet these obligations, now is the time to forget the idea of owning your own restaurant. You can reconsider at a later date, when the situation improves.

Preparing an Information Package

When you set out to obtain a loan, lenders will ask you for all sorts of information. It would be wise for you to prepare some material in advance, both to make your case convincing and to clarify the situation in your own mind. The various topics you should include in your package are discussed in the following section.

Type of Loan Needed

It is important to know what kind of loan you are looking for. There are:

First mortgage loans,
Second mortgage loans,
Construction loans,
Equipment (chattel) loans,
Loans for working capital.

First mortgage loans are loans using the real estate and building as collateral. These are the most desirable and, in most cases, the only basis on which you can obtain a mortgage from a bank. It is highly unusual for a bank to take a second mortgage. A mortgage is generally taken for a long period of time. The maximum for a restaurant would be fifteen years because of the speculative nature of the business. Payments are made monthly or quarterly and include interest and a portion of the principal. As with all mortgages, the early payments consist of almost all interest and little principal amortization.

Depending on market conditions at the time, you may receive as much as 85 percent of the appraised value of the property as a loan. You should borrow as much as you can in this manner.

The rate of interest will depend on the prevailing rate. If you feel you have a good basis for a loan, do not hesitate to shop around. A quarter or half percent does not sound like much, but it adds up in fifteen years.

Second mortgages are loans using the residual value of the real estate from the first mortgage and anything else that can be considered collateral, which usually includes the equipment, furniture, and fixtures. The residual value is the amount that would be left, if the property were sold and the first mortgage paid off. Obviously, a second mortgage is more risky than a first. Consequently, the rate of interest will be higher than that of a first mortgage. There is not much shopping around

you can do for interest rates, but you may be able to get a bigger loan.

Construction loans are those loans used for construction of a new building or remodeling of an old one. As mentioned earlier, you only want to pay for the actual money borrowed, *when* it is borrowed. You do not want to be paying for the total commitment in advance. Construction loans are usually made by advancing money for construction as it progresses. This is done by the issuance of notes. When the work is completed and all the tradespeople have been paid, the notes are usually consolidated or a mortgage is drawn. With this arrangement, you only pay for the money as it is used. If you borrowed a lump sum and then did the construction work, you would be paying for the money before it was put to use.

Equipment or chattel loans are made on personal property as opposed to real estate. Because personal property wears out, can be stolen or destroyed, and can be made worthless in various ways, a loan such as this carries a higher interest rate and can only be had for the predictable life of the item. In general, only items having a useful life of at least five years should be financed this way. Actually, any loan that finances a purchase of personal property is a chattel loan. This includes the ordinary department store purchase. If you are able to get a department store to finance your furniture purchases, for example, go to it. But, watch the method of computing interest that department stores use. It is not the same as the bank's.

Loans for working capital are more often used after you have been in business. There are times when your bills may be getting ahead of you, you may want to pay some taxes early to obtain the discount, or you may need to make an unusually large purchase. This is when working capital loans are usually made. However, you may take such loans in the beginning to conserve your cash for other opening purposes. Borrowing of this nature is usually done on a straight demand note. You pay the interest as it becomes due and pay off whatever you can on the principal amount as you are able. Demand notes do not have a specific date of maturity. They are payable on demand.

Description of Business and/or Property

A potential lender would like to know the purpose of the loan. For this reason it is necessary to make up an accurate description of the business. Not only does this give the lender a good idea of what the business is like, but it will help you in determining the business's good and bad points. Photographs, as well as a written description, should be included. The description should contain:

1. Real estate information concerning land size, number of buildings, attached or free standing, size or area contained, condition of building(s), current use, and necessary remodeling.
2. List of major equipment (if any).
3. List of furnishings (if any).
4. Other assets.
5. Other important factors or values that would tend to make the property worth more.

Appraisal

The purpose of an appraisal is to get an independent, objective opinion of the value of a business and its assets. An appraisal is pri-

marily intended to give the potential purchaser an idea of the real value of the property and/or the building, along with the business value.

When having an appraisal made, it is very important that the future value of the operation, as compared to the current value, is considered. If a business is worth $100,000 as it stands, it is worth $150,000 (or close to it) if you add $50,000 in the form of improvements. When a lender is able to lend 70 percent of the appraised value, for example, the loan will be $70,000 on the $100,000, but $105,000 on an appraisal of $150,000.

Upon receipt of the loan application, the lending institution will make an appraisal of the property on its own. This is done to ascertain the actual worth of the property for loan determination. It is, however, desirable for you to have an independent appraisal made. This will give you a good idea of the real value and also provide a comparison with the one made by the lending institution.

By including the independent appraisal in your loan presentation, the lender is aware you have a fair knowledge of the value of the business. This could have a definite bearing on the amount of the loan forthcoming.

Market Study

A market study is an objective analysis of a particular area with regard to the feasibility of locating a specific business.

It could be argued, and justifiably so, that the market study should be done before seeking financing. If this had been done and financing did not materialize, a great deal of effort might have been expended for nothing. On the other hand, financing will seldom materialize without a market study. The dilemma you are faced with is which should be tackled first. My suggestion would be to do them concurrently. It would be worthwhile to take some time off to devote to either or both of these projects. Without a doubt, they are the two most important aspects of getting started.

Before any large food service company will consider a location, it does a market study or analysis. An objective team of people will go out and survey the particular area and then make a recommendation. Objectivity is extremely important. Personal emotions must not enter into it. Many diverse details such as traffic flow, zoning, competition, economic activity, and ethnic grouping are considered. When all factors are weighed and evaluated, a decision is made.

In deciding on a location, there are two possible approaches. First, you can pick the area in which you want to locate and then study it to see whether it has the potential for success. Second, you can choose a wide area and determine where a restaurant would be most successful. This area could range from anywhere in the United States to a location in a particular town or city.

If the potential location is near your home, it is conceivable a good deal of the work may be done on weekends and evenings. However, this will not be the case if you will be locating some distance away. It might be desirable in such a situation to take a mini-vacation and really study the area completely. A few dollars spent this way will pay off in a more careful and less rushed survey. Money spent this way is tax deductible if you open the restaurant, and could save you many dollars later.

Consult the list that follows. Make up an itinerary so that you may utilize your time efficiently. Certain items can only be done on workdays. Other items can be done at any time. Perhaps there are others who can help you? Give them an itinerary as well.

A good bit of advice might be to keep your interviews low keyed. You will get much more information if you are polite and let other people do the talking.

When all the information is gathered, analyze it and put it into a comprehensive sales talk. Explain the reasons you think the operation will be successful, stress the good features, and downplay the bad ones or explain how you will overcome them. When you are finished, you should be as convinced as the person to whom you will be making the presentation. If you are not convinced, investigate the flaws of the presentation.

When conducting a market survey look for:

1. The general area. This could be a city, a seashore, a suburb, or a country area. Does it relate to what you have in mind?

2. Access. How easy is it to get to your location? Is it so complicated that it will discourage new customers? If you expect to draw from other areas, are you easy to get to?

3. Zoning regulations, taxes, and growth of area. Faster growing areas are advantageous but they will probably have restrictive zoning regulations and rising taxes.

4. Local and state laws. These pertain primarily to health, environmental, and liquor laws. There may be others that concern a restaurant as well.

5. Competition. Is there any that will affect your type of operation? Other restaurants will not necessarily affect you. As a matter of fact, some studies advocate that the more the better. Check with the local chamber of commerce, restaurant association, zoning board, and even the neighbors for information.

6. Population size. Depending on the size of your restaurant, this may or may not have a bearing.

7. Income level of the area. You do not want to have a fancy restaurant in a low income area.

8. Ethnic breakdown of area. This would have an effect if you were running a specialty operation. A German style restaurant in an Italian district may not be as successful as it would be elsewhere.

9. Where will your customers come from? Do you expect to get them locally, from a distance, or some combination of both?

10. The traffic survey done by the state will be of great help in determining how much traffic will go by your door. Depending on your operation, this may or may not be an aid.

11. Parking. Will you have a parking lot? Many communities require it. If not, is there enough on-street parking available? Can arrangements be made with a local parking lot if necessary?

12. What is the employment situation? Will you be able to get competent employees? Are wage scales higher than you would like?

13. What will be your price structure? Will the area sustain a restaurant with your prices?

14. Will your operation be seasonal or year round?

15. Capacity of proposed restaurant. Is it too big or too small to be supported in the area?

16. Will you be able to expand if you want to? Do not just consider space requirements. Also consider such things as local zoning and building laws. Are variances possible or are you locked in?

17. Municipal services. Do you have fire and police protection? Your own well or septic tank?

18. Proximity to markets. Are you located so far from the markets that deliveries will be a problem? Do the types of dealers you need deliver to your area?

Pro Forma *Statement*

A *pro forma* statement is a projection of sales and expenses over a period of time, usually a year. It can be based on past experience or no experience at all. In the latter case, the use of averages and known information is utilized to arrive at an acceptable statement. You should remember that a *pro forma* is only a calculated analysis of anticipated revenues and expenses. Any future event can make the entire analysis worthless. However, such a guide is an absolute necessity and cannot be ignored because of future uncertainties.

National averages are available from such organizations as the Small Business Administration and the National Restaurant Association. Because every restaurant is different due to such factors as location, labor market, rent, financing, and menu these averages can only be used as a guide.

It is difficult to project sales for a new operation. Many expenses (rent, insurance) can be accurately predicted and therefore are very reliable. Other expenses (food, beverage costs) will run close to averages. Still other expenses, such as payroll, can be determined rather accurately with some calculations. Therefore, it is easier to arrive at a *pro forma* by determining expenses than by anticipating sales. You will then know what sales are required to sustain an operation with the predetermined costs. You and the lending institution will then have a better idea of your chances of success.

Determining Expenses

Food and beverage costs are determined after arriving at all other expenses and anticipated profit.

Payroll expense is determined by an analysis of the future staff. Will you need a cook, a pantry person, a dishwasher, a waiter or waitress, a busperson, a bartender, a maitre d', a cleaner? If so, how many of each? What will be the rate of pay? How will you decide the rate for each of these positions (by local standards or your standards)? Will *you* need a salary? How many hours will each person work? Should you plan to be over-staffed at first (a good idea) to be sure the service is what it should be? What will you do later on? When you have multiplied all the positions by the number of hours to be worked and the rate of pay you will have a fairly accurate idea of the payroll expenses. On top of that, add on payroll taxes such as social security and unemployment fund. Fringe benefits such as hospitalization and life in-surance can be picked up here or under the insurance expense.

Other Expenses can be found listed in a later chapter. Some of the more involved ones are explained next.

Uniform costs can easily be provided by the supplier. If you require the staff to supply uniforms you can eliminate one expense.

Laundry includes table linens, towels, and kitchen uniforms. This expense can be computed by figuring how many tablecloths and napkins will be used during each meal, the number of towels needed in a day and the number of uniforms and aprons worn by the employees. You may also wish to consider jackets or the like for bus personnel. When table linens are rented, the cost of laundering is combined with the rental charge. This is usually figured under the laundry expense.

Linen expense relates to the purchase of linen. In most cases, it is more economical to purchase your own table linens than to rent them. It also allows you to pick the linen of your choice. Some laundry companies will purchase the linen you want and rent it to

you, but this is not a common practice. The one disadvantage in owning your own linen is loss. If it is stained, a hole is burned in it, or any other irreparable damage is done, you lose the linen. With proper training of per-sonnel this loss can be kept to a minimum. A linen purchase is a large initial outlay you may not wish to, or be able to, make. If this is the case, consider rental on a temporary basis. Purchase when you are able.

Utilities can only be estimated. With the help of your local representatives you should be able to come up with a realistic figure.

Hauling and contract cleaning, if you use it, costs are usually arrived at by a fixed monthly charge which can be ascertained very easily.

China, glass, cutlery, and utensils are discussed elsewhere in this book. You need only be concerned with yearly replacement costs in the *pro forma*. The initial purchases are usually considered in the balance sheet. Again, with good personnel training, replace-ment expense should be kept to a minimum. A distinct advantage for a small operation is that every time someone breaks something the owner is there to hear it. A definite de-terrent. Keep the soiled cutlery drop away from the garbage can. You will be amazed at how much cutlery you will save.

The cost of printing and menus can only be determined after you have decided on the menu format, the number needed, and what-ever other printing will be needed.

Paper and cleaning supplies can be de-termined quite easily by anticipated use. The person selling the cleaning supplies and dish-washing detergents can give you a reasonable estimate.

Repairs should be minimal during the first few years of operation, providing every-thing is rebuilt or replaced when you begin. You may need some additional plumbing or wiring but this expense should be minor.

The figure for rent is simply your rental cost each month. If there is a mortgage, the monthly payment can be calculated by the bank on the estimated mortgage.

The tax payments can be determined by using the previous year's tax bill. In addition, property improvements usually result in a reassessment and added taxes. This should be considered.

Insurance costs are obtainable from your agent.

Amortization of leasehold improvements can only be estimated after you have some idea of what will be undertaken. You should obtain competitive bids for an accurate idea. Even then it would be a good idea to add another 10 percent or so.

The remaining items to be entered in the *pro forma* statement are profit, sales costs, and sales.

Determining Profit, Sales Costs, and Sales

To arrive at these figures a number of calculations must be done. In order to do them certain information is needed:

1. Estimated operating expenses,
2. Estimated occupancy costs,
3. Estimated depreciation,
4. National averages for all of the above,
5. National averages for the cost of food and beverages.

For illustrative purposes let us say we will operate only five nights a week for dinner. The restaurant will have fifty to sixty seats, serve liquor and wines, and have a continental menu (as opposed to steaks, chops, and roasts). The atmosphere will be on the conservative side, catering to the service of fine food with well done appointments. Using this as a foundation, a fair estimate of labor costs will be about $40,500 per year and other operating expenses will run in the neighborhood of $30,000. Occupancy costs should run around $9,000 and depreciation about $3,000. These are arbitrary figures.

At present, the national average for the items mentioned are as follows:

1.	Payroll	27%
2.	Other operating expenses	20%
3.	Occupancy costs	6%
4.	Depreciation	2%
	Total	55%

The total in dollars for these items is $82,500.

To compute our food and beverage costs we must know our sales. To arrive at the sales figures we need a proportion. Because the aforementioned percentages are based on sales, sales must be 100 percent. If this is the case, we know what 55 percent of the 100 percent is but we do not know what the remaining 45 percent is. To find total sales we use the following ratio or proportion:

$$\frac{\% \text{ we know}}{\$ \text{ we know}} = \frac{100\%}{\$ \text{ we need to know}}$$

$$\frac{55\%}{\$82,500} = \frac{100\%}{x}$$

$$55x = \$8,250,000$$

$$x = \$8,250,000 \div 55$$

$$\text{Sales} = \$150,000$$

The national average for total cost of sales is approximately 36 percent of sales. Thirty-six percent of $150,000 is $54,000. We now have the following information:

Sales		$150,000
Cost of sales		54,000
Gross profit		96,000
Operating expenses		
Payroll	$40,500	
Other	30,000	
Total		$ 70,500
Profit before occ. cost		
and depreciation		$ 25,500
Occupancy costs		9,000
Profit before		
depreciation		$ 16,500
Depreciation		3,000
Net income		
before taxes		$ 13,500

What percentage is profit? Divide $13,500 by the total sales, $150,000 and you get 9 percent. This is a fair return and will be acceptable to any lending institution.

The *pro forma* is complete except for one item. The breakdown in sales and costs must be made between food and beverage. We must again refer to the national averages. The usual ratio between food and beverage is between 2.0 and 2.7 times. That is, for every dollar spent on beverages there will be between $2.00 and $2.70 spent on food. Again, for the sake of example, let us take a middle figure of 2.33.

Total Sales are $150,000
2.33 Food + 1.00 Liquor = 3.33

$$\frac{\text{Total Sales}}{\text{Total Ratio}} = \frac{\text{Food Sales}}{\text{Food Ratio}}$$

$$\frac{\$150,000}{3.33} = \frac{x}{2.33}$$

$$\$150,000 \times 2.33 = 3.33x$$

$$\frac{\$349,500}{3.33} = x$$

$$\$104,955 = \text{Food Sales}$$

$$\$150,000 - \$104,955 = \$45,045$$
$$= \text{Beverage Sales}$$

In order to break down the cost of sales between food and beverage for the purpose of the *pro forma* it is simplest to use national averages again. The average for food cost is 40 percent and beverage is 27 percent. By relating the percentage to the individual sales you will come up with the cost in dollars and cents.

Food sales	$104,955.00
	× .40
	$ 41,982.00
Beverage sales	$ 45,045.00
	× .27
	$ 12,162.00

This is approximately the $54,000 we determined earlier. The figures can be rounded off for the statement.

Goals and Method of Operation

This part of the presentation does not have to be very elaborate. As a matter of fact, it should be very general. After all, expansion can only be predicated on how successful you are, which is not something you can accurately predict. Describe briefly the direction you plan to take if your assumptions as to your success are realized. Without being overly detailed, describe the atmosphere, the menu, the price range of food and drinks,

YOUR RESTAURANT

Pro Forma Statement for the Year 19XX

SALES		
Food	$ 104,955.00	70 %
Beverage	45,045.00	30 %
Total Sales	$ 150,000.00	100 %
COST OF SALES		
Food	$ 42,000.00	40 %
Beverage	12,000.00	27 %
Total Cost of Sales	$ 54,000.00	
GROSS PROFIT	$ 96,000.00	
OPERATING EXPENSES		
Payroll	$ 40,500.00	27 %
Other	$ 30,000.00	20 %
Total Operating Expenses	$ 70,500.00	47 %
PROFIT BEFORE OCCUPANCY COSTS AND DEPRECIATION	$ 25,500.00	
OCCUPANCY EXPENSES		
Rent	$	%
Taxes	$	%
Insurance	$	%
Amort. of leasehold improvements	$	%
Total Occupancy Expenses	$ 9,000.00	6 %
TOTAL BEFORE DEPRECIATION	$ 16,500.00	
DEPRECIATION	$ 3,000.00	2 %
NET INCOME BEFORE TAXES	$ 13,500.00	9 %

Figure 2–2. Pro Forma Statement

and, in general, the type of customer you plan to attract.

You may come up with some sort of timetable for expansion, assuming you plan to expand. Lenders look for conservatism. They would rather see their loans paid off more quickly from unanticipated profits than have you reinvest. This actually works to your advantage anyway. By paying your obligations earlier than anticipated you improve your credit rating and convey a feeling of success. This will make future borrowing that much easier.

There is nothing to say you should expand. In my restaurant in Lancaster, Pennsylvania, I added a cocktail lounge because I did not have one. Other than that, I never increased my capacity. I operated at optimum most of the time. True, there were nights when I could have used more seats, but if I had them, I would have had to enlarge the kitchen. I was satisfied with my rate of return and found no reason to expand. So, if you are happy with your size, stay that way. Chances are you will be able to watch over the smaller business more successfully.

Lenders are interested in security. You have to show them you can provide it.

Business Structure

The importance of the business structure cannot be overlooked. It is of importance both to the lender and yourself. The reasons will probably be more obvious after a brief description of each.

There are three basic business structures:

1. Proprietorship,
2. Partnership,
3. Corporation.

The *proprietorship* is the simplest type of business structure. It consists of you and you alone. Legally, you are completely responsible for everything that happens in the business. The assets are all yours but so are the liabilities. The gains are yours but so are the losses. When you die, the business entity dies with you. The tax liability is one of a personal nature, the profit and loss is reflected in your personal return. The main drawback with this business organization is the unlimited liability you assume. If, for some reason, a suit is brought against your business, you are totally liable. This means the court can go beyond your business assets and claim personal assets in settlement of a legal claim.

The *partnership* is an agreement between two or more persons to conduct a business for profit. It is not always required, but it is preferable to have the agreement in writing. Each partner contributes something (labor, abilities, capital) to its operation. The liabilities are still on a personal basis. As far as the individual is concerned, the partnership is very much like the sole proprietorship with regard to taxes and liabilities. Each partner files his or her personal tax return considering his or her proportionate gain or loss from the partnership. A partnership remains intact after the death of a partner unless there is only one partner surviving.

The *corporation* is chartered by the state. It is considered a legal person, can be formed by two or more persons, and must have a president, vice-president, secretary, and treasurer. In most states, one person may hold two offices. Some states require a solicitor (attorney). There must be an annual meeting held once a year. Corporate tax forms must be filed with the federal and state governments. Incorporating is not a complicated procedure; any lawyer can do it for you rather quickly. Consider also, if you are operating under a different name than that of the corporation, the registration of a fictitious name. This protects your business name from having someone else use it. A registered name is similar to a trademark. However, it is only valid within a single state.

The big advantage to incorporating is the limited liability provided. Liability is limited to the corporate assets. The stockholders and officers are liable only for their total investment in the corporation. Their personal assets cannot be touched. The only exception to this would be fraud of some nature.

Because it is your company (called a closed corporation because the stock is not sold publicly), you may be an owner (stockholder) and an employee. This is like having all the advantages of working for a company and still being your own boss. Some of these advantages are fringe benefits (hospitalization, pension plans, and insurance), Workmen's Compensation, car allowance, and any other legitimate expenses. You do not even have to ask the boss for a raise anymore.

It is a good idea to pay yourself a salary so that the expense picture is not distorted. After all, if you had hired someone to do a particular job, you would pay him or her a salary. If the company is a little short of cash, you may defer payment to a later date. Furthermore, you went into business to improve your standard of living, not lower it.

The federal and state governments both levy a corporate income tax. This is usually at a fixed rate, but check with your state government. Of course taxes are only paid on profits, which you may not have in the first few years. Profits can also be paid out as a bonus at the end of the year to certain employees (namely you). They are no longer considered profits. They are now expenses. If the recipient of the bonus is in a lower tax bracket than the corporation, this is advantageous. Otherwise, it may not be. This is a field of discussion beyond the scope of this book.

A disadvantage of other business entities is that they are not perpetual. This means that the loss of a partner, for example, could result in the dissolution of the entire partnership. This could come about by death or the leaving of one of the partners for other reasons. This is not a problem with the corporate structure. It is much easier to sell a corporation for this reason. Sale merely requires a transfer or sale of the corporate stock. The stock may be sold at book value or whatever price the seller is able to obtain.

A further refinement, which is a plus for a small business, is the formation of a subchapter *S* corporation. A subchapter *S* corporation is one in which the tax liability reverts to the individual stockholders. In the early stages of a business, when the corporation usually sustains a loss, the stockholders may utilize this loss on their personal returns under a subchapter *S* corporation. Later on, when the business becomes profitable, this may not be as advantageous. When that time arises, the corporation may become a regular corporation again.

As you have probably concluded from the above discussion, the most advantageous business entity for a small business is the corporate structure. Although it may cost more to form initially, the advantages far outweigh the expense. The limited liability aspect alone is of utmost importance to the operator.

Paradoxically, this one distinct benefit to the corporation may actually hinder the acquiring of the money necessary to get it started. Lenders want assurances their money will be paid back. If you limit your liability, you limit their assurances. Fortunately, there is a way around this. Co-signers, discussed earlier in the chapter, may be the answer. Borrow the money in the company name, but make yourself personally liable by co-signing. If your assets cover the amount of the loan, you will probably have no trouble. If they do not, you may need additional co-signers.

Of course, arrangements such as co-signing are only necessary for the unsecured money needed. This is money usually used for the purchase of fixtures, equipment, repairs, and remodeling. If you are purchasing property or real estate, this in itself will be collateral for the loan or mortgage.

The ability of a corporation to issue stock may also be of advantage to you. There are always people around who like to invest in speculative ventures. In addition, there are others who have enough confidence in your ability to invest in it. You may want to take advantage of this form of capital. Be careful not to sell more than 49 percent of the outstanding stock, or you may lose control of the corporation.

The obvious disadvantages of this method of financing are some loss of profits for you and, possibly, having to answer to the stockholders. In a small business, these problems would probably be insignificant. The advantage of having interest-free money available could easily outweigh these difficulties.

Financing a business is a difficult task. It is especially difficult for those not versed in the means of obtaining money. It is time-consuming and expensive. You must be prepared to answer any and all questions regarding the venture, regardless of how personal or insignificant the questions may be. The best advice is, be prepared. Follow the procedures outlined and you will be able to make a sound and sensible presentation.

Do not make a commitment until capital requirements are met. Do not sign any leases or sales agreements or any binding contracts until you are sure you are able to finance the venture.

The Resume

Include in this section information about your past experience in restaurant work or related fields, particularly your management experi-

ence. If you have never worked in a restaurant, say so. Stress your management ability. This is all you have to sell. It will not be easy to convince someone that just because you are a great cook you will make a successful restaurateur. On the other hand, just because you have worked in a food operation, there is no assurance that you will be successful on your own. This will be a selling job on your part.

Lending institutions also like to know something about your personal life so do not make this just a business background resume. Include your age, marital status, how many children you have and whether or not they are dependent, and anything else you think may be important. You also should include information about your community activities and your business associations. Try to establish the fact that you are, or could be, an asset to the community. You could include newspaper clips and the like, if you have any. If you were looking for a new job, you would make the resume as interesting and informative as possible. This presentation is even more crucial to your life. The resume is the only written means you have to sell your case. It is your opening argument, so make it as impressive as possible.

If you plan to start your restaurant in an unfamiliar area it will probably be more difficult to obtain a loan. Therefore, you might include in your resume names of some persons or businesses in the new area who know you and would recommend you. The more influential, the better. Also include references from persons and businesses from your current location.

Personal Net Worth

Make up a financial statement of your net worth. This should include cash, securities, and assets, such as property and insurance, and any regular sources of income. Subtract your liabilities, such as mortages, notes payable, and car payments. What you have left is your net worth. How much of this will you be putting into the business? Lenders will want to know.

Unless you live in a very small community, the members of the loan committee probably will not know any more about you than that you are loan request #_____. The presentation packet you provide may make the difference between getting the loan or not. Do your homework, present them with the facts and you will increase your chances of success.

To Buy or to Lease

Instead of purchasing an existing business, you may choose to lease one. Leasing is essentially different from purchasing, because you do not obtain title to leased property.

Leasing (also called renting) is the right, for a given periodic payment, to the use of certain land, building, store, etc. over a period of time. How it is used and cared for depends on a Lease Agreement which must be in writing (for your protection). A lease may be a so-called "flat" lease (a fixed sum each period) or a "percentage" lease (usually, a fixed sum, plus a percentage of gross sales). Most leases are flat leases. Percentage leases may be used in times of tight money.

Purchasing is the conveyance of a piece of land, a building, equipment, furnishings, etc. for a consideration (usually money). This is done by the transfer of clear title (deed) or stock (in the case of a corporation). Except in very unusual circumstances, a purchase is a permanent transfer.

Leasing is an alternative to purchasing if:

1. Funds are limited,
2. You do not want a long time commitment,
3. Nothing is available for purchase.

There may be times when you choose to purchase and lease in concert. This would be the case if you leased a tract of land and built a restaurant on it. You would own the building and lease the land.

Advantages of Leasing

1. No immediate large outlay of cash. No down payment.
2. Fixed amount of rent for each month for a given period. No fluctuations due to taxes, increased insurance premiums, etc.
3. Major, and often minor, repairs done by landlord.
4. Flexibility. You can pick up and leave as soon as lease expires.
5. No rent until premises are actually taken over.

Disadvantages of Leasing

1. After the current term expires, the new rental figure could be so high as to force you to go elsewhere.
2. Repairs may be slow.
3. You build up no equity. All the money you pay as rent is gone.
4. If leasing of equipment and furnishings is involved, the physical condition may not be very satisfactory. Equipment breakdowns can be serious and poor furnishings reflect on your reputation.

5. If, during the lease period, you decide to sell the business, it may be more difficult because the buyer has less flexibility as to what he or she can do with the property. He or she will be governed by the terms of the lease. Also, if future lease terms are not spelled out, there is the uncertainty of the new terms. This is especially important with regard to rental payments.
6. Improvements may be at your expense and you may not be able to take them with you when you leave.

Advantages of Buying

1. You build up equity.
2. Your business assets become collateral.
3. More times than not, you will have obtained real estate that will increase in value. I bought the property for my first business at $300 per front foot. When I sold it five years later, it had increased to over $500 per front foot.
4. If you would decide to sell, for one reason or another, you can always sell or lease the property and sell the restaurant equipment and furnishings separately. This would be advantageous if you had to sell quickly.
5. You would not have the problem of your lease being renewed or your rent being increased at the end of the lease period.
6. You can make changes and additions quickly (assuming you have the money).

Disadvantages of Buying

1. You need a large amount of cash as down payment. This is usually the most troublesome problem when starting out.

2. It takes longer to relocate or sell because you will, in all probability, have to sell the current location in order to make the change. However, you could lease it. This would likely be quicker and you would have additional income.
3. If you have chosen an unsuitable location, you do not have the option to move quickly to a new one.
4. Usually tax rates, and insurance premiums increase each year. You would have to absorb all these increases. In a lease, you may be able to forestall some of them.
5. Your bank payments may begin from the moment you assume the property. If you cannot open right away this can be costly.
6. All repair bills are yours.
7. Buyers are more difficult to find than sublessors, because of the necessary cash outlay.

Leasing

When leasing, be sure to have an *Agreement to Lease* drawn up by an attorney. You and the landlord can decide on all the items you want in this lease, but your attorney will write it in terms that will protect you in case the landlord decides to change something. No matter how friendly you are with the landlord, have this agreement. Times and personalities have a way of changing. Also, there is always the possibility that you or the landlord may die or the property may be sold. If this should happen, you will need a well defined agreement. Be firm about the items you want defined in the document. Ask questions if there is something you do not understand. I can remember a very amicable meeting with my landlord when we were drawing up terms for a lease. I can also remember my attorney cautioning me on certain aspects of it. I was later grateful for his advice. When you are new and naive in the ways of business, you need the help of an experienced attorney. If your terms are reasonable, there is no reason a landlord should not agree. If he or she does not, you should be a little suspicious. Remember, a valid contract is satisfactory to *both* parties. The owner is just as anxious to rent the property as you are to lease it. I think we sometimes lose sight of this and become much too accommodating when we want something very badly.

When making up a lease agreement, include at least the following items:

1. Exact description of what is to be leased.
2. Monthly rent. Can it be increased? How?
3. What is included in the rent? Heat, water, electricity, equipment, etc.? What is not included?
4. Term of the lease. A long lease with a firm rental figure is most desirable. If not, get options to renew. Try to pin down future rental figures to some limits. Otherwise, you may be forced to move out because of an exorbitant rental figure later on.
5. Who pays for maintenance? This includes such items as plumbing, heating, wiring, painting, and repairs to equipment.
6. Leasehold improvements. Who pays for them? Who keeps them?
7. Right to hang a sign.
8. Local laws. Is the owner in conformance? If he is not, will he accept the responsibility at a later date? If he will not, will he release you from your agreement? Will he aid you in petitioning for a variance in the future, if it is needed?

9. It is assumed you will carry insurance to cover what you own. Who carries and pays for what the landlord owns? Liability must be clearly indicated.
10. Right to sublet. Suppose you are not successful. Will you be able to sublet the premises to someone else?
11. Termination notice. How much time before the lease expires does one party have to notify the other of his intent to renew?
12. What happens to the lease in case of catastrophe? Is it cancelled?

If you are considering leasing, you will need the same information as you would if you were purchasing. After all, your objective, whether leasing or purchasing, is to be successful. To be successful you need to know exactly what the situation is.

An existing business has certain advantages over a new one, whether you lease it or purchase it. The most significant is that you know what you are getting. You will be able to examine past sales and expense figures, from which you should be able to determine if a profit is really being made (and how much). The condition of the building, equipment, and furnishings can readily be determined. In addition, there is a staff to help you generate income immediately. Finally, it is easier to finance an existing business than a new one.

On the other hand, there are a few disadvantages to an existing business. You may be paying for an operation that needs a considerable amount of remodeling to be efficient. Whether leasing or buying, you will be paying additional dollars for such improvements. The business may be badly run down, and it is always more difficult to rebuild an image than to develop a new one. You may be paying for a built-in clientele you are not looking for.

There are many decisions to be made when entering the restaurant business. It is difficult to say which is the most important. Certainly, one such decision is the manner in which you acquire the premises. Give it serious thought because it can make the difference between success and failure. Do not rush into it, as most of us are prone to do. Step back, disregard your immediate desires and look at it from a truly objective viewpoint. If necessary, consult with friends, associates, family, your banker, and any others who may have more experience than you. Do not be carried away with your emotions. You may lose everything you worked so hard for.

Buying an Existing Business

There are many sound reasons for purchasing an existing business. Probably the most overriding one is simply that you have found one you like and feel you can be successful with.

You probably will not be too concerned about how the current owner is operating because you have plenty of ideas of your own. This approach would be fine if you were guaranteed success, but even with the necessary money and ability there can be no such guarantee. Consequently, you must set about purchasing this business cautiously. Gather together all the available facts and information to increase your chances of prospering. After this is done, the picture may be less cheerful, or it may be even more encouraging.

The first step is to check with the owner or a realtor to see if the property is for sale. There is not always a sign out front. Next, get the selling price. Try to obtain a comprehensive list of what is included in the sale. At this stage, such information may be sketchy but it will help to some degree. If you feel the asking price is within a sensible range, think about financing. Talk to lenders and get a commitment as to loan possibilities.

If you are satisfied that financing will not be an impediment, do a market study. If you are pleased with the results, approach the owner or realtor, inform him of your seriousness and ask for more detailed information. If a realtor is involved, it is advisable to have him step aside at this point. The realtor will only be functioning as a middleman anyway and much time can be saved if you and the owner work directly with each other. When negotiating time comes around, the realtor can re-enter the picture.

When the owner becomes aware of your seriousness to purchase, he should be cooperative. If he is not, forget the deal immediately. Chances are good he is either hiding something or does not really want to sell. For you to pursue the matter with an uncooperative seller would be a genuine waste of time.

The owner has a price. It is up to you to determine whether it is the price you want to pay. If it is not, you must come up with a new price. This is called the "offering price." The offering price can only be arrived at by a careful analysis of the information available. The following list will give you a good idea of what to look for.

1. Why is the business for sale? Is the reason truthful and understandable or do you get the feeling the owner is trying to hide something?

2. Sales and all other operating data for the last three to five years. This should be in the form of a certified year-end statement, done by an accountant. Also a balance sheet for the current year should be available. Federal income tax statements would be highly desirable, but may not be forthcoming this early in the negotiations.

3. Bank references and five or six purveyors' names. These can be used to check credit and verify purchases. If purchases are out of line, the sales figures may not be correct either. Also, the quality of the purveyor will indicate the quality of the restaurant.

4. Inventories of food and liquor the owner is planning to sell with the business.

5. Inventory of equipment, furnishings, supplies, china, glassware, silver, and linen that go with the restaurant. How old is it?

6. Is the liquor license included in the sale?

7. Check the condition of items listed in #5. Try to find out who services the equipment. Check with the servicer about the condition of the equipment.

8. Try to find out (as discreetly as possible) from the local health department whether there are health problems at the location. Do not give them incentive to come up with new ideas.

9. How is the heating system, plumbing, wiring, insulation, pest control, and building structure? It might pay you to have someone check the various systems. Would the systems be adequate if you planned additions at a later date?

A few additional words concerning food and liquor inventories are in order. If you have been in any retail business, you are aware there is a certain amount of dead stock. When buying a restaurant business you must be very careful about purchasing food and liquor inventories. The quality may not be of the character you will use; some of it could be spoiled or bug infested, or it may be adulterated. Therefore, it is strongly recommended you do not purchase inventories of food and beverages. If you do, never purchase fresh or frozen food, opened containers, or any other item that looks damaged or short in fill. In addition, do not purchase anything for which you will never have a use. If it is necessary to purchase any food or liquor stock, do so only at a discounted price to allow for future waste.

If, after examining all the facts, you want to proceed, the next step is the appraisal. It may take a few days to complete, so start it as soon as possible. It will be needed to help you decide on the offering price.

Unless you are well versed in restaurant management, the financial information you receive may be of little value. This is where your accountant can be of service. Pass all available data on to him or her. Some of the items to be focused on are listed below:

Profit and Loss Statement

1. Realistic sales. Is it possible the reported sales could be distorted? Made larger to enhance the sale or made smaller for tax purposes?

2. Relationship of costs to sales. Are they within nationally accepted criteria? If not, why not?

3. Is the payroll too high or too low? Too high could mean padding of the figures or an expensive labor market. Too low might mean the owner is working in the business and not drawing a salary.

4. Insurance rates. Are they in line? May be high because of some liability you have not been told about (e.g. fire hazard).

5. Utility costs. If they are too high, may indicate worn equipment, poorly insulated building, or leaks in the plumbing.

6. Repairs. A high figure here can only mean one thing.

Balance Sheet

1. Current assets. Do these stay with business?
2. Fixed assets. Land and building should be handled like any other real estate transaction (conveyance of a deed) unless a corporate transaction. Furnishings, china, glassware, etc. should be valued at 50 percent of cost if used, 100% if new.
3. What is value of goodwill?
4. Current liabilities. Do they stay in business?
5. Taxes. Are adjustments necessary? Is a large increase anticipated?
6. Liens, notes, or mortgages. How are they to be handled?

Goodwill is the value placed on a good reputation or location, and is determined primarily by the owner. This value means a higher purchase price or rental payment for you.

To illustrate how goodwill is arrived at and how it is reflected in a selling price, let's take the following example:

Real estate	$75,000
Equipment	20,000
Furnishings	10,000
Inventories	3,000
Other assets	1,000
	$109,000
Sale Price for business	$125,000

(For the purpose of simplicity, there are no Current Assets or Liabilities and no real estate commission.)

The sale price for the business is $16,000 more than the value. Assume a 10 percent profit (about $11,000) and you still have $5,000 left. This is goodwill. This is what the owner thinks the business is worth, over and beyond a fair profit on the sale. After all, isn't he or she presenting you with a going business, with built-in customers? Isn't this worth something to a prospective purchaser? The answer is yes, *if*. This "if" is what you must consider.

If you are purchasing or leasing the restaurant with the intention of running it as the current owner is, then the goodwill is a valid cost, and you too will have to put a value on it.

The chances are great however, you do not plan to run your restaurant in the same manner as your predecessor. If this is the case, the goodwill may be next to worthless for you. Under your management, every one of the previous customers may be displaced with new ones seeking an entirely different cuisine. You will then have paid for goodwill and derived absolutely no benefit from it.

It is imperative that you examine the asking price carefully. Determine what you are being asked to pay for. Is the price based on physical worth and inventories or is it inflated with goodwill, seller profit, and, perhaps, other meaningless items?

By this time, you should have received some commitment from your financing source and have completed a market study. Once you have made an offer, you are obligated to go through with the deal if the owner accepts.

Before an offer can be made, you should have a good idea of the cost of operation when you own it. Now is the time to complete the *pro forma* statement. Using the form in Figure 2–2, write in all the information you have. Use national averages for that which you do not have. Will you be able to make a profit? The answer must be yes or do not proceed any further.

Now you must decide what the restaurant is worth to you. This can be determined by asking yourself one question: what would this business be worth if *I* started it from the beginning? Using the information you have already gathered, compile a list of assets and determine their total value. Add in a fair selling profit and, perhaps, some goodwill and you will have an idea of what the business is worth. How does this compare with the independent appraisal? The estimates should be rather close.

Now, consider any improvements or additions you are planning. How much will they cost? How much do you need for operating capital for the first two or three months? Add these figures to the value you placed on the business and you will have a fairly accurate idea of the amount you need. If your available capital is insufficient, you must raise more capital, reduce or eliminate your improvement program, or hope the owner will accept a lower selling price.

If the improvement program is an integral part of the purchase plan and cannot be reduced appreciably, the only alternative is to offer less than the asking price.

Therefore, the logical first step would be to submit your offering price based on the capital you have available. If this is accepted, fine. If it is not, the seller will probably come up with a new price. This will then give you a better idea of how much additional capital you will need to obtain. If you can only acquire a portion of this amount, submit a new bid and, perhaps, something will work out. If it does not, then it will be time to end the deal.

If you have never experienced a real estate transaction you would be surprised to know it is a regular cat and mouse game. One person says, this is what I want, knowing he won't get it. The other person says, this is what I'm prepared to pay, knowing full well it is ridiculously low. The first person says, well, I'll consider this, and so on. Finally, they get down to the real figures and the bargaining really takes place. Therefore, never consider the original selling price as the real price and never give your final offer first. It is advantageous to have an agent to pass the bids back and forth because he can keep you aware of the feelings of the other party (works both ways, remember).

Never reply to a new offer before the deadline. By doing this, it appears you are only reluctantly considering the new price and are almost ready to end all the negotiations. This is supposed to shake the other person up. It is to be hoped that the seller wants to sell a little more than you want to buy. This gives you an edge. If it is the other way, never let the seller become aware of your feelings. You'll be able to tell when the negotiating is becoming very serious. When this happens, if you are close to agreement, a small compromise can close the deal. Many a deal has died, only to be rekindled when the owner finds he cannot get a better price than yours.

Reminder: Do not enter into any legal proceedings such as an offer to purchase or settlement without the help of an attorney.

When making an offer, place a time limit on it. Otherwise you may be sitting around for a long time waiting for an acceptance, by which you are legally bound, and the seller will have time to look for a better offer.

Do not purchase a business without insisting on a covenant not to compete. The previous owner agrees not to open another restaurant or similar operation within a given area around the one you are purchasing. It can restrict the former owner to within blocks (in a city) or miles (outside a city). Do not make the area too large or it may be considered in restraint of trade and be invalid.

The transaction at the time of sale will be much simpler if certain things can be determined beforehand.

1. The seller keeps all cash and money in checking accounts.
2. The receivables are kept by the seller or at least he is responsible for their collection.
3. The seller pays the accounts payable and any interest due on notes, mortages, etc. The purchaser should start out with no prior current assets or liabilities.
4. Unless other arrangements are made, the seller should cancel all notes and other loan obligations and release the business of all liability.
5. The seller should reimburse the purchaser for taxes collected (payroll, sales, etc.) or pay the taxes himself.
6. Utilities use should be computed until the day of sale and payment made at the closing.
7. Prepaid items (e.g., insurance, real estate taxes) should be prorated and adjusted at the closing.
8. If there are any inventories, settlement should be made at this time. They should be verified by the purchaser.
9. An adjustment must be made on the federal and state income taxes to be paid year-end. If not, the purchaser will find himself paying tax on profits made by the seller.

If settlement involves only a single proprietor, it should go rather quickly and easily. If you are dealing with a partnership, be sure all partners are in agreement (this is also true during early negotiations). At the very least, be sure the one with whom you are dealing speaks for all of them. It is necessary for all partners to sign for the sale to be completed.

When the business is incorporated there are two ways in which it can be purchased. One is through liquidation of the corporation and the other is by a stock transfer. The latter is by far the simplest. The necessary transactions are made by the stockholders. They may then sell their stock back to the corporation or to the purchaser of the business.

These are the basics you have to know to purchase a business. Arrange the financing, do a market study, get an independent appraisal, gather as much information regarding the physical and financial aspects as possible, complete the *pro forma* statement, decide what the business is worth, make your offers and consult with your accountant and lawyer, and then you can take over.

Setting Up an Operating Statement

When starting in a new business it is essential that you know where you stand financially. This information should be available at the beginning of every month, which makes keeping complete and accurate records during the month necessary. The method used to set up a current operating statement may also be used in setting up a *pro forma* statement for the initial financing requirements of the business. The only difference is that actual figures instead of estimated ones are used. (See Figure 2–3.)

The data needed to set up a statement are:

1. Sales figures,
2. Inventory figures,
3. Cost of sales,
4. Operating expenses,
5. Occupancy expenses,
6. Other information.

Sales Figures

It is important that you keep a sales journal or register. Each day's sales will be recorded

```
                        YOUR RESTAURANT

             Operating Statement for Month of_____19XX


                                    Month        To Date

      SALES
         Food                   $_____ __%  $_____ __%
         Beverage               $_____ __%  $_____ __%
         Other                  $_____ __%  $_____ __%
           Total Sales          $_____100%    $_____100%

      COST OF SALES
         Food                   $_____ __%  $_____ __%
         Beverage               $_____ __%  $_____ __%
         Other                  $_____ __%  $_____ __%
           Total Cost of Sales  $_____          $_____

      GROSS PROFIT              $_____          $_____

      OPERATING EXPENSES
         Payroll                $_____ %    $_____ %
         Other                  $_____ __%  $_____ %
           Total Operating Expenses $_____ __% $_____ %

      PROFIT BEFORE OCCUPANCY COSTS
         AND DEPRECIATION       $_____         $_____ __%

      OCCUPANCY EXPENSES
         Rent                   $_____         $_____ __%
         Taxes                  $_____         $_____ __%
         Insurance              $_____         $_____ __%
         Amort. of leasehold
           improvements         $_____         $_____ __%
           Total Occupancy Expenses $_____       $_____ __%

      DEPRECIATION              $_____         $_____ __%

      NET INCOME BEFORE TAXES   $_____         $_____ __%
```

Figure 2–3.   Operating Statement

here. At the end of the month, the columns are totaled and the monthly sales are obtained. Sales should be broken down in categories of food, liquor, wine, and miscellaneous. In some states, a further breakdown as to beer and cigarettes is necessary. Use whatever breakdown suits you, but remember to consider sales tax requirements.

Inventories

On the last day of every month an inventory should be taken of all food, liquor, wine, and miscellaneous. Amounts should be entered in an inventory book. The price paid for each item is entered. The value of each item or items is then computed and a value placed on the entire inventory.

Cost of Sales

The cost of sales is important to the operating statement because it gives you a true picture of the amount of food, liquor, etc., that was used during the month, or whatever period you choose to use. An individual who is not familiar with business accounting would probably assume the cost of sales was equal to the monthly purchases. In most cases, this would not be true. The true cost of sales comes about only after inventory and credit adjustments. As mentioned elsewhere, an inventory that has decreased in value from the preceding month indicates usage. Conversely, an inventory that has increased in value indicates that something has been added to it. This would have to have come from the purchases made during that month.

To compute the cost of sales, the *opening inventory* must be taken into consideration. The opening inventory figure is the same as

the closing inventory figure of the previous month. The *closing inventory* is the figure arrived at after taking this month's inventory. *Purchases* are those made during the month. *Credits* would be for breakage and spoilage.

Illustration

Opening Inventory	$1525.82	
Closing Inventory	1213.51	$ 312.31
Purchases		3364.29
Total Consumption		$3676.60
Credits		− 4.25
Cost of Goods Sold		$3672.35

Operating Expenses

Operating expenses are those expenses directly related to sales. Because these expenses do not always fluctuate in the same direction as sales, they must be watched constantly. Listed next are most of the expense categories you will encounter. If you have others, just add them to your statement.

Payroll Expenses
  Salaries and wages
  Officers' salaries (corporation)
  Payroll taxes (Social Security, Unemployment Insurance, Workmen's Compensation)
  Other (e.g., hospitalization)
Laundry
Uniforms
Utilities
  Electric
  Gas
  Water
  Telephone
Hauling and waste
Contract cleaning

Utensils

China, glass, and cutlery

Linen (if purchased)

Printing and menus

Office expense (include postage)

Automobile expense

Paper supplies

Cleaning supplies (include dishwashing)

Licenses and permits

Professional fees (attorney, accountant, etc.)

Insurance expense

Repairs and maintenance

Advertising

Bank and finance charges (monthly)

Dues and subscriptions

Credit card commission

Travel expenses

Miscellaneous expenses

Bar expense

Interest

Organization expense (corporation)

Occupancy Expenses

Occupancy expenses are those expenses that continue whether or not you are operating. They do not fluctuate with sales, and include:

Rent

Mortgage payments

Depreciation

Administrative (corporation)

Leasehold improvements (if leasing)

Insurance (not included in operating)

Taxes (e.g., real estate)

For a very small restaurant as you may be starting, it is not necessary to list all these categories. Some of them can obviously be condensed. Utilities and payroll are two good examples. Once the actual structure of the monthly statement is decided on, forms can be printed on a copy machine and merely filled in. Keep in mind that a "year to date" and "percentage" column should be included.

Two items that may give you some trouble, if you are not familiar with accounting, are leasehold improvements and depreciation.

Leasehold Improvements. When you rent or lease a building you may decide you would like to do some remodeling. Normally, any changes, additions, or repairs you make on the structure become part of the structure and belong to the landlord. In some cases the agreement to lease may read that these additions are retained by you when the lease expires. In any case, any changes you make are called leasehold improvements. If they are relatively minor, they may be written off immediately. In most cases, however, they are not that small. Good accounting procedure and the IRS say they should be written off over their expected life. For example, if the expected life is three years and the cost is $1,800, then the cost per year would be $600. Divided by twelve you have a cost of $150 per month. This is how much you write off each month under Leasehold Improvements. If you purchase something at a later date, add it to the schedule you have drawn up.

Depreciation. Depreciation is calculated on the equipment and furnishings you purchase. If you buy $30,000 worth of equipment and the expected life is ten years, you have a yearly expense of $3,000. Unfortunately, all items do not have the same expected life. Therefore, each one must be computed separately to find the correct charge. For example,

Item	Cost	Life	Charge/Year
Stove	$2,000	10 years	$200.00
Mixer	200	7 years	28.57
Refrigerator	1,200	12 years	100.00
		Total	328.57

After seven years, you remove the mixer charge. After ten years, you remove the stove, and so forth.

There are different types of depreciation. The one illustrated is called the straight line method. I feel it is the best one for a small businessperson.

Keep in mind, when you purchase a piece of equipment, for example, you may have to pay cash for it right away but it is paid for over a period of years in the accounting procedure.

A schedule may be obtained from the Internal Revenue Service that outlines the expected life of your equipment.

If you own the real estate, you may also depreciate the buildings but not the land. The theory is land does not lose its value through obsolescence but the buildings do. The same method as outlined above should be followed.

Inventories

Inventories are an essential part of any restaurant operation, large or small. Larger operations may utilize computers but smaller ones will find this a luxury difficult to justify.

Inventories serve three functions:

1. Accounting,
2. Information,
3. Deterrent to dishonesty.

Accounting Function. Before an accurate profit and loss statement can be completed, inventories of food, liquor, and other supplies must be taken. This aids in determining the value of the supplies consumed during the period.

Information Function. Inventories may be taken informally (counted and not priced) to keep you informed of what is in stock. If the grocery company calls on Tuesday, then you can take an informal inventory on Monday. This enables you to order whatever is needed. There is nothing more frustrating than going to storage and finding an item missing when it is needed. For this reason, it is a great idea to train the employees to tell you if an item is getting low. Keep a running list on the wall, or somewhere, to list items as they are needed.

Daily inventories of food in the refrigerator are also helpful. They are a big aid in helping to control leftovers and waste. Leftover food should be used as quickly as possible. The longer it is around, the more the quality deteriorates. Eventually, it is only fit for the garbage can, which is costly.

By watching the inventory book each month, you will have a very good idea of how much of each item is used. This may vary due to some unusual occurrence but generally, it stays rather constant. This will help you in ordering. It also helps you determine some of the slower moving items.

Deterrent to Dishonesty. Inventories not only act as a real deterrent to pilferage but also a psychological one.

By taking monthly, or more frequent, inventory, you are able to keep tabs on what is being used. If usage of certain items deviates from the normal, taking inventory will make you aware of it. This is discussed more fully in the chapter on security.

The very fact employees see you taking an inventory is a psychological deterrent to pilferage. They know you are concerned and watching.

Inventories should be kept as low as possible (and practical). Money tied up in inventory for a long period of time cannot earn money for you. In addition, excessive inventory takes up valuable storage space and invites pilferage. It is always tempting to take advantage of a good deal when it comes along, but consider the financial aspects carefully before tying up money in inventory.

When starting out, you will tend to under-order and over-order. Don't be discouraged; eventually you'll get a hold on it.

How to Compute an Inventory

Computing the inventory is not a difficult task. The taking of it is most time consuming, however.

What is needed are:

1. Two well-sharpened pencils,
2. An inventory book or inventory pages,
3. A small calculator,
4. An adding machine,
5. Invoices from month being covered.

A few preliminary steps can make the job easier. If frozen foods, for example, are weighed and identified on the outside of the package when they are placed in the freezer, your task will be easier. Arrange storage shelves properly and logically. Keep refrigerated food together in groups, such as dairy products, vegetables, and meats, instead of having these items intermingled and scattered every which way.

Taking the Inventory

Figures may be entered directly into the inventory book or they may be entered on preprinted sheets. (See Figure 2–4.) The latter method is more helpful with large and scattered items such as wines which may be found in two or three locations. I find it easier to carry a few pages on a clip board than to carry a bulky inventory book.

When using preprinted sheets have holes punched along one side and fit them into a looseleaf binder. If they are neat and legible, this can serve as an inventory book.

Items should be entered on the page as they are encountered on the shelf. Do not say, "I'll add these in when I get to the ones at the other end." Too many items are forgotten or miscounted that way. Jot the amount down in the book and add to it when you find more of the same item. Just use a plus sign between the numbers. When pricing is done, they can then be added together. By using this system, you are able to check back more easily to detect any errors. *Never erase.* The figure is lost forever if you do. If an error is made, cross it out with a single line. This way, if you have to check back, the error can be detected.

If you find items that are not listed in the inventory book or on the pages, write them in. Be sure to identify them carefully so they can be priced properly.

When taking inventory, travel in a straight line. Do not skip from one shelf or location to another. Shelves too should be arranged in a logical order, with items in groups whenever possible. The inventory sheets or book should be made up in the same order as the shelves. Leave a little extra space for the addition of new items. When the counting is over, give one last general look around the room to be sure you have not overlooked something. Check floors and high shelves.

	INVENTORY					
				Date_____		

Unit Size	Item	Qty		Unit Price		Amount
			Balance forward			
	CANNED FRUIT					
#10	Apples, sliced	4		2	79	11 16
#2½	Peaches, halves	1+7 ⑧			72	5 76
#2½	Pears, salad cut	3			87	2 61
#10	Pineapple, chunks	1+3+1 ⑤		3	16	15 80
#2	" "	14			64	8 96
	CANNED VEGETABLES					
#10	Carrots, Belgium	8		3	44	27 52
16 oz.	Mushrooms, sliced	11+2+1+1 ⑤		1	92	28 80
			Total forward			

Figure 2–4. Inventory Sheet. This is an example of the type of inventory sheet you can make up yourself. The items can be written and the entire page can then be photo-copied. The center column can be for case prices or other information. If holes are needed, they can be punched in on left side.

When taking inventories of unpackaged goods, be consistent in your measurements. Do not count whiskey in tenths one time and in quarters the next. Always be consistent whenever counting anything that has to be measured.

Opened and prepared items are generally not counted in food inventories unless they are very large quantities or very expensive. If this procedure is constantly adhered to, it will balance itself out over the year.

If not prepackaged, food items should be weighed or counted. Certain items, such as ice cream, are more easily estimated. Usually, spices are not counted in the inventory until the last month of the year.

Computing the Value of the Inventory

Now that you have everything entered in the book or on the preprinted sheets, the value of the inventory must be determined.

It is necessary to price every item by entering the last purchase price in the column next to the quantity counted. These prices are obtained from the monthly invoices. Some items may be left over from a previous month. In this case, their price will not change. Prices should be entered as unit prices, not case prices.

1 cs. 6/#10 cans Tomatoes $12.84
   One can costs $2.14
If the count was 14 cans, the value would be:
      14 × $2.14 = $29.96

It is easier to make all these calculations at one time. Do not find the unit cost and later multiply it with the quantity. Do all the calculations at one time. It is much less time consuming.

When all unit prices have been entered and extended, total each page. It is not necessary to total each page separately, just use a running total to the end.

Using the Operating Statement

There is little sense in compiling an operating statement (also called profit and loss) unless you use it. The statement is valuable as an analytical tool.

Initially, to analyze your operation you will have to rely pretty much on national standards. Sometimes, regional standards are available as well. Such statistics can be obtained from the National Restaurant Association or from the accounting firm of Laventhol & Horwath.

When you have completed the preliminary work of collecting the figures, enter the correct amounts next to each category in the preprinted statement. These figures should be entered under the column "Month." If this is not the first time for the statement, add the "Month" figures to the past month's "To Date" figures to get the current "To Date" amounts. Total each column where indicated.

The next step is to compute the percentages. This is done by dividing each category of expenses by sales.

Food costs should be divided by *food sales*, liquor costs should be divided by *liquor sales* and other costs should be divided by *other sales*. All other expenses, operating and occupancy, should be divided by *total sales*. The proper percentage should then be entered in the column to the right of the expense.

Illustration

Assume Total Sales of $10,000, Food, $7,000, Liquor, $3,000. Cost of sales for food, $2,800; for liquor, $840. Payroll costs $3,500; rent, $650.

Food percentage   = 2,800 ÷ 7,000 = 40%
Liquor percentage =   840 ÷ 3,000 = 28%
Payroll percentage = 3,500 ÷ 10,000 = 35%
Rent percentage   =   650 ÷ 10,000 = 6.5%

The first month's statement will be of little value. It probably will not be a full month, nor will sales be of a meaningful amount. It will however, give you some idea of your cash flow. In addition to the inadequacies mentioned above, expenses will be inflated because they will not be geared to income. The payroll will most likely be very high until you are able to streamline the staff schedule. Some of the other expenses will be high because you had to purchase blindly, and probably purchased too much. The occupancy costs will be high in relation to sales. Because of these factors, and others, the bottom line will most likely show quite a loss.

The second month should be better and the third month should become meaningful. There is little use considering anything more than the bottom line for the first two months. During that time you will doubtless have a loss. By the third month, sales should be improving and the loss should be mitigated. You can now start to analyze the statement.

When analyzing an operating or profit and loss (P&L) statement, look primarily for improvements and trouble spots. In most cases, improvement can be determined by month-to-month and year-to-year comparisons. Month-to-month sales comparisons in the restaurant business are generally of little value because sales fluctuate so greatly. Some operations may have good summer months and poor winter months or vice versa. Others may have a good January and a bad December. In such cases, a comparison of continuous months does not really tell you anything. The best way in which to compare sales is yearly. Compare this year's month with the same month last year. In this manner, it is easy to discern a sales trend. Sales should show some trend upward each year. The amount will depend on how new the operation is, how successful you are in fulfilling the public's desires, and how much you want to grow. (See Figure 2–5 for a sample statement of income.)

After you have completed a year of operating, another column should then be added to the statement. Title it, "Last Year."

Costs and operating expenses should be monitored month-to-month, as well as year-to-year. If not, they may get so far out of hand it will be difficult to correct them.

Earlier, when the *pro forma* statement

was made, you set up certain percentage guidelines. If the food percentage was set at 42 percent and you are running at 45 percent, something is wrong. If payroll was to be 33 percent and you are running at 38 percent, better look into it. If you predicted sales of $150,000 for the year and you are only running $100,000 on an annual basis, something should be done (more advertising, perhaps). Remember, you predicted a profit based on a certain amount of sales. If sales do not measure up to this amount, you may find yourself short of cash and unable to pay your debts. If the percentages or sales figures are not in line, do something immediately before things really get out of hand.

If sales increase and costs go down, percentages go down.

If sales increase and costs go up, percentages can go either way.

If sales increase and costs stay the same, percentages go down.

If sales decrease and costs go down, percentages go either way.

If sales decrease and costs go up, percentages go up.

If sales decrease and costs stay the same, percentages go up.

The importance of the above chart can be easily understood if you realize:

Sales = Income

You cannot pay out more than you take in. That is why the concept of percentages is based on sales.

Sales = 100%

When all the percentages are added, they cannot equal more than 100 percent. If

STATEMENT OF INCOME

THE LEMON TREE RESTAURANT, INC.

| | YEAR ENDED | | | |
	SEPTEMBER 30, 1969	PERCENTAGES	SEPTEMBER 30, 1968	PERCENTAGES
SALES				
Food	$114,425.42	72.34	$115,677.12	73.63
Beverages	43,275.80	27.36	40,938.65	26.06
Miscellaneous	481.35	.30	489.10	.31
TOTAL FOOD AND BEVERAGE SALES	158,182.57	100.00	157,104.87	100.00
COST OF SALES				
Food	37,692.96	32.95	40,666.65	35.15
Beverages	13,512.12	31.22	13,157.41	32.14
Miscellaneous	348.37	72.35	426.05	87.12
TOTAL COST OF SALES	51,553.45		54,250.11	
GROSS PROFIT				
Food	76,732.46	67.05	75,010.47	64.85
Beverages	29,763.68	68.78	27,781.24	67.86
Miscellaneous	132.98	77.65	63.05	12.88
TOTAL GROSS PROFIT	106,629.12	67.41	102,854.76	65.47
OTHER INCOME	64.36	.04	35.72	.02
TOTAL INCOME	106,693.48	67.45	102,890.48	65.49
CONTROLLABLE EXPENSES				
Officers' Salaries	24,450.00	15.46	23,130.00	14.72
Salaries and Wages	36,683.42	23.19	30,714.54	19.55
Laundry	3,331.33		3,405.06	
Stationery and Printing	1,305.02		753.88	
Supplies and Expense	2,355.12		2,530.14	
Advertising	1,860.04		2,658.99	
Utilities	3,247.55		3,031.31	
Licenses and Permits	327.00		56.00	
Payroll Taxes	2,480.88		2,191.37	
Bar Expense	585.94		439.84	
Dues and Subscriptions	236.02		190.65	
Hauling and Waste Removal	1,046.68		1,000.84	

Page 4

Figure 2–5. Illustration of an Actual Operating Statement

| | YEAR ENDED | | | |
	SEPTEMBER 30, 1969	PERCENTAGES	SEPTEMBER 30, 1968	PERCENTAGES
Professional Fees	$ 1,075.00		$ 1,446.00	
Insurance Expense	1,661.11		1,703.75	
Commissions to American Express	681.36		-	
China, Glassware & Linen Expense	713.46		943.94	
Repairs and Maintenance	1,908.24		2,044.94	
State Capital Stock Tax	197.47		168.16	
State Corporate Loans Tax	12.51		85.42	
Automotive Expenses	869.96		647.50	
Interest Expense	601.11		1,431.97	
Amortization of Orgnization Expense	369.24		369.24	
TOTAL CONTROLLABLE EXPENSES	85,998.46	54.37	78,943.54	50.25
PROFIT BEFORE RENT AND OCCUPANCY COSTS	20,695.02	13.08	23,946.94	15.24
RENT AND OCCUPANCY COSTS				
Rent Expense	8,800.00		8,400.00	
Insurance on Building	1,278.50		1,235.02	
Property Taxes	998.23		866.39	
Amortization of Leasehold Improvements	198.00		198.00	
TOTAL RENT AND OCCUPANCY COSTS	11,274.73	7.13	10,699.41	6.81
PROFIT BEFORE DEPRECIATION	9,420.29	5.95	13,247.53	8.43
DEPRECIATION	2,924.07	1.85	2,549.32	1.62
NET INCOME BEFORE STATE INCOME TAXES	6,496.22	4.10	10,698.21	6.81
PROVISION FOR STATE INCOME TAX	424.99	.26	699.88	.45
NET INCOME FOR THE YEAR	$ 6,071.23	3.84	$ 9,998.33	6.36
Earnings Per Share of Common Stock Outstanding	$6.07		$10.00	

See notes to financial report

Page 5

Figure 2–5. (Continued)

they do, you are operating at a loss. If sales decrease by 2 percent, costs must be decreased by 2 percent in order to maintain the *status quo*. There may come a point when sales have decreased so drastically there is no longer a possibility of reducing costs to that level. This is when you are out of business.

You must constantly monitor the financial aspect of the business. If costs increase, the increase must be offset with added income or reduced expenditures. There are five possible alternatives to meet this challenge:

1. Increase sales in some manner,
2. Raise selling prices,
3. Decrease portion sizes,
4. Pay less for ingredients,
5. Take a smaller profit.

If labor costs increase, the alternatives are:

1. Cut the size of the staff and train those remaining to be more efficient,
2. Streamline the hours of operation (thereby reducing the number of hours worked),
3. Increase prices,
4. Increase sales.

None of the possibilities outlined may be particularly desirable from a customer point of view but if you have excellent food and service you should not lose customers. If you are just another one of the group of average restaurants, customers will go elsewhere. Another good reason for a quality operation.

The operating statement then, should be used as an early warning device to keep you abreast of the financial condition of your business. It should tell you when you are doing well and when problems are beginning to develop. The first time a problem arises, investigate it immediately. If it recurs you must take corrective action. By using the monthly statement in this manner, you will be able to keep your operation on a sound financial footing.

Other Financial Aspects

Balance Sheet

The *balance sheet* (see Figure 2–6) is a statement of the financial condition of a business *on a particular date*. This varies from the *profit and loss statement* which states the financial data of a business over a *period of time*. Unless you are well versed in accounting principles, I suggest you have an accountant prepare this statement. In a new business, it should be prepared quarterly if possible.

The purpose of the balance sheet is to tell you whether or not you are in sound financial condition. In broad terms, sound financial condition means if the business is dissolved, the debts of the business could be completely paid for with the assets the business owns.

The following equation is the basis of a balance sheet:

$$\text{Assets} - \text{Liabilities} = \text{Net Worth}$$

Assets are all things of value owned by the business. They can be current or fixed. Examples of current assets would be cash, accounts receivable, and inventories. Examples of fixed assets would be land, buildings, equipment, and furnishings.

Liabilities are the amounts the business owes. These are generally classified as current, due in less than a year, and fixed. An example of current liabilities would be ac-

Figure 2–6. A Simple Balance Sheet

Assets

Current Assets
Cash	$12,000	
Accts. Receivable	1,000	
Inventories	2,000	
Total Current Assets		$15,000

Fixed Assets
Building	$60,000	
Land	10,000	
Equipment (less depreciation)	20,000	
Total Fixed Assets		90,000
Total Assets		$105,000

Liabilities and Net Worth

Current Liabilities
Accts. Payable	$11,000	
Accrued Expenses	2,000	
Other expenses	3,000	
Total Current Liabilities	15,000	

Fixed Liabilities
Mortgage	7,000	
Other	13,000	
Total Fixed Liabilities	20,000	
Total Liabilities	35,000	

Net Worth
Stock	$60,000	
Retained Earnings	10,000	
Total Net Worth	70,000	
Total Liabilities & Net Worth		$105,000

counts payable. An example of a fixed liability would be a mortgage.

Net Worth is what is left after the liabilities are deducted from the assets. In the case of the corporation, this would include the corporate stock in addition to the retained earnings (profit kept in the business). Net worth is also called *equity* or *capital*.

Current Ratio

The current ratio is the current assets divided by the current liabilities. The minimum result should be 1:1. Most businesses operate around 2:1. However, in a restaurant there is little need for surplus cash. Consequently, 1.5:1 is usually sufficient. All the current ratio indicates is an ability to pay off the current debts. To have extra, unneeded cash lying around in a bank account is unsound. Surplus cash, or working capital, might better be used in reducing long term obligations such as notes and mortgages. This does not say you should not keep an adequate "cushion" in the cash account for the unexpected.

Cash or Accrual Basis

A business is either on a *cash* basis or an *accrual* basis. There are very few businesses operating on a cash basis. On a cash basis, all expenses are counted *when made* and all income is credited *when received*. This is not a satisfactory method of operation for a business. Consequently, most businesses operate on an accrual basis. With this method, income is accounted for when it occurs (whether it is received or not) and expenses are considered when incurred, rather than when paid. This means that even though the monthly invoices are paid on the tenth of the month following the month they are incurred, they are charged to the previous month.

Sometimes, certain expenses are paid in advance. These are called *Prepaid Expenses*.

There are times, usually at the beginning of a month, when certain expenses are paid that should be partially charged to the preceding month, as well as the month in which they are paid. When this happens, there is an *accrued expense*. Such expenses appear on the liability side of the balance sheet.

An example of an accrued expense would be wages. If a weekly payroll check is made out and some of the charge is from one month and the remaining charge is for the following month, the balance sheet must take this into account. If this is not done, all the wages would be charged to the month in which the wages were paid. This would distort the fig-

ures of that period. The adjustment is also made in the profit and loss statement.

Illustration

Assume payroll period ends April 3
Assume payroll amounts to $1,500
Assume payroll is for 5 days

⅗ of 1500 = 900

Then $600 goes into the March payroll and $900 goes into the April payroll.

Reporting Year

A business can end its year on a calendar year or a fiscal year. A calendar year always ends on December 31. A fiscal year may end at the end of any month. If it is more convenient to close the books in November for example, then the year may end at that time. Once the date is decided, it must be followed every year. You are required to file tax forms within a specified number of days after that date.

Budget

During the first year of operation, the *pro forma* statement will act as the budget. However, after the first year you must draw up a new budget based on anticipated sales and expenses. It may not seem necessary but it is good business procedure. It is the only way in which you will be able to tell if you are on the right track during the year. The budget is made in the same manner as the *pro forma* except that now you will have more reliable figures on which to base the estimates.

What to Do with That Extra Cash

Believe it or not, there will be times when you will have more cash available than you need.

This happens usually about the twentieth of the month through the last day. The reason this happens is because this is accumulation time. You are now accumulating the cash needed to pay the monthly bills. This money is not available to pay any long term obligations but it is available to earn interest. The very least you should do is put it in an interest bearing account at the bank. At this writing, there are money market funds which pay a high rate of return. Such funds allow quick

withdrawals as needed. If you find yourself with a surplus that can be invested for more than a few days, put it in U.S. Government securities for as little as thirty days. As the business progresses, from time to time, you will find a surplus of cash. Such surplus should be used to reduce long term debt. This is essential to improve your credit rating more rapidly. Never let money sit idly by. It should always be working for you.

Chapter Three

Legal Requirements and Office Systems

One of the most time consuming and costly tasks the small businessman has to perform is the periodic filing of tax and miscellaneous government forms. For the beginner, the work is mind boggling. There are two ways you can handle it—one is to hire an accountant, the other is to do it yourself. If you do not have the time or inclination to file yourself, you may decide the expense of an accountant is worthwhile. You may decide (as I did) after a period of time, to take on the job yourself.

Taxes are collected on three levels: 1) federal, 2) state, and 3) local. There are taxes you collect for employees and taxes you pay for your business. In addition to tax forms, there are licenses and permits that must be periodically renewed. Just about all of these, including liquor license and health certificate, require payment of a fee.

The collection of taxes, the payment of taxes, and the procurement of permits is the responsibility of the individual business. It

would be wise to contact your nearest IRS office and your state and local governments to determine your responsibilities in this regard.

Federal Government

Upon opening a business, you must immediately obtain an *Employer Identification Number* by filing Form SS-4. The form is available at your local IRS office. Once you have obtained a number, the government will automatically mail all necessary forms as they are needed.

As an employer, you will be collecting social security and income taxes from your employees for the federal government. This money must be paid to the government on a monthly basis and reconciled quarterly. Make out a check for the proper amount and take it to an authorized bank along with a copy of a *Form 501*. This must be done by the fifteenth of the month following the month the money was collected. At the end of each quarter, file *Form 941*, which reports social security, tips, and withholding tax information.

The employer is required to match the amount of social security taxes collected from the employee. The current tax rate is 6.65 for both you and the employee. Keep in mind that you ·do not have to add a matching amount on tips collected. Only match the amount collected that resulted from taxation of wages earned.

By February 1 of each year you must furnish all your employees with a *W-2 Form*. This form contains all the information needed regarding federal, state, and local taxes collected the previous year. If an employee leaves during the year, you are required to provide this form within thirty days of termination. Be sure to keep the duplicates in a safe place throughout the year, because you will need them at year's end. By the end of February, all completed *W-2* forms are mailed along with a *W-3 Form* to the regional IRS office. If you keep good payroll records, the *W-2 Form* is not difficult to complete, although it is a time consuming job.

Another year end report, *Form 940*, for Federal Unemployment Tax (FUTA) must be filed by January 31. In most cases, small restaurant owners will not be liable for quarterly payments because their payroll will not be large enough. If such payments would be required, *Form 508* would be used. The tax rate in 1979 was 3.4 percent. A credit of up to 2.7 percent is allowed for state unemployment taxes paid. Consequently, the year end payment may be as low as 0.7 percent. What you pay is determined by an experience rate which is determined on the basis of wages paid. The employer pays all of this tax.

If you have a liquor license and dispense liquor, you must have a permit from the federal government, which must be renewed an-nually. An application will be sent to you each year, after you apply for the first permit. The application is very simple to complete and is just mailed back with a check.

In addition to the above requirements, there are income tax forms to be filed. Of course, the individual files a personal income tax form. There are special returns for partnerships, corporations, and subchapter S corporations, all of which tie in with your personal taxes in some way depending on the circumstances.

The federal government provides a very fine booklet, *Employer's Tax Guide* (Circular E) to help you compute and complete your tax forms. In addition, there is a *Tax Guide for Small Business* (Pub. 334) which is very comprehensive and helpful. I strongly advise you to get copies from your local IRS.

If you are starting a new business or adding new equipment to an existing one, you do not want to overlook the investment tax credit. Since the form and procedure are quite involved, consult your accountant before preparing the form.

State Government

Each state has its own requirements for taxation. As a result the discussion here will be brief and general.

Sales taxes are currently collectible in all but five states. At the end of every month or quarter, a check for the amount collected is mailed to the state, along with a form showing the amount of your sales. Some states require special breakdowns on sales of food, liquor, beer, and cigarettes. Some states give a small percentage discount for collecting the tax.

In most states, there will be business income taxes to be paid. In addition, there is the state unemployment tax which is similar to the federal tax. Income taxes for the employees are collectible through withholding provisions. A portion of the *W-2* form must be filed with the state at the end of the year.

In most states, you will need a license to sell alcoholic beverages, a health inspection license, and a cigarette sales permit. Other licenses may be necessary in some states. New operations require special building permits.

Local Government

Some local governments have income and occupational wage taxes which must be deducted from the employees' wages. In addition, there may be personal property taxes which are paid by the business entity. Permits from the health department, licenses to sell liquor, and fire permits may be required. Also, special permits for new or remodeled structures may be required.

Insurance Coverage

Unless you are financially able to cover any unusual expense due to accident, negligence, or fire, you need insurance. Insurance can take two forms, self-insurance, or insurance purchased from a company, broker, or agent.

Self-Insurance

Self-insurance can either replace outside insurance completely or supplement purchased insurance. The former method would best be used for something with a predictable cost. A TV antenna is a simple example. Divide the item's cost by a certain number of years. The result is the amount of money you will set aside each year to build a fund to pay for a new antenna should anything happen to the one you have.

There are several problems with this method. First, how many years do you use to figure your annual payment? The decision might not be too difficult for a TV antenna, but could be quite complicated for something more expensive and involved when you consider such things as installation costs. Second, you might be required to replace the item before you have enough money in the fund to pay for it. There is no way to predict such an event. The only way you can protect yourself against it is to start out with some money in the fund. This, of course, ties up capital that you could use more profitably when beginning your business.

I am sure the real and potential problems of this method of self-insurance are apparent. It is not generally recommended for the beginning business. However, I would recommend taking advantage of deductibles.

The most common example of a deductible policy is the one you probably have on your automobile. A fifty dollar deductible policy costs more than a one hundred dollar deductible, which costs more than a two hundred dollar deductible, and so on. By assuming some of the risk yourself, you can reduce the annual premium you pay to an insurer. This type of self-insurance is advantageous as long as you do not self-insure for more than you can handle. As in the above example, self-insurance becomes more useful as your financial position improves. However, you are always fully insured. You do not reduce the amount of insurance; you merely assume part of the cost of coverage.

Purchased Insurance

Insurance may be purchased directly from an insurance company, through an agent, or through a broker. There is not much distinction between an agent and a broker. Generally, an agent sells insurance for one company and a broker sells for a number of companies. However, you may find agents that sell for a number of companies.

It has been my experience, both in my personal and business life, that purchasing insurance from a broker is preferable to purchasing directly from a company. There is no additional cost to you, but there are advantages. Large companies by nature are more complicated and less understanding than smaller ones. The local insurance broker is always available to give you service and satisfaction. He or she is closer to you and the community and is, therefore, more understanding of your problems. He or she wants your business and, most important, is there when you need him or her. In addition, a single broker may be able to handle all your insurance needs.

Shop around for insurance, as you would for any other item. Price and service must go hand in hand. When comparing policies, be sure they are identical. A slight difference in coverage can make a distinct difference in the premium you pay. Your broker should make the alternatives clear to you. Do not be afraid to ask around about brokers and the companies for which they underwrite. Be sure both are reputable. If your business is large enough, do not hesitate to use more than one broker. Competition may encourage brokers to give you the best possible service.

Take advantage of group insurance whenever possible. It is almost always less expensive than private insurance. Examples of group policies are the plans available through the National Restaurant Association and Blue Cross-Blue Shield.

Finally, reevaluate your insurance coverage annually. There are always innovations being made in the insurance field. In addition, your property and equipment become more valuable each year as the replacement value increases.

If you are not familiar with the insurance industry, contact your state insurance commission for information.

Types of Insurance Coverage

The following outline of various types of insurance is complete enough for the beginning restaurant owner. I strongly recommend that you invest in all these types of insurance as soon as you are able. Your broker will advise you about the amount of coverage you need, which varies with each individual operation.

Fire and Extended Coverage covers you for losses due to fire, vandalism, and malicious mischief. You must insure for at least 80 percent of the value of the property and equipment. If you do not, you will not receive full value for your loss (it will be prorated). Try to insure for 100 percent because replacement always amounts to more than you estimate.

Comprehensive Liability generally covers two main areas of liability. *General Liability* covers injury to a guest or outsider on your premises. This is important to note because if an employee is injured on the property or premises, he or she is covered under workmen's compensation. Of course, if an employee is a guest at the establishment, he or she will not be covered under workmen's compensation. *Products Liability* covers you in case of illness resulting from consumption of one of your preparations.

Liquor Liability covers you if someone does something wrong while under the influence of alcohol that he or she received from your establishment. This is becoming an increasing problem as more and more states are passing laws making the alcohol dispenser a liable party.

Auto Liability covers bodily injury and property damage caused by a vehicle owned by your business. Your business would be liable for damage if any one of its employees were driving. You may want to include *collision* and *comprehensive* insurance, depending on the age of the vehicle.

Theft Insurance is often a separate policy. It covers breaking and entering and what is stolen or destroyed.

Umbrella Policy is additional coverage used to cover excess liability.

Fidelity Bond covers dishonesty by employees.

Business Interruption Insurance is expensive and is not needed immediately. It reimburses you for your sales loss when you are closed down through no fault of your own (e.g. fire). In effect, it gives you the income you lose when you are not operating.

Workmen's Compensation covers your employees (and yourself, if you are incorporated) if they are injured or become ill because of their job. This policy or its equivalent is required by most states.

Medical Insurance is generally a group plan. It is a fringe benefit provided by the employer, and not required. However, it is hard to get employees to work without it. It can be contributory, with the employee and company sharing the cost, or the company can pay the entire premium. Medical insurance pays all, or a portion of, the expenses incurred due to illness or injury of an employee or a member of his or her family. This is a personal insurance, not a business type of insurance.

Dental Insurance pays for dental care of the employee or members of his or her family. It too, is a personal type of insurance.

Retirement Fund is another fringe benefit.

If you provide it for yourself, you must provide it for your employees. It, too, can be either contributory or noncontributory. A retirement fund is money put aside for the eventual retirement of an employee. The amount put aside may be "vested" or not. This means the employee has the right to take the money with him if he leaves your employ before retirement takes place.

Life Insurance is insurance placed on an individual which is payable to a beneficiary after the employee's death. It is a low cost fringe benefit paid by the employer.

Key Person Insurance is life insurance on the key person or persons in the company. The life of the individual(s) is insured by the corporation. If he or she dies, the corporation can use the proceeds, for example, to purchase his or her stock in the corporation. If the business is a partnership, this form of insurance is handled a little differently, but accomplishes the same purpose.

Handling Charges and Cash

A restaurant can be operated on a strictly cash basis (this includes checks), or it can be operated with charges. Both the cash system and the charge system have inherent problems. Although cash may be simpler for bookkeeping, without strong controls a great deal of money can be lost. On the other hand, if customers are allowed to charge and do not pay their bills promptly, the company can lose money too. In today's business atmosphere, it is still better to extend some means of credit to your guest.

There are two ways to allow your customers to charge: in-house systems and third-party (credit card) systems. With the former, you take all responsibility for billing and collecting. With the latter, you accept credit cards supplied by outside companies, who do the billing and collecting for you—for a fee.

In-House Charges

It is not difficult to set up an in-house charge system. All you need is a typewriter, letterhead stationery, and envelopes. One person should be free on a weekly basis to type and mail invoices. Unless there are a great many charge customers, billing should not take very long. A sample billing is shown in Figure 3–1.

If bills are not paid within thirty days of the invoice date, send another bill. After a further two weeks, send a bill with an interest charge added. Follow up, two weeks later with a firm but polite letter. After three months, threaten legal action. After three and a half months file for collection. Make telephone calls if necessary. Never just forget a bill.

Credit Card Charges

Credit cards are issued by banks or private companies. Banks generally charge a lower fee than private companies.

When you inform the bank or company that you would like to use their system, a representative will be sent to outline the program. All systems are different, but basically, the company charges you a percentage of the money (your sales) they collect, which amounts to from 3 to 6 percent. This expense is offset by the following advantages:

1. You save billing time and money when someone else collects for you.
2. Customers may pay bills from an impersonal third party more quickly than those from small businesses.
3. You do not have to wait for customer payment. The bank or company you use will determine the speed with which you are paid. Many banks accept charge slips with your bank deposit, as cash.
4. There is little bookkeeping involved. One entry will cover any number of charges.
5. The private companies do a great deal of advertising and promotion. This can be an advantage to your restaurant.
6. Major credit cards have a certain amount of prestige. People often seek out businesses that honor a particular card.

Credit cards create some extra work for service personnel, who must check a list of cancelled credit cards before accepting one. In addition, if the bill exceeds a certain amount, telephone verification must be made for your own and the credit company's protection. If this check is not made and a charge is uncollectible, you are responsible.

Charges should be handled in the same way as cash. Losing a charge slip is the same as losing money. Employees should, therefore, be held 100 percent liable for charge slips. Because of this, in many restaurants, the waiter or waitress tends to hover over a guest until he signs the charge slip. Granted, the salesperson is responsible for the slip, but they are also responsible for cash, and they usually do not linger then. Many guests become annoyed at a hovering server. The server should stand at a discreet distance while they watch, if they feel it is necessary.

A charge system of some form or other is an integral part of a restaurant's service to the customer. A large number of people will not patronize a restaurant that does not accept credit. Some people consider credit a status symbol. Others do not like to carry large amounts of cash. Finally, the advantage to you is that people who charge spend more and tip better.

You will have to choose which credit

802/457-1818 • 24 Elm Street   **Woodstock, Vermont 05091**   T. F. CHIFFRILLER, JR., *Proprietor*

November 26, 1981

Mr. Robert Customer
Box 2100
New York, New York

<u>STATEMENT</u>

Restaurant Charges $83.21   Gratuity $16.64   <u>$99.85</u>

Thank You,

THE BUTTERNUT TREE

Sophisticated Dining in a Country Setting

Figure 3–1. A Sample Bill

This invoice was adapted from regular stationery. It is simple to make up and contains all the information necessary for a complete billing. For new customer charges, make an additional note about interest charges for bills not paid in thirty days.

system to use. The in-house system is more personal and will probably cost less to administer. The third-party system may have a larger appeal and limit liability somewhat, but may cost more.

Recording Charge Sales

All sales, regardless of whether they are cash or charge, must be entered in the sales journal. Use the following calculation:

Sales = Cash + Charges ± Overages
& Shortages

Figure 3–2 shows only the bank deposit columns of the sales journal. A more detailed analysis of the sales journal itself appears later. For the time being, take note of the following information.

On 10/1 charge is made for $99.85 and there is a shortage of $.05. The charge has no effect on the deposit, but the shortage reduces the deposit by $.05.

On 10/2 there are no charges but there is an overage of $.25, which increases the deposit by that amount.

On 10/3 there are two charges made. They have no effect on the deposit.

On 10/4 the $99.85 is paid back (no brackets). The amount is added to the day's cash, for a deposit of $552.25.

At the end of the week, make a list of all outstanding charges for control purposes. This record aids you in determining who owes how much money to you and the length of time the debt has been outstanding. These amounts are called *Accounts Receivable*.

Handling Cash

From an accounting point of view, cash sales are by far the easiest to record. However, keeping track of cash requires a system of controls.

If you do not serve liquor, it is possible to set up a very simple control system. Have a prix fixe menu. A single, predetermined price is listed on the menu for an entire meal. You merely multiply the number of guests you had by the menu price to find out how much money you should have collected. However, if you serve liquor the system is much more complicated.

In fact, unless the owner personally checks every bit of food and every drink that is served, presents every check, and makes the change for every guest, there is *no* simple system.

Many owners are victimized by dishonest employees. This problem can be almost completely eliminated by a good system of controls. The first step is setting up a Pre-Check System.

The Pre-Check System

The general system is the same in all restaurants. The food and liquor dispensed are balanced with the amount of cash or charges recorded. Individual operations may vary, so it would be best to contact the company that will supply your register(s) and have a system tailor-made for your operation.

Figure 3–2. *Sample Journal Entries*

Date	Charges			Cash		Over/under		Deposit		
10/1	Customer	(99	85)	396	55		(05)	396	50	
10/2				524	50		25	524	75	
10/3	Mr. Good	(21	35)	491	25		—	491	25	
	Mr. Friend	(10	85)							
10/4	Customer	99	85	452	40		—	552	25	
10/5	VISA (3 slips)	(46	30)	505	20		—	505	20	

A pre-check system (PCS) will only work if you insist on complete accuracy down to the last penny. One register is used by the person collecting cash, the other by the salespersons. In a small operation, you may start out with one register for both functions and add a second later.

An accurate system of "dupes" (or receipts) is necessary to implement any pre-check system. Handwritten dupes are most commonly used in restaurants not utilizing a PCS, as a memo rather than as a control. Originally, a dupe was a carbon copy of the salesperson's order. This was presented to a particular station in the kitchen or to the bar to obtain the needed food or beverage. Thus, the salesperson had a copy of his or her order and the department had its record. At the end of the meal the department dupes were compared to the items sold (which appeared on the guest check). This assured the owner that no item left the kitchen or bar without being accounted for. In the vast majority of today's restaurants, the dupe is just a written order which is thrown away after the order is completed. This negates the control aspect of the dupe system. The PCS returns this control to the owner along with many other benefits as well.

The pre-check system is performed as follows:

The order is first taken on a small pad by the salesperson. The waiter or waitress then goes to the register and enters the menu items in the machine. Some of the newer machines may have the item listed on the keyboard for instant touch or a specific number may be assigned to each item.

As each item is entered in the register, a small piece of paper (the dupe) is ejected. In some recent models, the dupe is ejected only after all the items are entered. If desired, and the menu item is not printed on the dupe, it may be written in by the salesperson. De-

pending on the age of the machine or the manufacturer, the check is inserted during the entry of the items or after all the items are entered.

There is no way a dupe can be obtained without the transaction being imprinted on the check. If the kitchen and bar staff are instructed not to give anything without a dupe, nothing can leave the kitchen or bar without being accounted for.

This system has proven extremely successful when followed to the letter. It is essential that a single person have complete charge of any cash or charge transactions or corrections during the meal period. If just anyone is allowed to make adjustments, the control aspect is completely lost.

At the end of the meal, the dupes are turned in and placed with the cash. They can then be used for a later check, if needed. The person in charge takes a reading from the machine(s). The machine is then cleared and the tapes are removed. The tapes are placed with the cash for the bookkeeper. The tapes have recorded *every* transaction that went into the register. Consequently, if a check or dupe has been altered it can be caught.

When the meal has been completed and the register cleared, there will be an accurate breakdown of all sales by categories. When the categories are added together, the total should equal the amount of money and charges collected by the person receiving the cash. Of course, errors are sometimes made by the person operating the register(s). If they are found before the check is presented, they can be corrected by the person in charge, *not* by the salesperson.

The bookkeeper must check a number of items to insure the accuracy of the system. Initially, this may be time-consuming. However, after a time, a trained person will be able to spot errors very quickly.

It should be a hard and fast rule that

employees are responsible for their errors. In addition, they should be held accountable for lost checks.

The Register

There are any number of companies that have registers available. These machines offer many more features, are simpler to operate, can be programmed, and cost less than those of the past. In addition, they can be tied in with other registers and transmit data electronically to the kitchen or the bar. With such a setup, the order often reaches the kitchen or bar before the service person does. However, such sophistication may be a little expensive for the beginning operator.

Whether one machine will be sufficient for you depends somewhat on the physical size of your operation and the distance between departments. If two registers are used, one should have a cash drawer and the other should be used as the checker machine. The checker will have categories for such items as food, liquor, and beer. There are many features which can be incorporated into the checker machine; among them are previous balance pick up, automatic line finder, and an error correction key.

The design of the cash register will vary depending on how you use it. In most smaller operations, the bartender will act as the cashier. If this is the case, the bartender will need keys to ring up the sales. There must also be keys for checks paid, cash, charge, and tax (optional). If you have a separate cashier, you will need another small register for the bartender.

The register should be installed at the proper height (the top of a table or counter is too high) and with sufficient lighting. The keyboard should be within easy reach of shorter people.

Guest Checks

Any type of standard preprinted check may be used. The only requirement is that it fit the machine. Because different machines space lines differently, you may prefer checks without lines. Having special checks printed with your business's name is an unnecessary expense. The check is seen for a very brief time by the guest. Its major purpose is internal control. Having a different colored check for each department, however, makes sorting easier.

Checks should be consecutively numbered so that you can easily keep track of them and be sure duplicates have not been used.

Checks should be issued by the person in charge. The numbers should be recorded, and each salesperson should be responsible for the return of all unused checks. Never allow erasures or heavy crossing out. Employees should be instructed to run one heavy line through any errors they make.

Tax and service charges may be written in at the bottom of the check rather than entered in the register.

Writing on checks should be in ink.

Checks should be dated, and include the salesperson's name or initials and the table number.

A two-part check can be useful for a receipt. However, a separate printed receipt with your name, address, and telephone number makes a good piece of advertising. Include all pertinent information for tax purposes, such as the amount of the check and the date.

Pricing

Have a complete menu and price list for all food. Also have a list of drinks and their prices along with a wine list. Placing a copy of these lists by each register will save a lot of errors. Unusual items not on the lists are sometimes ordered. The person in charge should determine the price of each of these. The price should then be noted on the check as "special." Try to keep away from specials. They cause extra work and confusion among the staff.

Supplies and Operation of Register

Be sure to have enough supplies on hand. This includes not only the guest checks, but tape and ink pads as well. The system sometimes turns into needless pandemonium when the tape runs out. A mark on the tape warns when the end is near. Train your personnel to notify the proper person when the mark becomes visible.

It is important that the person in charge is trained to change tapes and correct minor problems such as check jamming. Such problems can really throw salespeople off pace in the middle of a busy evening.

No piece of machinery is guaranteed to last forever. For this reason, it is a good idea to obtain a yearly service contract with the company from which you purchase the machine. The first year is usually covered by the purchase warranty. After that, a service contract entitles you to priority service in case of failure. Without such a contract, you may wait days for service.

Errors

It would be impossible for the very best employee never to make an error. *No one* except the person in charge should be allowed to correct an error once it is printed on the check.

When an error is made (and found before the guest receives the check), the salesperson must bring the dupe containing the error to the person in charge. This person will authorize the removal of the amount. The correct amount should then be added to the check. The dupe that was in error should be initialed by the supervisor and put with the cash for that meal. This is important because the amount will have to be accounted for in order to balance out.

It is important that this routine be followed from the beginning. If it isn't, there will be no way to guarantee your figures at the end of the meal.

As mentioned previously, never allow erasures or obliterations of the printed figures. It can be time consuming and costly tracing these amounts. A single line through the item is sufficient.

By following this method for the treatment of errors your work will be kept to a minimum.

Employees must be held accountable for their errors. Otherwise, there is no incentive not to make errors. In addition to the money directly lost, the bookkeeper's time is costly. Employees should be responsible for overcharges as well as undercharges, since an overcharge results in an unhappy guest who may not return.

An incentive program might help reduce errors. If a week goes by without an error by anyone, offer some type of bonus. Let the employees know you appreciate their hard work and effort.

The pre-check system is designed to save you money. I do not know of anyone who has tried the pre-check system and gone back to the old method. Even the employees are happier with PCS than with the old carbon-duplicate system.

The cost of instituting the PCS demands that you pay attention to every detail of the system. To overlook any one is to decrease the value of the system to a degree. The work involved to make it succeed must be done daily and not allowed to pile up. The following errors can all be avoided if the system is properly used.

1. Charging an incorrect price for an item.
2. Errors in addition.
3. Errors in calculations.
4. Missing checks.
5. Listing of items incorrectly, resulting in an incorrect charge.
6. Items not on check.
7. Item listed twice, when served only once.
8. Incorrect tax and gratuity (when added to check).

There are various ways to make employees aware of their mistakes. One is to make up a weekly list of their names and the amounts of their error to be posted. Make it the employee's responsibility to pay before the next week starts. If an amount is particularly large, do not post it. Tell the person privately to avoid embarrassment. Make the checks containing the error available for employees to see. Any other method of notification that results in obtaining the money due the company is satisfactory.

No system is completely foolproof when human minds are looking for a way to beat it. However, the pre-check system is about as close to perfect as you can get in controlling sales. It is not inexpensive to install but the money saved, due to the elimination of errors and dishonesty, is considerable. The fact that so many restaurants are willing to install the system speaks for itself.

In addition to control, the system produces a sales breakdown with no additional effort, comprehensive tax records, a supplement for other records, a neat, creditable check, and fair treatment of the guest. There isn't much more one can ask of a system.

For those who simply cannot afford the cost of a register when starting out, the old dupe system may be utilized. It is a very poor substitute for the PCS but it is the only viable alternative.

Accountability is the key. In order to gain any semblance of control, it is essential that all checks and dupes be consecutively numbered.

Salespeople must be held strictly accountable for all checks and dupes. To facilitate this end, the employee must sign for any checks he or she receives and return the unused checks after each meal. Erasures and alterations should not be permitted. At the end of the day, the items listed on the dupes should be compared with those listed on the checks. They should be the same. As with the PCS, no item should be dispensed from the kitchen or bar without a dupe. Pricing and arithmetic must also be verified. Sales figures can be obtained with the use of an adding machine and entered in the sales journal.

Safeguarding Cash and Checks

Up to now, we have been primarily concerned with the bookkeeping function of cash handling. We spoke of it in terms of recording, so we could be assured of receiving all that was due us. Now, we will discuss the acutal handling of cash and how to safeguard against its loss.

The pre-check system precludes stealing from the business or the guest by manipulation of the check. However, additional procedures should be implemented to insure against any dishonesty whatever.

The areas to be considered are:

1. From the time the salesperson receives the guest's money (or charge), until it is in the register,
2. While the money is in the possession of the cashier,
3. From the time the cashier turns it over to the house to the time it is placed in the bank.

Control of the Salesperson

It is wise to set up a routine to be followed once the guest makes the actual payment to the salesperson. One such routine might be:

1. Check is presented.
2. Check and cash (or bank check, credit card, or signed check) are picked up by service person. The cash is counted.
3. Check is taken to cashier and turned over with the payment. If a credit card is used, a voucher is properly filled out and returned, with the check, to the guest. The guest then signs both the check and the voucher. Both are returned to the cashier.
4. Cashier verifies amount and rings up the amount paid on the check. If a credit card is used, this step is not completed until cashier has the credit card voucher. If a security check on the credit card amount is necessary, it should be done before this step is completed.
5. Cashier gives the service person the necessary change. If it is a credit card sale, the customer portion of the voucher is returned to the salesperson. The change is counted when received.
6. Change or charge voucher is returned to the guest.

Counting the payment in front of the guest protects both guest and salesperson. Recounting by the cashier, protects both you and the cashier. Finally, the salespersons' counting the change protects them and the cashier.

Gratuity Payout

Sometimes the gratuity is included on house charges, credit card charges, or bank check payments. This must be paid to the service-person. Because no actual cash is changing hands, the tip is paid from the cash drawer. When this is necessary, just use a standard petty cash form obtainable from an office supply house. Have it filled out with: 1) date, 2) amount of payment, 3) signature of person receiving payment, 4) guest check number, and 5) reason for payment (gratuity). The completed slip is retained by the cashier and counted in the cash deposit at the end of the meal.

Control of the Cashier

Even with the pre-check system, there is not complete control over the bartender. If he or she does not ring up a sale or undercharges,

Figure 3–3. Petty Cash Slip

NO. _____	AMOUNT $ _____
RECEIVED OF PETTY CASH	
DATE _____ 19 __	
FOR _____	
CHARGE TO _____	
APPROVED BY _____	RECEIVED BY _____

it can go undetected. Consequently, it is imperative the cashier and bartender are of unquestionable character. These are two jobs for which you must absolutely check references.

The cashier is given a starting bank, for which a signed receipt must be obtained. A bank is an amount of cash entrusted to an employee in order to transact the daily business. The amount should be kept to a minimum. It can be fifty, seventy-five, or one hundred dollars, or whatever is needed to facilitate the easy flow of business. The bank should consist of pennies, nickels, dimes, quarters, singles, and fives (tens, if needed) in the proportion necessary. At the end of the day, the bank should be replenished and made ready for the next day's business. The daily make-up of the bank may change but the total amount will not.

At the end of the meal or day, the cash drawer will usually contain the cashier's bank, cash from sales, credit card vouchers, checks, and, possibly, some miscellaneous cash. This must be reconciled with the day's business (See Figure 3–4.) The simplest way to do this is:

1. Count the bank out.
2. Count remaining cash.
3. Total amount of checks.
4. Total cash and checks.
5. Total all charges. Keep house charges separate from credit card charges. Add to total in #4.
6. Total petty cash slips, if any.
7. Add totals from #4, #5, and #6.
8. Person in charge clears register. Remove and retain tapes.

If no mistakes have been made, the total in #7 should equal the amount of the total sales for the meal or day.

Sometimes, there may be some extra cash because of money received from the service personnel in payment of errors. This should be deducted from #7.

When the cashier has completed the "cashing out," the money and checks should be placed in an envelope. Note the amount enclosed and the date on the outside. The charges, petty cash slips, voids (if any), guest checks, and register tapes should be bound with a rubber band and wrapped with another band to the cash envelope. This should then be turned over to you (or the person you designate), along with the cashier's bank.

After the money is removed from the register for the day, leave the drawer open. If someone breaks in, there is not much sense in having the empty register pried open and damaged.

Handling Cash and Checks

The final step in safeguarding the currency in your possession is to get it in the bank, or in a safe place until it can be deposited. Some owners have a metal safe or a "secret" hiding place on the premises. Others take the receipts home with them. The best procedure is to deposit the money in the bank at the earliest opportunity. Use the night depository, if necessary.

Try to choose a bank convenient to your business location. This makes it easier to make deposits and to obtain needed change.

To make a deposit, recount the money and checks given to you by the cashier. If both counts agree, there is no problem. If they do not, count it again. If they still do not agree, count the cash bank. Sometimes money is put in the wrong place after it is counted. If there is still a problem, note the difference by listing all the cash denominations and the check amounts. Then, make the deposit as is.

CASH REGISTER REPORT

Initials _____   Date _____

Bank $ *100.00*

Cash

    Coins $ *80.25*

    Singles   *15. —*

    Fives   *35. —*

    Tens   *90. —*

    Twenties   *140. —*

    Other   *- O -*

       Total Cash $ *360.25*

Checks

    First Bank $ *20.45*

    State Trust   *46.20*

       Total Checks $ *66.65*

Subtotal $ *428.90*

Charges

    House $ *- O -*

    Credit Cards   *40.36*

       Total Charges $ *40.36*

Petty Cash slips $ *4.36*

Subtotal $ *471.62*

Other Cash (plus/minus) $ *(1.10)*

       NET TOTAL $ *$470.52*

Figure 3–4. Cash Register Report

The next day speak to your cashier regarding the difference. Be sure to make a duplicate deposit slip when putting money in the night depository, or you will have no record of the amount. If the bank disagrees with the figures on your deposit slip, someone will call the next day to reconcile the difference.

Here is a way to count the cash at the end of the day and remove the cashier's bank at the same time. Once this system is mastered, it will save time, because the cash is handled only once. With most other methods, the bank is removed in large bills, the remainder is counted and then the large bills have to be exchanged for change for the next day's business. With the method described here, the change from the current day is utilized the next day. This may save an extra trip to the bank.

1. Remove the pennies from the register. Count them to the nearest nickel and place the extra to the side.
2. Add the amount of the pennies to the nickels and bring to the nearest dime. Put the remainder to the side.
3. Add the above sum to the dimes and bring to the nearest quarter putting the remainder aside.

4. Add the sum above to the quarters and bring to the nearest dollar. Put the remainder aside.
5. Add the dollar figure to the dollars from the drawer and put aside any amount over a multiple of five.
6. And so on, until you reach the amount of the bank.
7. The money put aside becomes part of the cash receipts.

Illustration

Assume you have sales and tax of $540.58 on the register at the end of the meal. The cash bank is $100.

When the amount of change is added to the amount of paper money (and no errors have been made), the total will equal the sales and tax figure on the register. If there are checks or charges, they are added to the total cash and the resulting figure is the sales and tax. (See the table at the bottom of this page.)

The Bank

The last item to be considered in handling cash and checks is the bank account and the deposit.

#1	Pennies	$	.28						−	.08	=	$ .20
#2	Nickels		.85	+	$ .20	=	$ 1.05		−	.05	=	1.00
#3	Dimes		1.70	+	1.00	=	2.70		−	.20	=	2.50
#4	Quarters		9.75	+	2.50	=	12.25		−	.25	=	12.00
									.58		
#5	Singles		63.00	+	12.00	=	75.00				=	75.00
#6	Fives		25.00	+	75.00	=	100.00					100.00 (Bank)
	Tens		180.00									
	Twenties		360.00									
	Other		-0-									
			$640.58									
#7			− 100.00 (Bank)									
			$540.58									

Opening a business account is no more complicated than a personal account. You supply the necessary information to the bank and they give you an account number. This number is printed on your business checks and deposit slips to facilitate handling and to give you a means of identification if any problems should arise. The bank furnishes a monthly statement, usually at the end of each month, which you use to reconcile your accounts. Whether you use checks made up by the bank or some other source is up to you. This is discussed more completely in the sections on cash disbursements and the payroll system.

The deposit slip will have space to enter change, bills, and checks. Count the change and bills from the daily receipts and enter the total in the proper column. Loose change should be placed in a small envelope provided for that purpose. Large numbers of coins of one denomination should be placed in separate envelopes to save time in counting.

Each denomination of bills should be counted separately. The bills should all be facing in the same direction and the face should be on top. When bundling the various denominations together, the larger bills should be on top. On some deposit slips, there is space to break down the paper currency.

Checks should be listed separately on the deposit slip. In the upper right corner of all checks there are a group of numbers. These are there to identify the various banks. When listing checks, use the top group of numbers for identification. List the number and then the amount. All checks must be endorsed on the back with the company name and account number. It is a simple matter to have the bank make up a rubber stamp for this purpose. Be sure the stamp says, "for deposit only." This prevents anyone from cashing the check.

Total the deposit slip and attach it to the cash and checks. Depending on the system used by the bank, you may need a duplicate deposit slip. If this is the case, the bank usually furnishes the proper deposit book which contains a carbon. Fill in your name and the date and make the deposit as soon as possible. By doing all the paperwork before you arrive at the bank and following the proper procedure, you save yourself those extra minutes standing in line unnecessarily.

The deposit slips should be retained for recording in the Cash Disbursements Journal and as a record of the deposit.

Reconciling or Balancing A Checking Account

One of the less important items of everyday life is the balancing of the monthly bank statement. More often than not, the bank's balance is accepted as correct and we dutifully adjust our book balance. We reason that banks do not make mistakes.

In business, this approach is unacceptable. You must know where the mistakes were made and who made them. Banks sometimes do make mistakes. Besides, you will need accurate documentation at tax time.

Here is a list of reasons a checking account might not balance at the end of the period:

1. Checks are outstanding.
2. A check is written but not entered in the checkbook or registry.
3. A check is written for a different amount than the one that is recorded.
4. The bank records the check incorrectly on the statement.
5. You, or the bank, have incorrectly entered a deposit.
6. A deposit has been omitted either on your records or on the bank statement.

7. A deposit you have considered in your balance does not show on the bank's statement because it was made after the closing date on the statement.

8. Charges, such as service charges, printing of checks and deposit slips, postdate checks, and insufficient funds penalties, were made by the bank.

9. A check you deposited was not collectible, and has not been credited to your account.

10. One of your checks has been altered.

11. Errors that have been caught by either you or the bank on a day-to-day basis have been overlooked.

Reconciling a bank statement is not really that difficult after you do it a few times and get to know where the mistakes occur most frequently. If you are careful when writing checks and making your deposits, errors seldom happen. It is important to remember that if you find the same mistakes happening frequently, you are being careless. Correct yourself and save a lot of extra work in the future.

Here is the procedure to follow to balance your bank statement:

1. Get a full-size, lined sheet of paper and a colored pencil.

2. Have last month's statement, your bankbook or registry, the deposit book or bank slips, and any other pertinent material you may have collected since the last statement at hand.

3. Open the bank statement and remove the contents. Be careful not to misplace anything.

4. Separate the checks from the statement. If there are deposit slips, separate them as well.

5. Open the statement. Starting at the top of your pile of checks, tick off on the statement each amount that corresponds to the amount of a check. This assures that you have each of the checks that is debited to your statement. (This step is optional. I don't really find it necessary. If you are new to balancing, it may give you some reassurance to do it.)

6. Check the balance on last month's statement. The opening balance on the top of this month's statement should be the same amount. If it is not call the bank immediately.

7. Arrange the checks in numerical order.

8. Compare *your* deposit slips with the amounts on the statement. Tick off each amount on the statement that agrees with your slip. You will probably find you have more slips than the bank has entries. This is because the bank may close out the statement before your deposits are credited. If this is so, make a list of the amounts and total it. If there are any errors, note them too.

9. Make a list of all outstanding checks. These are checks you have written but have not been charged to your account as yet. Set up a list with the heading o/s (outstanding).

   a. You probably had o/s checks on last month's statement. These will be on the top of the pile of checks. Tick them off last month's list of o/s checks. If some are still outstanding from last month, enter them in the new list you have set up. List by check number and amount. It's a good idea, if these checks remain o/s for two consecutive months, to check with the company or person involved as to why they have not been cashed.

b. The remaining checks should now be compared with the bankbook or check register. As each check compares with the one in the checkbook, tick it off. If you come upon a number in the checkbook that you do not have a check for, place o/s next to it and list it (by number and amount).

c. You now have a list of all outstanding checks from last month and this month. Total them.

10. If there were any errors, such as the incorrect amount in the comparisons of the checks to the book or register, these should have been listed. List them as (+) when they are to be added to your book balance or (−) when they are to be subtracted.

11. Make notes on your sheet of paper of any other charges.

12. Write down the balance from your bank statement.

a. Deduct the total of o/s checks from step #9c.

b. Add the total of the deposits in step #8.

13. Write down the balance from the checkbook or register.

a. Add or deduct any errors as noted in step #10.

b. Deduct any charges as noted in step #11.

14. Compare total in #12 with #13. They should agree.

15. If they do not agree:

a. Check the arithmetic on your worksheet.

b. Sometimes, the difference is the amount of a check or deposit you may have overlooked when comparing your checks and slips against the bankbook or statement. Go back over your work and see if this is the case.

c. The next possibility (and the most likely) is that you have made a mistake in the arithmetic in your bankbook. You must now go to your checkbook or register and double check all your addition and subtraction.

d. You may wish to do this step before the one above. Go through the entire reconciliation process again. You may have overlooked something the first time. Chances are, if you are careful, this will not be the case. That is why I prefer doing #15c first.

16. Assuming you are in balance, you must now make the necessary adjustments to your book or register balance. If there are any bank errors, the bank must be notified. They should send you confirmations of any corrections they make. If you have made any errors, they should be added to, or subtracted from, your book or register balance.

Reconciling the Payroll Account

Basically, payroll accounts are reconciled in the same manner as the general account. There should always be some differentiation between payroll and general account checks. Usually, this is done by using a different color check or a different series of numbers, or both.

Cash Disbursements

A cash disbursement takes place whenever you make payment for something in cash (or check). When the money is paid out, you have reduced your cash holdings. An example may be found in your daily life. If you use your credit card to pay for a purchase, you retain the money in your pocket. When you pay the statement at the end of the month, you have used the money you had in your pocket and, therefore, reduced your cash holdings. Even though the obligation was incurred earlier, the cash disbursement did not take place until you actually paid the bill.

In business, cash disbursements should always be made by check. This acts as an element of control and gives you a permanent record of the payment. Granted, there will be times when payment by check will not be practical and cash will be used. These exceptions should be held to a minimum.

A petty cash bank may be kept on the premises. Generally, about twenty-five dollars is sufficient. This can be adjusted as you see fit. When the cash is used up, it is replenished by the issuance of a check for the amount needed to bring the fund back to the original amount. For example, if the bank is $25 and you spend all but $2.73, write a check to petty cash for $22.27. The check is then cashed and the petty cash fund replenished. After this is done, you will have a complete record of all the expenditures.

You can take money from the day's receipts *if* you make a receipt or voucher for the amount removed. However, as you will see later, this will result in a loss of control, confusion, and extra work when the expense must be entered in the books. The petty cash fund is the best method to use to ensure the necessary control.

In a small business, cash disbursements are limited to two categories: general expenses and payroll. General expenses are broken down into categories (e.g. food, beverage, laundry) when the check is made. Payroll is much more involved and requires exact computations before a check can be drawn. See the section concerning payroll for a detailed description. You can set up both systems yourself. However, I strongly recommend a complete system by a company such as Safeguard Business Systems for simplicity and accuracy. The cost may be greater in dollars laid out but you will save in many ways.

To set up your own general account, you will need a bank checking account and some columnar paper. The bank checks should be colored (different from the payroll checks), numbered consecutively, and marked, "General Account." In addition, they should have your name, address, account number, and a place for an authorized signature. Only one person should have authority to sign checks. The checks should be bound in a large book with as many to a page as possible. The check stub should be attached to the check (it is much harder to forget to list one this way). Checks are written in the same general manner as other checks. On the stub, carefully note the amount of the check, the date, the purpose of the check, and the name of the company or person receiving it.

Next, you will need some columnar sheets for the journal in which the checks will be recorded. In addition to the information found on the check stubs, the columnar sheet will also contain a breakdown of the expense. It is possible to have any number of categories or accounts. However, it is more practical to limit the number of columns used. For example, food, beverage, and payroll will have a number of entries during the month. For this reason, it is a good idea to have a column for each. Items such as telephone, electricity, and water can be grouped under one column called "utilities." They can be picked up by name at the time the financial statement is prepared.

At least once a week, more often if you have the time, the information contained on the check stubs must be transferred to the

Cash Disbursements Journal. To do this, list each check by number on the breakdown sheet. Record the date, check number, name of company, and the amount of the check.

The check amount should be broken down and extended to the proper account (column). There are times when a check amount may be for more than one category of accounts and thus, be apportioned to various columns.

Listing checks is a straightforward procedure. There are two categories which require some explanation. These are the petty cash fund and the payroll account.

As we discussed earlier, in order to replenish the petty cash bank, a check is written for the amount covered by the vouchers. When the check is written, the amounts for the various categories or accounts are listed under the proper heading. This is accomplished with one entry. If money had been taken from the daily receipts as was suggested, an entry would have to be made in the cash receipts book for each amount and an offsetting charge would have to be made to the Cash Disbursements Journal. This would have to be done each day an amount was taken from the daily receipts, regardless of how small or large—an unnecessary waste of time and bookkeeping.

The payroll account is a special account which is discussed elsewhere. However, when the payroll check is written to the general account it is broken down somewhat differently than other checks. Suppose the entire payroll is $400. Ninety-six dollars is withholding tax and $24.20 is FICA. This must be reflected in the journal breakdown because your immediate cash disbursement is only $279.80 ($400 − $96 − $24.20 = $279.80). You do not pay out the withholding and FICA until a later date. To indicate this when making the journal breakdown, list the sum of the entire payroll and deduct the amounts of the withholding

tax and FICA. Bracket the amounts to indicate a deduction to the account.

Although the payroll account is a completely separate account, the money to fund it comes from the general account. That is why a check must be written. This check is then deposited in the payroll checking account.

Each page of the Cash Disbursements Journal should contain the month and year at the top. In addition, the pages should be numbered consecutively for ready reference and filed in a special binder.

Balancing the Cash Disbursements Journal

At the end of each month the journal is closed out. (See Figure 3–5.) The columns are totaled vertically and then these totals are added together. This total should equal the total in the column containing the check amounts. If it does not, an arithmetic mistake has been made. To find the error, first check to see if you *subtracted* the withholding and FICA taxes. This is a common mistake. Second, check the total of the vertical totals. Third, check the vertical totals themselves. Fourth, check the horizontal totals (if a check amount was entered in more than one column). The improper addition of the petty cash check is the most common error in this test.

You do not have to wait until the end of the month to total your figures. It can be done weekly. Each new week's total is then added to the previous week's for a subtotal. Errors are easier to uncover when totaling is done more frequently.

When the cash disbursements journal is in balance, there is one additonal check you must make. Is the journal in agreement with the checkbook? This can be determined very quickly by running a total of the check stubs for the month. If this total agrees with the

Figure 3–5. Cash Disbursements Journal

CASH DISBURSEMENTS JOURNAL

PAGE 12
MONTH MAY
1979

CK. NO.	DATE		NAME CHECK ISSUED AND PURPOSE		AMT. OF CHECK	FOOD	BEVERAGE	PAYROLL	FICA	WITHHOLDING	FOOD SUPPLIES	MISC.	
223	5	4	PETTY CASH		21 14	8 63	4 52				5 98	2 01	(TACKS)
224	5	8	COLONIAL OFFICE SUPPLY (OFFICE SUPPLIES)	Apr.	46 50							46 50	
225	"		MONARCH INCORP.	Apr.	196 23	122 50					73 73		
226	"		PAYROLL ACCT.		279 80			400 00	(24 20)	(96 00)			
227	"		GOOD MEAT COMPANY	Apr.	780 29	780 29							
228	"		ACME BEER DIST.	Apr.	27 40		27 40						
229	"		PETTY CASH		17 24	6 72					3 29	7 23	(PAPER)
230	"		NANCE'S PRODUCE	Apr.	329 10	322 10					7 00		
			ETC.										
242	5	14	STATE NATIONAL BANK		2385 70							2000 00 385 70	PRIN INT
243	5	15	PAYROLL		334 36			478 00	(28 92)	(114 72)			
			ETC.										
					4417 76	1240 24	31 92	878 00	(53 12)	(210 72)	90 00	2441 44	

amount in the total of the check amounts, you are in balance. If it does not, recheck the figures you just ran. If no error is found, the problem is in the transfers from the checkbook to the journal. You must now compare each entry in the journal with the corresponding one in the checkbook. There is no other place a mistake can be made if the journal has balanced.

When the error is located, the amount in the journal must then be changed and the necessary corrections made in the various categories and totals.

When the month is completed and everything is in balance, the totals of the various accounts are then used to compile your operational statement.

Life being complicated as it is, restaurant accounting must follow the pattern. Unfortunately, some of the accounts in the Cash Disbursements Journal are for last month's expenditures, while some of the current month's figures will not appear until next month. Consequently, the operational statement cannot be completed until the current month's expenses are paid.

While you are waiting for all the expenses to be recorded, you can list on the operating statement form whatever expenses you have available for the current month. When the remaining items are paid (before the tenth of the month), add these amounts to those which you already have. This will then give you all the expenses for the current month. You are ready to compile the statement.

Analysis of Figure 3–5

1. Note the information from the check stubs contained in the first four columns (check number, date, account name and check amount).

2. Page number and date appear in upper right corner.
3. Checks are listed in consecutive order.
4. The amount for petty cash checks is spread among various accounts. The items in "misc." column are identified. Any items in the "misc." column should be labeled. Notice, when the amounts from all the columns are added together on a particular line, they equal the amount of the check.
5. The payroll check is written for the difference of the total payroll minus FICA and withholding.
6. Certain checks are marked with "Apr." This indicates they were last month's expenses and will be used in preparing that month's operating statement.
7. For the purpose of illustration, the totals are made with the figures contained on this sheet. However, it is obvious that other figures have been omitted.
   a. Each column has been totaled from "Food" through "Misc."
   b. When the above totals are added (or subtracted) together, the total will equal the total under "Amt. of Check."
   c. The total under "Amt. of Check" should equal the sum of the check stubs.

Commercial Business Systems

There are two reasons for suggesting a commercial business system for cash disbursements instead of the do-it-yourself type. First, by eliminating the double work of writing the check information on the stub and check and then again in the journal, considerable time is saved. The need for a cash disbursements book is also eliminated because the information can be included in the disbursement journal. Second, an opportunity for errors is eliminated. Whenever you have transfers, you have an opportunity for error. Figures can be copied incorrectly, omitted or duplicated, or transferred to the wrong line. Any of these errors will throw your balance off, making rechecking necessary.

By using carbons or NCR paper with both the cash disbursements and payroll, the commercial business system eliminates extra work and the conditions for transfer errors. In addition, everything you need in the way of supplies, such as checks, and columnar sheets, can be obtained from one source. The

forms are preprinted and designed to fit a standard work board. Look into this concept *before* you start operating.

Compare the simplicity and time saving features of a system such as the one in Figure 3–6 with the do-it-yourself system described earlier. Note the necessity of only having to write the information on the check one time. It then appears on the journal sheet with all the information you need for your records. You can extend the check amount to the proper account at the same time you write the check. Also note the way the system can be adapted for a cash receipts journal.

Figure 3–6. A Commercial Business System for Cash Disbursements. This system contains: 1) check, 2) disbursements journal, 3) bank balance and deposit section, 4) columns for accounts, 5) space for balancing totals, 6) extra columns which can be used for cash receipts. (Artwork courtesy of Safeguard Business Systems Inc.)

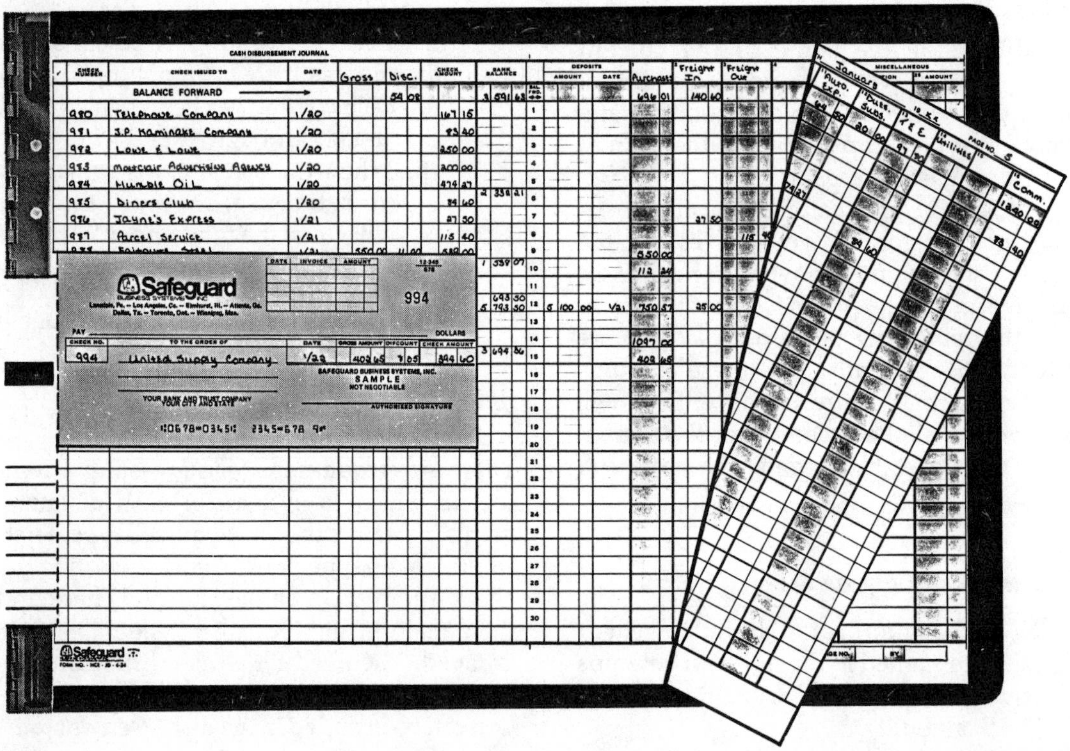

Sales Journal and
Cash Receipts Journal

In a small business there is no need to do more bookkeeping than necessary. I do not believe in keeping a great number of records that will never be used. If certain information is required for good bookkeeping and tax purposes, it should be recorded. Time is precious when you are in business for yourself. As the business grows and gets more complicated, your bookkeeping will become more elaborate.

Fortunately, small restaurants lend themselves nicely to so-called "single entry" bookkeeping. Because of this, small restaurateurs can keep most of their own records without too much difficulty.

Sales receipts must be broken into components to compute percentages and make comparisons. The usual breakdown is food and beverage. However, wine and beer sales can be added, if a sales comparison is needed. In some states, for tax purposes, additional breakdowns may be required.

At the end of each meal or day, the register provides the information needed for the sales breakdown. This information will be subject to corrections you may find after auditing the guest checks for the period. Once the necessary corrections are made to the register readings and you are in balance, you are ready to enter the figures into the journal. Do not make entries until you are in balance. Enter each amount (food, liquor, wine, etc.) in the proper column. Add these amounts together to arrive at the amount to be placed in the column headed "Total Sales."

The next item to appear in the journal is sales tax. It is a good idea to check this amount each day. Simply multiply the taxable items by the tax rate and compare the figure with the amount collected. If the two are not within a few pennies of one another, better go through the guest checks for mistakes.

Errors are not uncommon when service personnel compute their own tax.

The sales journal portion of the combined books is now complete. At the end of the day, the cashier should have either cash or charges equivalent to the sum of the sales and sales tax.

The procedure seems simple, but, unfortunately, it must be modified at times to take into consideration the following:

1. Mistakes by the cashier in making change,
2. Pricing errors on guest checks,
3. Tax errors,
4. Payments for errors made by service personnel.

Here are some general guidelines to use when recording in the cash receipts journal:

1. When errors occur on the plus side (overage), they are deducted from the o/s (over-short) account. If they are short, they are added to the o/s account. Such errors usually are due to incorrect change being given out by the cashier.
2. Pricing errors uncovered when the checks are audited are handled in the same manner. If the incorrect charge is less than the proper amount, the amount is added to sales. If it is an overcharge, it is subtracted from sales.
3. Tax errors are recorded the same way as sales and o/s errors.
4. Employees should be held responsible for all errors, whether they are over or under. When the amount of the error is paid back (to the restaurant), the entry should always be a deduction from the day's business because it has nothing to do with the day's sales.

5. When a charge is made, it is a plus because eventually it will be collected. Consequently, charges are added in the journal. As mentioned elsewhere, they are "receivables." They are considered part of current assets.

6. Later when the charge is paid, it is deducted from the journal. This offsets the original entry to take it out of receivables.

7. Whenever a charge is made or paid, the name of the person must be included next to the charge or payment to identify it.

Essentially, this is all the information you need to set up the cash receipts journal. Following is a practical application of the information outlined.

Instructions for Making Entries

In all cases, it is assumed the given data for sales and tax will be entered. Except for 12/10, the amounts will be the same as given in the illustration.

12/5 Sales and tax equal $361.84. This is the only money collected this day. There were no adjustments to be made. The deposit will then be $361.84.

12/6 Sales and tax equal $402.50. Cash plus charges are $402.40. The cash is $.10 short. It is entered as a plus transaction in the o/s column. There was no other money collected, therefore, the deposit will be $319.00.

$$\$402.50 = \$319.00 + \$83.40 + \$.10$$
$$\$402.50 = \$402.50$$

12/7 Sales and tax equal $541.10. Cash is $541.35. There were no charges. The cash is $.25 over. It is entered as a minus transaction. The deposit will be $541.35, plus the check for $20.12 (received on account) or $561.47. Because the check had nothing to do with the day's sales, it is entered as a minus transaction (a deduction).

$$\$541.10 = \$561.47 - \$.25 - \$20.12$$
$$\$541.10 = \$541.10$$

12/8 Sales and tax equal $481.70. Cash and charges are $481.70. The cash is cor-

Figure 3–7. *Cash Receipts Journal*

		SALES						RECEIPTS				PAGE 12 MONTH DEC. 1979
1979	FOOD	LIQUOR	WINE	MISC.	TOTAL SALES	SALES TAX	DEPOSIT	O/S	MISC.	EXPLAIN
12 5	219 40	99 60	30 00		349 00	12 84	361 84			
12 6	232 30	108 20	47 60	50	388 60	13 90	319 00	10	23 35 / 60 05	RUDOLPH TREE
12 7	365 70	112 20	40 00	1 25	519 15	21 95	561 47	(25)	(20 12)	MONTY
12 8	321 90	110 50	30 00		462 40	19 30	372 80		40 15 / 75 15	VISA M.C. O'NEIL
12 9	406 10	128 90	56 00	2 00	593 00	24 36	403 94		13 99 / 185 91	CHARG-PD VISTARS
12 10	736 20	280 70	75 50	1 75	1094 15	43 80	905 88	35	72 31 / 12 86	VISA WRIGHT
									6 00	ERROR
TOTALS	2281 60	840 10	279 10	5 50	3406 30	136 15	2924 93	20	617 32	

rect. The deposit will be $372.80. The charges should be entered in the "Misc." column as plus entries because they are additions to the day's business.

$$\$481.70 = \$372.80 + \$108.90$$
$$\$481.70 = \$481.70$$

12/9 Sales and tax equal $617.36. Cash and charges are $619.16. Cash is $12.00 over because extra money was collected due to the payment of employee errors. Therefore, this is a minus to the day's business. It is also short $10.20 because a tip was paid out. This must be accounted for by adding the tip to the charge on which it was incurred. Thus, Mr. Peters' charge will be entered as $200.31 ($190.11 + $10.20) to compensate for the cash shortage. The reason we know it is Mr. Peters' tip is because tips are not broken down on credit card sales.* Also, it would be noted on the petty cash slip. The actual cash collected is correct. The deposit will be $403.94.

$$\$617.36 = \$403.94 - \$12.00 + \$25.11$$
$$+ \$200.31$$
$$\$617.36 = \$617.36$$

12/10 Sales and tax equal $1131.95. Cash and charges are $1131.60. The cash is $.35 short. There is a pricing error you have uncovered after the close of business for $6.00. This is entered as a plus (addition) to "Food" and also to "Misc." Whenever an addition is made to Sales, it must also be made to the Receipts or you would not be in balance. This will increase "Total Sales" by $6.00. The deposit will be $905.88.

---

*Some credit card companies do not charge a fee for the collection of tips. Tips would then be broken down.

$$\$1131.95 + \$6.00 = \$905.88 + \$225.72$$
$$+ \$.35 + \$6.00$$
$$\$1137.95 = \$1137.95$$

The Payroll Account

One of the more complex duties in starting a new restaurant is the computation of the payroll. If you are not familiar with the payroll operation and all the accompanying taxes and deductions, it will be very confusing to you at first. Care is of the utmost importance because a very simple mistake can cause extra minutes locating it. There are outside firms that can do the entire payroll for you and provide adequate records at the same time. However, this is another added expense which you may not be able to afford. If you have any familiarity with figures, I suggest you tackle the job yourself. Do not wait until you are in business; try a dry run before then.

There is no difference among computing a payroll for a proprietorship, partnership, or corporation. Employees can be paid by cash or check. The easiest and most reliable method is by the use of checks. The paperwork involved in computing the amount each employee receives is the same whether you pay by check or cash. Paying by cash involves money counting and there is no absolute proof in case of a dispute involving accuracy. In addition, you run a security risk by having a great deal of money about. No one can argue with the amount written on a check and writing one is a lot less time consuming than counting money. In addition, it is more secure. Many areas have banks that will make up your payroll, which would eliminate some of the problems of handling.

When employees are paid you have a responsibility to deduct certain items from their pay. This can be anything from taxes to a retirement fund. In order to maintain strict accuracy, it is important that you keep very careful records. You will be periodically asked to submit reports to various levels of government, along with your remittance for taxes owed and collected. The possible deductions are:

1. Federal income tax (withholding),
2. FICA (Social Security),
3. State income tax,
4. Local taxes (e.g., wage tax),
5. Meals,
6. Hospitalization,
7. Life insurance,
8. Retirement program,
9. Pay advances,
10. Union dues,
11. Tips.

As you may have noticed by now, making up a payroll is a rather involved chore. Because of this, it is advisable to make a worksheet rather than work directly onto the checks. In this way, you can find and correct your errors before making any entries on the check stubs. The worksheet is done in pencil which is easy to change. Once it is in balance, you can transfer the correct figures to the check stubs. If a simplified payroll system is used, because of the use of carbons, one entry on the check stub is all that is necessary.

A small payroll is not difficult to process once you become accustomed to it. However, initially it is somewhat confusing and involved. Basically, you are talking about money earned on one side and deductions on the other. Errors occur most frequently in arithmetic. Because of this, there must be some cross check on your work. Two other areas in which you may make an error that will affect your balance are in transferring to the check stub and in the typing of the check.

There are a number of commercial payroll systems available. The advantage of these systems is that they provide all the materials you need from one source. This can be a time saver when you first begin operating. In addition, they can also provide a computer service. The system with which I have had the best results is the one provided by the Safeguard Corporation in Fort Washington, Pennsylvania. This company provides a local representative who will help you with your problems. Systems such as this one simplify your work and save time.

How to Compute a Simple Payroll

What is Needed to Get Started

Worksheet;
Sharp pencil with eraser;
Checks, ledger sheets, payroll summary sheet, ledger;
Control sheet;
Tax tables, withholding (federal, state, and local), FICA;
List of other deductions;
List of employees to be paid and their rates;
Time worked by each employee (advise a time book).

How to Do Payroll

1. Date the worksheet. This is usually the last day of the payroll period.
2. List the names of all the employees to be paid.
3. Open time book and enter the number of hours or days worked next to each employee's name on the time sheet.

4. By referring to the list of employee rates, multiply their time by their appropriate rate. Enter this in the first column labeled "Regular Earnings."

5. If there is any overtime, follow the above procedure and put this figure in the appropriate column marked "Overtime."

6. If there are tips reported or paid by you, record these in the column marked "Tips."

7. Total boxes (regular pay, overtime, tips) and put amount in column marked "Total Pay."

8. Compute withholding tax by using tables provided by IRS. Enter in column marked "Withholding."

9. Compute FICA tax by using IRS tables. Enter in proper column.

10. Compute any state or local taxes. Enter in the appropriate column or columns.

11. If there are any other deductions, put them in the proper column.

12. Add all the deductions together and subtract from "Total Pay." Place this figure in the column marked "Net Pay."

Steps 1 through 12 should be carried out for each employee. When this is completed, you will have figures running horizontally next to each name.

13. Total all columns vertically.

14. When totals under "Regular Pay," "Overtime," and "Tips" are added together, they should equal the total in "Total Pay."

15. Add totals of all deductions together. Subtract this figure from the "Total Pay" total. This should be the same as "Net Pay" total. If it is, you are in balance. (If you are even one penny off, you are not in balance and you must find the error.) Determine how much you are off by subtracting one figure from the other.

To find an error always check back from the last step completed. Check your adding machine tape. You may have made a wrong entry.

Completing Checks

Once the worksheet is in balance you are ready to complete the paychecks. Carefully transfer the figures for each individual to his or her check stub. If you are using a commercial system, you will be setting up the individual's ledger card and the payroll summary at the same time. If you are not, the ledger card must be completed for each employee. Your worksheet will suffice for a payroll summary sheet. Be sure to enter the check number next to each worker's name.

After this is done, you complete the face of the check by typing in the employee's name, date, and amount from the "Net Pay" column. When this is completed for all employees, run a total on all the checks from the figures you have typed in. This total should agree with the total found in step 15 above. This indicates that you have not made a transfer error. The checks are now ready to be signed by the authorized person and distributed.

Payroll Control

You are required by the federal and state governments to submit quarterly reports concerning the taxes you have collected from your employees. Because of this requirement and because good accounting procedure demands it, you must keep accurate records.

The weekly payroll summaries (if you are paying weekly) are in balance at the end of each pay period. It is now necessary to set up some sort of control to see that the figures throughout the year are correct. (See Figure 3–8.) You do this by taking a ledger card and transferring the weekly figures to it. These figures will be exactly the same as the weekly amounts. At the end of each quarter (13 weeks), total all the columns vertically just as you did in step 13 when you were doing the weekly payroll. When these columns are added (and subtracted) vertically and horizontally, the total net pay figures should be the same. This is similar to step 15 in payroll computation. If they are not, it is because you made an arithmetic error or did not transfer an item completely or correctly. These correct figures are then used to compute your tax obligations for the quarter. If you are careful in recording your transfers each week, you will have no trouble at the end of the quarter.

The same procedure must be followed on the individual employee ledger cards. Total vertically and check horizontally. They, too, must balance. Add all the totals within the group (e.g., regular pay) from each card to arrive at the complete total for that category. This is done for all categories including tips, withholding, and FICA. These totals should agree with the totals on your control ledger sheet to be in balance.

A Special Situation

Tips are a special situation. Tips made by the employees must be reported to you by the tenth of every month after the month in which they are earned. If the employee does not report them, you are not responsible. If the employee does, it is up to you to withhold FICA and withholding taxes.

Due to the amount of tips an employee may report, it is possible that the wages paid will not be sufficient to cover the tax obligations. In such a situation, it is the responsibility of the employees to make up the difference on their own year-end tax statement.

If tips are collected by you, the employer (e.g., in the form of a service charge), they are treated the same way as wages for tax purposes.

Figure 3–8. Payroll Summary

	Name	Pay End	Ck. No.	Time Reg.	O/T	Tips		Total Pay	FICA	W/H	State		Net Pay
1													
2													
3													
4													
5													
18													
19													
20													

PAYROLL SUMMARY   Page No._____   Year_____

Correcting Errors

Simple arithmetic errors occurring in your work must be corrected immediately. This is the only way you can stay in balance. However, some errors can be more easily corrected at a later date. An example of this might be a paycheck that was incorrectly computed due to a misinterpretation. Perhaps the wrong tax amount was used, the hours were not correct, or the pay scale was not the right one. These types of errors do not directly affect your figures.

When such errors do happen, the simplest way to correct them is to make the adjustment the following pay period. If the person was underpaid or overpaid, simply add the amount to or subtract it from the "Regular Earnings" column of the paycheck. Do not include the amount in the regular pay figure, as this may be confusing. Note it just above the regular pay. Use the same technique to adjust for advances against pay.

Correct errors at the earliest opportunity. They may be forgotten or become difficult to correct later on.

Payroll Ledger Sheet

The payroll ledger form in Figure 3–9, or a similar one, can be obtained in any large stationery store or from special companies that cater to the food service industry. The forms found locally are not usually geared to the restaurant business, but they can be adapted.

The following numbered explanations refer to the numbers found on the sample form in Figure 3–9.

1. This information is necessary for tax computation.
2. Record the pay rate for the individual in this box. You may wish to include the date.
3. This indicates the last day of the pay period.
4. These three columns are added together to arrive at "Total Pay."
5. If there is no state tax, this column can be ignored. The blank columns can be used for any other deductions (e.g., hospitalization).
6. Indicates incomplete section of drawing. This would be completed on a standard form.
7. This line is used for totaling the vertical columns at the end of the quarter.
8. Same as number 6 above.
9. This line is used to total the entire page. The total is then carried over to the other side of the sheet and continued.

At the bottom of the sample ledger page the letters *a* to *f* are listed. These indicate the proper order to use when balancing out at the end of the quarter.

To arrive at the totals on the line marked "Q" each column must be added vertically. The totals found on the line marked "T" are found by adding the totals from each of the "Q" totals. When totals *a*, *b*, and *c* are added together, they must equal the total in box *d*. When all the totals found within the bracket marked *e* are subtracted from *d*, the result will equal the total *f*.

This balancing method is used for the individual payroll ledger cards and for the control ledger card. The information for the ledger cards is found on the payroll summary. The information for the control ledger card is the totals at the bottom of the summary page.

Payroll Checks

If you are using your own system, it will be necessary to order payroll checks from the bank. If the bank can provide checks with

PAYROLL LEDGER SHEET

Name_____Dept._____   Marital St._____ ① Pay Rate ②

Exemptions _____

Address_____   S.S. #_____

Telephone_____ Date started_____ Date left _____

	Per. End	Reg. Pay	O/T Pay	Tips	Total Pay	FICA	W/H	State					Net Pay
1													
2													
3													
4	③		④			⑥		⑤					
⑦													
13													
Q													
14													
15													
⑨						⑧							
26													
Q													
T													
		a	b	c	d			e					f

Figure 3–9. Payroll Ledger Sheet

attached stubs containing the necessary payroll information, you should use them. If the bank cannot, be sure there is room on the check to write this information. If this cannot be done, you will have to provide the information separately.

Commercial systems (see Figure 3–10) for payroll accounting are available.

General Office Needs

Use this list as a checklist when setting up your office:

Adding machine, extra ribbon, extra tape rolls

Calculator

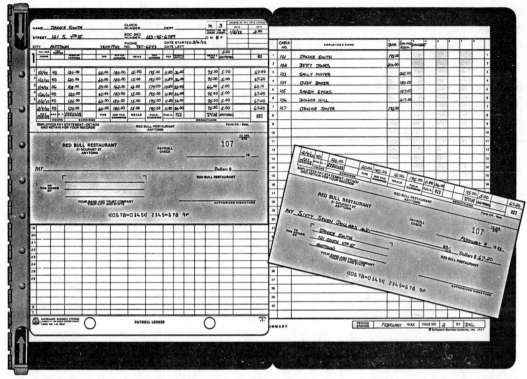

Figure 3–10. A Commercial Business System for Payroll. This system includes: 1) the payroll check with all the boxes imprinted at the top of the check, 2) the payroll ledger sheet, 3) a payroll summary sheet. Simply by writing the check, you have the information needed on the individual's ledger sheet and the payroll summary sheet. All you have to add is the employee's name and the check number. When the checks are written, you then total the vertical columns (not visible in Figure 3–10) on the summary sheet to balance out. If each check is proven as it is written, there should be no problem in balancing. The totals are then transferred to the control ledger card. If you would like to have a breakdown of the payroll by departments, this can be done by utilizing the columns on the left of the summary. (Artwork courtesy of Safeguard Business Systems Inc.)

Typewriter, extra ribbon, correction fluid or tape

Filing cabinet, file folders, index

Desk and chair

Writing paper and envelopes (#5s and #10s)

Pencils, pens, marking pencils, colored pens, sharpener

Stapler, staples, extractor

Paper clips, large and small

Rubber bands

Paper pads, various sizes

Cellophane tape (½" and 1"), dispensers

Scissors

Ruler and yardstick

Letter opener
Postage stamps
Money box (optional)
Petty cash slips
Book to record employees' time
Magnifying glass (handy, when you need one)
Thumbtacks

Stamp and envelope moistener (invaluable)
Glue
Small dictionary
Clock (optional)
Bulletin board (this may be located anywhere)

Chapter Four

Personnel

The two biggest challenges facing any business today are material costs and finding competent personnel. Of the two, the personnel situation is the most difficult. Although the cost of materials may be high, there is no cost to you after the items are purchased. Employees are not only expensive initially, but become progressively more expensive due to training costs and salary increases. Furthermore, there is no way to measure employees' contribution to the final product until they have been tried over a period of time. Add to this the human relations problems involved in dealing with individual personalities and you will understand labor's enormous challenge.

The restaurant business has traditionally received the "leftovers" of other businesses in the labor market, making the situation even more severe. In industry, wage scales are higher. In white collar work, the surroundings and environment may be more pleasant. In just about any other business,

the hours are better. Because employees prefer the better paying jobs, nicer surroundings, and more suitable hours, they tend to seek out those jobs first. The restaurant job is often a last choice.

The small restaurant has some advantages over the larger operator in attracting and holding employees. In larger restaurants, employees are just numbers on timecards. In a small restaurant, there is the potential for closer relationships among the workers. They are more apt to work together, which results in happier and more efficient employees. The smaller staff and limited area of a small operation make supervision simpler. Because of their size and longer hours, larger restaurants must employ more full-time workers. Most small restaurants are so limited in the number of hours they operate that part-time employees are far more satisfactory. Because there are many more part-time workers than full-time workers available, it will be easier for you to find satisfactory personnel.

Potential employees can fit part-time work into their schedule, and you can take advantage of the market in people who want to supplement their current income. In addition, having several part-time employees gives you more people to call should you need a short-notice replacement for a shift or two.

Of course, there are a few disadvantages to hiring part-time employees. One is the turnover rate. Because part-time jobs are usually supplemental, the employee is in a position to leave your employ more easily. They may leave because of family pressure, lack of physical stamina, or because they no longer need the extra income. A second reason is the difficulty in communicating with a large number of employees who work at different times. In most cases, this difficulty can be overcome by posting all changes in procedure on a bulletin board. Do not hire seasonal workers unless they fit into your business schedule.

It is important to hire and train the best workers you can find, full-time or part-time. Take time to make your selection, pay as well as you can, and *train well*. Good training will produce a happier employee, owner, and guest.

Training, of course, is not the only thing that makes a happy employee. There are four other ways you can make your employees happy.

Discuss expectations. At the time of hiring, tell your employees what you expect of them. In addition, tell them what they can expect from you.

Be fair. Make sure you treat all of your employees the same way. If you have a rule, stick with it. Never bend it to fit the individual. Employees like to have rules, because rules provide a structure for their behavior.

Be consistent. Follow the same procedure each time you do a particular thing. If employees know how you will react in a given situation, they will be much more at ease. Employees will make a greater effort to please you if they know what behaviors are likely to accomplish that purpose.

Be friendly. Try to understand the problems your employees may have, without, I should stress, getting too deeply involved. A smile and a cheerful word from you as your employees arrive could make the difference for the entire shift.

Camaraderie, the guests' attitudes, and surroundings all contribute to employees' happiness. However, the only element over which you have complete control is your own behavior. If your employees like you, they will withstand a lot of the other problems.

I have tried to simplify a very complex subject. In a small restaurant, you are dealing eyeball to eyeball and have to act instinctively. If you try your best to hire the right employees, train them properly, and give them pleasant working conditions, you will then have solid, long-time employees who will be working for the house and not themselves.

Hiring Personnel

There are two ways you can fill a vacant position, hire from outside or promote internally. The advantages of the latter are that the employee is already familiar with your policies and the responsibilities of the new position and is probably available immediately. The possible disadvantages are that you have two people to train in new jobs, you are still left with a position to fill, and you or the employee may not be happy with his or her performance in the new job. Furthermore, because of the last reason, you may lose a good employee because he or she would feel uncomfortable returning to the old position.

Hiring should not be done in a haphazard manner. A careful, thought-out approach to hiring new employees will pay dividends. Consider each applicant's background and qualifications carefully and you will save both money and time.

First of all, it costs money to hire and train an employee. It costs money to advertise. Wages are paid to this employee, whether he works out or not. It costs you money to advertise again. There may be wasted food or liquor.

Secondly, it costs you wasted time. Generally, you do not have the luxury of extra time to start a new employee. Even with the conventional two weeks notice, there isn't much time to find a new employee and get him trained before the old employee leaves. So, if you make a poor selection, it may be a few wasted, precious days before you can start someone else. It is also wasted time and money for the persons doing the training. Don't forget you are paying them to help train this new person and it is bound to slow up their work. It's time consuming to explain every step you take and why to take it.

Advertising

There are three ways to obtain employees: formal advertising, word of mouth, and agencies.

You may advertise in newspapers, trade journals, local publications, or any other written form. Pick your medium carefully. When you need experienced preparation personnel, advertise in the larger newspapers. When you need unskilled labor, advertise locally. You must reach a larger audience to obtain skilled people. The chances of finding a skilled salad person in a small town are rather remote. The chance of finding a dishwasher is much greater. Try to reach the appropriate audience.

The ad layout (the way the ad is presented on the page or column) is important. Try to catch the eye of the reader. Remember, you are competing against other restaurants. The elements you should consider when designing your ad are space, typeface, borders, and artwork. (See Figure 4–1.)

Space. This is the simplest method of making your ad stand out. Try to have *white space* setting off your ad. This merely means blank space and can be most effective. If you are just another listing on the page, you may be easily skipped over.

Typeface. Put the important information in large or bold letters.

Borders. Heavy, curly, wavy, or other kinds of borders may be used to make your ad stand out. You can use them on the sides or bottom of the ad or to box in an ad.

Artwork. Artwork can be expensive. However, the results can more than offset the cost. An interesting sketch or picture is certainly an eye catcher.

When preparing your ad, consider content after design. Once you have caught the readers' eyes, you must get them to read on. Use a boldfaced headline at the beginning of the ad. The headline should clearly state the nature of the position you wish to fill. Do not expect readers to search through your ad to find this information. Use letters that are large and easy to read, and do not squeeze them together. Use more than one line if necessary.

When composing the body of the ad,

is looking for a weekend maintenance person. We offer good benefits which include:

Good starting wage
  Meals
  Uniforms
  Paid retirement
  Paid Profit Sharing
Apply in person at 516 W. Lancaster Avenue. EOE.

Not exactly fine dining, but a very fine ad. Note: white space, large letters, border, art work.

COOK

1st COOK

Excellent opportunity at prominent medical center for cook with minimum 3-5 years experience in multi-national food preparation or graduate from a recognized school specializing in food preparation. Individual should have supervisory experience or related formal training. Bakery and catering experience would be helpful. Call or write Personnel, XYZ Medical Center, an equal opportunity employer

Good use of
WHITE SPACE

WAITRESSES EXPERIENCED for weekends — Fri., Sat. & Sun. 11:30pm to 7am shift & 5pm to 11:30PM. Apply in person. NO PHONE CALLS

WAITRESS/wtr Expd only Good working conds. Good tips.

WAITRESS/WAITER — Cocktail. Pt time. Nights. Apply in person 10/6 between 5pm–11pm

WAITRESS/m Must be exp'd. Nites, good working conditions.

WAITRESS M/F. Exp'd. day work. CC, good tips. No Phone Calls.

WAITRESSES/Walters Exp only Apply in person

WAITRESSES/WAITERS Exp'd only. For appt. call

WAITRESS/M. Exp'd. Very good tips.

Competition
is keen

RESTAURANT
Very well-known established bar & restaurant looking for across the board new management personnel. Top notch, gets top dollar. Willing to train serious minded workers. Openings are for:
   HEAD CHEF & 2nd CHEF
   HEAD BARTENDER
   MAITRE'D/HEAD HOSTESS
   2 ASST. MANAGERS
We need responsible people for responsible jobs. Others need not apply. Send letter of intro/resume to Box 000, Boston MA, applications will be answered.

Cluttered
Lacks drawing power

Figure 4–1.   Examples of Help Wanted Ads

put yourself in the position of job seekers. Think the way they think. What interests them are hours of work and scheduling options, locations, salary, and the way to apply. If the job is not aptly described in the headline, there should be a brief explanation of it in the body of the ad.

I do not generally include the rate of pay in the ad. I seldom even give it over the telephone. Sometimes I will give a range, but I never give a definite figure. I prefer to interview the person and determine her or his capabilities before deciding where to start a person in the range.

Put your name, address, and telephone number at the end of the ad. State whether or not you want interviews. It is usually advisable to have them or else people will be dropping in on you at all times of the day and night.

The best days to run your ad are weekdays, Monday through Friday. If you have part-time positions to fill, weekends are usually good as well. Depending on your location, a morning paper may be better than an evening paper or vice versa. Local weekly papers are also effective.

Be certain someone is available to answer the telephone. It does not make much sense to be away from the phone when you are trying to fill a job. Have time open in your day to interview the applicants. It works best to schedule interviews in immediate succession. If the interviews are strung out all day long, you may waste a lot of time waiting for people. In addition, you cannot make a valid decision about who to hire until all applicants have been interviewed. The faster you can get the interviewing function completed, the faster you can fill the vacancy.

Another way to obtain employees is through an agency. There are two types of agencies, public and private. The public agency is generally run by the state. Sometimes, local organizations will set up an agency in an area where employment is particularly difficult. Seldom does either of them charge a fee. I have found a number of well-qualified, unskilled individuals through an agency of this type.

To obtain its help call the agency, tell the agent the type job you have to offer, and give pertinent details. The agent will search the agency's files or advertise and call you when a suitable person is found. You interview the applicant and make your decision. There is no obligation on your part to accept the individual if he or she is not the type you are looking for.

Private agencies work somewhat differently. They charge either the applicant or you

a finders fee. Hence, only use this type of agency for a skilled individual. It has been my experience that a good agency will carefully screen applicants before it sends them to you. On the other hand, a poor agency will send anyone that comes close to your description, regardless of qualifications.

Some private agencies specialize in temporary help. Such agencies will send employees on a short-term basis. The employees will be trained in their particular job duties. The quality of these temporary workers varies greatly, so they should be closely supervised. One advantage to using temporaries is that you have no financial responsibility toward them. The agency pays and insures them.

Finally, you can obtain new employees by word of mouth. The best people to pass the word are your employees. Make it clear that you will not hold current employees responsible for the individuals they recommend. A good incentive for employees who bring in successful candidates is some kind of remuneration. Sales representatives and delivery people can also be valuable as recruiters.

Reviewing Applications

As you get more and more experienced in interviewing candidates, you will develop a feeling about people. This, coupled with the more formal information you have, will enable you to make a reliable decision. When you first begin, you will not be right everytime you select an employee, but do not let this discourage you. Even experienced interviewers make mistakes.

The first thing you must have is an application form. It saves a great deal of time and gives you some insight into the person's ability.

Standard, ready-made forms may be purchased from any office supply company or you may tailor your own. The problem with the former is that they often provide for unneeded information. The simpler the form, the more useful it can be. It is faster for the employee to complete and it is easy for you to get the information you require quickly.

Because of state and federal laws, the information you may solicit from a potential employee is limited. Basically, if the information you seek has no connection to the job, you are not allowed to ask for it. Therefore, requesting information regarding an applicant's race, religion, nationality, age, or marital status is generally not permitted. The question of age may be modified in certain cases. If, for example, there was a legal age at which a person may tend bar, it would be permissible to ask this person's age.

At least the following information should be included on all application forms:

Name

Address

Telephone number (or numbers)

Social Security number

Means of transportation

Who to call in case of emergency and telephone number

Educational background and highest grade completed

Job applying for

Amount of experience

Special training in job

Personal references (2)

Past job history (3)

When applicants call for an interview, give them specific appointment times. You will then be able to plan your work schedule around the interviews. You will also have an opportunity to evaluate the reliability of the applicants based on whether they appear on time.

There will always be people who do not show for interviews. Keep this occurrence to a minimum by giving as much information about the job over the phone as is practical. Include hours, days, and the duties of the position. When an applicant has finished asking questions, ask whether this job sounds interesting. If the response is not enthusiastic, push a little to find out why. Better to reject an applicant over the telephone than waste time with an interview. On the other hand, if the applicant is interested, schedule an interview at a convenient time for both of you. Ask the applicant to call, if he or she has a change of mind.

When applicants arrive, greet them in a cordial and friendly manner. Making them feel at ease will result in a much more productive interview. Make a note of dress and appearance on the application after it is completed and returned to you. Such observations can give you a good idea of the applicant's attitudes. Give the interviewee an application form and explain how you would like it filled out. If you are interviewing a number of applicants at one time, you can interview one while the others are completing their forms. If you are interviewing individuals at intervals, the best thing to do is leave the applicant alone to complete the form. People tend to feel ill at ease when someone is hovering over them.

Try to conduct the interview in a quiet area or room. Also, try not to be interrupted during the interview. You should give your undivided attention for the best results. Give yourself a few minutes before the interview to look over the application.

When you have the completed application, you should take note of:

The Address. Applicants may live too far away to make travel to your restaurant worthwhile. Consider also, that you may need an employee in a hurry sometime. The type of neighborhood the person lives in may also provide some insight into their personality. Deducing from this information takes a little experience, but can be helpful.

Age. You cannot discriminate on the basis of age. However, the age will alert you to ask more pertinent questions. A person who is obviously too young may not have the experience you are looking for. A person who has retired may not be capable of doing heavy work. On the other hand, retired persons are generally very reliable and are flexible in their work schedule.

Transportation. Without adequate transportation, how does the employee get to work? Public transportation may be reliable during normal working hours, but can be very unsatisfactory at off hours. On the other hand, automobiles have a way of breaking down. Ask about the condition of the car. Try not to hire anyone who relies on friends for transportation. This method is undependable.

Health. Ask questions if you have any suspicions. Sometimes you may have to read between the lines to catch a problem. You only want employees who are in good health. Hiring someone with a contagious disease could result in a problem with your insurance carrier. People with handicaps are not considered in this category.

Educational Background. For full-time employment, do not hire highly educated people for an unrewarding position. They will be bored and will not stay very long. For part-time employment, this is not always the case. On the other hand, too little education can also be a problem. The person with a high school education is probably at about the best level for a restaurant.

Experience and Special Training. This tells you whether you are going to spend a lot of time training. You may not have the time to do it.

Personal References. References give you a little insight into the applicant's thinking, but should not be given too much weight since they will always be favorable.

Job History. This item provides the most information about the applicants. Are they job jumpers? What did they do at jobs in the past? Why did they leave? What were they paid? Always check with past employers to verify the information the applicant gives.

When you have finished looking over the application and asking whatever questions you have, give the particulars of the job, including pay scale, opportunities for promotion, and whatever benefits you provide. Give the applicant a copy of the job description. Then, give the applicant a chance to ask questions. There are always a few, and you can get a little insight into people from the type of question they ask. Conclude the interview by telling the person you will be in touch after you have interviewed all applicants. Even if you only send postcards, let all applicants know you have someone else.

Be sure to make plenty of notes. You cannot expect to remember everything about each individual who applies for a job.

Interviewing

The interview is your means of determining whether the applicant is suitable for the job you want to fill. During this brief time, you must make a judgment based on the individual and the information he or she provides on an application. To judge each applicant on an equal basis, you must set up specific criteria. Decide what you are looking for, and list these characteristics. All too often, when this sort of thing is left to memory, one of the items is forgotten. One master list can be made and referred to during the interview, or it can be mimeographed and used as a checklist. Keep the information with the individual's application. The blank back of the application is an excellent place to record the information. You may wish to use a code designation so that the applicant is not aware of what you are trying to find out.

There are four items you should look for when conducting an interview:

1. Attitude,
2. Appearance and physical characteristics,
3. Intelligence,
4. Experience.

Attitude can be the most important element of any employee's future success with you. A positive attitude is invaluable to you. You need people who sincerely want to please. You must determine whether the person being interviewed will fit into your organization. Will he or she be able to get along with you, the other employees and, most importantly, the guests?

Appearance and physical characteristics are indicative of the applicant's attitude. If a person comes for an interview and is not neatly dressed and free of offensive odors, you can be sure the situation will not improve once this person is working for you. In addition, personal untidiness will be manifest in the person's work. You do not want to have to worry about sloppiness and unsanitary work, so think carefully before hiring this type of individual.

Look also for such things as nervousness and other physical problems such as skin rashes. It is normal for a person to be nervous early in an interview, but the nervousness

should eventually disappear. Nervous employees do not usually stay at a job very long. Do not hesitate to inquire about any apparent physical or health problem.

The *intelligence* you are looking for here is not necessarily the type which is obtained from schooling. You need to determine whether this person can be trained to do a job. Remember, the number of years of schooling does not transfer directly into intelligence. Common sense is important too. You need an employee who can make decisions when necessary.

Does the *experience* this person has fit what you are looking for? A busperson who worked in a fast food operation, for example, would not be qualified to work in a formal dining room just on the basis of experience. Always ask questions about the work the applicant did in the establishments listed on his or her application. Keep in mind that this person will have to be retrained for your system. Therefore, his or her experience should relate in some way to the position you are trying to fill.

In addition to digesting the formal application and the information provided by the applicant, you must do a certain amount of reading between the lines. Only you can provide the insight necessary to determine whether this person will fit into your organization. If you rely solely on the information provided by the applicant, you will often find you have hired the wrong person. Trust your judgment and let it help you with decisions.

Observation by/of Potential Employees. To show a potential employee your concern for his or her happiness on the job, have an observation session. The employee comes in to observe the job, the other employees, and the restaurant in general. This gives him or her an idea of what you expect. At the same time, it gives you some idea of his or her ability.

Observation sessions should be arranged on a purely voluntary basis, at no cost to you.

Panic Hiring. Panic is the feeling you get when the chef decides to quit without notice. Your stomach tightens, your head begins to ache, you become irritable, and you wonder what you will do now. Your first inclination is to talk the chef into coming back. When this does not work, you are ready to hire the first person who comes along.

Everyone in a small restaurant will go through this at some time. Unless you are a really calm person, just about anything you do under these conditions will be wrong. It is not easy to be calm in a crisis situation. But if you are to make rational decisions, you absolutely must try. Dropping your established criteria for hiring is never justified. If you hire unqualified individuals, you will learn by experience that the practice seldom pays off.

After the initial shock of an employee abandoning a job is over, sit down and analyze the possibilities available in obtaining help. Is there someone in your employ who can fill in temporarily? Do you know someone who has the skills to fill in for you? Can you do the job yourself and have someone do your own work? Are there temporary help agencies available? Can you limit your operation until a replacement is found? Should you close until the position is filled (a very, very last resort)?

Establish a plan of action. First, decide how to limp along, at least temporarily. Second, decide how to go about filling the position.

When you have the situation under control, try some retrospection. Ask yourself why the employee left. Perhaps you made mistakes, such as not checking with past employers or asking the right questions, when you hired the individual. Did you ignore indications of the person's unhappiness? Was

there something about the job which was wrong (work load was too heavy, poor pay, bad hours)? Of course, it just might have been the employee. The quitting may have been the result of a personal crisis. Regardless of the reason, learn from it to lessen the chance of it happening again.

You should never beg an employee to return. Make a reasonable effort, but no more. An employee who returns under these circumstances has you on the defensive. It will be almost impossible to criticize her or him again.

If you have to hire someone who is not qualified, do not allow yourself to slow up looking for the proper replacement. It is easy to let yourself relax once the pressure is off. Principles are easy to live with when everything is going smoothly, but hard to maintain when things are rough.

Training

Training is important in operations of all sizes. Granted, the small operator does not need the elaborate training program the larger one does. However, it is essential that you have some method of telling your employees what you expect of them.

There are three important reasons for training your employees: 1) getting the work done your way in a consistent manner, 2) projecting your image to the public, and 3) saving money. If you are hiring persons with no experience you must teach them the job from the beginning. In the following discussion, I am assuming that you are hiring experienced personnel.

Job Descriptions

The first step in a training procedure, writing a job description, takes place even before you hire someone. I cannot stress the importance of this step too strongly. Only you know what you expect of an employee. As a matter of fact, there is a distinct possibility that you are not sure yourself.

Make a list of all the positions you will have available. In a very small operation, this may only be one other person. List all the jobs you expect each individual to perform. Analyze the list. Are you expecting too much or too little? Tie each position with other jobs you have available. Does one dovetail into the other or is there duplication of certain functions? If you are satisfied the description is clear, you have a blueprint for hiring. Have it typed and copies made. When people come for interviews, you can hand them the job description and say, "This is the job." This is much easier than trying to explain verbally.

The job description in Figure 4–2 is both

Figure 4–2.
Job Description and Duties for Waitresses/Waiters

Because you deal directly with the guest, the job of waiting on tables is one of the most important functions at The Inn. You are in a position to convey the feeling and concern the owners have for the guests. If your attitude is not one of pride and concern, then the guest gets the impression that the owners also feel this way. Obviously, this isn't the case and this is why you should know your duties well.

Due to the seasonal nature of business at The Inn, we do not have many full-time or regular employees. Because of this, it is necessary to have an outline of the duties of those who work here. You will find these duties listed in the following paragraphs.

For those of you who have never waited on tables before, it will be necessary for you to go through a training period. When you have completed your training, you will be given a part of a station and eventually, a complete station. Remember, speed is an essential part of being a good waitress/waiter, but never sacrifice quality of service for it.

Waiting on tables is much like "show-business." Even when you are unhappy, the guest must never know. This can be extremely difficult at times, but a pleasant approach almost always results in a more satisfied guest. This, of course, has its financial rewards.

Personal Appearance

Your appearance makes an impression on the guests. If the impression is bad, it may be difficult to overcome. These guidelines are to be followed:

a. Generally neat and clean.
b. Waitresses' hair should be tied back if long. Men should keep their hair well trimmed. All service personnel should have hair which looks neat and clean.
c. Rings, if worn, are to be small and limited to one on each hand. No other ornamentation should be worn.
d. Strong smelling perfumes or after shave lotions are not permitted. Waitresses should wear only clear nail enamel and light makeup.
e. Shoes should be kept polished.
f. Waitresses' skirts should not be more than two inches above the knee cap. Waiters are to wear long sleeve shirts only.
g. Uniforms should be clean and pressed for each meal.

h. No gum chewing.

i. No smoking, except in the proper area.

General Duties

a. Be properly attired and groomed.

b. Set up stations, plus any side duties for entire setup.

c. Know the menu for the meal.

d. Greet guest. Get cocktail order and serve.

e. See that guest has a menu. Tell guest of any changes or additions.

f. Take order and place order in the kitchen.

g. Present the wine list.

h. See that the guest has the necessary *extras* (relishes, rolls, butter, etc.).

i. Serve meal. Observe table for anything that may be missing.

j. Check back with guest.

k. When ready, clear the table.

l. Present dessert menu, take order and serve.

m. Check for coffee.

n. Ask for cordials.

o. Present check. Pick up as soon as possible and return change.

p. See that table is made ready for the next party.

There will be times when you will have the assistance of a busperson or a relish server. These people are here to assist you at your job. If you use their services, it is your responsibility to see that they do things correctly. If they misplace something, clear a table improperly, or forget something, it is your responsibility to see that these errors are corrected. Naturally, this assumes that you know your job.

The difference between a good server and an excellent server depends on how well he or she takes care of the guests. The server who spends time in the employees' dining room when there are guests in the dining room will find it very difficult to do even a good job, let alone an excellent one. Your place is in the dining room when you have people at your tables. If you take careful note of it, you may be surprised at how your tips will increase when you give that extra amount of service. The server who refills the water or wine glass, empties a soiled ash tray, replaces needed silverware quickly, sees that the guest has the needed extra butter or bread, refills a coffee cup (don't forget the cream, too), and presents the check quickly, is truly a rarity and will be compensated accordingly.

Before guests are seated, you should check and see that your station is impeccable.

a. Clean linen, silver, glassware, china, ash tray, salt and pepper, sugar bowl. Sugar bowls and salt and pepper shakers should be filled before each meal.

b. Tablecloth clean and well pressed.

c. Chairs clean and dusted.

d. Large crumbs removed from floor.

e. Flowers and/or candles checked.

f. Everything properly placed.

g. Clean tray on tray stand.

Remember, we use tray service at The Inn. This means that all items taken into, or out of, the dining room are to be carried on a tray.

Cocktail Service and Order Taking

It is extremely important that you greet the guest as quickly as possible. There is nothing more annoying to a guest than to be seated and then ignored. If you cannot get to them right away, tell them. For example, "I'm sorry. I'm tied up right now, but I'll be with you in a few minutes." This will probably take care of them for as long as five minutes. Maybe someone can bring them a relish dish, or something, until you get there. Of course, if there is a relish server or busperson, they can do this.

a. Greet the guests. (Good morning, good evening.)

b. As soon as guests are seated by the host, get the cocktail order. Do this by saying, "May I take your cocktail order?" Do not say, "Would you like a cocktail?" This is a negative approach. If they *do not want* cocktails, go to step *c.*

c. Remove extra place settings from the table as soon as possible.

d. If they *want* cocktails, get them and serve them to the right of the service plate. When the drink is low, return to table and ask if they would like another. *Now* go to step *c.*

e. When ready to take the order, go to the table and inform guests of any changes or additions to the menu and what the soup is. Then ask them if they are ready to order. Don't just stand there and wait for them to say something. If a guest is hesitant about what to order, help by making suggestions. If they haven't ordered an appetizer or soup, don't let this go by. Ask them if they would like an appetizer. For example, "Wouldn't you like an appetizer? We have wonderful fresh fruit today." You'll be surprised how many more appetizers you will sell this way.

f. At this point, the wine list should be presented. Do not *ask* about wine; *always* present the list. This is an essential part of positive selling. Don't forget to get the order. Special details about selling wines will be presented to you on a separate list.

g. Make your order as efficiently as possible. When writing the order, develop some sort of shorthand, so you can write quickly. Start with one person and go to the right at multi-person tables. This avoids mixups later.

Ordering and Picking Up

A great deal of your time will be spent in the kitchen getting your order together, ordering in the different departments, returning soiled tableware, and picking up your order. It is essential, for your own peace of mind and for the guests' satisfaction, that you develop a system to save yourself steps and mistakes.

We use a dupe system at The Inn. This means that all food and drinks must be written down on a dupe in order to be received. Don't miss anything.

Due to the layout of our kitchen, it would probably be simpler to order your cold food and then your hot food. This is always the way in which food should be picked up for service, cold food first, hot food second.

After you have ordered your appetizers, entrees, etc., it is time to develop in your mind how you are going to serve. In addition to picking up your food, you may have:

a. Cocktails to serve.

b. Other appetizers.

c. Wine to get and serve (along with glasses).

d. Entrees to serve to another table.

e. Desserts to serve.

f. Bread and butter or relishes to put on tables.

g. A check to present.

h. After dinner drinks.

As you can see, if you had only one table, it would be very easy. There is no way that your system can be developed for you. You must do this yourself. The important thing to remember is that you must utilize every moment as completely as possible. Get in the habit of doing this when things are slow, and it will come naturally when you are busy. Always keep in mind what you are going to do next. It is always a temptation to stop when you finally place an entree or check in front of a guest. Don't do it unless your guests are completely taken care of. There are times when you can save yourself time, *if* they are ready. Sometimes it is possible to take the cold appetizers (or bread, etc.) for one party along with the entrees for another party. You'll see these shortcuts as you get more experience. Never serve cold food to one table at the expense of another table. For instance, don't serve soup and other appetizers to one table while the hot entree for another table sits. The same is true in reverse. Something has to get cold.

Serving Sequence

Remove service plate

Relishes—serve immediately

Bread and butter

Appetizers—serve before soup

Soup

Salad

Pick up relishes

Entree

Beverage

Dessert

Be sure appropriate silverware is given with each course. If the guest uses something that is needed in the next course, be sure it is replaced.

Always be sure *all* hot food coming from the kitchen is covered.

Food that is presented to the guest should be as attractive as possible. Wipe spots from plates if the cooks miss them. Don't forget to garnish your plates with watercress or parsley (whichever is provided). Wipe the sides of soup cups. Soup belongs in the cup, not in the saucer. Always pick up your cold food first when setting up your tray. This includes such items as bread and butter, in addition to the more obvious items.

When you go to the range or salad area for anything, be sure to say whether you are ordering or picking up.

Serving and Picking Up Dishes

How you serve food and beverages is very important. Basically, all food is served from the left and beverages are served from the right. There are times, however, when this is not possible. If this is the situation (for example—against a wall table), serve the best way possible. If you always remember never to reach across or in front of anyone, you'll have no difficulty in serving correctly. At the end of this description, there is a diagram showing the proper place setting.

Placement of dishes, glassware, and silver are an important part of good service. Always remember that the meat, fish, etc., goes at the bottom when placing the plate. The reason for this is that these items generally have to be cut.

When guests have finished dinner, the table should be cleared. Do this by starting with one person and continuing around the table. Clear all the dishes from one person before going to the next person. Stack dishes in your hand, not on the table. You may remove as many dishes as you feel and look comfortable with. Therefore, it would be possible to clear more than one person's dishes at a time without returning to your tray stand. When you have as many dishes as you wish to hold, return them to the tray. Then return for more. Be sure that after clearing the individual settings, you remove items such as the bread basket, butter, etc. Pick up all silverware except the coffee spoon when clearing the entree. After this is done, the table should be crumbed. This is done by taking a clean, folded napkin and brushing the crumbs onto a small plate. When this is completed, repour water and check for clean ash trays.

At this point, present the dessert menu. While doing this, ask if anyone would like coffee, tea, etc. While you are getting the coffee and cream, they can read the dessert menu. After you have served the beverage, get the dessert order. This is done in the same manner as the wine by saying, "May I take your dessert order?" You then pick up your desserts in the kitchen and serve them. Check for more coffee at this point, and again later. When it looks like the guests are finished, return to the table and ask if they would like an after dinner drink (cordial). If yes, get it and serve it. If no, present the check.

Don't forget the check. Go back as soon as possible and pick it up with the money (or charge) and return the change (or charge slip) quickly. You are now finished with this party.

When they leave, reset the table for the next guests.

General Considerations For All Dining Room Personnel

1. Handle silverware by handles only.
2. Cups should be picked up by handles only.
3. Plates should be handled on edges only.
4. Glassware should be picked up by bottoms or stems only (clean or dirty).
5. *Never* put a glass or pitcher directly into an ice bin. If it breaks, you'll never find it. *The guest will!*
6. Keep hands out of ice; use scoops.
7. Water glasses should be filled to within ½ inch of top of glass, (or less). This also applies to coffee.
8. Empty cocktail glasses are to be removed as soon as possible.
9. When stacking trays during the clearing of a table, all china, silver, etc. should be placed on the tray with similar items together. This will help to cut down on breakage in dishroom.
10. Never scrape plates in the dining room.
11. Dining room personnel should be friendly and courteous at all times. However, do not get into lengthy conversations. This holds up your service to others.
12. Never put your hands on or lean on the back of a customer's chair.
13. Always stand straight.
14. Don't stand around and chat with one another when guests are seated. This applies to the dining rooms and bars.

15. Keep your voice down when talking in the dining room for any reason.
16. Don't chew gum or toothpicks.
17. Nothing should be placed on table, such as a tray or your order pad.
18. If you think there is something wrong with the food you must serve, tell the hostess. If *any* problem comes up, see the hostess.
19. Replace silverware quickly if a guest drops something. You'll be amazed at the guest's response.
20. The butter dish should have an underliner with a fork on it.
21. If it can be helped, do not pick up water glasses or coffee cups when repouring.
22. When coffee is spilled on saucer, replace the saucer.
23. Don't use fingers in butter. Use a fork (or spoon).
24. Do not save returned tartar sauce, bearnaise sauce, or mayonnaise. They are easily contaminated.
25. Don't reuse butter or cream in the dining room. It can be saved for the range.
26. If you see something on the floor that doesn't belong there *Pick it up.*

Figure 4–3. Basic Table Setup

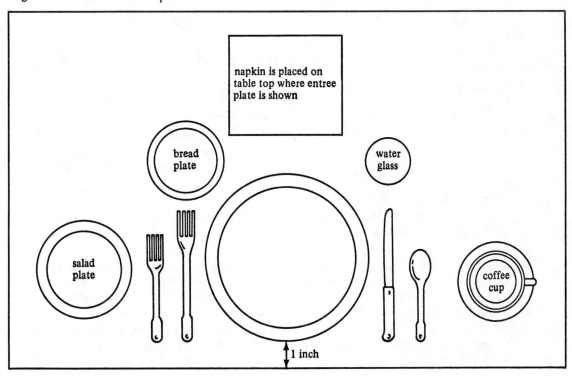

general and specific. Within the general structure are specific details about the procedure for certain duties. It covers how the employees are expected to look, what they are responsible for, and what their duties involve. Notice how the duties of this position are dovetailed into those of the kitchen. It is important to let employees know they are dependent on members of other departments. At the end of the job description, responsibilities of all dining room personnel are listed. This same list appears on the job descriptions for all other dining room positions as well. By doing this, each person has a better overall knowledge of the entire picture.

The second job description (Figure 4–4) deals with banquet personnel only. This description was written with the assumption

Figure 4–4.

Instructions to Banquet Personnel

1. All silver should be placed in a straight line. It should be 1½ inches from the edge of table.
2. Cups should be placed on the right, 2 inches from bottom of table. The handle should be at a right angle, in the direction of 3 o'clock.
3. The butter plate should be placed above the fork, with the crest on top at 12 o'clock. The butter patty should be placed just below the crest. When serving butter in bulk, use a regular, round butter dish. Have chipped ice and eight pieces of butter.
4. The water glass should be placed directly above the knife.
5. Napkins should be placed on the left, next to fork (unless there isn't enough room, then place them on top of fork).
6. Salads should always be placed to the left of the fork, one inch from the edge of the table. For parties over 40, the salad may be placed on the table beforehand. Unless otherwise stated, salad dressing will always be in goose-neck bottles.
7. Ash trays should be placed in the center of each table in front of each fourth person.
8. Large cream pitchers should be half-filled only. Small ones should be filled to within a ½ inch from top. Cream pitchers, sugar bowls, and salt and pepper should be placed together in the center of table.
9. Chairs should be dusted and placed in one straight line.
10. When tables are completely set, you should be able to stand at one end and look down at a straight line of dishes and glassware.
11. When base plates are used, pick them up before serving the first course.
12. Soup cups should be on a saucer, with crest showing in the proper direction (towards you). The cup and saucer should be on an underliner. Waverly Wafers should always be used. Fruit, fish cocktails, and juices are all served on underliner with appropriate garnish.
13. Dinner plate should always be placed with crest at 12 o'clock and the meat at 6 o'clock.
14. Service of rolls and coffee should not be begun until the entree and vegetables are served. There will be times, with large parties, when this will not apply because of a special serving sequence.

that all banquet personnel were trained in regular dining room service. It was specifically written for banquet servers to ensure consistency of setup and service. When a new banquet server received a copy of these instructions, there was no excuse for an incorrect setup.

The third description (Figure 4–5) is a good example of a general type of job description. Because this person had a multitude of duties, the outline could not be specific. This position is usually filled by a less educated person or one of low incentive. In such situations, it is better to have a general outline of duties and give specific on-the-job training.

Training Procedure

The training procedure I have found most effective is:

1. Present the job description when people are hired. Have them take it home and read it. Tell them they should be familiar with its contents when they begin work.

2. The first day at work, have them observe. If it doesn't interfere with someone else's work, they may do some small tasks. Observe them carefully. You'll get a feeling about whether they can handle the job. It doesn't take an expert to tell if a person is clumsy or too slow. Don't

Figure 4–5.

Job Description for Utility Worker

Hours
11 AM—4 PM Mon.—Sat.   4½ hr/day   27 hr/wk
    Evenings—when needed

Duties
1. Wash dishes and put them away.
   Keep dishroom area, including tables, shelves, sinks, etc. cleaned up.
2. Wash and sanitize utensils.
   Keep sinks and tables clean.
3. Empty trash, garbage and empty boxes, etc.
   Replace plastic liners.
   Periodically wash plastic cans.
4. Keep outside trash area clean.
   Keep hopper closed and clean.
5. Floors:
   During Operating Hours—Keep papers, etc. picked up. Mop water spills.
   After Operating Hours—Sweep floors. Thoroughly (under equipment, etc.) mop entire kitchen. Leave mop outside building when finished.
6. Keep all refrigeration equipment cleaned on outside and inside. Wipe doors each day.
7. Keep shelves in kitchen wiped.
8. Put all grocery, produce, and meat orders away. Check all orders first.

overreact because it is their first day. However, if you don't think they'll be able to do the job keep a close eye on them.

3. Each succeeding day give them more tasks to perform until they know the entire job. Don't rush them. Some people work more slowly than others. Some work well under pressure; some do not. This is what you will determine after a reasonable period of time.

Training is much easier for everyone concerned if there is someone other than yourself for the trainee to work with. Employees seldom feel comfortable working with the boss. Besides, you will probably be constantly interrupted and this does not make for good training.

The important thing in training is to give new employees as much time as you (or your assistant) can. *Never* just throw people into a job and forget about them. They will become discouraged, frustrated, and bewildered, and unless they are of very strong character, will probably just quit. This does not help you one bit, and it has cost you time and money. Some people are quite capable of doing a fine job under controlled conditions. However, put this same person under pressure and you may get disastrous results. It is one thing for an employee to work well with a trainer. It is another for that employee to be able to work alone.

Do not hesitate to tell new employees when they are doing a good job. On the other hand, tell them when they are not doing something correctly. Bad habits can be built up quickly. You really have to strive for balance in this. Too many compliments are not good, nor is a barrage of complaints. Do not be impatient when training. Remember, good, reliable help is hard to find.

The importance of good training can never be overstated. A restaurant with well-trained personnel is a rarity. Guests will be aware of it immediately and sing your praises. The employee will know his or her job and be happier for it.

Terminating Employees

Terminating an employee is one of the hardest jobs you will have to face. For this reason, it is essential that you are prepared with all the facts when the moment of action arrives.

Before we consider the actual termination interview, let us first find out just how an unsatisfactory employee ever got in our midst in the first place. After all, didn't we use the best of interviewing techniques, check references, and train this person right from the start? Of course we did. Well, what went wrong?

One very good possibility is that the person was never quite fit for the job in the first place. Even with all the proper procedures, you could never tell if the employee was emotionally sound for a particular position. Furthermore, during the interview, he or she may have colored the truth a little bit, giving you the impression he or she was really better than the facts indicated.

A second, and very common, possibility could be that something changed in the life of the individual after he or she was hired. Perhaps a family problem developed, for example. This is quite often the case when the quality of the work of a good employee slips for no apparent reason.

A third possibility could be boredom or dissatisfaction with conditions or fellow employees on the job.

Regardless of the reason, performance is affected over a period of time. Because it is a gradual metamorphosis, the employee may not be aware of his or her poor performance. Consequently, it is up to you, the employer, to point out the problems. If the employee's performance does not improve, you have a valid reason for discharging him or her.

Keep in mind that good employees are difficult to find and that you have expended a great deal of time, effort, and money training this person. These are two excellent reasons for trying to salvage this employee. You should not reduce your standards to this person's level, but you should do all *you think* is reasonable to make a good employee out of one who is not quite working out. If you decide to go no further, then enforce your decision with a termination.

First, be sure your mind is made up. If you are satisfied you have really tried with this person, your decision should be firm. Do not be swayed by more promises to do better. Second, compile all the facts. Everything must be in writing (date of the warnings, time they were made, the place, the subjects, etc.) for two reasons: 1) it presents your case to the employee and 2) it provides documentation for the Unemployment Compensation Bureau. Third, get the termination check made up. Fourth, call the employee into the office (or to a quiet corner, when no one else is around) and make the termination.

The exit interview is not easy for you or the person being discharged. Get to the point as quickly as possible. State the case and make the termination. Before giving the employee the termination check, ask whether the employee has anything to say. Sometimes, valuable information about your operation can be obtained at this time. The employee no longer has anything to lose and may give you some interesting and helpful information about problems you are not aware of. This is also the time to have the employee turn over any company property he or she may have, such as uniforms and keys.

In addition to inability to perform, you may have to discharge an employee for disobedience. When a person directly disobeys an order, the situation usually becomes a tug-of-war between the two of you. When this occurs, your first inclination will be to end the relationship right then and there. If you do not, you may feel your standing will be diminished in the eyes of the employees. In such situations try not to let your emotions get the best of you, because if you do you are more likely to make a poor judgment or decision, which can lead to a minor disaster for you. There are two basic ways to handle such a highly charged situation.

The first way is the easiest and in 90 percent of the cases, the worst. Simply blow your stack and fire the person on the spot. This leaves you with an immediate vacancy and a clear case for paying this person's unemployment claim. The second method is to give the person a warning. Tell him or her to improve his or her attitude within a specified time period, or face being terminated. The most difficult situation the owner of a small restaurant has to face is to have an immediate and unexpected vacancy. You should strive to reduce the possibility of such an occurrence whenever you can. Delaying tactics are imperative, even if a temporary loss of prestige is suffered. When such vacancies occur, you invariably suffer the most anguish.

In most instances, when you terminate an employee you must have his or her final paycheck ready. If the employee quits, the check must be available at the next payday. Again, be sure all company property is returned at the time the paycheck is given. When an employee who has had access to important locks leaves, the tumblers should be changed for your protection.

The final consideration when terminating an employee is whether to give notice. Notice is simply informing the employee of your decision to terminate him or her and setting a date in the future on which the termination will become effective. Unless you have reason to believe an employee will leave immediately, notice should be given to all but those who have worked only a very short time or who have been overtly disobedient. Unfortunately, in almost every instance, once an employee has been given (or gives) notice, performance slips. Because of this, it may be best to pay him or her something extra and let him or her go as soon as possible.

There is no reason to be apologetic about terminating a worker. To condone poor performance is both demoralizing to the other employees and costly to you. Discharging an employee is not easy, but it is something that must be done occasionally.

The Bureau of Employment Security

Every business, large or small, must deal with the Bureau of Employment Security some time or other. This is where ex-employees receive their unemployment checks.

If an employee is out of work and meets the necessary requirements, he has the right to receive unemployment compensation. Most states have an unemployment compensation fund. The employer contributes—the employee does not. At the end of each quarter you make a contribution based on your experience rating. Initially, and until your experience brings about a change, you will be assigned a general rate. If you have employees leaving you and receiving unemployment benefits, your rate may be adjusted upward. Each year, in January, you must also file and contribute to the Federal Unemployment Tax Fund (Form #940). You will receive a credit for the amount you contributed to the state fund at this time.

At one time, it was difficult to deny an employee unemployment compensation if he or she was discharged. Today, the system is more realistic. It recognizes that an employer has the right to discharge an employee for just cause and that such cause may be reason enough to deny the individual claim benefits.

If you discharge an employee, have *complete, accurate documentation*. If you do not, the board will decide in favor of the employee most times.

Briefly, the system works like this:

1. Employee is terminated.
2. Employee goes to the nearest unemployment office and applies for compensation. He or she fills out a form stating the reason for being discharged.
3. A copy of this form is sent to your business. If it is accurate, you sign and return it. If it is not, you write out your story and return it.
4. The case is reviewed and a decision made. If the decision is against you and you are not satisfied, you may appeal. The same opportunity is provided the employee.
5. If it is appealed, there is a hearing before a referee. This is where you present your facts. The referee hears both sides and later makes a decision.
6. Usually, it stops here but both parties still have the right for further appeals.

If the decision is against you, and the employee worked for you only during the designated period, your account will be charged for all the compensation the employee receives. If he only worked for you half the period, you are charged 50 percent, and so on. So you see, it behooves you to be careful about discharging an employee. It can be very expensive to have a great deal of unjustifiable turnover.

Each quarter, a statement is sent to you by the Bureau. It lists all the charges against your account by employee's name. Look it over carefully. Be sure you are not charged for someone incorrectly and that proper charges are for the correct percentage.

You cannot help discharging employees, but you can keep claims charges to a minimum by maintaining careful records and keeping a check on the system. The best place to keep such records is with the payroll ledger card. When an employee is terminated, enter on the ledger card the date he or she last worked, the rate of pay, the reason for leaving, and your opinion of his or her work. Attach all supporting documents to the card. Be sure you have a current mailing address for all discharged employees.

Resignations

When an employee is discharged you are more or less in control of the situation. You are not in such an enviable position when an employee decides to leave you. At the very least, it is a difficult situation to be in.

Sometimes, an employee has a simple gripe which can be easily reconciled by talking about it. The problem is eliminated and the employee decides to stay. Other times, it is much more complicated and such a satisfactory solution is not possible. There may be times when an employee does not even show up for work to give you the opportunity to talk about it.

Let us discuss some of the reasons an employee might leave.

1. *Work is unsatisfactory.* Maybe it never was what he wanted or he is no longer satisfied.
2. *Personality conflict.* This could be between the employee and other employees or with the boss. If the problem is with you, think about it. Can anything be done without compromising your standards? If the problem is with another employee, check the story out. You may find a certain employee is giving others reason for consternation as well. Of course, it could turn out that the employee who is leaving is the one giving everyone the hard time. Personality conflicts are very difficult to resolve.
3. *Outside problems.* Usually, such problems are family related. The spouse may be transferred to another city. Perhaps, a serious accident or a death occurred which changed the family's plans. If the employee provides only supplementary income, it may be that the money is no longer needed or that the employee's spouse does not want the person working any longer. These are only a few of the many outside influences that could cause an employee to leave.
4. *Physical and psychological aspects.* Working in a restaurant produces problems that do not occur in any other occupation. Some people can never adjust to such conditions. It takes a strong person to put up with such irritants as kitchen clamor and difficult guests.
5. *Pay, other remuneration, advancement.* What would be a better reason for leaving a job than needing more money? If you are paying a competitive wage, there is not much more you can do to alleviate this problem. Employees should understand the opportunities for advancement when they are hired. Point out the other advantages to working for your restaurant (friendly staff, employee parties, bonuses, etc.).

This list is far from complete, but it gives

you some idea of why people leave jobs. In most cases, there is little you can do about their leaving. Perhaps, you could pay them a little more money or provide some other financial incentive, but you can seldom do anything about the outside or family problems they may have.

An employee leaves in one of two ways: with notice or without notice. The latter is devastating, the former is almost as bad. Either way, you have an unexpected vacancy to fill. This is especially disheartening if the employee is a good one.

The first thing to do, assuming you wish to retain the employee, is to talk with him or her. It might be a problem which can be ironed out. If not, the employee may agree to stay a little longer to give you more time to find a replacement. Even if losing the employee is not serious, the extra time makes the job search less pressing. During the discussion with the employee, point out some good reasons to stay with you. If remuneration is the problem, you may be able to offer a little more money or shorter hours. Never beg an employee to stay. Offer whatever you can, give him or her time to think it over, and then accept the decision.

Rehiring

Simply stated, I would never rehire an employee terminated for disciplinary reasons or who quit without giving notice. Generally, the rehiring of employees is not sound practice. If a person leaves for such reasons as moving from the area, pregnancy, sickness, or the like there has not been a conflict with the job. Under such conditions, rehiring will usually work out. It *almost never* works out in other situations.

Rehiring an employee can have detrimental effects on other personnel. Rehiring

a person who was fired for disciplinary reasons indicates a weakness on your part. Further, if employees can leave for *any* dissatisfaction they may have with their job and then be rehired, you will end up with no discipline at all.

Sound Employment Policies

It does not seem to matter much in which occupation a person is employed, the majority of people are working because they have to. They are primarily concerned with earning the highest pay possible in the most pleasant working conditions. It is quite possible that a person will consider lower direct remuneration if working conditions are more desirable.

Desirable working conditions can mean different things to different people. A cook, for instance, may consider new equipment the most desirable working condition. A waitress or waiter may be happy with nice surroundings. All, however, seem to have one requirement in common—they must like the people with whom they work. This includes the employer as well as their peers.

It is sad to say that the hospitality field in general does not provide pleasing working conditions. To compound the matter, it does not provide good compensation either.

Many large companies in other industries go all out to give their employees every benefit imaginable. Of course, this may be overdone to some degree. However, due to the enormous competition for capable personnel, it becomes imperative to provide the best possible working conditions and benefits.

A small business cannot afford the elaborate benefits and substantial pay scales provided by larger concerns. Consequently, all it can offer is an adequate fringe benefit plan, fair financial compensation, and friendly and satisfying working conditions. In comparison, this may not seem like much, but it may be all that is needed to obtain the type of employee you are seeking.

Determination of the Pay Scale

What is adequate pay? To arrive at the rate employees are to be paid may be difficult at first. This is especially true if you are starting a new business, as opposed to one that is established and in which the employees are already working.

First, break down your staff requirements. Some will be on salary and some will be paid hourly. There will be those who receive tips and those who do not. There are the professionals and the non-professionals. Finally, some will be full-time and others part-time.

Contact the local restaurant association, chamber of commerce, and state employment agency for the information they can provide. If possible, talk to other restaurateurs. When you interview people for the job openings you offer, ask them what they are being paid and what they feel would be adequate. Sometimes your bank can help provide this kind of information. Look in the want ads of the local newspaper. Find out what is being paid by local industry as well. This will tell you what you are competing with. Also to be considered is the federal Minimum Wage Law.

Preferably, all wage rates should be established before you start your business in order to predict payroll expense. If this is not possible, at least establish tentative rates to act as a guide. It would not be unusual if you had to adjust some of the rates soon after you started due to unforeseen circumstances. This is normal in a new business.

The only way in which you can hope to attract qualified applicants for the positions you have is to offer a good rate of pay. If you do not, no one will come to be interviewed. The labor market for trained personnel is very competitive. You must be prepared to pay at least the going rate and preferably a little better.

When determining the rates for service personnel, take into consideration whether or not they receive gratuities. When tips are received regularly, the government currently allows you to pay approximately one-half of the minimum wage. However, you may find this is not enough to attract people to the job. In this situation, you will probably have to pay a higher rate until you can establish how good or bad tips are. Later on, the hourly rate can be lowered if the tips are adequate.

In a highly successful restaurant, company pay may amount to only 15 or 20 percent of the service person's earnings. The remainder will be gratuities. Of course, the amount each person earns will depend on how well he or she performs.

Also to be considered is the rate of pay while training. No matter how experienced new employees are, they are not worth full pay when they start. They must learn your method of doing things. Because of this, it is necessary to have a lower rate for the initial training period. This period can be for a matter of days or for as long as a month. It depends on the individual and the amount of experience involved.

Pay rates should never be absolute. There are times when one person is clearly worth more than another, so you need a certain amount of flexibility. Rates should be stated as a range. For example, the rate for a kitchenperson could be from $3.35 to $3.75. A range such as this gives you the opportunity to start the individual where you think appropriate.

Starting employees are not as efficient as longer term employees. Because of this, it is a good idea to increase pay at intervals, until an employee reaches the top rate you have established for the job. Intervals of one month, three months, and nine months seem to work the best. As each interval ends, review the person's performance with him or her and give an increase based on performance. After the first two or three reviews you should give performance reviews annually.

The last consideration is merit increases. Rates should be set-up for those who do exceptional work. During the first year, this can be accomplished by accelerating the normal intervals. After that, you will have to establish specific rates.

Rate increases may be described in dollars and cents or in percentages.

If you have a very small restaurant, fewer than five employees, you can probably get by without a formal rate structure. The problem is, however, that you are very apt to forget to advance those who work for you. This is one reason a more formal approach is desirable. In addition, you will find when you try to hire employees that very few will be happy with, "we have no set policy for advancement." Knowing where you stand financially is a part of good working conditions.

Fringe Benefits

Now that the rates are set up, other forms of remuneration must be considered. These are primarily the fringe benefits.

Basic fringe benefits which should be available to your employees are:

1. Hospital and medical insurance,
2. Major medical insurance,
3. Vacation pay,
4. Sick pay.

The listed benefits are usually available to all regular employees after a specific waiting period. A regular employee is usually defined as a full-time worker and/or one who works on a regular basis at least twenty hours a week.

Hospital and major medical insurance can be set up on a contributory basis. You and the employee divide the cost. The division is up to you, but the more you pay the more desirable the benefit will be. The advantage of a contributory program is that an employee will not pay for unnecessary or unwanted benefits. A program in which you pay all the cost may be wasted on those who do not need the benefit.

I recommend getting the best possible plans available. Pay what you can afford for the employee and let the employee pay the remainder. Remember that group insurance provides lower premiums than individual plans. Both you and the employees will benefit.

Vacation pay is usually provided after an employee has completed one year of service. It should be available to both part-time and full-time workers. Full-time workers' pay would be based on their regular weekly salary. Hourly workers would have their pay computed on the average number of hours they worked in a week over a period of a year.

Sick pay is a benefit that can be abused, so make the guidelines for receiving it stringent. An employee should be with you for at least six months before this benefit is made available. Limit the coverage to a certain number of days per year to protect yourself from those who abuse it. You can always give more if you have a really good employee who deserves it.

There is little question that you are increasing your operating costs with fringe benefits. However, if you do not offer them, you will be increasing your operating headaches. The more you can do to arrest turnover, the better off you are. It is expensive to train employees to do things your way and then to have them leave you. Good fringe benefits are just another way of getting solid employees and keeping them.

Working Conditions

Good working conditions are not a single element but a conglomeration of elements. They include the tangible, along with the intangible. Restrictions, guidelines, freedom to express yourself verbally, financial advancement, a feeling of appreciation, and friendly co-workers are just a few of the elements that make up a satisfactory working environment.

Small restaurants have a tremendous advantage over large ones. They have the opportunity to promote an esprit de corps the large restaurant could never hope to develop. This is a big advantage because it will result in a staff that will pull together for you. Do your part as an owner and employer to foster this feeling.

Of course, you cannot let the togetherness aspect go too far. There must always be a leader and the leader must be you, the owner. Employees are happier when they have someone they can come to with their problems. They also like a boss to tell them when they are doing a good job.

Your own behavior is an important part of the working environment. You should strive to exhibit the characteristics of a good supervisor. If you can weigh all the evidence and make a fair decision, treat everyone equally, stand up for yourself when you are right, admit mistakes, listen to unsolicited suggestions, stand behind an employee when he is right and remain cool under the most difficult circumstances, then you are a good supervisor (or employer).

In addition, you must not be so friendly with the employees as to lose their respect, but you must be friendly and understanding enough for them to come to you when problems arise.

Physical Facilities

In that large company we talked about earlier physical facilities would indicate a plush lounge with all the amenities. In a small restaurant, you may be lucky to provide employee restrooms. Don't worry a great deal about this. Most restaurant employees do not expect much in this regard. Try to provide some area away from the public area in which they can have a smoke or a few quick words with one another. Keeping the "back of the house" facilities as clean, neat, painted, and maintained as the public areas indicates you care.

Performance Standards

Performance standards are a necessity. An employee will be happier when he or she knows what is expected and can strive for fulfillment of the criteria you set. High standards will result in top performance on the part of the employee and high praise from the guest.

Performance standards include personal performance as well as job performance. Employees should never be allowed to smoke in the public rooms or near food preparation. The same restrictions should apply to eating and drinking. Uniforms should be clean and pressed. List your rules on the job description and point them out to new employees.

When it comes to performance, be firm. Let one person slip and the others may feel they can start slipping too. An employee is constantly projecting your image and it is up to you to set and maintain the standards.

Owner-Employee Relations

It is important to have an amicable relationship with your staff. A boss who never cracks a smile or shows any understanding will never get the sincere cooperation of the employees. Deciding just how friendly and understanding you should be is not easy. Too much and you lose respect. Too little and you lose their cooperation.

A sense of humor can go a long way when the pressure is heavy. A little joke at the right time can do a lot to relieve the tension. On the other hand, do not be afraid to let someone know when you are angry about something they have done incorrectly.

Do not become too involved with the personal problems of any member of the staff. It creates a tendency to be less objective. This, in turn, influences your decisions regarding this person. Never become involved socially with any employee.

Once in a while, give the staff a little something extra when they do an exceptional job. After a particularly difficult time, you might buy them a drink. An extra few dollars as a bonus after a hard week is an appreciated gesture. Have birthday cakes on employees' birthdays. Let each employee bring a one dollar silly gift to make a party of it. At Christmas, have an informal party. In the summer, have a cookout. There are many inexpensive ways to show your appreciation to a loyal staff.

Distractions

Restaurant kitchens are traditionally very noisy for several reasons. First is the physical structure. Health regulations in most states require surfaces which are hard, non-porous, and washable. By nature, such surfaces, instead of helping to absorb it, actually help sound to bounce around the room. Second is the human voice. Waiters and waitresses always like to get their orders in promptly, so they yell them out the minute they are in the kitchen. In addition, it seems the cooks seldom understand the waitresses and waiters and a good deal of spirited conversation ensues for each order. Third is the sound of the movement of dishes, glassware, silver, pots, pans, and serving utensils. Finally, there are the mechanical contributors. The refrigeration units banging away, the ice cubes dropping in the bin, the exhaust fans whirling at tremendous speeds, the steamer ejecting its vapors, the dish machine spraying and belching its liquid, and the mixer whirling in a metal bowl.

To keep the noise level down you can ask the service personnel to wait until they reach the range before calling their orders (softly), you can ask the pot washer and dish washer to be a little more quiet in handling their wares, you can even use soft water to make ice cubes; but you cannot stop the machines from running or the hard surfaces from bouncing sounds.

Well, I hope by now you are getting the idea. There is more to a good job than the money. Consideration on the part of the employer for the employee is also essential to a smooth-running operation.

Unless there are some special needs, happy employees will not leave their jobs. Even if they are making a little less money, as long as they like their employer and fellow employees, they will think long and hard before making a move. It is up to you to provide this type of atmosphere. All it requires is some thoughtfulness and consideration on your part.

Maintaining high standards and keeping employees happy in today's labor market is a real challenge.

How the Owner Puts It All Together

We've had a good deal of discussion involving the needs of the employee. It is, without a doubt, a very important aspect of a smooth-running organization. But, where does good employee relations end and sound management begin? Too often, this aspect of running a business is overlooked. An employer should be able to demand certain performance criteria without being branded selfish or hard to work with. In order to satisfy such a requirement, let's first discuss why good management and employee relations go hand in hand.

If one is to have a well run organization from the customer's, employee's and owner's point of view, there must be definite, high standards for performance. These can only be obtained by sound training. Such training is costly to any owner in time, effort and money. Consequently, it is fair to say an owner has an investment in each of his employees. It follows, therefore, an owner would have no valid reason to constantly harass his employees and force turnover among the staff. If an owner should do this, he is hurting his investment and creating an unnecessary expense to himself and his business.

You have probably heard it said, "He is a difficult person to work for." It's hard to generalize, but certainly such criticism may be unwarranted in a large number of cases. There are two reasons a person may be difficult to work for. One is that he *really is* difficult to work for and the other is that the employee does not want to perform by any imposed standards.

The former is something only the employer himself can change. To be difficult, in this day and age, is pure idiocy. There is nothing to be gained and everything to lose. Without a doubt, such an attitude will not attract good employees.

The latter reason is probably a more likely explanation for a person acquiring such a reputation. It is unusual but gratifying to find a restaurant with definite operational standards. It would be a challenge to visit ten restaurants at random and find more than one with definite operational standards for all the employees. If such a situation exists (and it does), it is understandable why the owner with standards may be called difficult to work with.

If you are, or expect to be, one of these "way out" individuals; don't apologize. You deserve a medal. By having high standards, you have set your operation far above all others. You have provided an excellent reason for guests to return again and again. And, you have provided a place your employees can be proud to be a part of.

How you implement these standards is important. I do not advocate being soft. If you set high standards, you are justified in having those who work for you adhere to them. This does not mean you should just give them a sheet of paper with the instructions written on it and expect them to perform. You should instruct them carefully, be considerate and fair in your expectations of them, and give each a reasonable amount of time in which to perform.

There is no question that an employee has the right to voice his or her unhappiness with a particular condition of the job. If it is a valid criticism, you may wish to make a change. However, never sacrifice a standard if it will result in a disservice to the guest.

It's your reputation. Set the high standards necessary to achieve a good one, both for your restaurant and yourself. The care in which you run your restaurant will determine its success.

Chapter Five

The Heart of the Matter —the Kitchen

Because the kitchen is the most important element of the restaurant, it should be an initial consideration. If it is a new kitchen, or if you are planning to remodel an existing one, a list of the equipment required must be completed before the operation can be started. Even if you are purchasing or leasing an operating business, an inventory of what is needed will have to be made. Make this inventory at the outset to give you some idea of the amount of money involved. It will be necessary in order to determine your overall financial requirements. Once the amount of equipment is decided on, its layout must be determined. In order to accommodate the equipment, remodeling of the premises may be required.

Once the kitchen is planned and installed, the actual day to day operation, including sanitation, purchasing, receiving, storage, controls, pricing, menu making, and food preparation, must be considered.

Equipment List

There are basic pieces of equipment that every kitchen must have. Beyond that, additional equipment will be determined by the individual restaurant's needs. Therefore, it is first important to decide on the type of menu you will use. The more elaborate the menu the more elaborate the kitchen equipment. For example, a steakhouse would require a charcoal type broiler, a French style restaurant would not. If a restaurant features elaborate desserts and baked products, it would surely need a good bake oven. A small restaurant could get by with a five quart mixer, while a larger one would be needed in a bigger operation. It is important, then, to determine the type of food to be served and the quantity in which it will be produced before considering the equipment purchase.

Listed below are the pieces of equipment

necessary in every kitchen, regardless of size or menu.

> Cooking surfaces
> Ovens
> Hot food service counter and heat lamp
> Slicer
> Refrigeration, walk-in
> Refrigeration, reach-in
> Freezer
> Ice maker
> Mixer
> Blender
> Work tables, metal and/or wooden
> Sinks (3 compartment, single, and hand)
> Dishwasher and tables
> Hood and exhaust system with filters
> Fire prevention equipment
> Shelving for storage
> Pot rack or shelving
> Refrigeration shelving

This list is by no means comprehensive. It merely illustrates basic needs. Complete lists of equipment for preparation and baking, kitchenware, supplies, and general sanitation can be found in various sections of this chapter.

It is better to under-purchase when equipping a kitchen. If there is a doubt as to whether a piece of equipment will be needed, do not buy it. Kitchen equipment is an expensive investment and until you, or your cook, have actually worked in the kitchen area for a few weeks, you will not have a really good idea of the necessary changes or additional equipment needed. You may want to leave open space for any equipment in question so that it can be easily added at a later date.

Generally, unless you build the building new, kitchen space is limited. If it is not limited in footage, there are always limitations such as entranceways, pipes, and support columns.

If you are purchasing or leasing an existing business it will probably be difficult to relocate the kitchen area. However, if you are purchasing or leasing a store or house, you may have some leeway as to the kitchen's location. Here are a few considerations to help you make a decision:

1. Do you want an open or closed kitchen? Do you want your customers to see you work? Do you want to see your customers?

2. Accessibility. The service personnel have to be able to get in and out with a minimum of trouble. Purveyors have to be able to make their deliveries without walking through your dining room. For this reason, most kitchens are located in the rear of the building.

3. Storage. Where are you going to store the food, the liquor, and the supplies? This area should be near the kitchen if possible.

4. Location of utilities. The more plumbing and wiring you have to have done, the more you are increasing your costs. For this reason, it is best to stay as near to the present utilities as possible. However, do not let this influence you too greatly. Many times, the steps saved will more than offset the extra cost of installation.

5. Local codes. Check into these carefully once you have considered the other factors.

Once the equipment list is compiled and a decision has been made as to the kitchen's location, you can proceed with the kitchen layout or plan.

Layout

A preliminary layout can be done by a non-professional without too much effort. (See Figure 5–1.) If you feel you are not capable of making one, contact a restaurant supply house which offers this service or a professional architect. Architects are the most expensive and seldom know much about restaurant operations. If you think you may purchase the necessary equipment from a particular dealer, go to this company. Usually the company providing the equipment will supply free planning.

If a dealer or architect is doing the job, all you have to do is provide the list of equipment you need. A member of the staff will then come to the location and take accurate measurements and then submit a preliminary

plan for the kitchen. Go over this layout carefully and make necessary changes. The plan will be revised and resubmitted. Do not be discouraged if you do not see eye to eye right away. I went through this back and forth procedure seventeen times for one operation. Keep in mind that it is much less expensive to do the changing on paper than it is to do it after everything is in place.

Some general principles to be followed when planning are:

1. Keep plumbing installations as close together as possible. Plumbing can be difficult and involved. With careful planning, it is possible to save yourself considerable expense.

2. Electrical installation is similar to plumbing. If a central panel can be installed in the same room as the equipment to be used, it may save installation costs. At the very least, it will be more convenient than having to run to the basement each time a problem arises. When installing

Figure 5–1a. Building Plans—The Owner's Sketch

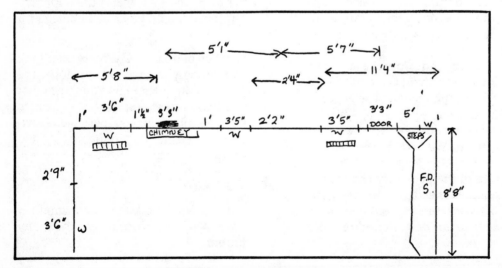

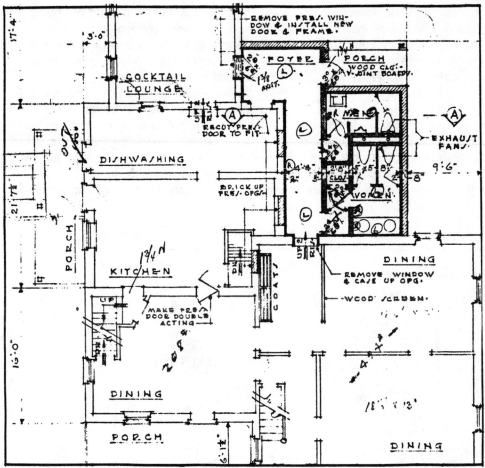

Figure 5–1b. Building Plans—The Architect's Drawing

a new panel be sure to use breakers and not the old style fuses. Both breakers and wiring should be of adequate size to sustain the load they will carry. This is very important when heavy equipment is involved. Consider the power supply as well. It too should be adequate. 120/240 volts or 120/208 volts are the most common installations. Three phase wiring is slightly more expensive to install initially but it can save operating costs later on.

3. A kitchen should be laid out in areas. Have the hot food area in one place, the cold food section in another, and so on. This not only simplifies preparation but allows service personnel to move about more efficiently and quickly.

4. If a door or window creates a problem because of its location, consider moving it or covering it. Doors that swing in the wrong direction can be changed.

Doing your own preliminary layout

drawings is not really difficult. However, it does take time. The time saved can be directly translated into money saved by you. Follow the directions outlined below and I'm sure you can come up with a passable sketch.

1. Obtain spec sheets (Figure 5–2) for all equipment wherever possible. These can be obtained from any restaurant supply company or directly from the manufacturer. Such literature gives you complete data as to size of equipment and electrical and plumbing information for each piece of equipment.

2. Assemble any other information you have collected regarding equipment for which a spec sheet is not available.

3. Make a rough sketch of the room or rooms on a large sheet of paper.

4. Use a six foot or longer rule to measure the room. A wooden folding rule is the easiest to use. The job will go much more quickly if two people are available to do it. One can measure while the other writes the measure-

Figure 5–2.   A Typical Spec Sheet (Reprinted with permission from Scottsman Ice Machines.)

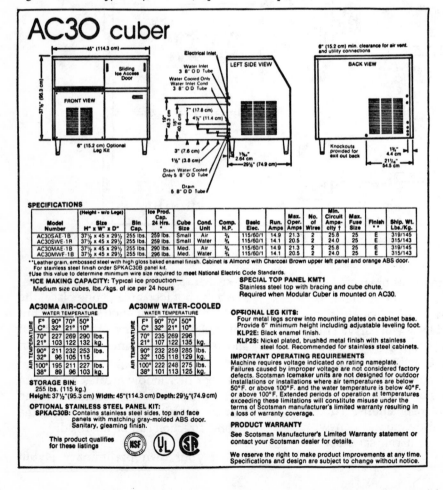

ments down. Proceed to carefully measure the circumference of the room to the nearest inch. Be sure to put in door and window openings, partitions, pipes, shafts, and conduits. Place this information right on the rough sketch you made in step three.

5. Make an accurate drawing of the kitchen area. To do this, reduce everything to a common scale. This scale, for our purposes, will be ¼ inch equals 1 foot. Here is an example of how 6′ 9″ translates into the scale for your drawing.

$$6 \text{ feet} = ¼″ \times 6 = 1½″$$
$$9 \text{ inches} = \rule{2cm}{0.4pt} \quad \tfrac{3}{16}″$$
$$6′ 9″ = 1\tfrac{11}{16}″ \text{ (on the drawing)}$$

You can make your life easier by purchasing an architect's scale, which has the scale all laid out for you and eliminates laborious conversions. When you are finished, the entire sketch should be a reduced schematic view of what you see when looking into the room. If it is not, go back and check your figures.

6. Take all your equipment specs out. Get some firm, cuttable cardboard, shears, and a sharp pencil. Using the measurements in the specs, proceed to make cardboard cutouts, to scale, for each piece of equipment for width and length. It is helpful to write the height on each cutout. Label each piece so you know what it is.

7. Using the scaled drawing you completed in step five, fit the cutouts into position. You will find that things do not always fit where you would like them to. Remember, that little piece of cardboard is just like a piece of stainless steel, you cannot bend it or cut a piece off. It has to fit exactly as it is.

8. Now that everything is in place, trace an outline of all the equipment directly onto the room diagram. Note the heights of each piece on the drawing.

9. Take the drawing, your rule, and scale and walk around the room checking the specs with the layout. You may even want to draw in each piece of equipment on the floor. Check the height of the equipment as well, to be sure there is no obstruction. If everything fits in, you are in business. If not, start arranging again.

10. The one remaining task is to check on utility hookups. If an item needs electricity, is there a receptacle? Have you concentrated your hookups as much as possible to cut down installation costs?

If you have never worked in a restaurant or a restaurant kitchen you should have a professional do the detail work. Content yourself with making the scale, room drawing, setting up the general areas, and deciding what equipment is needed. To attempt anything beyond that could result in serious and costly mistakes.

For those who have had kitchen experience, here are a few guidelines to be considered when doing the layout:

1. A minimum service aisle is 48 inches. This barely allows two people to pass one another.

2. A work aisle should be approximately 36 inches. An example is the aisle between the range and the hot food section.

3. Never locate a fryer near a water source such as a sink. Serious accidents could result.

4. Doors to refrigerators and closets should open in the direction in which they are most frequently entered.

5. When two pieces of equipment, such as a range top and a broiler are located side by side, try to have a work space (called a spreader) of at least 18 inches before the next piece of equipment is placed.

This provides room to set utensils down.

6. The placing of equipment in a particular area should be as compact as possible. This saves extra walking. However, be sure to provide as much work surface as possible beside it. This saves time during the heavy preparation period.

7. A small sink in the serving/cooking area is invaluable during serving time.

8. Provide adequate reach-in refrigeration near the serving area for the cook to use during the meal hours. It is faster and reduces the opening and closing of the walk-in refrigerator.

9. If the cooking equipment is placed along side a wall, a smaller exhaust system is needed than if it were placed in the center of the kitchen area.

10. In a small kitchen, try to locate equipment used by both the hot food and cold food sections in the center. This eliminates extra steps and the need for people to cross in front of one another.

11. Items used primarily by service personnel, such as soup, rolls, coffee, and ice cream, should be placed where they can be easily reached without disturbing the prep personnel. If there is adequate space in the dining room, many of these items can be placed at a service station in that room.

12. Two doors are required for service personnel to leave and enter the kitchen from the dining area.

13. Keep noisy sections such as the pot washing area away from dining room doors.

14. Do not forget to provide storage area for clean china and glassware.

15. If there is not a separate room for food storage, build some shelves in the kitchen or use pre-made metal shelving.

After you have decided what equipment will be needed and how it will fit into the existing area, give a professional architect the fact sheets and scale layout. He will make a drawing that will be acceptable to all the necessary governmental agencies. Submit the drawing(s) for approval. Once the drawings are approved, you are ready to begin construction and to purchase the equipment.

There are all sorts of codes and restrictions on building and remodeling. The Health Department, Bureau of Building Codes, Zoning Commission, Fire Department, and Bureau of Labor and Industry are just a few. These departments should be considered from the beginning. You do not want to tie yourself into a long lease or the purchase of a piece of property if there is a possibility that some ordinance will deny you the right to open.

Used Equipment

A new business venture usually has limited capital and by purchasing used equipment the restaurateur is able to spread his or her capital in more directions. The used equipment will perform the same function as new equipment would, even if it is not as shiny. As the business develops, a new replacement can be purchased.

In many instances, used equipment can be a very good buy. However, it is important the purchaser knows what she or he is buying.

If possible, try to determine:

1. Why it is being sold,
2. Something about the operation it was used in,
3. When it was purchased,
4. How well it was cared for and serviced,

5. If any warranties are still in force,
6. How well it works and what would be needed to put it in good operating condition,
7. Whether or not it will fit your requirements,
8. The average market price for such used equipment,
9. What a comparable new piece would sell for.

You are assuming an unlimited risk when purchasing used equipment. Therefore, the price you pay should reflect this and be considerably below the cost of new. If you purchase from an individual, as opposed to a dealer, more than likely you will have no recourse if something should go wrong immediately after purchase. A dealer has a reputation to protect and, consequently, would probably be willing to make some kind of adjustment in such a situation. This is an important consideration when you are not certain about the condition of a particular piece of equipment.

Certain categories of used equipment are good buys and others are not. As a general rule, it is not wise to consider any used equipment which would leave you with a serious problem if it should fail.

Refrigeration fits into the category of risky buys. There are so many things that can go wrong with refrigeration that an older piece should not be considered unless it is used only as a back-up. This includes all forms of refrigeration such as freezers, ice makers, and refrigerators. If a warranty is provided by a dealer, this rule does not apply.

It is also risky to purchase used mixers. Although a mixer can give you many years of solid service, once they start to deteriorate, they go quickly. You will end up investing more in repairs than the cost of a new mixer.

Gas equipment is simple to operate and easy to repair. However, gas ovens and dishwashers have a burn out problem. In an oven, it is the floor. In a dishwasher, it is the bottom of the tank(s). The condition of these sections should be checked carefully before a purchase is considered. Also check for warping. The constant heat from gas flames and pilots tends to warp flat surfaces.

When purchasing a used oven, whether gas or electric, check doors and wall insulation and thermostats. Poor insulation and malfunctioning thermostats can cost you extra in energy expenses. In addition, poor insulation will keep your kitchen much warmer than necessary in the summer months. With electric equipment, you should check the elements to see if they are functioning. A burned out element could be costly to replace.

Used items that are usually safe to purchase are tables, sinks, slicers, fryers, and toasters. This assumes that you check each out carefully before purchasing.

It is often possible to obtain old spec sheets for used equipment by writing to the company. Just include as much information as possible about the piece. Serial and model number are absolutely essential.

Before you consider purchasing any used equipment, take accurate measurements so you are sure it will fit where you want it. Remember, you cannot take it back in most cases.

Try to use an authorized dealer for repairs if possible. At the very least, use authorized parts. This may be more costly, but unless you are dealing with an expert repairperson, it is absolutely necessary.

Do as much of the cleaning up and minor repair work as you can. This will save you money. Do not attempt anything you are not familiar with. This will cost you money.

Used equipment can be purchased from many sources. Most large cities have people who just specialize in selling such equipment. Many new equipment dealers have used equipment that they have taken in as a trade. These can be particularly good deals. Sometimes a local restaurant or hotel is going out of business and has equipment for sale. Check your newspapers. Consider running an ad yourself for what you are looking for.

New and Used Equipment Combined

From the foregoing you have probably concluded there is a place for both new and used equipment. It certainly is true. With a careful selection of used equipment and the purchase of new essential equipment, you should be able to come up with a minimum outlay of capital.

Kitchen Equipment

To Be Used in Preparation

Cooking tops
Ovens
Metal overshelves to keep food and plates warm
Broiler, conventional or char-broil
Grill
French fryer, filter or strainer
Microwave oven
Steamer or pressure cooker
Hot food table and counter
Sandwich and/or salad unit
Food warmer lamp
Walk-in refrigeration and shelving
Reach-in refrigeration for storage
Reach-in refrigeration for working

Freezer, cabinet or walk-in type
Slicing machine, gravity-feed type
Mixer, five quart minimum, ten quart preferred—extra bowl, grinding attachment, whip, dough hook, and paddle
Food processor
Toaster, four hole
Blender, extra parts
Soup warmer, plus two insets and cover
Wooden work table or large work board
Metal work tables
Tray rail
Storage rack for trays
Small sink at salad area, eighteen to twenty-four inches in diameter, plus drainboard
Small sink at hot food prep area
Ice cream freezer and dipper well with water
Ice maker
Bake oven

Support Equipment

Storage shelving and/or overhead, hanging pot rack for storage of pots, pans, and other utensils
Shelving for storage of china, glassware, and other items
Hand sink
Coffee maker or urns
Portable rack to use with eighteen by twenty-six inch pans for preparation
Roll or bread warmer
Two wheel cart or hand truck
Storage area or room with shelving
Exhaust fan, hood, and automatic fire extinguisher system
Adequate lighting

Compactor

Portable fire extinguisher(s)

High stool to sit on when working

Cooking tops and ovens can be gas or electric. Gas equipment is less expensive to purchase and service but is not as efficient as electric. Some people find it easier to cook with. Electric equipment is easier to keep clean. Generally, electric equipment is sturdier in construction and better insulated. Gas may require a special tank in the ground. Electrical equipment may require a larger service. Gas may be more or less expensive than electricity.

Some cooks prefer to cook on a flat surface, while others prefer burners. If you use burners, try to have at least six. You may want to consider having both burners and a flat surface. There should be two ovens. You will be severely handicapped with only one. Cooking tops and ovens come combined as a unit or they may be purchased separately to be built in or to be placed on top of a counter. Stainless steel is highly recommended because of its ease of cleaning. The added expense is well worth it. If you cannot afford to purchase good equipment right away, this is a good place to consider the purchase of used equipment. Do not buy cheap ranges, they are not worth the money and will not hold up.

Convection ovens are more expensive than conventional ones, but have many advantages. Among them are faster baking, a better baked product, and less waste. They can be used effectively for food preparation as well as for baking. Convection ovens are more energy efficient than standard ovens.

Consider a see-through door and a light in the oven as extras.

Metal overshelves are shelves that fit over the cooking top area. Sometimes they are built into the range. If not, it is advisable to have them. They are a great place to keep food warm for a short period and make an excellent area to keep dinner plates if no other is available.

Broilers heat from the top or bottom. The ones that cook from the bottom are called char-broilers. They cook just like an outside barbecue. The others are radiant broilers. The char-broiler is easier to keep clean and uses less fuel. A broiler is an item you may not need. If there is any doubt do not buy one. You can always add it later. You may want to consider leaving space for one if you have extra space.

A *grill* is another item you may not need. If you have a flat surface cooking top, you could reserve a section of this for grilling.

The *french fryer* is a great help when you need it, but if you will not use it often enough, do not buy one. In addition to the cost of the piece of equipment, it requires a special hookup on the fire extinguishing system. In some states, it may even increase your insurance rate. If you do have one, be sure to purchase a filter system to filter the grease. If you cannot afford a system, at least buy filter papers and a holder. The fat will last longer and give you a much more desirable product if it is filtered.

Microwave ovens are very useful for reheating prepared items in addition to cooking fresh ones. It's far better to reheat an item in this manner than to keep it sitting in a hot food table throughout the meal. This oven has its limitations but is extremely useful for fast preparation.

A *steamer or pressure cooker* is a good item to have but you can get by without one in a small operation. Its big advantage is speed. There are also energy saving features as well. Vegetables can be cooked satisfactorily in boiling water if you do not have a cooker.

A *hot food table and counter* is used to store

and serve hot food. It is a must. Be sure to include an overshelf. Above this will be the *food warmer lamp* to keep the food hot after it is dished.

The *sandwich and/or salad unit* is a refrigerated unit from which cold foods are served and prepared. This too, should have an overshelf or serving shelf. If you will not be doing much in the way of sandwiches and salads, such a unit may not be needed. The unit's uses are really very limited.

The *walk-in refrigerator* is indispensable. A small, 6' × 6' size, would be the smallest I'd recommend. Equip one side with metal shelving and save the other side and rear for bulk storage. If you find you need more shelving, add it later. These units are usually prefabricated and can be made to fit almost any area. They can even be placed outdoors with the entrance inside the kitchen. The refrigeration compressor can be located anywhere there is a free and adequate circulation of air. Get a door latch that can be locked. Do not forget a built in thermometer and an interior light. If you are fortunate enough to be able to find a used one, be sure the compressor is sound. If there are any doubts, have it rebuilt or purchase a new one. You cannot afford to have troubles with this piece of equipment.

Reach-in refrigeration is used primarily for storage of prepared food. In addition, it saves steps and the opening and closing of the walk-in. Such refrigeration should be located close to the person using it. For example, the cook's box should be near the range so he or she can have the mise-en-place readily available. The size of such refrigeration depends solely on your needs and the space you have available. There may be times when you will want to have as many shelves as possible in these refrigerators, so provide for adjustable shelving. This type of refrigeration is usually self-contained and does not require drainage.

Check this when you consider the equipment.

The size and type *freezer* will depend on your operation. Usually, a small operation does not need a large freezer. However, if you plan to use a lot of frozen items, you will need an adequate size. This is one piece of equipment which should be purchased new, unless you are absolutely certain of the condition of the used one. A failure of a freezer can be *very* costly.

A *slicing machine* is also indispensable. The uses you will find for this piece of equipment will amaze you. It is great for portion control and uniformity of product. It is one of the few pieces of equipment that will last forever, if properly cared for. A rebuilt slicer is almost always a good buy. Do not buy anything but a gravity feed type. Be sure, if you purchase a used one, the sharpening gear is included. If it is not you can get it from the manufacturer.

When buying a *mixer* be sure to get all the attachments listed. Do not buy a used mixer. They are very expensive to repair and once they start to deteriorate they do so quickly. The ten-quart is the best all-around size for a small kitchen. You can survive with a five-quart. Do not skip this piece of equipment.

A *food processor* is nice to have, but not necessary.

Do not buy a *toaster* unless you really need it. You can purchase a rebuilt one with confidence, if it has been carefully rebuilt.

A *blender* is a really versatile piece of equipment. Commercial ones are very expensive. If you do not expect to use one too frequently, an ordinary home-type will do. For the money, this is a wonderful piece of equipment to have around when you need it. It is much better for liquids than a food processor.

A *soup warmer* is really necessary if you serve soup. It frees the cook from dishing soup out and allows the waiter or waitress to do it. Do not forget a location for the soup bowls or cups. Keep the bowls warm if possible. There should be two insets to facilitate replacement of soup. Round ones are better than square ones. The best capacity is five to seven quarts. It must have a thermostat.

A *wooden work table* is easier to chop on than a metal one with a chopping board. Some states do not allow wooden table tops any longer, so metal ones are used. There is no doubt that metal is an easier table to keep clean. Regardless of which you use, it should be a minimum of six feet long (unimpeded) to get any real use out of it. Permanent piles of supplies on the tabletop limit its use. Use other tables for the equipment. The work table should be used for direct preparation only. If you use a metal table with a board, get a large board so that you are not cramped in your work. It should be the depth of the table, at least three feet wide, and one inch thick. There should be a board of about the same dimensions in the cold food section. These boards are made of pure plastic or combined with rubber or wood. The old-fashioned hardwood boards are also available, but you should check with your local health department before buying one of these.

Table tops should be at least 14 gauge stainless steel. If any lighter, they bounce. The legs should be sturdy and well braced. Preferably, there should be at least one shelf and a drawer underneath. The edges of the table should be rolled to prevent injury and the feet should be adjustable. The height should not be over thirty-four inches.

Tray rails are located on the service side of the pick-up area and attached to the hot food unit to enable the waiter or waitress to rest a tray while picking up food. A length of from six to ten feet is ample, depending on how much area you have.

A *storage rack for trays* is very useful. It provides a place for trays to be stored when they are not in use and gives them a chance to dry out and deodorize somewhat. Trays should always be cleaned and wiped before being placed in the rack.

Work sinks in both the hot food and salad area are very important. They do not have to be very large. The salad sink will be used primarily for cleaning greens. The other sink will be used as a water source and to cool food. It is handy to have a filler hose for filling large stock pots. The hose could be installed over the range instead of at the sink. The salad sink should have a drainboard. The one in the hot food area can be built into a table or be free standing, with or without a drainboard.

Ice cream freezers come in a variety of sizes. The one best for you will be determined by how many flavors of ice cream you will carry, whether other frozen desserts will be stored in it, and whether it will be used as additional storage capacity for other foods. The smallest size available is a four hole cabinet. This will hold six cans of ice cream. If you are not using ice cream, you do not need an ice cream freezer.

In addition to the cabinet, you will need a dipper well with running water. This is required by health departments in almost all states. If your health department does not require one, you can do without it very easily. A stainless steel, two quart bain marie pot will serve the same purpose.

Ice makers have capacities of from one hundred pounds up. Purchase one that makes a little more ice than you need. Ice makers make ice in all shapes and sizes. If you have a bar, it is best to have smaller pieces of ice. The shape is irrelevant. Most machines come with a storage bin slightly larger than the ice making capacity of the machine. It is possible to buy a bin with a larger capacity. This is highly recommended if you expect to have high peak periods of ice usage. A one hundred pound machine with a two hundred pound bin will assure you of an extra day's supply of ice.

Do not buy a used ice maker unless it is relatively new. They are very expensive to repair once they start to deteriorate. Also, check the bin of a used machine for holes.

Bake ovens will not be needed by most small restaurants because of the limited number of desserts offered. If you have good roasting ovens or a convection oven, you can probably get by without a special bake oven.

Storage shelving is probably one of the most neglected areas of consideration when planning a kitchen. Shelving is needed for the storage of dishes, glasses, pots, pans, and food, both in the storeroom and refrigerators. Plan on having shelving wherever you have available space. Metal shelving is costly but well worth the money. It is indispensable in the walk-in refrigerator because of its resistance to moisture and ease of cleaning. Wooden shelving should never be used in refrigerators. In the storage area, wooden shelving is quite acceptable. Try to obtain a depth of at least twenty inches. This depth will accommodate three #10 cans in a row, two rows will take care of a case. Shelves should be about eight inches apart. Have some shelves with a higher opening to take care of gallon containers, boxes, and bulk items. All supplies should be stored off the ground. To conserve floor space, pots can be hung on a rack over the preparation area. Flatter pans can be stored under tables and on shelves. Wooden shelving is satisfactory for china and glassware storage if it is painted or covered. Be sure all shelving is well secured.

A *hand sink* will probably be required by your local Board of Health.

Whether you use a *coffee maker or urn* will depend on how much space you have and how many people you serve. The coffee urn

is used in larger operations where a great deal of coffee is needed at one time. If you have a fairly even demand, a coffee maker or brewer will prove very satisfactory. In addition, it provides fresher coffee and is less involved in brewing. Further, the brewer can be hooked up with or without a water source. So, for the small inconvenience of having to get water elsewhere, you can save the expense of additional plumbing. Such brewers come in all sizes. One that holds three pots should be more than adequate. An electrical connection is required.

A *portable rack* to use with eighteen by twenty-six inch pans is a luxury which should be considered if you have the space for one. This is a cart, on wheels, with slides to hold the pans. Such a cart can be wheeled around the kitchen and is particularly useful for preparation which takes a great deal of horizontal space.

A *roll or bread warmer* is a handy item to have but is not needed immediately. Such warmers come as table top units or free-standing units. They usually contain one to three drawers. The size you should purchase will depend on your needs.

A *two wheeled cart or hand truck* is a wonderful item to have around the restaurant. It saves a great deal of lifting and carrying. A cart with two handles is easier to use than one with only one center handle. The price differential is quite small for the extra handle. The wheels should be approximately eight inches in diameter for easier handling.

Any *storage area* should be free from moisture and extreme temperature changes. There should be no holes in the floor, walls, or ceiling through which vermin or bugs may enter. The floor should have a smooth finish which can be easily cleaned. Have adequate lighting and ventilation.

The *exhaust fan and hood* are among the most important items in any restuarant. The fan must be designed to remove all cooking odors and smoke from the cooking area. The proper size should be determined by an engineer who is aware of the dimensions of the cooking section. The hood should extend six inches or more beyond the edges of the cooking equipment. It should be made of an easily cleaned material. Stainless steel is excellent but, of course, more expensive than regular steel. The necessary fire extinguishers, nozzles, and filters will be inside the hood (see Chapter Thirteen).

Remember, air that is exhausted must come from somewhere. Be sure air intake is also considered when designing the exhaust system. In some cases, air intake may be an integral part of the exhaust system. In other cases, you will simply leave a window open. In any situation, be sure the intake air is not so cold and does not flow so rapidly that it cools the food or produces unnecessary drafts.

Adequate lighting is essential if everyone is to work at top efficiency. A dull, poorly lit kitchen is difficult to work in. Check with the local power company and have one of their engineers prescribe what is needed. Do not make your kitchen so bright that the light overflows into the dining room.

A *compactor* may be needed in certain locations due to the poor availability of refuse pick-up. There may also be a lack of space to store refuse and garbage.

Kitchenware

Hot food table pans
12″ × 20″ × 2½″, start with 12
12″ × 10″ × 2½″, start with 12
12¾″ × 10⅜″ × 2½″ plus dividers, start with 6
10⅜″ × 6⅜″ × 2½″ plus dividers, start with 6
There may be times when a few of the above pans may be needed in 4″ and/or 6″ depths.

Covers for above pans
Hinged 12″ × 20″ cover, if serving roasts
Sauce pans and lids
1½ qts., 2¾ qts., 4½ qts., 7 qts. (2)
Saute pans (coated)
8″, 10″, 14″ (may need more than one of each)
Brazier, 16″ × 5½″ (may need cover)
Stock pots and lids
10 qt., 20 qt.
Roast pan with lid, 16″ × 20″ × 4½″
Bains-marie and, possibly, lids
1½ qts.
2 qts. } 3 of each
Larger ones, if needed
Prep pans, 10″ × 14″ × 2″ (start with six)
Collander, 12″ or china cap, 5½″
Prep pie pans, 9″ (2 doz.) for use under broiler or in oven.
These can be of very thin gauge and made of steel.
Cutting boards, composition
18″ × 12″
24″ × 18″
Larger one, if butchering
Food mill, 10″
Prep pans to use in microwave, non-metal
Au gratin dishes and/or casseroles, if needed
Metal bowls for mixing salads with dressing
Small, 3 qt. or 5 qt.
Large, 12 qt. or 20 qt.

Kitchen (Small wares)

Thermometers: oven, refrigerator, meat, pocket
Knives:
French, 6″, 8″, 12″

Boning
Paring (2)
Serrated
Grapefruit
Clam or oyster (optional)
Slicing (optional)
Sharpening steel
Cleaver, 8" blade
Tenderizer, 3" square, 2 sided
Tongs (for removing food from grill, broiler, and pots)
Grater, coarse and fine
Potato peelers, hand (2)
Strainers, fine and coarse mesh, 6" and 9"
Turning spatulas, 3" × 6" and 3" × 8" blades
Spreading spatulas, 6", 8", 10" blades
Skewers, 6", 12" (optional)
Egg beater, hand
Nut cracker
Whisks, thin wire, 10", 14", 16"
Egg slicer (2)
Small juicer (to fit over cup)
Slotted or perforated serving spoons, stainless steel
    Long, 13" or 15" (3 or 4)
    Short, 11" (3 or 4)
Solid serving spoons, stainless steel, long (2) and short (2)
Wooden spoons, 10" and 15"
Forks, 2 prong (2) (in different lengths)
Wooden soup paddle (optional)
Skimmer, stainless steel, 4" and 6" diameter
Mesh skimmer for use with french fryer, 5"
Ladles, stainless steel,
    2 each of 1 oz., 4 oz., 8 oz.
    1 24 oz.

Scrapers, rubber, 4 each, 9½", and 13½"
Dishers (also called dippers) various sizes
Scoops (for flour, sugar, etc.)
Shakers or dredges (for salt, pepper, flour, etc.)
Pastry brushes (2)
Ice scoop, large (32 oz.)
Ice cream spade
Racks for cooling and baking
Zester (optional)
Portion scale
Scale, 25 pound capacity
Can opener, #2 size, plus extra blade and gear
Scissors
Small timer
Plate covers for entree plates, fiberglass (metal is too noisy), 1 dozen should be adequate, 2 dozen would be better
Large wall clock
Punch type can opener

Baking Utensils

Layer cake pans, 9" (start with 6)
Pie pans, aluminum, 9" (start with 12)
Spring form pan
Angel cake pan
Cake pans, 10" × 14" × 2"
Loaf pans
Muffin pans
Cookie sheets or jelly roll pans
Flan pan
Flour sifter
Shakers
Rolling pin, 24"
Rolling surface (board)
Wire racks for cooling

Pie server
Large gelatin molds
Individual molds for desserts
Thermometer
Hot pads (cloth)
Paring knives (2)
Bench scraper
Rubber bowl scrapers (small and large)
2 each

Kitchen and Baking Use

The items listed below can be used in cooking preparation or in baking. They are not specifically allocated to either department.

Bun pans, 18″ × 26″ × 1″ (start with 12)
Half pans (as above), 18″ × 13″ × 1″ (start with 12)
Measuring cups and other containers
  Cups, ¼ to 1
  Containers, 1 quart and 1 gallon
Measuring spoons, 2 sets
Salt, flour, sugar containers
Mixing bowls, metal, 1½ qts., 3 qts., 4 qts., 5 qts., 8 qts.
Plastic storage containers and covers
  2 qts. (12)
  6 qts. (12)
  22 qts. (1)
(Note: the plastic containers used for cottage cheese and sour cream are excellent for this purpose and don't cost anything.)
"Drip-Cuts," 6 oz., 14 oz., 30 oz.
Funnels, various sizes

Kitchen (Supplies and Paper)

Uniforms (purchased or rented) include hats, aprons, trousers, dresses, and jackets; except for paper hats, rental is the way to go
Side towels and rags (purchase or rent)
Pads and pencils
Plastic wrap, 18″
Aluminum foil, 12″ (may need 18″), expensive item, use sparingly
Freezer wrap, 18″
Wax paper, 12″ or 18″ (depends on use)
Parchment paper (optional)
Plastic bags for storage, various sizes
Plastic or paper cups for pre-portioning and control, 4 oz. and 8 oz.
Paper baking cups (optional)
Cheese cloth
Butcher twine
Hot pads (4)
Pastry bags and ends, various sizes
Toothpicks
Sandwich picks or frills
Anti-oxidant (1 or 2 jars)
Blackboard and chalk (to notify service personnel when items are running low or are exhausted)

Equipment Maintenance and Repair

There are four reasons for good maintenance:

1. Preservation of equipment.
2. Prevention of costly and inconvenient breakdowns.
3. Reduction of operational expense.
4. Safety.

Every restaurant owner has a great deal of money invested in equipment. It is advantageous to maintain it and prolong its life as long as possible. It is, therefore, particularly important that you establish a maintenance program.

Maintaining equipment reduces the need for large capital expenditures and reduces the possibility of a serious breakdown which could put you out of operation.

The failure of any important piece of equipment, from an exhaust fan to a walk-in refrigerator, can put you out of business for a few hours or a day or more. If you are located in a remote area, where parts are hard to obtain, you may wait days to be back in operation. Furthermore, if the breakdown occurs after hours or on a weekend, you may not be able to get emergency service until the service company reopens. Obviously, breakdowns can occur even to well cared for equipment, but the chances are greater if the equipment is not maintained.

The cost of operating certain mechanical equipment will increase if periodic maintenance is not performed. For example, if refrigeration coils are not periodically cleaned to eliminate the dust which collects on them, they become less efficient. Less efficiency means more power is used, the motor works harder (causing premature wear), and temperature recovery is slower.

Belts must be tightened, gears oiled, and filters cleaned if operating costs are to be kept to a minimum. Anything less than this will result in increased repair costs.

Finally, improperly maintained equipment can be a safety hazard. A leaking french fryer can suddenly burst into flame, burning the operator. A worn gasket on the steamer can unexpectedly allow a burst of steam to shoot out at a cook. Why create risks when preventive maintenance will help to eliminate them?

A maintenance program certainly will not solve all your problems when it comes to equipment breakdowns. However, it will re-duce the number and limit the inconveniences associated with such breakdowns.

In establishing a maintenance program, you must first decide which work will be performed by your staff and which will be performed by an outside firm. As a general rule, if the equipment is complicated or beyond your scope, have an experienced outside firm do the work. Good examples of this would be maintenance of refrigeration and convection ovens. Be sure the firms you employ are reliable and competent.

To help you decide who will perform the maintenance tasks, make a complete list of all equipment involved. Such a list will give you a better understanding of what has to be done and who should do it.

When employing an outside firm, contract with the firm yearly for the work to be performed. The contract should clearly spell out: 1) the services they are to perform, 2) how often the service is to be given, 3) the annual cost, with a breakdown, 4) what work or parts are not included in the contract, 5) the charge for extra services and parts, 6) details on emergency service, and 7) cancellation terms.

When determining the costs for doing a job yourself, include such items as payroll costs, fringe benefits, workmen's compensation, supplies, and energy costs. When these are added up, you may find it less expensive (and less bothersome) to employ an outside firm.

There is one intangible benefit to having an outside firm which should not be overlooked. In many instances, employees of outside companies are trained in many facets of work. Because of this, they may discover potential problem areas which your people are not capable of uncovering. Consider this along with the direct costs.

Most maintenance jobs performed by

outside firms will not be done very frequently. Some may be carried out quarterly, yearly, or seasonally. The exact day and time is seldom spelled out. Because of this, it is a good idea to make a list of the companies and the services they perform, approximately when the work is scheduled, and exactly what they are to do. This will act as a reminder for you to call them, if they do not call you.

In addition to the list of outside firms, a calendar should be made up noting the jobs to be performed by your own staff. In doing this, try to have certain jobs performed on the same day each week. This system is easier for the employee to remember and gets him or her into a routine. The calendar should list the job to be done, the time, and, possibly, the person expected to do it. Such a visual reminder makes everyone aware of the tasks to be fulfilled. Always check to see that the work is done correctly. Keep the calendar as a permanent record of the work performed.

Even with the best maintenance program, equipment will break down. If this happens, you will want to reach the service company quickly. Therefore, a list of all service companies should be compiled. Hang it where it can be seen by everyone. Keep it updated. Service calls should never be made

by anyone but yourself, unless there is an emergency and you cannot be reached.

Keep a record of all maintenance performed by outside companies. This is the only means you have to help you determine when the cost of repairs is reaching the point where replacement should be considered.

Items on the following list of maintenance work can usually be performed by the owner and staff. If you are not handy or have no one on your staff who is, even the simple jobs should be done by an outside firm. Do not attempt any job unless you are absolutely sure how it is to be done. In some cases, it may be wise to have a serviceperson show you how the first time. After that, you can do it yourself. Many companies are so overloaded with work that they are only too happy to do this.

Do-It-Yourself Jobs

Cooking Area
1. Cleaning of grease filters over cooking area.
2. Checking accuracy of thermostats. Do not attempt adjustment unless you know how.
3. Cleaning of burners (gas) and/or heating

Sample Service List

Service	Company	Telephone Normal	Emergency
Refrigeration	J.W. Ramsey Co.	555-1663	555-2794
Gas problems	Pa. Gas Co.	555-2964	same
Ice maker	Colonial Equip.	555-3769	—
	Joe Rudy	—	555-6873
Electrician	City Electric Co.	555-1616	555-1674

(Note: The type of service, not the company name, is listed first. Company names do not always indicate the service they perform.)

element (electric) in french fryer. Changing fat.

4. Cleaning of burners and/or elements in range tops.

5. Cleaning of ovens. Use of foil on deck reduces necessity of cleaning.

6. Checking conditions of door gaskets and tightness of oven doors.

7. Checking door springs in oven. Replace if broken.

8. Checking motors and blowers in convection ovens for proper operation.

9. Checking operation of gas pilots. Have gas dealer do adjusting.

10. Cleaning broiler. Check for easy and smooth movement.

11. Checking steamer gaskets' condition. Replace if needed. Checking for correct pressure. Checking timer.

12. Adjusting legs to keep equipment level.

Other Equipment

1. Slicer. Will need occasional sharpening and oiling of moving parts.

2. Mixer. Seldom needs maintenance if cleaned well after every use. Check condition of attachments.

3. Coffee makers, urns, and stoves. Makers and urns need occasional de-liming. Bowls and urns need to be cleaned with urn cleaner periodically. Check burner elements. Replace if burned out. Check switches.

4. Toasters. *Carefully* check operation. Have repaired by professional.

5. Exhaust fans. Lubricate, when necessary. Check, tighten, or replace fan belts.

6. Refrigeration (coolers, freezers, ice cream chests). Keep coils free of dust and built-up dirt with vacuum cleaner.

7. Plumbing. Have pipe leaks repaired. Fix leaking faucets. Are drains working satisfactorily? Clean grease trap when needed.

8. Intake air grills. Keep cleaned.

9. Dishwasher. Most detergent suppliers will handle maintenance of the dish-machine and related equipment.

10. Air conditioning. Keep filters clean. Check belts and lubricate larger units.

11. Fuse box. Frequent power failures indicate wiring deficiency. Have electrician check out wiring.

The most commonly neglected maintenance is that which should be performed daily. If all equipment is *thoroughly* cleaned at the end of each day's use, more expensive maintenance will be minimized. The persons using the equipment should be reponsible for cleaning it. They will be much more careful in their work procedures if they know it is their job to clean up at closing time. *You*, as owner and manager, must insist on this. It's your investment.

The key to the success of a good maintenance plan is its cost. The more you and your staff can do, the greater the savings. Conversely, the more outside help you employ, the more costly the program will be. It is essential then, to know the costs involved so you can determine when it is no longer practical to continue the plan or some portion of it.

Miscellaneous Maintenance Equipment

Set of tools (hammer, screwdrivers, pliers, wrenches, saw, etc.)

Step ladder and, possibly, larger ladders

First aid kit

Garden hose (optional)

Outside tools (optional)

Light bulbs and fluorescent tubes, various sizes

Heavy duty extension cords

Three prong adapters (2)

Flashlights (kitchen, dining room, and bar)

Extra fuses, if you use them

Sanitation for Kitchen and Related Areas

Sanitation includes cleanliness, sterilization, and waste removal. It is important not only from a health and aesthetic point of view, but also from a financial one. Sales can be lost simply because a restaurant looks unsanitary. In addition, think of the consequences of a guest becoming ill because of food eaten in your restaurant. It would certainly result in bad publicity and a subsequent loss in sales, perhaps in a permanent loss, and, possibly, in an image-damaging law suit. Such notoriety is difficult and costly to overcome.

Because of public pressure, the health departments of more and more states and municipalities are becoming concerned with the responsibilities a restaurant has to its public. There is a growing trend to enact a uniform health code which would be used throughout the United States. Such regulations, enforced universally, can only aid the restaurant industry in the long run.

There are four general areas of sanitation in a restaurant: 1) the kitchen area, 2) the dining area, 3) the bar, and 4) the public areas. Kitchen sanitation will be discussed in this chapter.

Kitchen sanitation is broken down into:

1. Food handling,
2. Refrigeration and storage,
3. Dishwashing and warewashing.

Handling Food

If all food handling was performed by machines, we could eliminate many of the problems inherent in restaurant kitchens. Unfortunately, it is not. Therefore, our first consideration will be the human factor.

Employees must be trained in proper food handling techniques and should understand why they are required. It is not practical to give an employee a book of rules and simply expect him or her to fulfill your requests. A training program must be set up and then followed through, to ensure that the employee is actually putting into practice what he or she has been taught.

Harmful (as well as non-harmful) bacteria are transmitted by people or utensils. They are not capable of their own movement. Such transmission is done directly or indirectly. When a person sneezes in your face, there is little doubt you are being contaminated. However, when transmission is indirect it is hard for an employee to understand the danger of infection. It is up to you to make the dangers clear. Take the time to get subject information and explain it to them. Two good sources for this information are *Sanitation for Food Service Workers*, Richardson, CBI Publishing Co., and *A Self Inspection Program for Foodservice Operators*, National Restaurant Association, Chicago.

Here is what you should require of all employees handling food or drinks at your establishment.

1. Good health. You may require a physical examination before employing an individual. A person who is sick can infect others. It is better this person not work.

Neither fellow workers nor guests want this person around. In some cases, you may require a note or call from a person's doctor indicating it is safe for an individual to return to work. No one should be allowed to work with unbandaged cuts or sores.

2. Clean hands. Hands are the most frequent carrier of germs. They should be washed whenever they come in contact with contamination. This is particularly important with kitchen workers. Hands should always be washed after the toilet is used. When a person is forced to use a hand to cover a sneeze, the hands should be washed immediately. Hands which are not washed after becoming contaminated, may touch glassware and utensils and pass the bacteria on to others. For this reason, glasses and cups should not be picked up at the rim, nor silverware picked up or placed by anything but the handles. Hands should not come in direct contact with food during preparation. Use spoons or other utensils for mixing.

3. Personal hygiene. Employees should be bodily clean. They should have no body or breath odor. Fingernails should be short and clean. Preferably, hair should be short. If it is not, it should be tied back. It should also be kept clean. Hats should be worn by kitchen personnel. Rings or jewelry, which can fall into food, should not be worn.

4. Uniforms. All employees should wear clean uniforms. There is nothing less appealing to a guest who looks into the kitchen than the sight of someone doing the cooking in jeans and a plaid shirt. Who knows where those garments were before they were in the kitchen? All kitchen personnel should wear clean aprons. They should not be used to wipe the hands on (another source of contamination). Hand towels should be used for all wiping. Neither legs nor feet should be bare. Stockings should be worn by the women and men should wear socks.

5. Smoking should never be permitted, except in specified areas set away from food preparation and out of sight of the guest. Hands should be washed after smoking.

6. Miscellaneous. Hands should never be used in place of a scoop to remove ice from the bin. Fingers should not be used to taste food. If tasting is required, the food to be tasted should be removed to a small plate and then tasted. It should not be returned to the batch. Eating should not be permitted in the preparation area.

By insisting your employees follow the above guidelines and procedures, you can eliminate one source of food contamination. There are still other factors to be considered, but at this point, it might be a good idea to explain how food poisoning occurs.

In order for bacteria to survive, they must be introduced to a desirable medium, one in which they can grow and reproduce. Second, the proper conditions or atmosphere must be present to allow them to multiply. If either of these requirements is not met, little, if any, growth can occur. During its life cycle, the living organism throws off wastes which are called toxins. It is these toxins that cause the illnesses associated with food poisoning.

Illustration

Suppose a cook has an infected cut containing staphylococci on his face.

While he is mixing the ingredients for a meatloaf, he inadvertently touches the cut, transfers the germs to his fingers, and continues to mix the meatloaf. The meatloaf mixture is now infected with the bacteria. The mixing is completed and the mixture is placed to the side, in the warm kitchen (78° F) uncovered, for an hour before it is used. Finally, the meatloaf is made and baked. Because the cook is planning to reheat it later, he does not bake it completely. The internal temperature never goes above 125° F. The loaf is removed from the oven and placed in the back of the kitchen to cool. It is later reheated and served. The next day a call is received from the health department. Seven (ex) customers have reported the restaurant for serving impure food.

What happened? The meatloaf ingredients (ground meat, eggs, bread crumbs) provided a perfect medium for the staphylococci to reproduce. The temperatures from 78° F to 125° F were just the right atmosphere for growth. Combine the perfect medium, the temperature, and the amount of time the ingredients were exposed and you have a classic example of food poisoning. It is obvious from this example that it does not take much effort to get a small epidemic going.

In addition to the personal hygiene of the food handler, there are two other ways in which contamination can come about. One is outside contamination and the other is the improper treatment of food on the premises.

Outside Contamination. The proper treatment of food begins at the back door. Allowing fresh food to sit out back for hours before processing or refrigerating it is just inviting problems. When fresh food is delivered, it should be taken care of immediately.

Frozen items should be placed in the freezer without delay. Delivery vehicles sometimes do not have freezer capacity and frozen foods are mixed in with fresh produce. Such foods may have already started to defrost en route. If your restaurant is at the end of the delivery route, it is possible that your entire frozen food order may be defrosted. If you discover that this has happened, return the order. If the thawed food is refrozen, it is possible that the product has developed enough bacteria and toxins that additional mishandling could result in food poisoning. It is important, therefore, that all food deliveries are carefully checked before they are accepted.

Every case and package of fresh produce should be opened and checked before it is placed in the refrigerator. Look for deterioration of the product. A single spoiled item can contaminate an entire case or package.

Raw meats provide an excellent medium for the growth of bacteria. An even better one is provided by fresh fowl such as turkeys and whole chickens. Seafood deteriorates rapidly when left at room temperature for just a few hours. All these items should come to your restaurant in a refrigerated vehicle or be iced while in transit.

All fresh food should be refrigerated as soon as it is received to reduce bacteriological growth. Do not leave the food out with the intention of working on it right away. "Right away" can be an hour or more.

Fresh foods should also be protected from other types of contamination including dirt, sprays, and detergents. Do not store onions or potatoes under the pot sink to be splashed with detergent or waste water. Store then in a protected area or cover them.

If you check fresh and frozen foods carefully for deterioration and/or other potential or real contamination, you will have eliminated another source of infection.

Improper Treatment of Food on Premises.
The last source of contamination attributed to the food handler is improper treatment of fresh, frozen, and cooked foods. Frozen foods, such as vegetables, entrees, and prepared meats, cannot become infected while held at the proper frozen temperature (0° F). How and where such foods are defrosted, however, can be critical in eliminating contamination. Proper defrosting of foods takes planning on the part of the food handler. The correct method is to place the frozen item in the refrigerator to defrost well ahead of the time it is needed. The time required will depend on the particular product and the refrigerator temperature. The food defrosts slowly and naturally, reducing the amount of juice lost. Food defrosted in this manner cannot become contaminated with new bacteria while defrosting.

Using some foods without defrosting results in a better flavored product after cooking and also eliminates spoilage. Examples of such items are vegetables, breaded products, uncooked entrees, and unbaked hors d'oeuvre and pastries. Meats such as steaks do not have to be defrosted before cooking. However, some cooks prefer to thaw them. If this is the case, such products should be kept well wrapped and used as soon after defrosting as possible.

Seafood and poultry are particularly prone to infection because of the quality of the meat. These items can be safely defrosted in either of two ways: the refrigerator method mentioned above or the water method. Without question, the refrigerator method is the recommended one. When the food is needed in a hurry, the water method can be utilized. Simply place the items to be defrosted in a suitable vessel and allow cold water to run over them until they are defrosted. Never use hot or warm water, which breaks down the tissue, causing a loss of juices, and provides a medium for contamination.

As a general rule, do not refreeze any food. Refreezing causes tissue breakdown and an increased potential for infection.

Tissue breakdown occurs in frozen foods because of ice crystal formation. Ice crystals have sharp points that can puncture the cell walls of the food, causing loss of juices. The higher the temperature at which freezing takes place, the more ice crystals are apt to form. The speed of the freezing process also has an effect on ice crystal formation. Commercially frozen food is frozen so quickly and at such a low temperature that ice crystal formation is almost nonexistent.

If you are forced to defrost food in a warm kitchen because of a lack of refrigeration space, be sure it is kept tightly wrapped with plastic film. There will still be an increased loss of juices and flavor, but the risk of contamination will be minimized.

Once foods are defrosted, they should be treated with the same precautions as fresh food. The cardinal rule for the proper treatment of fresh food is keep it refrigerated, if you are not working with it. Never allow food to sit in a warm kitchen for any length of time. Food that is ground, such as hamburger, paté and stuffing should be kept covered at all times. These products are easily contaminated. Whenever you place food in an area where dust or dirt can fall on it, cover it with plastic film.

Cooked foods probably present one of the largest potentials for bacterial invasion because of the desirable temperatures. In addition, the preparation of such foods presents another opportunity for infection.

It is essential that all utensils be sterilized and free from grease and caked-on food particles before they are used. The surfaces on which food is placed, chopped, sliced, or mixed should be sanitized and free from contamination. The same is true of equipment such as slicer, range top, and mixer. Clean towels and rags should be provided, along with the proper cleaning agent, to enable the food handler to keep equipment clean.

Food should always be cooked to an internal temperature high enough to destroy harmful bacteria (above 140° F). Unless the temperature is obviously above 140 ° F (e.g., a boiling liquid), it should be checked with a thermometer. This is especially true of roasted items such as meats, and of cream soups and certain cooked desserts.

Leftovers are another candidate for contamination. Because they are usually reheated to a temperature lower than 140° F, bacteria grow in them very rapidly.

Once preparation is completed, all food should be refrigerated immediately. Do not allow it to cool in the kitchen. The shallower the layer of food, the faster it will cool. Therefore, the same amount of food will cool more quickly in a 12" x 20" x 3" pan than in a two quart bain-marie. The proper temperature to stop bacteriological growth is 45° F or lower. It takes varying amounts of time to cool food to this temperature. The temperature of the refrigeration, amount of food, size and type of container it is placed in, and the temperature of the food when placed in the refrigerator all affect the speed of the cooling process. It is best to cool food as quickly as possible. Prepared food placed in the refrigerator should always be covered. Plastic film is particularly satisfactory for this because it allows the transfer of heat and cold to take place more rapidly. The film can later be replaced with a more permanent cover. Food in metal containers cools more rapidly than in plastic or china, because metal is a better conductor.

It is important to remember that food should be stored at or below 45° F and cooked to a temperature of 140° F or higher. When you do not allow food to remain at temperatures between 45° F and 140° F, you eliminate another means of infection. (See Figure 5–3.)

If correct procedures for proper handling are instituted and followed, the possibility of infection to food served in your restaurant is virtually eliminated. If there is such an occurrence, it will be the result of carelessness on the part of the individual, not ignorance of food handling techniques.

Refrigeration and Storage

Adequate and proper refrigeration is one of the most important ways to limit contamination. Every operation, regardless of size, should have a walk-in type refrigerator. A unit as small as six feet wide by six feet deep is sufficient for most smaller restaurants. Fitted with open, metal shelving, it can be of immense value in cooling foods quickly. Because of its wide, open area it is capable of reducing temperatures more quickly than a reach-in unit. The refrigeration unit should be fitted with an accurate thermometer, preferably one that can be read from the outside without opening the door. However, a simple hanging type hung in the warmest section is sufficient, even if it is not as convenient. Thermometers should be checked periodically for accuracy. Employees should be instructed to be aware of the refrigerator temperatures and report any problems immediately. Refrigeration problems must be taken care of as rapidly as possible to prevent food wastage and down time, both of which can be quite expensive.

In addition to a walk-in refrigerator, there should be reach-in refrigerators at the cook's station, cold food section, and one for the service personnel to work out of. If space

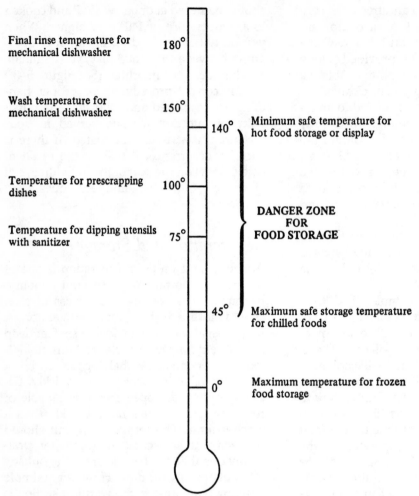

Final rinse temperature for mechanical dishwasher — 180°

Wash temperature for mechanical dishwasher — 150°

140° Minimum safe temperature for hot food storage or display

Temperature for prescrapping dishes — 100°

DANGER ZONE
FOR
FOOD STORAGE

Temperature for dipping utensils with sanitizer — 75°

45° Maximum safe storage temperature for chilled foods

0° Maximum temperature for frozen food storage

Figure 5–3.   Critical Temperatures (Fahrenheit)

is a problem, the latter two can be combined.

It is essential that all refrigeration be kept at the proper temperatures. In the case of the walk-in, a temperature of about 36° F is necessary for proper preservation of foods. The temperature of reach-ins should not go above 36° F because the doors are constantly being opened and a proper temperature is difficult to maintain. The cook's box should be kept at 36° F because of the proximity to the hot cooking equipment. This is one of the

most important refrigerators on the premises. It allows the cook to keep foods chilled at all times. Without it, food would be left in the warm kitchen and be exposed to all kinds of contamination. In addition, there would be a significant loss of quality and flavor.

In addition to the refrigeration, an adequate size freezer should be available on the premises. It can be located anywhere safe and accessible. The temperature should be at 0° F or less for safe storage. When food is put in the freezer, it should be dated and rotated.

All refrigeration units, including freezers, should be equipped with accurate thermometers.

Refrigerated food should be wrapped or covered with plastic film (never towels). The only exceptions are certain raw vegetables and fruit, which do not become contaminated as a result of their raw state. Wrapping prevents contamination from bacteria and other matter. It is best to store raw food away from cooked or prepared foods.

Processed food should never be put in the freezer without heavy wrapping, which prevents freezer burn (dehydration). Food placed in a freezer cannot become contaminated with new bacteria when wrapped. However, there is still the danger of outside contamination from cardboard cases and other types of containers. Before placing new packages of food in the freezer, look for breaks in the packaging which will allow the contents to be exposed to the air.

All boxes and crates should be cleaned before they are placed in a refrigerator or freezer. This is especially true if they are stored on shelves above other foods. Large boxes, such as lettuce cases, should be stored on the floor of the walk-in. If you purchase wire baskets to store produce in, you can eliminate the cardboard boxes and wooden crates and the accompanying outside contamination.

It is important to maintain good air circulation in both the refrigerators and the freezer. From a practical point of view, if the cold air is not allowed to circulate properly, the compressors have to work harder to cool, thereby shortening the life of the machinery. From a sanitation point of view, it is important for the air to circulate so the chilling of the food will take place more quickly.

Opening and closing refrigerator doors introduces warm air into the units. This raises the temperature and increases the time needed to chill food. Teach your employees to open the doors only when necessary.

All freezers and refrigerators should be cleaned periodically, outside and inside. Spills should be cleaned up when they are made. To maintain efficiency, the outside cooling coil should be vacuumed as dust builds up on it and a program of preventive maintenance should be instituted.

Non-Refrigerated Storage. Two types of foods can be stored without refrigeration: perishable items, such as raw potatoes, which have a relatively short life, and non-perishable items, such as canned goods, which have a shelf life of many months.

Basic rules apply to the storage of both perishable and non-perishable food items.

1. The storage area must be dry and well ventilated, have little direct sunlight, a stable temperature, be well lit and kept clean.

2. Food should not be stored near pipes, windows that leak, or sewer openings. It should also be kept away from walls that get damp.

3. Food should *never* be stored on the floor. Bulk food or cases should be stored on platforms six to eight inches above the floor. Other food (e.g., canned goods, packages) should be stored on shelving. Shelving should not be close to walls. This hinders air circulation. Wooden shelving is to be sealed or painted. Shelving should be kept clean.

4. Storeroom floors should be of a material that is easily cleaned (e.g., asphalt tile). Spills should be cleaned up immediately.

5. Food should be rotated. The oldest used first and the newest placed behind the

old. If necessary, date the items to be sure.

6. Check merchandise for cleanliness when it is delivered. Roaches enjoy hitchhiking on cartons.

Perishable items, such as potatoes and onions, can be kept in the storeroom or in a safe area in the kitchen. Such items should be covered and kept six inches above floor level on a platform. They do not require refrigeration but should be checked periodically for deterioration and possible infestation.

Semi-perishable items, such as apples, bananas, and oranges, may be temporarily stored outside of refrigeration. However, such storage results in definite flavor and quality losses.

Eggs and cheeses must always be refrigerated. Many operators still store them at room temperature, which may result in bacteriological, insect, or rodent contamination.

Bulk items, such as sugar, flour, rice, and dried legumes, should be stored off the floor in tightly closed, marked containers.

Dishwashing and Warewashing

Dishwashing and warewashing are traditionally treated as one subject, probably because both use water, detergent, and sanitizers. However, there is a difference between the two. Warewashing provides clean preparation utensils for the kitchen staff. Dishwashing provides clean serviceware primarily for the guest. Although sanitation is the prime consideration for both, there is also an aesthetic appeal to sparkling china, glasses, and tableware.

Proper Warewashing Procedures. Pot washing is considered the most lowly of jobs in restaurant kitchens. It is unfortunate that it

has inherited such a stigma, because the importance of this position cannot be overlooked. If the warewasher does a poor job, all our previous concern for sanitation can be thrown out the window. If only one pot is contaminated with a strain of infectious bacteria, the infection can spread throughout the entire preparation cycle.

The warewasher should be trained and relied upon to do the work consistently, as it is described. Anything short of this could result in problems for everyone concerned. Sometimes, this same employee is called on to perform the dishwashing and general kitchen cleanup functions as well. If this is the case, even more intelligence, reliability, and cooperativeness is required.

The next requirement for warewashing is satisfactory facilities—adequate sinks, hot water, supplies, and detergents.

The pot sink should have three compartments and a drainboard at each end. The compartments should be twenty-four inches square with twenty-four inch drainboards. The drainboards should slope toward the sink compartments so waste water flows back into the sink. The drain opening should be two or three inches in diameter and be screened to prevent food particles from entering pipes. The old-fashioned plug type drain, although not as convenient as the lever type, is the most trouble free. The sink should be made of 16 gauge, 18-8 stainless steel with cove corners inside and tubular, adjustable legs. The faucet should be a heavy duty, mixer type with a swing nozzle.

Because of space limitations, you may have to modify some of the above specifications. If length is a problem, you can reduce the size of the drainboards or eliminate one completely. If the local health department will allow it, a two compartment sink can be used. This is better than reducing the compartment size. Compartments which are too small make some warewashing difficult.

Adequate hot water is essential for good warewashing. Although modern day detergents allow you to wash in almost cold water, the ease of washing is greater with warm water. In addition, the hotter the rinse water temperature, the faster the drying. If a sanitizing agent is not used in the final rinse, water of 170° F is required to sanitize utensils. A good reason to have that third compartment in the sink is that 170° F water requires a special, and expensive, hot water heater. If your dishwasher is adequate in size and the food is not baked on, pots and other utensils may be washed in it.

The proper detergent is another factor. One which cleans, dissolves grease, and sanitizes is what you should look for. The detergent dealer can help you with this. Detergent can be in powder or liquid form. In many cases, automatic dispensers can save you money.

Pots and utensils can be cleaned with cloths, sponges, or brushes. Experience shows that pot brushes are the most efficient. They clean with a scraping, as well as a rubbing, action and are, therefore, more efficient. Stubborn soil can be removed with nylon scouring pads. Stainless steel pads are not recommended because pieces of the pad can be left on the pot or utensil and end up in the food. Scouring powder should only be used as a last resort. If not properly washed off, it can contaminate the food.

Racks or shelves are needed for clean storage. Clean items should not be placed on the floor unless they are on a platform, at least six inches above the floor. Overhead racks at the range are excellent for storage of smaller pots and pans with handles. Other items must be stored on shelves.

Having all the finest equipment in the world would be of little use if it were not used properly. The correct washing procedure is:

1. Place all soiled pots and utensils on one drainboard (or nearby) at one end of the sink. Do not place them *in* the sink because it is then necessary to remove them in order to fill the sink with water and detergent, which takes extra time.
2. Half fill wash sink with water and add the detergent. More water and detergent can be added as the work progresses.
3. While sink is filling (or before), scrape heavy grease and large food particles from utensils. Stack items of similar size and shape together.
4. Begin washing.
5. Place drain plug in second sink. Rinse detergent from items with very hot water and leave them in second sink until adequate room is no longer available. With this method, the sink is filled, as utensils are rinsed, and less water is wasted.
6. Half fill third sink with the hottest water available. Add sanitizer. Dip utensils in sanitizer. Place them on drainboard to dry. If utensils slide on drainboard, place a clean towel on top of surface to stop sliding.
7. When items are dry, place on shelves or rack. Do not towel dry. Do not nest wet pans together. Stand vertically until dry, then nest.
8. Change wash water periodically as it gets dirty. At end of cycle, drain water and wash out sinks.

Hard to remove and burnt on food can be removed more easily if the cleaning is done in stages. Remove as much of

Sorting tray or tote box for tableware.

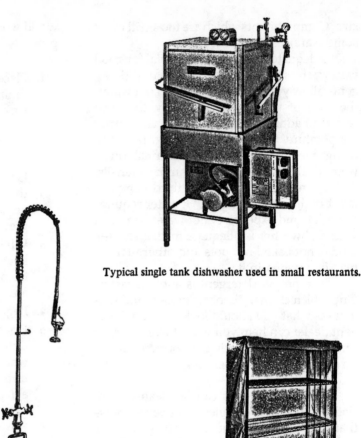

Typical single tank dishwasher used in small restaurants.

Spray rinse flexible arm for pre-scrapping.

Perforated cannister for the washing of tableware.

Metal storage racks on wheels.

Figure 5–4.   Some Kitchen Sanitation Equipment

this food as possible with one washing. Then allow the pan to soak. Repeat this procedure as many times as is necessary to remove all food. Cleaning such a utensil all at once is difficult and time consuming. Doing it in stages saves time and makes the work less frustrating.

If the proper technique is followed, pots, pans, and other utensils will be germ-free and clean of grease and food particles. Caked-on soil should not be allowed to accumulate. Such accumulation can be a breeding ground for bacteria. Encourage cooks to cooperate with this program. A little more care in cooking and a little pre-scraping on their part will reduce the hours needed for the warewashing personnel.

Proper Dishwashing Procedures. On the surface, dishwashing appears to be a relatively simple, uncomplicated, and uninvolved function. In fact, the procedure is quite involved. You will need to consider:

1. correct equipment and its location,
2. the efficient layout of the equipment and area,
3. specialized cleaning and other products,
4. special plumbing and, possibly, wiring,
5. supplies,
6. storage for soiled and clean serviceware,
7. proper personnel selection,
8. careful training of personnel.

For purposes of our discussion, unless otherwise stated, the term dishwashing will refer to the handling and washing of glassware, tableware, and miscellaneous items, as well as chinaware (dishes).

The first requirement for any dishwashing area is the dishmachine. There are a number of factors to be considered before you buy. Dishmachines can be square, rectangular, or round. They can be under-counter or freestanding. Loading can be done by hand or by belt. The rinse temperature can be 180° F or 140° F. There are many options. Before deciding on the type of machine you want, determine the location and the amount of space available.

The location should be as near to the kitchen door as possible, without having the noises generated enter the dining room. If you are fortunate enough to be designing the kitchen from the start, try to locate the dishwasher and the warewashing sink in close proximity to one another. This not only saves on plumbing but enables one person to work both dishwashing and warewashing when necessary.

Once the approximate location is decided on, determine how much space is available. If you only have a small corner, you might consider a round dishmachine. If you have limited space along a wall, consider an under-counter model. Finally, if you have ample room, install the unit you think will do the job most effectively.

A recent innovation in dishwashers allows you to use 140° F water for rinsing with the addition of a sanitizing agent in the final rinse. The advantages of the new machine are:

1. Elimination of need for a hot water booster,
2. Lower operating costs,
3. Use of less energy,
4. No hot water (180° F) problems.

If you are opening a new restaurant or replacing old equipment, consider installing this type of machine. There is one drawback with this type of machine; silverware cannot be washed in it (it turns black). There is no problem with stainless steel.

In addition to the machine, you will need dish tables to receive the soiled dishes, glasses, etc., provide a stacking area and to allow space for filling and emptying the racks. These are an integral part of the dishwashing setup and must be considered in the planning stages. Incorporate as many undershelves in the tables as possible to provide additional space to place trays of soiled dishes, which tend to back up at busy times. Shelves also provide space to store dish and glass racks, thereby keeping them off the floor. Table top and shelves should be 14 gauge stainless steel.

Overhead shelves are another important feature to help you gain space. Generally, they are used for receiving soiled glassware.

Keeping glass items separate from other materials eliminates a good deal of breakage.

A hole in the top of the dish table at the soiled dish end can be topped with a rubber collar and used for the disposal of trash and scraps as trays are unloaded. The hole should be located near the edge of the table so it does not interfere with the movement of the wash racks. A garbage can should be placed beneath the hole. (See Figure 5–5).

All small and medium size dishmachines use racks to hold dishes, glassware, and other items during the wash process. Dish racks and the flat open racks which are sometimes used are standard. However, racks for glassware are not. They come in a number of sizes and must be purchased carefully to obtain the correct size for your glassware. Shorter glasses use short racks, tall glasses use taller racks, and so on. If an incorrect rack is used, the results will be poorly washed and water stained glasses.

Figure 5–5.

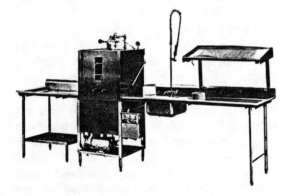

A typical dish area arrangement in a small kitchen, containing the machine, dish tables, spray rinse, scrap block, overshelf, and sink. It was probably designed to be operated from the side facing you. Some of the things wrong with this arrangement are: clean and soiled dishtables are too small; there are not enough undershelves; stacking area is inconvenient; there is no place to unload trays brought from the dining room; and the location for the garbage hole is inconvenient.

The most efficient method of washing tableware is to use plastic cylinders specially designed for this purpose. Because the tableware is placed in the cylinder standing up, the changes for spotting are almost completely eliminated.

Soiled tableware, whether silver or stainless, is usually placed in a pre-soak container or tub as it is removed from the dining room tray. It is later loaded into the wash cylinders and run through the machine. Space must be provided for this container.

Place the trash or garbage can to the side of the dish table. This location facilitates the disposal of waste materials, but limits the accidental discarding of tableware into the garbage can.

There should be a hamper, or other container, for soiled linen as it is returned from the dining room. Linen should be carefully checked for stray pieces of tableware before it goes to the laundry. When linen is removed from the table, it should never contain paper or cigarette stubs. Both items tend to raise havoc with the appearance of linen after it is laundered.

In sections of the country where heavy lime is found in the water, it is advisable to use a water softener. This will eliminate all natural spotting and reduce the amount of detergent used. If you cannot use a softener, you should have the dishmachine de-limed periodically. The procedure is not difficult, but it requires the purchase of a special solution.

It is helpful to have a small sink in the dishwashing area in which to soak items with stubborn food (e.g., casseroles, egg dishes). It also provides a source of water for cleaning. Never allow the use of scouring pads on china, glass, or tableware. Scouring will scratch glass and tableware and remove the glaze from chinaware.

Matting should be used on the top of

the dish tables to reduce breakage and noise. The most common matting is a neoprene webbing which is easy to wash and keep clean.

Detergent and wetting agent dispensers are almost always supplied by the company that supplies the detergents. Usually, there is no charge for the use of this equipment. Each company has its own type of equipment. Be certain the dispensers are installed in such a way that their removal will present no problems to you later.

A rack should be provided to place dining room trays after they have been emptied and wiped clean. Such a rack facilitates handling, enables trays to dry out and helps to rid the trays of odors.

Detergents and Other Compounds. The purchase and use of the proper detergent is another important consideration in the washing and sanitizing procedure. Do not purchase detergents or related dishwashing compounds from a general supply house. Purchase such items from a company which specializes in dishwashing and warewashing compounds. Such companies are concerned *only* with the results you have with their products.

Shop carefully before making a decision regarding the purchase of the needed compounds. Consider service (most important), price, ease of use, range of products, and availability. There are only one or two companies that can fill all these requirements satisfactorily.

Detergents are formulated to do an optimum job under specific conditions. An operation with very hard water will require a different formula than one with softer water. The type of machine also makes a difference. There are many variables. A good sales representative will supply a detergent to fill your particular needs.

The amount of detergent used is determined by the efficiency and size of the dishmachine, water hardness, amount of soil, water temperature, and the machine operator. All major suppliers install automatic feed devices on the dishmachine for the accurate dispensing of their product. Such installations may require alterations to your plumbing. If so, be certain the changes can be repaired if you decide to change suppliers. These dispensers regulate the amount of detergent added to the wash water. Their operation is relatively trouble free.

Pre-washing (scrapping) removes soil from dishware before it enters the machine wash, reducing the amount of detergent necessary. It can be accomplished manually or mechanically. If done manually, the operator does the rinsing with a spray extension attached to the sink. If done mechanically, the front end of the dishmachine is equipped with the scrapper.

Pre-washing lessens the amount of detergent needed by reducing the amount of soil and grease allowed to enter the wash tank. It also reduces the amount of hot water used because warm water is used to flush the serviceware. In addition, because the wash water is kept cleaner, fewer wash tank changes are necessary.

A wetting agent can be used to reduce the amount of detergent consumed and to speed up drying. A wetting agent reduces the surface tension of water. When surface tension is reduced, an action called sheeting takes place. Practically speaking, this allows water to spread out and run off serviceware without leaving droplets. Because of this phenomenon, drying takes place much more rapidly. An added bonus is the elimination of spotting on serviceware. The wetting agent is injected into the rinse water automatically, from the dispenser, at the beginning of the rinse cycle.

Pre-soaking is another important aspect of dishwashing. It can perform three functions: remove difficult and baked on soil, hold tableware in solution until it is ready to be washed, and fulfill the detarnishing function.

Some food items, such as those baked in casseroles, adhere so strongly to the dish they are cooked in that the soiled dish cannot be cleaned by regular dishmachine action. Because of this, the dish must be pre-soaked. Usually, a little dishwashing compound added to the soak water will do the job. The dish is then manually scraped with a pot brush or rag and the food particles are loosened. The dish is then put through the regular machine cycle. Never use scouring powder or nylon pads to remove soil from dishes of any kind. Use of either of these products results in scratching and removing of the glaze from china products.

Racking of tableware for washing is a time consuming task. Unfortunately, no one has been successful in coming up with a method to make the task less laborious. The dishwasher usually allows the tableware to accumulate before washing it. While it is accumulating, the tableware should be soaking, not left in a dry state. Soaking softens the soil so that it can be easily washed off in the machine. If silverware is used, it can be detarnished while it is being soaked. Simply line the soak container with aluminum foil and add a detarnishing powder to the water.

You can also lessen the consumption of detergents by having the correct water temperature and water pressure.

Water pressure should be approximately 20 psi (pounds per square inch). If it is less, the washing action is reduced and more detergent is needed to do the job. A gauge should be attached to the water inlet so the pressure can be monitored. If the psi is much greater than 20, a pressure regulator should be installed to protect the machine.

When a high temperature dishmachine is used, the rinse temperature must be 180° F. 140° F is satisfactory for a low temperature machine. The wash water in either machine can be between 140° F and 160° F, although 120° F is satisfactory for the low temperature machine. If the water is not at the correct temperature, more detergent will be necessary to properly wash the serviceware.

Dishwashers contain built in heaters to maintain the proper temperatures in the wash and rinse tanks. Heaters are capable of maintaining a temperature, but are not designed to heat cooler water. This function is performed by a special booster heater attached to the water line. Such a heater may be gas fired or electric.

Overall savings may be obtained in the dishwashing area with constant supervision on the part of the owner. Some additional items you should look for are:

1. Thermometers (or dials) should be periodically checked to be sure they are operating and that they are accurate.
2. Switches should be turned off when machine is not in use.
3. Indicator lights and buzzers should be replaced as soon as they stop functioning.
4. Employees should report problems as soon as they occur.

Miscellaneous Recommendations

1. When purchasing a new machine, be sure it is equipped with a low water cutoff. This turns the power or gas off if the machine should be accidently drained. (There are also times when an employee will drain a machine and forget to turn it off.) Without this cutoff, the bottoms of the tanks will eventually

burn out. A new tank bottom costs hundreds of dollars to replace.

2. In hard water areas, the dishwasher should be periodically de-limed. The machine will operate better and serviceware will come out cleaner if this is done.
3. Replace broken dials immediately. Broken dials are health department violations. You have no way of knowing what is going on without them.
4. Store detergents well off the floor and away from water sources.
5. Fix small leaks quickly so they do not develop into big problems.
6. Chipped and cracked chinaware and glassware should be discarded. It harbors bacteria, looks unsightly, and is an accident hazard.

The Dishwashing Function. Just as any other task in a restaurant, dishwashing must be performed correctly. The person(s) employed to fill this job must be properly and adequately trained. In addition, the job procedures must be posted so they can be readily referred to. All too often the person employed is literally shown the dishmachine and told to go to work. This is not only discouraging to the employee, who may be completely bewildered, but the results are likely to be less than satisfactory.

You cannot expect persons applying for the job of dishwashing to be very elegant, but they should be neat. Generally, people who are neat with themselves are neat in their work. Check their work record. It should indicate reliability. You need someone you can be sure will show up for work every day. Finally, look for someone who has the ability to learn. This can be ascertained at the interview and by a check with past employers.

Employees in this department must

wear hats. In addition, uniforms of some sort are required. The bare minimum would be a white jacket and an apron. However, a full uniform is preferable. The apparel should be changed each day and during the day, if necessary. Unless covered by another garment, street clothes should not be worn by the machine operators. Long hair must be restrained or tied. Preferably, men should be clean shaven but if they have beards, they should be well trimmed.

Setting Up

1. Garbage and trash cans should be properly placed. Each should be lined with a plastic bag.
2. Machine tanks should be filled (if machine has such tanks).
3. Activate heater switches.
4. Check dispensers for detergent, etc. and activate.
5. Fill soak sink(s). Add compound.
6. Pre-rinse hose faucets (if one is used) should be turned on with the proper mix of water (lukewarm).
7. Put racks in place.
8. Landing area should be cleared of unnecessary items. Dishes left previously should be properly stacked.
9. Wiping cloths should be made available, along with pan of cleaning solution.

Procedure for Unloading Trays and Racking

1. Remove paper and linens from trays and place in proper receptacle.
2. Place silverware and difficult items in soak sinks.
3. Stack dishes on landing table according

to size and shape. Cups, glassware, etc. should be racked. These functions may be performed by a dishwasher, bus personnel, or service personnel.

4. Trays should then be wiped and properly stored in a rack.

5. Scrap and pre-rinse dishes manually if machine is not equipped with a scrapper.

6. Rack dishes by size. Rack same dish size, side by side in rack. More than one size dish may be loaded in same rack but sizes should not be mixed together. This saves time when unloading.

7. Place only full racks in dishmachine for washing. Replace full rack with an empty one. As much detergent, hot water, etc. is used to wash a partially filled rack as a full one. Therefore, it is wasteful to run partially filled racks.

8. Tableware should be placed in cannisters for washing with handles on the bottom. Mix forks, spoons, and knives together. Do not rack only spoons, for example, in one cannister. When racked in this manner, similar items have a tendency to nestle. This results in only partial washing.

9. Miscellaneous items (e.g., casseroles, dessert dishes, ramekins) are racked and washed in flat racks.

Although modifications may be made to the above procedures, the concept of sorting and racking must never be lost sight of. When dishes and glassware are dumped on the landing table without sorting, breakage and increased labor costs will result. There is also a certain psychological value to seeing a well cared for dish table. It conveys a feeling of order and neatness.

As racks become filled, they should be placed in the dishmachine. Some dishmachines have curtains (for doors) and run con-

tinuously once turned on. Others require a door to be closed to activate the machine. Some machines automatically turn off at the end of a cycle. Others run constantly and eject the rack after it reaches the end of the run. When the latter type is used, there is a tendency, when in a hurry, to push racks through, instead of allowing them to feed normally. This practice should be eliminated because it shortens the wash and rinse time and the items will be improperly washed and rinsed.

During the time the first rack is placed in the machine (and periodically, after that), check the water temperature and general operation to determine if everything is functioning correctly.

When the cycle is ended, the rack should be removed from the machine, put to the side and the contents allowed to dry.

Tableware (in the cannisters) should be given a few gentle shakes to remove excess water clinging to it. This will speed the drying process.

Glassware with concave bottoms (looking at it), can be patted with a clean towel when removed from the machine. This drys up the little pool of water which pockets there and sometimes runs down the side of the glass when tilted.

It is not necessary to remove glassware or cups from the wash racks. Both can be stored in the racks. If they are to be stored on shelves, be sure they are completely dry. Storage should be with the open end down, on clean shelves. Constantly check glassware and tableware for proper drying. If these items do not dry properly, spotting will result. Incorrect drying is usually caused by too low a rinse temperature or the improper amount of wetting agent.

Remove dishes from the racks and stack. Again, it is important to keep sizes and shapes together when unloading. This saves extra sorting time later.

Tableware can be unracked in two ways. The first method is by dumping the cannisters onto a flat, clean surface. The handles should all be kept in one direction. Each piece of tableware is then picked up by the handle and deposited into another cannister or into a sorting tray. In either case, spoons are kept together, knives are kept together, etc. If cannisters are used, the handles of the tableware should be up. In either method, it is important that the tableware is handled only by the handles to eliminate contamination.

When tableware is washed, it is washed with the handles on the bottom of the cannister. After washing, the clean business ends should not be touched. In order to sort the pieces, the handles must be on top. This is accomplished by placing an empty cannister over the top of the washed cannister containing the tableware. The bottom cannister is then inverted and the tableware falls into the empty cannister. The top cannister is then removed and the handles are available for sorting.

If the person doing the washing is also doing the unloading, he or she should always wash his or her hands before going from soiled to clean serviceware.

Miscellaneous items can be removed from the dishmachine, stacked and placed on trays, and later distributed to the proper location.

End of Operating Day

1. Turn off all switches (*very important*).
2. Drain machine (if it has tanks).
3. Clean inside of machine (e.g., strainers).
4. If curtains are used, remove from machine for drying.
5. Wash tables, shelves, and walls near machine.
6. Wipe machine—sides, top, and bottom.
7. Empty and clean soak sinks and rubber ring at garbage hole.
8. Clean other sinks.
9. Discard trash and garbage. Re-line cans with plastic liners.
10. Sweep and mop *under* and around equipment area.
11. Wash cleaning cloths and place to dry or in laundry.
12. Remove soiled linen to appropriate area.

At least once a week (more often, if necessary), the rinse and wash arms should be removed and taken apart for cleaning. As mentioned earlier, if you operate in an area that contains hard water, a periodic rinse with a lime dissolving solution is necessary.

Dishwashing and Warewashing Equipment and Supplies

Large equipment

Dishwashing machine

Dish tables with hole for pre-scrapping

Overhead rack area

Undershelves

Three compartment warewashing sink with drainboards

Small sink in dishwashing area, if possible

Hot water heater to provide ample hot water

Hot water booster (for some hook-ups)

Pre-scrap, spray hose

Small equipment

Automatic dispensers for detergents and wetting agent

Racks for dishes, glasses, tableware, and miscellaneous items

Holders for tableware after washing

Shelves to store chinaware, glassware, etc.

Pans for pre-soaking

Table and sink drainboard matting to reduce noise and breakage

Small length of garden hose to wash down area

Supplies

Detergents for dish and ware washing

Rinse additive (wetting agent)

De-liming solution (in hard water areas)

Detarnisher for silverware (not needed for stainless)

Degreasing compound for heavy grease removal

Grill cleaner (if you have a grill), water base is easiest

Pot brushes, fiber or nylon

Scouring pads, nylon only (never steel)

All purpose cleaner and spray bottle

Stainless steel cleaner

General Kitchen Sanitation

General kitchen sanitation takes in all cleaning maintenance other than warewashing and dishwashing. It involves such tasks as sweeping, mopping, and general cleaning. It is important that these functions be performed according to a definite timetable. Such timetables should be in writing and posted where the employee can see them.

The entire kitchen area must be swept and mopped once each day. Certain sections may require additional sweeping and/or mopping. The dishwashing and warewashing areas are two sections that usually require extra mopping throughout the day. The range

and pantry sections usually require extra sweeping. If the kitchen is used for luncheon and dinner, it should be swept and mopped in the afternoon, as well as in the evening.

Cooperation of the cooks can help to minimize the extra maintenance needed to maintain a spotless kitchen. Many cooks have the habit of wiping food particles from work table tops onto the floor. This is totally unnecessary. Anyone doing it should be reminded of the extra work it entails. There is nothing more indicative of a sloppy worker than a messy floor.

Personnel doing the cleaning may have to be reminded to sweep and mop *under*, as well as around, equipment. They should also be instructed to move non-stationary equipment and furnishings when cleaning, not just clean around them.

Kitchen walls should be periodically washed with a suitable cleaning solution. Both soil and grease must be removed. How frequently this is to be done will depend on the particular kitchen area and its usage.

Lighting fixtures provide another area for cleaning. How involved this will be depends on the type of lighting or fixture. Free hanging fixtures will require more work than recessed lighting. Whether fluorescent or incandescent lighting is used, the tubes or bulbs should be kept clean. The more grease or dust they accumulate, the less efficient they are in lighting the area.

Shelving, whether wood or metal, should be periodically wiped and cleaned. Metal shelving can be dismantled and washed in the sink or, possibly, in the dishmachine. The larger sections can be cleaned outside the building somewhere. Metal shelving is particularly easy to maintain, *if* it is wiped clean immediately after something is spilled on it. If spills are allowed to accumulate, cleaning can be a chore.

Wooden shelving must always be painted or sealed in some manner. Otherwise, it will absorb spills and dirt and eventually have to be discarded. Painted shelving is easy to maintain but may have to be cleaned more frequently.

Refrigerators usually require weekly cleaning, depending on the fastidiousness of the people using them. Walk-in floors *do* require weekly cleaning. Remove everything on the floor and then sweep and mop it.

Reach-in refrigerators should have the shelves removed and washed. All surfaces should be cleaned with a non-odorous, sanitizing solution.

Freezers (food and ice cream) should be defrosted and cleaned every six or eight months. An added bonus to the cleaning of the freezer is a review of what it contains.

When refrigeration is being cleaned, the doors should be kept closed as much as possible or the unit turned off. This will conserve a great deal of energy. The food products which have been removed to facilitate cleaning must be placed in another refrigerator to maintain their temperature. If this is not done, it presents a desirable temperature for the growth of bacteria. Frozen food can be placed in a refrigerator and covered with newspaper if no other freezer is available.

Even with daily cleaning, range tops and ovens tend to accumulate baked-on soil. Once every week or two a strong degreaser should be used to remove this soil.

Clean broilers with a wire brush after every use. Periodically, they must be taken apart and thoroughly cleaned in much the same manner as the ranges.

French fryers require filtering after every use. This not only keeps the fat clean, but extends its life. Simple filter arrangements are available from the kitchen supply dealer for this purpose. Depending on use and the type of fryer, the unit should be emptied periodically and given a thorough cleaning. How frequently this is to be done will depend on the amount of use the fryer is given, the food fried in it, and the frying temperature used.

Equipment such as slicers and mixers is to be cleaned thoroughly each time it is used. If this is done, there is seldom any need for other cleaning.

Hood filters are cleaned *before* they start accumulating grease. How often this will occur depends on how often the cooking surfaces and ovens are used. Once this period is determined, it is vitally important that a cleaning schedule be established and observed. If your dishwashing machine is large enough, the filters can be cleaned in it. If not, they can be cleaned in the pot sink. If there is a local car wash with steam equipment, this works even better.

No cleaning program will be successful if definite cleaning schedules are not maintained. It is human nature to put off less desirable duties. Therefore, it is essential to assign specific days or times on which a task is to be performed.

Basic Floor Care. Proper floor maintenance involves more than dumping soapy water on a floor and mopping it. For a floor to be properly cleaned, definite procedures must be followed. In addition, correct cleaners and suitable equipment must be provided.

The essentials are a straw broom and or/ a push type broom, a good quality mop, a mop handle, a press type mop wringer, two mop buckets with wheels (or on a dolly), and a quality detergent.

The first step is to completely and carefully sweep the floor. Next, fill one bucket with water and the proper amount of detergent and the other with clear water only. Employees should be impressed with the fact

Mop buckets, dolly and Gearpress type wringer

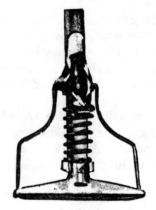

Spring type mop handle

Figure 5–6.   Some Floor Care Equipment

that detergent must be properly measured. A great deal can be wasted if it is just poured into the bucket. Furthermore, if enough is not used, the floor will not be as clean. Buckets should be filled approximately two-thirds full with hot water.

The water with detergent is then applied to the floor with the mop. Allow it to remain there for a minute or more for the chemical action to loosen the soil. When the floor is completely wet, return the mop to the wringer. Squeeze it as dry as possible and then place it in the clear water. Squeeze it again, as dry as possible, and remop the floor with the dry mop, until all the detergent water is removed. This will probably require a few dips in the bucket. If you prefer, another mopping of clear fresh water can be made. Finally, allow the floor to dry.

If your floor is large, it can be done in sections. Some like to do the range area first and then change the detergent water. Others like to do that area last, so they do not have to change the water. Keep in mind that if the water gets too dirty, it cannot do a good cleaning job.

When the floor is finished, rinse out the buckets and mop so that they are thoroughly clean and rinsed of all detergent and soil. Place the mop outdoors to dry and air, if possible. A mop that is not cleaned after every use develops quite an odor. This odor is then spread over the floor the next time the mop is used. Mops and brooms should be hung on a rack, off the floor. If this is not possible, lean them against a wall with the handle on the floor. The mop will dry more quickly this way and the broom will retain its shape.

Garbage and Trash Disposal

The first decision to be made regarding trash and garbage is where it is to be stored. The common method today is the dumper. This is a metal container which is placed at the restaurant site. Arrangements are made, on a lease basis, to empty the container as many times a week as needed. The rental cost is determined by the size of the hopper and the frequency of dumping. Although there are some problems relating to this method, it is probably the most advantageous for the small operator. It does provide a compact and relatively neat appearance.

With the present system, the dumper is emptied into a truck, on your premises and dropped back into place, with all the accompanying odors, spills, and grease. You must maintain and sanitize it, which is not difficult, if it has not sprung a leak at the bottom somewhere. A garden hose, a water source, a long handled brush, and some pine disinfectant will do the trick.

To clean and sanitize a dumper, first hose the inside with water. This will leave an inch or so on the bottom. Add one to two cups, depending on conditions, of pine disinfectant, stir well, and brush down the hopper. When finished, close the lid and the job is done. Leave the water in to continue its work as a disinfectant. It will be removed when the hopper is emptied.

Another disadvantage of this system is its size. Unfortunately, it is not an expandable unit. When you have more trash and garbage than the hopper will hold, you have problems. If this happens too frequently, you need a larger unit. If there is space outside the unit, you can stack cartons there.

The container should be placed on a cement or macadam pad to facilitate moving it and to make the area easier to keep clean. If the unit and the area surrounding it are kept clean and sanitized, the usual problems (odors, insects, rodents, and yellow jackets) will be eliminated.

Garbage and light trash must be contained in tightly closed, plastic bags. This is accomplished by tying a knot in the top of the bag or by using a metal tie. Even with all your care, bags will occasionally break open because of sharp edges. Nevertheless, waste placed in the hopper in plastic bags will reduce your cleaning problems and keep odors to a minimum.

Other methods of eliminating waste are the use of a compactor, a disposal, or an incinerator.

Regardless of which system you use for eliminating waste, always keep the area looking neat and as free of odors as possible. Usually, the dumper is located where guests can see or smell it. This can have a negative impact on your image if the area is not kept clean.

The other consideration in the handling of garbage and trash is how to deal with it within the restaurant.

To begin with, you need heavy duty, sturdy cans. Plastic ones are desirable because they are lightweight, easy to clean, and less expensive than metal. Although they may eventually crack, they do not dent (dents harbor bacteria).

Usually, the larger cans (twenty to thirty gallons) are used in the dishwashing area and for general use throughout the kitchen. The smaller cans (ten gallons) are used behind the range and in the pantry area where space is at a premium.

All cans should contain a plastic liner to eliminate daily washing of the can and expedite garbage and trash removal. Lids should be placed over cans when they are not being used for any length of time. Neither garbage nor trash should be left in cans overnight. The latter is a fire hazard and the former attracts vermin and insects and emits odors. Cans should be periodically washed, both inside and outside, to remove built-up soil.

Garbage and trash from the bar should also be emptied at the end of each day (or night). Trash in other areas, such as rest rooms, must be emptied after each meal. This not only presents a cleaner appearance but eliminates a potential for fire.

Restaurant owners must realize that a good restaurant is more than food and atmosphere. It is a place where management cares about its guests. Part of caring is providing sanitary facilities and food handling. On the surface, this appears to be a facet of the operation which yields no direct return. For this reason, it is difficult to convince many operators of its importance. However, losing customers because of poor sanitary practices can be damaging to your financial picture. Just one case of food poisoning reported in the newspaper with your name in the headline, and there will be little question as to whether or not sanitation directly affects the operation financially.

Rodent and Pest Control

One of the more vexing problems a restaurateur faces is the rodent and insect situation. It may exist because of an operation's poor sanitation practices or be totally unrelated to the operation. It may be an inherited situation or it may be developed by the current owner. One thing is for certain, it is not healthy or desirable. For this reason, it is important that it be controlled or eliminated.

The ideal situation would be, of course, to eliminate the problem. However, because you may not have direct control over it, this may be impossible. Such conditions might exist in a city with a serious rat problem or in a building in which other tenants harbor roaches. The next best thing, then, is control.

When we speak of rodents in a restaurant operation we are concerned with mice and rats. When we speak of insects, we are concerned primarily with roaches, flies, and ants. There may be additional problems from spiders, silverfish, and yellow jackets.

Pests can almost be completely eliminated inside the restaurant with proper sanitation and housekeeping procedures. The exception to this would be the hard core situations mentioned above. Even then, such sanitation practices will reduce the problem.

If a condition still exists, in spite of your efforts, then a professional pest control company should be employed.

Pests become "associates" of your restaurant only if you provide food, water, and lodging. Eliminate these amenities and you end the association. This is true of all pests, whether rodents or insects.

Rodents are doubly annoying because they cause direct damage in addition to contamination. They have sharp teeth which are capable of chewing wood and foodstuffs. The only protection from them is metal and/or cement.

To control rodents there are three steps to be taken: 1) close off the means of entrance, 2) eliminate those on the premises, and 3) close off any sources of water and food. By using this approach, you kill off those already in the building and insure against future infestation.

Rodents do not need a very large opening to enter your premises. A hole only an inch or so in diameter is large enough for a mouse. First, examine the outside of the building and plug any visible holes. Second, examine the walls from the inside looking out. If you can see light, plug the crack. The most effective plug is cement or a metal patch. In some cases, heavy steel wool is effective.

There is little sense in blocking interior holes at this time. If the animal is trapped in the wall or floor, it will only chew its way out somewhere else. The best thing to do next is set traps. When you think you have eliminated those in the building, seal the inside holes.

Flies are the most common insect nuisance found in a food service operation. They are particularly dangerous because of their ability to contaminate food and surroundings. They transmit disease, infection, and filth with ease. The types of flies most encountered in food service are the common house fly and the fruit fly. Flies are attracted by their sense of smell. So whatever you can do to reduce odors will be advantageous.

Direct spraying of flies with a safe insecticide is very effective if you can get within striking distance. Be careful not to spray foodstuffs when using insecticide. One problem with spraying flying insects is that you have no control over where they drop, which could present some problems. Screening is the most effective means of keeping flies from entering the building. All windows and outside entrances should be fitted with screen sash if they remain open for any period of time.

Fruit flies are very commonly found in the bar area because of the fruit garnishes used there. Because of this, all fruit should be kept refrigerated and covered when not in use.

Fruit flies must all be alcoholics because dead ones are found in open whiskey bottles more than anywhere else. For this reason (and others), it is advisable to be sure whiskey bottles are tightly closed each night.

Roaches may not be as numerous or as common as flies but they run a close second to fly infestation. In addition, they are far more difficult to get rid of. The sad fact about a roach problem is that it may not even be the operator's fault. All that is needed is one pregnant roach on a delivered carton and you end up with a family.

Cockroaches not only eat our food but contaminate it as well. They carry disease organisms which are transmitted to food, preparation surfaces, serving utensils, and tableware.

Dark, humid, and warm areas appeal to roaches more than any others. This is one reason you are apt to discover them in a dark kitchen when you suddenly turn the light on or when you pull out a drawer which has not been opened for some time. They are frequently found around sinks, garbage areas, storage areas, and ceilings.

Roaches are eliminated best with a residual type insecticide. This is usually applied to baseboards, around walls, near equipment, and in closed areas and lasts for days or weeks after it is applied. Once the roach touches it, it eventually dies. Exterminating cockroaches is not a job for the novice. Call in a professional before the situation gets out of control.

Ants, the other common insects found in many establishments, are probably easier insects to get rid of. They, like other pests, will all but disappear if you eliminate their source of food and moisture. The common brown ant and the carpenter ant are the most common types. The latter is the most destructive because its favorite food is wood pulp. It nests in, and eats, wood. The brown ant is more easily controlled because its sources are more easily detected and can be eliminated with a contact spray or a residual insecticide. Carpenter ants are eliminated more easily with a residual spray because it is difficult to find more than a few at one time.

Ant nests are often found outside a building. This area should be checked carefully and treated.

At the present time, a professional exterminator will inspect your premises, and put in the necessary traps and bait, and make regular monthly visits for about one hundred dollars per year. This is a small price to pay for the peace of mind you will enjoy.

Sanitation and Good Housekeeping

Just as good sanitation practices eliminated the hazard of contaminated food, good housekeeping and sanitation can eliminate the problem of pests.

1. Store garbage outside in tightly closed containers. Have frequent pickups.
2. Keep garbage container and area clean

and free of loose garbage and trash. Sanitize frequently to eliminate odors.

3. Inside garbage should be kept in plastic bags (in cans) and removed to outside storage container at night. Cans should be sanitized frequently.

4. Clean under and behind equipment, shelves, and tables so pests cannot build their nests there.

5. Leaky faucets should be repaired to eliminate one source of water for rodents and insects.

6. All food storage should be on platforms at least six inches above floor level and away from walls.

7. Get rid of cartons and other containers which harbor insects as soon as possible after deliveries.

8. Foodstuffs, such as flour, sugar, and beans, should be placed in closed bins as soon as possible after they are opened.

9. Clean up spills as quickly as possible after they are made.

10. Do not leave food on tables overnight in either the kitchen or dining rooms.

11. Follow sanitation practices as outlined in this chapter.

General Sanitation Supplies

Garbage and trash containers, plastic, heavy duty, with lids
    Smaller ones (10 gal.) in work area of range and pantry
    Larger ones (20 or 30 gal.) at dishwasher and outside area

Plastic liners for above

Brooms, straw and push types

Dust pan

Mops, 16 oz. (3) and handles (2), conventional spring type

Mop buckets (2) on dolly

Gearpress mop wringer

Floor cleaning detergent and measuring device

Cleaning cloths and rags

Paper towels and dispensers, one at range area and other at dishwasher or warewashing area

Uniforms (if required)

Hats (paper) and aprons

Wire brush for cleaning broiler

Plumber's helper

Insect spray

Container for soiled linen

Chapter Six

Finding the Real Cost of Food through Cost Management

Food cost management is understanding and controlling costs. It involves a complete knowledge of proper purchasing procedures, food handling, preparation, and labor utilization in both kitchen and dining room. You must consider all these elements combined to arrive at your true cost of food.

There is no subject you should be more familiar with than food cost management. The time you spend in this area can only lead to financial gains. A restaurant is a success not only because its sales are high, but because an adequate profit has been made on the sales.

Menu prices can only be determined if you know exactly what each particular item costs to produce. Remember, a restaurant is not like a retail establishment that buys a finished product and sells it. A restaurant is a manufacturer that purchases a raw product and converts it into a salable product. Every step of the manufacturing process has its costs and these costs must be reflected in pricing the final product.

Purchasing

Purchasing the right product at the right price is the first consideration in obtaining the real food cost. If the quality is poor or the wrong product is purchased, waste will result, thereby increasing the purchase cost. When the purchase cost is too high, you will have difficulty making a profit.

Quality

In the purchasing sense, quality means a near to perfect product. Such a product should be free from spoilage, blemishes, excesses, and other irregularities. Two boxes of tomatoes may both be of top quality, but one may be a 6-1 count and the other a 4-1 count. The difference in size has no bearing on quality. One variety of lettuce may be leafy and loose (Boston), while another may be compact (iceberg). The quality is not changed by these characteristics.

Price

Price is the monetary value the seller puts on a product, and is determined by quality, availability, production and transportation costs, and fixed costs. Prices fluctuate from dealer to dealer and season to season because costs fluctuate. A dealer with lower costs can usually sell at a lower price.

Dealers with high quality will usually command a higher price because their costs of selecting will be higher. It should be apparent that you get what you pay for.

Quality⇌Price

Your Needs

Along with price and quality, ordering the item that best fits your exact needs is also important. It is tempting to order the case of large sizes because the saving is greater. Unless you have a way to use up the extra product, the resultant waste may more than offset the saving. Whenever possible, order the size that fits your needs, unless you have a means of working off the surplus created. Otherwise, the money saved may just end up in the garbage can or remain on the storeroom shelf for a long time.

Purchasing food intelligently and carefully is the first step in good food cost management—the cornerstone for future cost savings.

Meat

Meat is the most expensive single item you will purchase. It will make up to 50 percent of total purchases, depending on your menu. Because of this, it is extremely important to purchase high quality. There is enough waste through trimming and cooking. You do not need the waste that results from poor quality.

You would do well to visit your supplier's meat plant in order to better understand the processing procedure.

Small restaurants generally use portion ready, primal, or oven ready cuts. Anything larger requires extra storage space and a competent knowledge of butchering. The National Association of Meat Purveyors, Tucson, Arizona 85704, pubishes two excellent guides to assist you in purchasing meat. They are: *Meat Buyer's Guide to Standardized Meat Cuts* and *Meat Buyer's Guide to Portion Control Meat Cuts*. Most meat supply houses have them available free of charge. The guides are particularly helpful because every cut is carefully described and numbered. Using such specifications assures that you are receiving exactly the cut of meat you ordered. A further advantage is in obtaining quotations. Each supplier will be quoting on the identical item.

The grade of meat is an important consideration. Prime beef is seldom used in restaurants today. The price is so high that guests are reluctant to order it. In addition, guests sometimes complain because the fat content is great.

Produce

Quality is the byword when purchasing produce. Extra money is almost always justified where better quality is concerned. Always check for freshness, color, and decay. To buy produce at the lowest price, without consideration for quality, is "pound foolish."

A problem encountered when purchasing produce is the multiplicity of sizes. There are:

Product sizes—items packed by size (e.g. lemons)

Package sizes—same products, packed in different types of containers (e.g. squash)

Weights—same products, same package, different weight (e.g. lettuce)

Package type—different sizes, shapes, and types of containers (e.g. string beans)

Be certain you and the supplier are speaking of the same size item when you order. With most produce, the larger the size the higher the price.

Finally, consider the age of the product. Green tomatoes may be fine if you have time to ripen them, but if you need them right away you want them ripe. On the other hand, you may want bananas a little green so they last longer. Be specific when ordering. It saves headaches later.

When purchasing produce from a local farm, you often have to sacrifice consistency and size for price and freshness. With lettuce, this may not be a problem because it is broken in salads. With an item such as melon, different sizes can result in various portion sizes when served.

Frozen Foods

Quality, flavor, and appearance are the main considerations here. If poor freezing or storage techniques are employed by the supplier, one or all of these may be lacking.

Fish and Poultry

Freshness is the key when purchasing fish or poultry. Deterioration is rapid as these products become older. Ordering the proper part of the fish or poultry is important. If you only need chicken breasts, do not order the entire chicken unless you are prepared to do something with the extra parts. Conversely, if you need a fish steak, order the whole fish, not the fillet.

Tell the supplier how you want the item prepared. Do you want the whole fish as is, or do you want it cleaned? Should the chickens be split or whole?

Do not forget to specify size. Fryers are smaller than roasting chickens. Do you need a pan size fish, or a larger one?

With the exception of freshness, the ordering recommendations will depend on how the item is to be utilized in the recipe. This information should be obtained from the cook before the ordering is begun.

Dairy Products

Quality and freshness are most important. Some items are ordered by size. The same quantity of eggs will weigh different amounts, depending on the size of the eggs. A thirty-dozen case of large eggs should weigh forty-five pounds, for example.

Grocery Items

The purchasing of canned goods should not be based on price alone. What is in the can after the juice is poured off is the important factor. Testing canned goods is discussed later in the chapter.

Sometimes suppliers have special buys that can save you money. Specials are difficult for the small operator to take advantage of, because of a lack of storage space and, sometimes, a lack of capital. However, if the specials are on items you use regularly, it may be worthwhile to work something out with your supplier.

There are times when items such as sugar and flour can be bought at the local supermarket for less than they can from your wholesaler. Keep an eye open for such opportunities.

When very small quantities of a product

are needed, it is better to pay a few extra pennies and buy it retail than to have it on your shelves for a long period of time. It does not make money sitting on the shelf.

Small restaurants are at a disadvantage when it comes to quantity purchasing. Most purveyors deliver only if an order is large enough to meet their minimum shipping requirements. For this reason, you must not only order the products you are out of, but you must anticipate your future needs as well. If an order can only be gotten together every two weeks, then you should anticipate needs for the weeks preceding the next shipment. In addition, you should take into consideration any expected change in business volume due to unusual circumstances such as holidays and seasonal fluctuations.

For the beginning restaurateur, purchasing is not an easy task. It is not easy to order just the right amount of an item. As experience is gained, these problems will be overcome. Keeping, and using, pertinent records will help immensely.

If you are so small that most of your shopping is done with the local market, you may wonder why you need to know anything about proper purchasing techniques. As you become more successful and volume increases, an adequate purchasing plan will be a necessity. Even if you never get any larger, you will still want value for your money.

Once a satisfactory purchasing system is established, effective receiving and storage procedures should be set up. A careful check of merchandise at the back door is the only way you can be sure you receive what you order.

If someone other than yourself receives an order, he or she should be trained to check quantities accurately and to sign every invoice. At a later time, *you* should check for quality and order accuracy.

Receiving and Storage

Receiving and storage are technical terms for what to do with food after it is ordered. Generally speaking, food should be checked for weight, quantity, freshness, and overall condition when it arrives. It should then be stored in the proper location.

Following are some receiving and storage recommendations for specific food categories.

Meats. Meats should be weighed. Some, such as portion control items, when purchased by the piece, must also be counted. Shortages mean money out of the operation, which can never be made up. Check for quality and freshness. Sometimes meats are shipped in unrefrigerated trucks. The loss in quality can be enormous under such circumstances. Off odors indicate something is wrong. Check carefully and do not accept anything that is not satisfactory. Be sure you receive everything that is listed on the invoice.

Meats should never be left in a warm room. They should be properly wrapped and immediately placed in the refrigerator or freezer.

Produce. Produce should first be checked for quality and freshness. Next, check quantities and weights. Open all boxes. Produce should be refrigerated (if required) or put in dry storage immediately. It deteriorates rapidly in a hot kitchen.

Frozen Food. When an item is purchased for the first time it is a good idea to open a box and check its quality and appearance. If the item is one you are familiar with, it is sufficient to check the quantity and weight and place it in the freezer.

Fish and Poultry. Handle in much the same manner as meat. Refrigerate immediately. Some items, such as lump crabmeat, require special attention. Both fish and poultry should be processed and used as soon as possible after they are received.

Canned Goods and Other Groceries. Canned goods, and most other items, usually arrive in cases. It is sufficient to check the number of cases with the invoice. Opening and checking each case would be time consuming and would serve no useful purpose. If the item is not what you ordered, do not accept it. Have the driver delete it from the invoice and give you a receipt or note the return on the invoice. Problems with the contents of the case should be discussed with the sales representative.

If it is not supplemented with an adequate receiving and storage program, careful purchasing will be ineffective. The time and effort expended in placing specific requests to your suppliers will be totally wasted if someone does not check to see that the product received is the product ordered. Further, even if the product is perfect when it is received, wasteful spoilage will result if it is not stored properly.

Perhaps the systems described are too involved for the very small restaurant owner. However, the concepts of using quality merchandise and checking to be certain that you receive all of it should not be lost sight of just because you are quite small. The money saved ends up in your operation and, ultimately, in your pocket.

Procedure for Handling Invoices

1. Invoices should be carefully checked with the goods received. *Any* discrepancy should be noted on the invoice, which should be signed by the driver for later credit.

2. If someone other than the owner receives merchandise, he or she should sign the invoice to indicate that the merchandise listed has been received.

3. A spindle should be provided to hold invoices. As soon as an invoice is checked and signed, it should be spindled. Invoices must not be lost, they are your only control and receipt.

4. Invoices should be removed from the spindle daily; the prices, extensions, and totals should be checked, and then the invoices should be filed alphabetically for payment.

5. Take advantage of discounts whenever you can. Discounted invoices should be held separately, ready for the payment date.

6. At the end of each month, invoices should be matched with the monthly statements, attached to them, and held for payment.

7. If the monthly statement is incorrect, call the purveyor immediately and straighten it out. Letting a bill remain unpaid can hurt your credit.

Testing as a Means of Establishing the Real Cost of a Product

The procedures you have set up assure you that the food received will be of the finest quality, fairly priced, and in the proper quantity. These are the first steps in controlling food costs and establishing a fair selling price.

The next step is to determine the real cost of the food product before preparation. This is accomplished by performing various tests on the most costly items, meats and canned goods.

Meats

Butcher Test. For those who will be doing any meat cutting at all, the butcher test (see Figure 6–1) provides an excellent means of determining the true cost (yield price) of a pound of meat or poultry. In addition, by finding the percentage of each cut to the whole, you are able to determine whether your cutting technique is correct.

By knowing the true cost (yield price) of a pound of meat, you can correctly price your menu items and accurately compare costs of your own butchering to the cost of portion ready cuts.

The only way to arrive at a true cost is to run a butcher test and estimate the cost of labor involved. The results of such a comparison will vary, depending on the purchase cost of the meat, the quantity, and the labor cost.

Too many beginning operators rely on guesswork to come up with a figure on which to base their menu prices. There is no simple method or shortcut; a butcher test *must be performed* to arrive at accurate prices.

When a butcher test is performed, the meat must be cut in the same way every time. If it is not, the percentage of each component to the entire piece will be changed. You should perform the test more than once to be sure your cutting method is consistent.

Example

If oven ready ribs can be purchased for $2.54 per pound and your cost, including labor, after doing your own butchering of the full ribs is $2.76 per pound, you are better off purchasing the oven ready ribs.

How to Use the Butcher Test

1. Enter the purchase information on top of 4" × 6" file card.
2. Determine the cut of meat to be costed (top round).
3. Break whole cut into sections (top, eye, bottom, etc.).

Figure 6–1.   *Butcher Test*

Date __3/29/81__						
Butcher Test for __Veal Leg__ ①						
Purchase Wgt. __49#2oz__ ① Cost/lb. __$1.90__ Tot. Cost __$93.10__ ⑨						

Item ③	④ Weight	⑤ %	⑥ Cost/lb	Cost of Item ⑦	Cost/oz
Top Round ②	4# 14oz.	9.9	⑪ ?	⑩ ?	?⑪
Eye	1# 7oz.	2.9	3.25	4.67	.2030
Tenderloin	1# 1oz.	2.2	3.75	3.98	.2344
Bottom Round	3# 5oz.	6.7	3.00	9.94	.1875
Other Meat	10# 13oz.	22.0	2.80	30.28	.1750
Waste	27# 10oz.	56.3	.10	2.76	.0063
				⑧($51.63)	
Totals	49# 2oz.	100%	$1.90	$93.10	

4. Weigh each section and record on card (this should add up to total weight—49 pounds, 2 ounces).

5. Calculate individual percentages (item weight ÷ total weight) and record.

6. Put a value (price per pound) on all sections, except the one to be determined—top round. These values are arbitrary and can be obtained from a price list or by inquiring of your supplier. Prices must be current.

7. Multiply weights by prices to arrive at the cost per item.

8. Add known costs to arrive at total ($51.63).

9. Subtract known costs from total purchase cost ($93.10).

10. This is the cost of the cut you are looking for (top round)—$41.47.

11. Compute cost per pound (item cost ÷ weight of cut). The cost is $8.51 per pound or $.5319 per ounce.

To arrive at a new yield price when market prices fluctuate and there is no need for additional testing, use the *cost factor*. Multiplying the new purchase price by the factor gives the new yield price (true cost).

Use the information in Figure 6.1 to arrive at the cost factor and, subsequently, the new yield price.

This procedure can be used for any cut of meat, as long as you know the original yield price and cost per pound.

Running a butcher test is not an easy task. It takes time and care, but there is no other way to determine the real cost of a piece of meat you butcher yourself.

Use of Portion Ready and Other Cuts. One disadvantage to purchasing larger or prime cuts of meat is the creation of by-products. Because all meats do not butcher or trim perfectly, there are scraps, which cannot be used with the primary product. In addition, some cuts (e.g. whole beef round) are made up of different muscle fibers. Each may have to be cooked in a special manner. If you purchase portion ready meats, you eliminate these problems. You purchase the piece you need and nothing more. The term portion ready includes such cuts as steaks, chops, and cutlets. Ready to use refers to such items as roasts and stew meat. Any item that requires no preparation other than cooking can be considered ready to use or oven ready.

Veal Top Round

New market price $2.10

Advantages of Portion Ready and Ready to Use

---

1. No by-products,
2. Little or no waste,
3. Known cost,
4. Weight consistency,
5. Leftovers minimized,

Step 1 $\dfrac{\$8.51 \text{ (yield price)}}{\$1.90 \text{ (cost per pound)}} = 4.48 \text{ (cost factor)}$

Step 2 $4.48 \times \$2.10 \text{ (new price)} = \$9.41 \text{ (new yield price)}$

6. No butchering skills required,
7. Control over butchering techniques, eliminating losses due to incorrect cutting,
8. Cutting labor reduced or eliminated,
9. Easy inventory control.

Disadvantages of Portion Ready and Ready to Use

1. High price per item,
2. Need to purchase items which would be by-products if own butchering were done,
3. No absolute control over quality except reliability of purveyor,
4. Some frozen items may require special cooking techniques to ensure proper results and yields,
5. If there is a need to defrost some items before use there may be a resultant loss of juices or tissue breakdown,
6. Preparation may be held up if items needing defrosting are not thawed in time to use,
7. Deterioration of product, resulting from incorrect defrosting techniques,
8. Need for increased freezer facilities.

It is obvious from these lists that a decision to use portion ready or ready to use meats will have to be based on the particular operation.

The beginning restaurateur, with little or no experience in butchering, will do well to purchase portion ready and ready to use meats. This should be done only through a reliable purveyor. As you progress, you may wish to experiment with some of the simpler, larger cuts, such as sirloin strip or full tenderloin. Only after a careful analysis of your skills, and other factors involved in your particular restaurant, can a decision be made as to which type of meat should be purchased.

How to Determine the Amount of Meat to Purchase

Number portions required ____50____
Size portion ____6 oz____
Purchased weight ____50 lb____
Final portion weight ____30 lb____

Method 1

a) $\dfrac{\text{Portion Size}}{16 \text{ oz.}} \times \dfrac{\text{Number to Serve}}{\text{Overall Yield \%}}$

b) $\dfrac{6 \text{ oz.}}{16 \text{ oz.}} \times \dfrac{50}{30 \text{ lb.} \div 50 \text{ lb.}}$

c) $\dfrac{6 \text{ oz.}}{16 \text{ oz.}} \times \dfrac{50}{60\%} = \dfrac{300}{9.60} = 31.25 \text{ lb.}$

d) Would need to purchase 32 pounds.

Method 2

a) $\dfrac{\text{No. Portions} \times \text{Weight}}{16 \text{ oz.}} \times \dfrac{1}{\text{Overall Yield \%}}$

b) $\dfrac{50 \times 6 \text{ oz.}}{16 \text{ oz.}} \times \dfrac{1}{30 \text{ lb.} \div 50 \text{ lb.}}$

c) $\dfrac{50 \times 6 \text{ oz.}}{16 \text{ oz.}} \times \dfrac{1}{60\%} = 18.75 \text{ lb.} \times 1.67 = 31.31 \text{ lb.}$

d) Would need to purchase 32 pounds.

Definitions

Portion weight = weight after butchering, cooking, portioning.

Purchase weight = original weight when purchased.

Overall yield % = final portion weight/purchased weight.

Canned Goods

When purchasing canned goods, consider both quality and price. Assuming satisfactory quality with all brands which are to be tested, we must then determine the real cost of the can's contents. Two tests which tell us this information are the drained weight test and the product count test. After running such tests, you may find significant differences from company to company. This is especially true of some of the higher priced items such as meats and fish.

Drained Weight Test. A drained weight test is easy to perform. In larger operations, six brands may be tested and compared at one time. This procedure cannot be used by the small operator, because he or she would have difficulty working off the contents of so many cans before spoilage set in. In such a situation, purchase a case of Brand A and run the test each time a can is used. The next time, purchase Brand B and do the test. It is a good idea to test two cans of each product to ensure consistency. When you have finished the testing, make the necessary comparisons and choose your brand.

Example of Drained Weight Test

Definitions

Total weight equals the contents in one #10 can. This includes juice and solids.

Drained weight is obtained by pouring contents of can into a strainer and allowing them to drain for two minutes.

Cost per ounce is obtained by dividing the purchase cost per can by the number of drained weight ounces.

Test Product: __whole tomatoes__

Company A

Total weight	6 #7 oz.
Drained weight	2 #14 oz.
Cost per can	$1.89
Cost per ounce	$ .041

Company B

Total weight	6 #9 oz.
Drained weight	2 #3 oz.
Cost per can	$1.64
Cost per ounce	$ .047

The above results indicate a saving of more than half a penny with Brand A for each ounce of tomatoes used ($.047 − $.041 = $.006). There is actually 12 percent more tomato solids in the can from Company A than in the one from Company B (45% − 33%).

Product Count Test. Some vegetables and fruits are packed by size or count. Peach halves, for example, are packed 30–40, 35–40, 40–50, indicating the number of halves per #10 can.

When using an item such as a peach half, the cost and size are most important. A certain size will be used because of its eye appeal or cost, or as an aid to pre-portioning. Once a particular size is decided on, it should be used all the time. Therefore, one consideration when purchasing peach halves (and other items as well) will be usage. The other will be the price of the particular size.

If you decide a peach half between 35 and 40 is the size you need, purchase a case of this size from Company X. Every time a can is opened, check the contents for count and quality. When you have used the entire case, add up the total number of peach halves and divide the total by six. This gives you an average number per can. Divide this amount into the cost per can to arrive at an average cost per half. You now have the cost for comparison purchasing and for computing the selling price. Now go through the same process with Brand Y. Compare prices and quality and make your decision.

Many buyers are fooled by purchase prices. The only sure way to determine what you are really paying for can contents is to run either or both the above tests.

Preparation

Until now we have only been concerned with the cost of food before preparation. We have obtained satisfactory price and quality through careful purchasing, reduced losses due to inaccuracies and product deterioration, and found the true cost of the purchased food through testing. The next step in the cost management procedure is to consider the savings through preparation.

Preparation is the process through which purchased food is turned into a palatable, salable product. Some foods, such as salad greens, may require very little preparation before becoming a usable product. Others, like meats, may require extensive preparation before the final results are attained.

Regardless of how involved the preparation is, all products go through basic processing: intitial preparation, incorporation with other ingredients, and final preparation. Utilizing proper methods throughout the preparation cycle can eliminate wasted costs.

Initial Preparation

Initial preparation is an important area for cost savings. Careful training of employees not to take shortcuts is essential if any cost reduction is to be accomplished. Once edible trimmings are in the garbage can, they can no longer produce income for the restaurant owner.

Following are some helpful suggestions and information.

Meats

Fats and undesirable fibers should be carefully trimmed out. No meat should be cut away with the trimmings. If it is difficult to accomplish this, save such trimmings and combine with other meat scraps for hamburger.

Nothing should be thrown out if it can be satisfactorily turned into a usable product.

Cut carefully when portioning. Expensive cuts, such as steaks, which are portioned before cooking must be cut with care. If you are cutting twelve-ounce sirloins and under cut, it will be impossible to use this meat unless you have it on the menu in another form. The meat can be frozen and when enough such "mistakes" are accumulated, it can be utilized in a special entree.

Bones can be used in making soup stock.

Waste fats are sometimes sold to renderers for additional income.

Poultry

Poultry is one item even an inexperienced operator will have no difficulty in cutting up. All that is necessary is a sharp knife to separate the breasts, legs, and wings. Use the carcass for soup stock.

Fish

Purchase fish ready to cut. Whole fish is cut into steaks and fillets are cut into the correct portion sizes.

Shrimp can be purchased shelled and deveined or in the shell. The purchase cost of in the shell is less than shelled and deveined, but the labor cost of shelling must be added in.

Cooking shrimp *after* they are shelled results in greater shrinkage. Cooking shrimp the proper amount of time reduces shrinkage and yields a more tender product.

Produce

Wasteful trimming should be avoided. Throwing away more of the outside leaves of lettuce, for example, than necessary increases your costs.

Small blemishes can be removed and the remaining portion of the leaf can be used.

Surplus leaves can be incorporated into soups (cream of lettuce) and other vegetables (petits pois a la français).

Fresh vegetables are usually less expensive when in season, but it takes longer to prepare them than frozen vegetables. In addition, some have more waste and require more time to cook. Such costs must be considered in the pricing structure.

Peeling vegetables can be quite wasteful if not done properly. Use the special peeler for potatoes on other items as carrots and root vegetables to reduce peeling wastes.

Vegetable trimmings can often be used in soups and stocks. Examples are celery leaves, beet tops, and asparagus stems.

Recipe Costing

The best means of reducing cooking costs is using standardized recipes and controlled cooking methods.

Standardized recipes produce these results:

1. Consistency of product,
2. Exact portion cost,
3. Known yield,
4. Reduction of overproduction.

There is no excuse for a restaurant operating without standardized recipes with all the advantages they offer. One of the most important benefits, consistency of product, can have a great impact on sales. How many times have you heard someone say, "You never know about the food in that restaurant—sometimes it's excellent, sometimes it's terrible."

When a recipe is used, you can be sure the product will taste almost the same, no matter who prepares it. This is a great advantage to you. If one cook leaves, the next one can produce the same dish, in the same way, at the same cost. No one will come into your restaurant and say, "What happened to the Veal Morengo, it was always so good?" If the recipe is followed (and it is up to you to see that it is), the dish will always be "so good."

Do not hesitate to develop your own recipes. If you see a recipe you like in a newspaper or magazine, put it on the menu as a special, at a low price, and get your guests' comments. Once you have it right, make it a permanent addition to your file.

Once a recipe is decided on, it should be "costed."

Recipe Costing

Suppose you create this beautiful chicken dish. You guess that its cost is $2.30 to produce. Using a 40% food cost, you come up with a selling price of $5.75. One day, you decide to really find out what the exact cost is. So, you write out the recipe and cost it. Much to your dismay, you find it costs $2.80 to prepare. Using the same 40% cost, you find it should be selling for $7.00. By carelessly arriving at a cost, you deprived yourself of $1.25 in sales.

It is foolish to produce any appetizer, entree, vegetable . . . any dish, without knowing exactly how much it costs.

Procedure for Costing a Recipe (Figure 6–2)

1. List the ingredients used in the recipe in the first vertical column.
2. List the quantities of each ingredient used in the next column.
3. List the cost of the ingredients next.
4. Break purchase unit cost down into ingredient measure cost.
5. Multiply cost by quantity to arrive at the total cost of the ingredient.
6. Total the amounts in step 5.
7. Divide total cost by the number of portions to arrive at portion cost.

Date 7-27-81

Recipe for Chicken Curry

Amount produced 6 quarts Total cost $16.93

Portion size 7 oz. Cost/portion .677

Number portions 25

Ingredients	Amount	Purchase Unit Cost	Item Cost	Total Cost
coconut	1 cup.	1.08/#	.180/c	.180
garlic	2 cl.	.15	.015	.030
onions, A.P.	½ lb.	.27/#		.135
curry powder	5 T	2.97/#	.046/T	.230
flour	1 C	.17/#	.043/C	.043
chicken stock	1½ qts.	n/c		
chicken, cooked diced	6 #	2.17/#		13.02
currant jelly	½ C	5.80/#/10 can	.892/#	.297
lemon juice	2/3 c	.12/ea.		.360
ginger	1 t	3.30/#		.014
apples	3	.12		.36
rice, E.P.	1 C	.20/qt.		.05

Cost of ingredients				14.719
Safety Factor 15%				2.21
Total Recipe Cost				16.929

Figure 6–2. Sample Recipe Costing Form

Cooking Methods and Cooking Yields

The method of cooking food will not only determine the taste and appearance of the final product, but it will also be a factor in determining the ingredients to be purchased. This is particularly true with purchased meats.

Meat cookery is a subject that cannot be adequately discussed in these limited pages. An excellent reference is *Foundations of Food Preparation* by Gladys C. Peckman, Macmillan Co., New York, 1967. There are two methods of cooking meats, dry heat and moist heat. Generally, dry heat is used to cook tender cuts of meat, while the moist heat method is used for the less tender cuts. Dry heat methods are roasting, broiling, pan broiling, and frying. Moist heat methods are stewing and braising.

In cost management, you are primarily concerned with purchasing the right product and utilizing it correctly. Consequently, you would not purchase a tenderloin to make a ragout. Conversely, you would not purchase a brisket to make steak sandwiches.

A further consideration is the cooking temperature. High temperatures tend to shrink and toughen meats. Cooking at lower temperatures reduces shrinkage and actually seems to tenderize meats in certain cases. Shrinkage is an important concern because the greater the shrinkage, the less meat there is for portioning.

Meat that is roasted generally loses less weight than meat that is braised or stewed. Thus, a pound of stew beef may weigh from eleven to thirteen ounces after cooking, while a pound of rib meat may weigh from twelve to fourteen ounces after roasting.

Meat cooked at higher temperatures will have a greater weight loss than meat cooked at lower temperatures. A twenty pound, oven-ready rib roasted at 350° F, for example, will weigh about one pound more than a rib roasted at 400° F. It is claimed that meat roasted at 250° F will have less than 9 percent shrinkage. This means that instead of a loss of approximately three pounds on a twenty pound rib roasted at 350° F, there will only be a one pound loss when it is roasted at 250° F.

Roasting can result in losses of as much as 20 percent depending on the cooking temperature and the preparation of the cut of meat. Braising and stewing will produce a loss of 32 to 35 percent. For this reason, you should be careful in calculating the true cost of a recipe.

It should be noted that in addition to the above losses, losses due to portioning can be as high as 12 to 15 percent.

It is evident then that, in addition to losses through butchering, you can expect further losses from cooking. How great these losses will be depends on the method of cookery and the temperatures used.

The more expensive meats and meat cuts are usually the most tender. Examples are beef ribs, sirloin strips, and tenderloins, and veal and most pork cuts. These items should be cooked in the manner which will yield the greatest return. Less tender and tougher cuts such as beef bottoms and some pork and lamb items, although lower in cost, must be embellished in preparation to warrant the higher selling price necessitated by their higher preparation costs.

In order for preparation to be a viable function of cost management, it must be performed with careful attention to detail. Sloppy initial preparation leads to irretrievable waste. The lack of standardized recipes results in an inconsistent product, overproduction, and little knowledge of real costs. Poor cooking methods result in high production costs and lost portions.

Waste Control in Preparation

Areas to be considered are:

1. Preparation waste,
2. Portion sizes,
3. Overproduction,
4. Utilization of leftovers.

Waste in preparation has been discussed. Food lost in this manner can never be recovered. Kitchen employees should not be allowed to discard any food that may have potential value.

Because menu prices are calculated on a particular amount of food, the portion size must not be allowed to vary. Any variance on the high side will reduce the return on sales. Consequently, all recipes should note the portion size. In addition, a chart indicating portion sizes should be posted in easy view.

Sometimes cooks can be quite careless regarding portion sizes when they are under fire on a busy night. One excellent method to reduce this problem is the use of pre-portioning.

The particular food item will determine the method of pre-portioning. Steaks for example, can be precut and weighed prior to service. Each steak is then carefully wrapped with plastic wrap and refrigerated. When a steak is needed, all the cook has to do is reach for a steak and unwrap it without worrying about cutting it to the correct size. Steaks that are not used can be marked and used the next day without fear of spoilage. Scraps from trimming can be accumulated and frozen until needed.

Prepared items such as Seafood Newberg can be pre-portioned in casseroles and heated in the oven or by microwave. Casseroles are extremely useful in pre-portioning. They may or may not be served in the dining room, depending on the appearance of the product.

Many other items lend themselves to pre-portioning. Two expensive items which we had on our menu involved cubed tenderloin of beef and lump crabmeat. When an extra ounce of either of these is served, the result can raise havoc with your food cost. To overcome this possibility, the ingredients (tenderloin cubes or crabmeat) were weighed and placed in plastic old-fashioned glasses. These were inexpensive and, because they were transparent, the contents were easily visible. The glasses were then placed in a 9½" × 13" baking pan for easy access, covered and refrigerated.

Items can also be portioned by count. Vegetables lend themselves to this method very nicely.

Using the correct size serving spoon can act as a control to portion sizes. Different spoon sizes will result in different portion sizes. Care should be taken not to mix up the spoons.

The use of a particular number setting on the slicing machine is another method of controlling portion sizes. In addition, it gives uniformity to a product. In some cases, weighing will still be necessary; in others, portion will be determined by the size of the slice. Once a particular size slice is decided on, it should be added to a list and the list should be posted near the slicer for easy reference. The slicing method is particularly useful for slicing boned beef rib roasts because of the uniformity of shape and size of this cut.

Standard size ladles and ice cream dishers may also be used to control portion sizes. A #10 disher will hold approximately 3½ ounces of liquid or 4 ounces of an item like ground beef or twenty-four scoops of ice cream per gallon. Instead of weighing the meat for each four-ounce hamburger, portioning can be done more quickly and just about as accurately with a disher. The added advantage is the speed with which such tasks can be performed. If you have ever made a few hundred cocktail size meatballs at one time, you will understand this time saver.

Another area in which waste can be costly is in production. Even with standardized recipes, a knowledgeable person must decide how much of a particular item should be prepared. If this is not done with some degree of accuracy, overproduction will result. Overproduction is never desirable, but it is not always a disaster. Most times, the leftover food can be converted into another salable item. However, such a conversion results in extra labor which would not have been necessary if the overproduction had not occurred.

Serious consideration should always be given to the use of leftovers. Often, especially where vegetables are concerned, storage and reheating ruins the flavor and texture. To serve such items would do little for your reputation. It would be better to discard the items immediately, rather than spend the money refrigerating them, if ultimately they will be thrown out anyway.

In order to intelligently decide how much to prepare, it is necessary to keep a count of the number of times an item is served. If you have a menu that changes every day, this can become a very involved task. Such factors as the particular day, the weather, and other menu items will influence the number of each item served. If you retain the same menu each day, or change it completely periodically, all you need do is keep a list of all the items on the menu and the number sold. These figures are then converted to percentages. The percentages are then related to the number of guests you are expecting for an approximate idea of how

many of each item will be sold. This procedure is more fully described in the section on menus.

Controlling waste is a very important element of cost management. It can mean the difference between an efficient, profitable operation and one that loses money.

Labor Utilization

The final item to consider on the topic of cost management is the cost of labor in the kitchen and dining room.

In most instances, kitchen wages are higher than dining room wages, because certain kitchen personnel are highly trained and skilled in their profession and command higher salaries. In addition, service personnel usually operate under the gratuity system. This enables the restaurant owner to pay them a lower wage.

In recent years, because of the change in the minimum wage laws, there has been a trend away from the gratuity system. In the new method, tipping is eliminated and a service charge is added to the guest's check. The amount collected goes to the restaurant, not the serviceperson. The serviceperson is then paid a competitive hourly rate and no longer must rely on adequate tips to supplement salary. In the majority of cases, after the service employee is paid, there is still money left from the service charge. This money is used to offset payroll costs in other categories.

Regardless of which system is used, kitchen payroll will still be higher than dining room, so extra effort must be made in the former area.

All personnel, kitchen and dining room alike, must be trained to do their jobs correctly. They must be made to understand that procedures which result in wasted time must be changed to more efficient methods. This cannot be stressed too strongly because inefficiency is one of the biggest factors contributing to financial failure in restaurants.

Improper working procedures are one cause of employee inefficiency. If you do not set up methods or procedures for doing particular jobs or recipes, employees often will not know how to handle the work efficiently. Under such circumstances, completion of the job may take two or three times as long as necessary. Written, step-by-step procedures are often necessary to produce efficiency.

Overproduction is another area worth looking into. When too much food is produced, labor is wasted in two ways. First, if the proper amount of food were prepared, the labor time would have been less. Second, additional labor is necessary because leftovers must be prepared in another manner to be resold. Employees should be given specific directions as to the amount to prepare. Do not allow them to make their own decision in this regard, unless this is a part of their job, as in the case of a chef.

Scheduling is the final area to be considered. Scheduling takes two forms. One involves the hours and days an employee works, the other is the amount of time needed to complete a particular job.

When an operation first begins, it is difficult to predict the amount of help that is needed. As experience is gained, the situation becomes clearer. Initially, it is probably better to have too much help. As the crew becomes more experienced, it becomes more efficient in its work. When this occurs, unnecessary hours and personnel can be eliminated. Such a hard line approach is needed, especially in the beginning, if you are to remain in business.

The other scheduling task is deciding how long it takes to do a specific job. This can be determined by your own observation and experience. Once you are satisfied a particular job should take a certain amount of time to accomplish, this should be the established criterion. If employees take too long to complete their work, they should be told about it. Slow employees are not only costly, they also make working difficult for the other employees.

From one point of view, it is more difficult to control labor costs in a small restaurant, because of the close relationship between the owner and the employees. However, it must be done if the operation is to be profitable.

Small restaurants, as we mentioned before, usually operate with a minimum staff. Because of this, all must be capable of doing their jobs effectively. If they do not, other members of the staff must work overtime or additional people must be hired to do the work. In either case, there is an unnecessary, additional cost to the restaurant.

Normal increases in the cost of labor are legitimate reasons for raising menu prices. Increases in labor, or any other, costs which are due to inefficiency are not. Such increases put you at a competitive disadvantage with other restaurants.

In summary, labor costs are an integral part of cost management. They must be analyzed as carefully and objectively as any of the other functions we have discussed. If they are not, substantial losses can occur.

Determining the Selling Price

The formula for arriving at the selling price of any menu item is:

$$\text{Selling Price} = \frac{\text{Cost of Item}}{\text{Food Cost Percentage}}$$

The "cost of item" is the actual or real cost.

The "food cost percentage" is an arbitrary percentage, set by you.

If, for example, you would like to determine the selling price for a ten-ounce sirloin steak that costs $3.75, you must decide the cost percentage you would like to have. Generally, 50 percent is acceptable for a steak, because a minimum of labor is involved in its preparation. By inserting these figures in the above equation, we arrive at a selling price.

$$\text{Selling Price} = \frac{\$3.75}{50\%} = \$7.50$$

Some operators prefer the factoring method. It is not quite as accurate, but it is faster if you do not have a calculator handy. The factor is obtained by converting the percentage to a real number. Thus, 50% is 2, 40% is 2.5, and 45% is 2.2. Simply multiply the "cost of item" by the factor to obtain the price.

$$\$3.75 \times 2 = \$7.50$$

Do not include labor, linen, or overhead. These expenses are picked up with the remaining percentage.

Most restaurants operate with a food cost percentage of between 40 and 45 percent. If this is not right for your operation, it can be increased or decreased according to your needs. This is an overall percentage, not necessarily the one for every menu item. With the steak, the factor was 50 percent. Some other item may only have a factor of 35 percent. As mentioned previously, the percentage can be changed by altering the portion size or by increasing or decreasing the selling price.

If the entree is garnished, the cost of the garnish should be included as well. Add it to the cost of the entree before making the price calculations.

Some restaurant menus include vegetables, salad, rolls or bread, butter and beverage with the entree. If you do this, you must include the cost of such items in the entree selling price. The simplest way to do this is to figure the cost of each item, add these costs together, and, with either of the above formulas, calculate the selling price. You will discover after doing this a few times that cost does not vary significantly. Because of this, it is quite acceptable to determine an average selling price for the "extras" and add this standard selling price to all entree prices. Thus, if it is determined that the accompaniments to the entree should be selling at $3.00, simply add this $3.00 to all entree selling prices. In the above example, the sirloin steak had a selling price of $7.50. Add $3.00 to $7.50 and the selling price for the complete meal will be $10.50.

If you find it necessary to change the standard add-on because of an increased cost, all you have to do is make the necessary cost changes and recalculate the selling price.

The formula for computing the selling price can also be useful in determining the food cost percentage and the cost of an item.

Food Cost Percentage

If you know the price you wish to sell a menu item for and you know its cost, you can come up with the food cost percentage very easily.

$$\frac{\text{Cost of Item}}{\text{Selling Price}} = \text{Food Cost Percentage}$$

$$\frac{\$3.75}{\$7.50} = 50\%$$

This is useful when you want to feature an item at a particular price. Using this formula, you are able to decide if the cost percentage is too high. If it is, you know the portion size will have to be reduced or else the selling price will have to be changed.

Cost of Item

The cost of an item can be determined if you know the selling price and the food cost percentage.

Selling Price × Food Cost Percentage = Cost of Item

$$\$7.50 \times 50\% = \$3.75$$

This information is useful in a similar manner. If you want an item to sell at a particular price and you must maintain a certain food cost percentage, then the cost cannot exceed the amount obtained with this formula. In the above example, the cost of a menu item which is to sell for $7.50 cannot exceed $3.75 if a 50% cost percentage is to be maintained.

The menu selling price should never be arrived at by guesswork. A price that is too low will mean a loss to your operation. A price that is too high may mean a loss of business.

Portion Size

The portion size is determined by aesthetic appeal and food cost. There are no formulas for determining the proper portion size.

Aesthetic appeal refers to how the food looks on the plate. If the portion size looks skimpy, make it larger. If the portion overwhelms, make it smaller. Eye appeal is one third of the battle of food presentation. The portion must not overpower, yet it must be ample.

Cost is the other factor to consider. When you have decided the size the portion should be, figure the cost. If the cost is too high, can the portion size be reduced without receiving complaints? If it cannot, do not use the item or do something to enhance the smaller size. In a fine restaurant, the size and appearance must be right. If this means the selling price will be unacceptably high, then do not serve the item. Any item which is not acceptable either in appearance or size can only hurt your image.

There is no subject more important to the operation of a small restaurant than cost management. It is the entire basis of a successful operation. Without a competent understanding of it, your chances of economic survival are greatly reduced.

Do not look upon the principles of cost management as only relating to the food department (although this is by far, the most important aspect). These principles can be applied to all aspects of the restaurant operation.

Good purchasing and receiving procedures are as important with janitorial supplies as they are with the production of fine food. The use of recipes will do the same for drinks in the cocktail lounge, as it will for the preparation of irresistible desserts in the dining room. Correct storage is just as important to the storage of wines as it is to the meat in the refrigerator or the groceries on the shelves.

From a financial point of view, success can only be attained by meticulous attention to costs. The most pleasing personality, the finest of food, the most capable staff can keep the money rolling in, but only capable cost management can put it in your bank account.

Chapter Seven

The Restaurant as Seen by the Guest

The primary objective of any restaurant should be the happiness and comfort of the guest. This can be accomplished by:

1. Serving excellent food,
2. Having well made drinks and an adequate wine list,
3. Providing correct and careful service,
4. Presenting a pleasant, relaxed, and well maintained atmosphere for the enjoyment of the above.

The creation of a fine restaurant is analogous to the composition of a beautiful painting: all the elements are blended together to create the whole. Remove any one of them and you risk spoiling the entire picture because each makes its own contribution to the overall image.

When people come to your restaurant for the first time, they will probably be in a somewhat critical mood. They will be looking for all the things they think are important.

From the moment they drive into your parking lot or enter the front door, they will be observing the "elements" of your picture. One by one, as they put the elements together, they will form opinions.

The guests' first impressions can be crucial. If they are not pleased with what they see, they might just turn around and walk out. Once past this initial point, they will relax somewhat and start to observe or, maybe, even feel, the restaurant's atmosphere. While waiting for the order to be taken or while sipping cocktails, they will begin to look around at the physical surroundings: the furnishings, the colors, and the decorations. They will begin to realize how comfortable the chairs are, how tastefully the lighting has been done, and so on.

It is obvious then that the smart restaurateur will create an atmosphere, or mood, that will satisfy. Follow this up with the right food and service and a faithful customer will have been created.

165

First Impressions

The parking lot (if you have one) will be the guest's first contact with your establishment. Parking lots do not have to be beautiful but they do have to be tidy. Assign someone the task of picking up loose debris before each meal period. If holes develop in the macadam, have them repaired before they become noticeable. Lines or markers should be kept painted or touched up. The lot should be adequately lighted.

Keep the exterior of the building in good repair. Repaint when necessary. At the very least, retouch as needed. If something is damaged or broken, have it repaired immediately. Be sure the garbage and trash area cannot be seen from the entranceway and that odors from this area are non-existent. Keep sidewalks and walkways swept constantly. If there is a lawn, trees, or bushes, keep them neatly trimmed. Plant a few flowers if a garden is available. Parsley makes evocative borders, as do many herbs. A simple addition of a window box, planted with bright flowers, under a few windows, can be eye catching and pretty even in a large city. Door decorations, such as New England dried corn, will add interest. Do not overdo it, but do make it interesting.

For many in-town restaurants, the first impression is not felt until after the guest enters the front door. Aside from the physical surroundings, which obviously have an important effect, the guest is expecting a clean, cheery, well maintained, and orderly environment. Anything less may act to downgrade expectations. Most important, at this time, is the manner in which guests are met. If a pleasant, courteous person meets them as they enter, they will be favorably impressed. If they are ignored or shown little courtesy, they will be influenced in a negative manner.

It is necessary then, that you do everything possible to present a favorable first impression. An unfavorable first impression can have an adverse effect on the guests' attitudes throughout the entire meal.

Atmosphere

Atmosphere is something people perceive. It is created by what they see and hear.

The first step in creating atmosphere in a restaurant is the formation of a basic theme. Have you ever noticed how few restaurants bother to do this? One gets the impression that the majority of restaurants are competing against one another to see how much they can look alike. They use the same color scheme (red), the same commercial furniture, the same lighting fixtures, the same chinaware and glassware, and, in some cases, even the same type of food (frozen).

Why not try something different? Create your own atmosphere. It is one of the few ways in which you can tell your guests, "this is me."

If you are fortunate enough to live near a large city, visit as many restaurants of your calibre as you can. Notice how the ones with a theme are more interesting to look at than the run-of-the-mill ones. In New York City, for instance, there is a restaurant with an enormous tree growing in the middle of the dining room. Another is fashioned as a greenhouse. Still another is furnished with automobiles. There are any number of unique ideas. Use your imagination or some hidden desire you may have to make your restaurant different. If you do not have an imagination or a hidden desire, you can still create a pleasing atmosphere by using consistency and good taste in decorating and furnishing. Whatever atmosphere is created, have it reflect *your* tastes and ideas.

An intangible part of atmosphere is having the guest feel comfortable. Fine food can only be appreciated and enjoyed in a relatively quiet and relaxed atmosphere. Such an atmosphere is not attainable without the assistance of the staff. They should be trained to be available to the needs of the guests and to be fast and efficient without being bothersome. Such a staff will create an impression of competence and concern for the guests.

Consideration of the preceding suggestions will result in a dining room that reflects your feelings for fine food, enjoyable surroundings, and a considerate staff.

Physical Surroundings

Colors. One of the first things to decide on is the dominant color scheme. Once this is determined, everything else will be tied in with it. This includes the color of the walls, the draperies (or curtains), the carpeting, and even the chinaware and linen.

Choosing a color may not be easy. If the room is naturally dark, light colors are needed. Yet, light colors soil easily and require continuous maintenance. If the room is bright, darker colors may be in order, but they tend to make a room feel closed in. This can be a problem in a small room. If a room is long, the colors will be basically different than if the room is square. If the ceiling is high, the color requirements are different than if it is low.

Wallpaper is very attractive in a home in which it gets tender loving care. In a restaurant it is equally as attractive, but, unfortunately, it does not get the same care. Food splashes and chair gouges are common occurrences. Wallpaper requires frequent cleaning and, often, replacing. If you use it, wallpaper should be heavily patterned and of the darker hues.

The way you use colors is important. Most reds, browns, greens, and yellows will enhance the presentation of food. Blues and blacks usually do not fit in restaurant decor.

Colors must be chosen with care. If you do not have an eye for color, speak to a professional.

Use top quality paint only. The cost of the paint is small compared to the cost of the labor needed to apply it. Good quality paint can be cleaned without appreciable wear, poor quality paint cannot. Use flat paint for walls (except in the kitchen) and semi-gloss for woodwork. If special colors are mixed, be sure the formula is available for duplication at a later date. When chipping of paint occurs, use a small artist's brush to touch up the spots. Few things look shoddier than chipped or worn painted woodwork.

Furnishings. This category includes such items as tables, chairs, lounge furniture, carpeting, draperies or curtains, and lighting. It would be impossible to discuss the requirements for each of these here. However, when purchasing furnishings, you should do a good deal of research before the actual purchase is made. Do not be content with the salesperson's recommendations, find out for yourself.

Chairs. Firm construction is especially important in the legs and chair backs. A dining room chair must have a comfortable seat and back because of the length of time a guest sits in it.

Dining rooms are usually limited in space and, therefore, chairs should not be overly large. Armchairs take up more space than those without arms. Be careful when purchasing armchairs that the arms fit under the table top.

If chairs are made of wood only, they should not be painted because of the wear they receive and the necessity for repainting. If upholstered seats are used, the upholstery should be of a color and pattern that will not easily show spotting. In addition, it is essential the upholstery be treated with a soil retardant to minimize the need for frequent cleaning.

Do not purchase a chair without actually using it for a week or so. It is not possible to judge a chair's comfort just by sitting in it, once or twice, in a dealer's showroom.

Chairs for the cocktail lounge must be exceptionally strong and well constructed, because some guests really like to relax in them. They hang their legs over the arms and lean back in them. This puts undue strain on any chair. If the chairs in the lounge are used with low cocktail tables, armchairs are recommended. If used with normal height tables, either style is satisfactory. Upholstered chairs should be of exceptionally strong and stain resistant material such as Naugahyde or leather.

It is a good idea to purchase a few more chairs than are actually needed. There always seems to be a time when someone wants to squeeze an extra person at a table.

Tables. These can be purchased ready-made or you can make the tabletop yourself, or have it made, and purchase the upright, or spindle, and base separately. This is advantageous when unusual size tables are needed. It may or may not be as economical using standard size tables.

The construction of the table will depend somewhat on where it is to be used. Naturally, the primary requirement is sturdiness. Tops should be at least one inch thick. Today, most tables are constructed of flakeboard and covered with a material such as Formica. This is durable and practical. However, if you plan to use the table without a table cover, and do not like the appearance of the Formica, your only alternative is a solid wood top. These are difficult to find because

they are not a standard product. In addition, if you are able to find them, they are more expensive. A local carpenter or lumber dealer may be able to make them for less.

If a table is to be kept covered at all times, a flakeboard top without the Formica is sufficient. However, if there is a possibility that the flakeboard top will be seen by diners, this arrangement would never be satisfactory.

The upright, or spindle, should be of solid construction. It can be seen below the tablecloth, so it should be attractive.

The base of the table is quite important. It must be of sufficient size to support the table under any conditions. In addition, it must be constructed so the table cannot be tipped if a person leans heavily on it. Very large table tops may require two bases. This also can be seen beneath the tablecloth and should be attractively made.

Tables in the cocktail lounge can be low or of normal height. This decision depends on space requirements and your own individual taste. Generally, they are not covered and require a finished surface. Such a finish should be capable of withstanding alcohol spills and cigarette burns.

Table decorations. The more items on a table, the more have to be removed each time a table is reset. Table decorations should be limited to a flower vase, a candle or lamp, and an ash tray. Anything more is superfluous.

Room decorations. The use of room decorations is essential to complete the decorating scheme. Interesting pictures and other knick-knacks can be hung on walls. Various items can be placed on sills and tables to enhance your decorating. Unfortunately, such items have a way of disappearing, so some discretion should be used in their selection and placement.

Other Furniture. If room is available, additional furniture, upholstered chairs or sofas and side tables, can make your restaurant look more comfortable. Such furniture should be covered with durable fabric and be well constructed.

Carpeting. Select carpeting for durability, stain resistance, and color. Carpet fibers should be relatively short and rather tightly packed. If they are too long, the carpet will be extremely difficult to keep clean. The more fibers per square inch, the better, and the more expensive the carpet, and the longer it will wear. Be sure the backing is strong or the fibers will pull out. Some thorough research into carpet construction, before a purchase, would be worthwhile.

Wool is still the best all-around fiber. It resists burns, water, and soiling.

Choose a color and pattern that fits in with your overall color scheme. Solid color carpeting should never be used in a restaurant. It is next to impossible to keep clean.

Carpeting should be thoroughly cleaned with shampoo at least once a year, depending on traffic conditions.

When the time comes for installation, choose a competent installer if you want to keep waste to a minimum. Leftover pieces can be made into runners and small rugs to be used in heavy traffic areas to preserve the underlying carpet. Some types of carpeting should be laid with both glue and holding strips. Seams should be sewn and taped for extra security. Carpeting always looks good after it is first installed. How it looks a year later is the important test. Ask to see a few jobs done by the installer before deciding on a purchase.

Floor Covering. Other floor covering will be needed in the bar, rest rooms, and kitchen. Such covering can be purchased in sheets or in individual tiles. A competent installer should be found to install the sheets. Tiles are an easy do-it-yourself job, if you have the time. If you like to redecorate an area every four or five years, the use of one-eighth inch thick tiles is sufficient. If you do not, use heavier material. Write Armstrong, Lancaster, Pa. 17604 for all the information you will need.

Lighting. In addition to making seeing easier, lighting is important in other ways. It can help create a particular mood or atmosphere and enhance a decorative scheme.

Lighting is available as overhead hanging or attached fixtures, overhead or recessed spots, side brackets, and as table or floor lamps. The lighting may be incandescent or fluorescent. Each comes in various sizes, shapes, and colors.

Dining room and lounge lighting should always be on dimmer switches so the amount of light can be regulated as needed.

Window Coverings. Draperies, curtains, roll shades, drop shades, blinds, and shutters are the options for window coverings. They can be used decoratively as well as functionally. Occasional cleaning or washing will lengthen their life and make them look fresher.

As with other things in a restaurant, window coverings do take a lot of abuse. It would be wise, therefore, to choose good quality fabrics or other materials.

Ventilation and Temperature Control. During the last few years, the public has become more conscious of ventilation, air conditioning, and heating. This has come about because of the increased cost of energy. In addition, the anti-smoking forces have made people more aware of the inconvenience and dangers of breathing secondhand tobacco smoke.

No one enjoys eating or drinking in a

stuffy or smoke-filled room. Therefore, proper ventilation is essential. If central heating and air conditioning are used in your restaurant, the outside air flow can be regulated to rid the room of smoke and odors. If heating or cooling is accomplished by other methods, another means of exhausting smoke and odors must be used. The least expensive is a properly located exhaust fan. Such fans can be quite effective but they have one major drawback. They remove heated (or cooled) air, as well as the objectionable smoke and odors. A more expensive, but far more useful, method is to use an electronic air filter. Such a filter removes smoke, odors, and dust particles and returns the cleaned air to the room. The saving in heat and cooling will help offset the cost of such a unit. Electronic filters can also be attached to central ventilating systems.

The placement of heating and/or cooling units, ductwork, and louvres should be carefully planned. The units themselves are noisy and should be located where their sounds are not annoying. Ductwork can be unsightly and, possibly, uncomfortable to those sitting nearby. Locate ventilating louvres so they do not spill their heated or cooled air directly onto the guests. The same is true for window or wall air conditioning units.

As of July, 1979, the federal government decreed that the temperature inside buildings cannot exceed 65° F when heating or be lower than 80° when cooling. There has been a good deal of controversy regarding these limits. Needless to say, there are those who are ignoring them.

It should be noted, however, that when the humidity is properly controlled, these temperature limits can be livable. Certainly, individual situations will develop in which some discretion must be used.

China, Glassware, Tableware, and Linen. The careful selection of each of these items will complement the overall decor. Proper colors, textures, and materials must be tied together to maintain the continuity of the entire restaurant.

Table Arrangements. Small restaurants always seem to be in need of more table space. To compensate for this, many owners crowd in extra seats. This is a mistake. People who eat out regularly expect to be crowded in a diner or fast food store, but they do not expect it in a finer eating place. Always try to keep adequate space between tables and chairs.

Further, once a table arrangement pattern is established, do not change it. Moving tables together for large parties, as is often done, destroys much of the atmosphere of the dining room.

Restrooms. Toilet facilities should tie in decoratively with other parts of the restaurant. They should be kept spotless and odorless. Many a restaurant has been judged on its restrooms.

If employees are allowed to use the guest restrooms (only if no other facility is available), they should be instructed to help keep them clean.

Menus and Service. Both subjects are discussed in depth elsewhere. Menus should also tie in with the decor. In addition, they should be interesting to look at.

The service should be perfect, helpful, and friendly.

By giving careful thought to each of the individual items mentioned above, you will create a central theme or atmosphere. With pleasant surroundings and facilities, the guests will be relaxed and comfortable, ready to enjoy your fine food and hospitality.

Chapter Eight

The Mechanics of a Smoothly Running Restaurant

In the preceding chapter, we spoke of the expectations of the guests when they visit a restaurant. The means of fulfilling these expectations were outlined and discussed in some detail.

This chapter will follow up on these topics and discuss them from the operating point of view. In addition, supplementary material will be presented to help the restaurant function smoothly and efficiently with a minimum of confusion.

Before supplementing the subjects discussed in the previous chapter, we will consider basic introductory procedures which involve guest and restaurant communications. The subjects include hours of operation, the telephone, and the reservation system.

Hours of Operation

There are five issues to be considered before deciding upon the hours of operation.

The customer. When is your restaurant needed—luncheon, dinner, weekdays or nights, or weekends? When will it attract the largest market? Will you lose a significant amount of business by not being open at certain times?

Profitability. Which days, and which hours of these days, will volume be the largest? Would it be wise to close on off days and off hours or should you attempt to build business during these off periods?

Labor market. Can you obtain a sufficient number of employees to work the hours you would like to be operating? If you cannot, will this mean cutting back on services while you are open?

Preparation time. If you are open for most of the day and night, is there time and space to prepare everything that is needed? To accomplish this, will it be necessary to increase the size of the preparation staff to the point where profitability will be decreased?

Your own welfare and happiness. Close at

least one day per week. You need time to relax even more than your employees. In addition to the day for relaxation, you may find a day is necessary just to do the bookwork and other chores that cannot be done while you are in operation.

Do not expect to be able to make the ultimate, correct decision as to the proper hours of operation the first day you are open. The information to help you make such a decision is too limited at this time. This is also true if you have purchased an existing operation. Just consider all the facts at your disposal and come to the best possible conclusion. Later, as you operate, more information will present itself and you may alter your thinking.

Be consistent in your operating hours. Do not change them without serious thought. Advertise changes well in advance. No one likes to come out for dinner and find his or her favorite restaurant closed.

During the early weeks of a new operation, minor changes may be made in the operating schedule. After six months have gone by, it is a good idea to sit down and analyze the situation carefully. You may find certain days (or nights) of the week are particularly slow. The same holds for the hours of the day. If this is the case, decide whether these off periods are the result of something within your control. If they are, come up with a plan of action to increase volume at these times. If the reason for the slow periods is beyond your control, consider revamping the schedule to eliminate the unprofitable or low volume times.

In the majority of cases, if your food and service is beyond reproach, consistently bad days or hours are out of your control and no amount of effort will have an appreciable effect. If there is no consistent pattern, the off times are due to the nature of the restaurant business and you will have to live with them.

The Telephone

The telephone is a very useful piece of equipment. Without it, the restaurant business would be terribly limited. In most cases, a telephone call will be the first contact a guest has with your restaurant. For this reason, it is important that whoever answers the telephone does it correctly.

Do not allow just anybody to answer the telephone, because the restaurant's image is reflected by the person answering and the information transmitted must be properly handled. We had a policy that only two of us could answer the telephone. If, for some obscure reason, neither of us were available and someone else answered, he or she was only allowed to take a message. Employees were instructed to always get the telephone number of the person calling. We later returned the call. All messages were put in writing and placed where they could be found.

A telephone conversation with a guest must be polite and to the point. The telephone should be answered by first giving the name of the restaurant, followed by "Good evening," or "Good day." If a person wishes to make a reservation, check the reservation book. Do not say "yes" unless you have the opening available. When hanging up, always say thank you.

Calls should never be placed on hold and forgotten. Keep an eye on the line until the call is completed.

The telephone is a very versatile device. Make use of its versatility. Investigate the conveniences offered by your local company.

Do not allow the employees to use the telephone for personal calls except in emergencies. Better to inconvenience employees than guests.

The Reservation System

It is not practical to run a small restaurant without a reservation system. The limited number of seats must be allocated to get the best possible turnover. Without a reservation system, you will actually lose business. People will not travel any distance unless they are assured of a table when they arrive. Even local customers do not want to wait an indeterminate amount of time to be seated. They will just go elsewhere.

To further compound the difficulty, the majority of diners all want a table at the same time, either from noon to 1 P.M. or between 7 and 8 P.M. This leaves you with empty tables during the fringe periods, which might have been sold if the potential guest was aware of the seating situation.

First, decide who will manage the system. This person, and only this person, should confirm reservations. No one else should be allowed to accept them. If this practice is not painstakingly adhered to, a number of problems, including over-booking, duplications, and incorrect arrival times, can result. There is nothing more embarrassing, or impossible to resolve, than two parties waiting for the same table at the same time.

There are two ways in which reservations can be handled. One allows parties to come at staggered intervals. The other has everyone come at the same time; this is sometimes called sittings. Decide which is best for you. Some owners find the staggered system is easier on the kitchen staff, others like the ease of serving all one menu item at one time.

Determine the number of tables and the maximum number of seats available. Do not squeeze in extra chairs unless you tell the guest you are doing it. Most people do not like to be crowded when eating.

Decide from the beginning that you will not move tables around the dining room to accommodate guests. Table moving disrupts the entire room to make a few people happy. If your largest table is for six and the party is eight offer them two tables of four, but do not move tables together.

Determine the amount of time to be alloted to each party. A general rule of thumb is one and a half hours for a party of two and two hours for a party of three or four. Larger parties, five to eight, may require as much as two and a half hours, because it takes longer to get their orders and to serve them.

Next, decide how many turnovers (for each table) you would like to have in an evening. Turnovers are the number of times a table is used in an evening. This will depend on the hours of operation, the menu, and the service style. To get a double turnover from a table of four, you would need about four hours. If you are open from 6 P.M. until 9 P.M., this will be no problem. You could take a reservation for that particular table as late as 7 P.M. and still use it again at 9 P.M.

When establishing the hours of operation, decide if the closing hour is serving time or seating time. It should be seating time. If it is not, that fact should be stated to anyone making a late reservation. Be sure the staff understands this as well. Guests should not be rushed just because they like to eat late.

Decide on how long reservations will be held if a party does not arrive at the specified time. Hold tables for fifteen minutes on busy nights. If someone without a reservation is waiting for a table, give the party the table. If the late party finally arrives, they will have to wait until a table is available. If no table is available, you will lose them. This is a necessary policy for self-protection. There will be times when a party does not show up and the reservation is not cancelled. You then end up with an empty table for that period of time. This can be costly in a small restaurant. The only way you can protect yourself is to get the telephone number from everyone who makes a reservation. No shows do not happen too frequently in a fine restaurant.

Two bits of advice which may be helpful are: 1) reservations are usually for later hours on weekends than on weekdays or nights and

2) tables are much easier to designate if they are numbered.

The following illustration shows how to set up a reservation sheet.

Illustration

Assume the dining room has forty-five seats. The hours of service are 6 to 10 P.M. It is a Saturday night. The table breakdown is:

3 tables of five (#3, 9, 12)
6 tables of four (#4, 5, 7, 8, 10, 11)
3 tables of two (#1, 2, 6)

The first step is to make up a seating chart. (See Figure 8–1.) This is done by using vertical columns for the arrival times and horizontal lines for the table sizes to produce a series of boxes, each of which should be large enough to list the names of the guests and the number in the party.

Next, enter the number of tables available at each specific time. To determine this consider:

1. You do not want everyone to sit down at one time. Therefore, spread the reservations out.
2. A reservation sheet is not started until you begin to get reservations. This gives you a nucleus to begin from. You can then expand outward in both directions. (A table for four at 8 P.M. can be ex-

RESERVATIONS — Dinner, Sat. Sept. 12

	6 p.m.	6:30	7 p.m.	7:30	8 p.m.	8:30	9 p.m.	9:30	10 p.m.
(3) 2's	~~(1)(2)(3)~~ Ross-2 Baird-2			(3)			(3)		
(6) 4's	(3)	~~(2)(3)~~		Rudsill-4	(3)	~~(2)(3)~~ Barron-3		(1)	(3)
(3) 5's	1 ~~(2)~~ Sears-5	~~0~~ Marion-5				(2)	(1)		

Figure 8–1. Seating Chart

panded to a table at 6 P.M. and one at 10 P.M. Once you have a half dozen reservations, you should designate tables.

3. You may have a pattern that works better than anything else (arrived at over a period of time). If you do, this should be used.

4. There may be a special event going on. If so, everyone may want to eat before (or after) it. This is advantageous to you because you know exactly when the table will be free again.

When reservations are taken, insert the name of the party and the number expected in the appropriate box. At the same time, reduce the number of available tables by one.

If a person calls for a particular time and it is not available, tell the caller so and suggest an alternate time. Do not allow people to talk you into giving them a table when one is not available. You will only have to live with it at the hour of reckoning. Better to take a name and telephone number, with a promise to call if a reservation is cancelled. Sometimes, when you are hopelessly booked, it is a nice gesture to suggest another restaurant in town.

The sheet is kept by the host or hostess. When a party arrives, check the name on the list to be sure they really have a reservation. If all is in order, cross the name out and lead the party to their table.

If a party's table is not ready, tell them so. Let them know approximately how long they will have to wait. Suggest the cocktail lounge. If the wait is longer than anticipated, bring them menus in the lounge and have someone take their order. In this way, they will at least get fast service once they are seated.

No system is perfect, but no system at all is worse. The one outlined is quite basic

and modifications should be made to suit your operation.

Whenever advertising is used, mention reservations. "For reservations, call . . ." is sufficient. It tells everyone that reservations are needed, but it does not completely discourage people from coming without them. It is always nice to have walk-ins to fill in the empty spots in the schedule.

Because I know no system is perfect, I thought it would be reassuring to list some of the "little things" you will encounter. The sentences in parentheses are the solutions you hope for.

1. A party shows up late, putting you behind for the whole evening. (Another party eats in half the time you expected and you're saved.)

2. A party of two arrives as a party of three and you just gave away your last four to a party of two. (They're nice people and offer to change tables.)

3. You cross out a name on the sheet by mistake and use a table you don't have. (Fortunately, a reservation doesn't show up on time and you tell them you had to give their table away.)

4. Someone swears they made the reservation for tonight and in fact, it was made for next week. (You'll have to get out of this one.)

5. One of your best customers calls and wants to know if you can squeeze him in with five out of town guests (on a busy night). (So why don't you come down and sit in the cocktail lounge and I'll see what I can do.)

6. The person who insists he made a reservation two weeks ago (but really didn't). (Throw him out. This is an old one.)

Creating the Mood

Previously, we spoke of what it is a guest would like to find in a restaurant and of the surroundings necessary to fulfill these expectations. It is time now to discuss in detail these surroundings, which create the ultimate mood of enjoyment and satisfaction.

First, we will discuss the physical aspects of the restaurant, followed by the human factor (service), and, finally, the presentation of what it is we have to offer.

Furnishings

The primary room furnishings will be the tables and chairs. The construction and other details of these items were discussed thoroughly in the previous chapter. However, another important consideration is how they are placed in the room. They must be located so they are:

1. Not directly in front of doorways, air conditioners, fireplaces, etc.,
2. Away from service areas such as the kitchen,
3. Convenient for service,
4. Not too close together,
5. In an attractive pattern.

Accomplishing all this is no easy task. If you purchase a restaurant furnished, you will have to do the best you can with what you have. If you are starting anew, a table plan can be made up. The information needed to do this follows.

Spacing

If there are *no aisles* you need a minimum of thirty-six inches behind chair back from wall or chair.

Table Shapes

Round   Rectangular   Square

Table Arrangement

Square   Angular

Floor Location

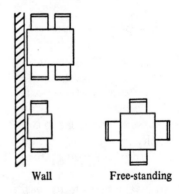

Wall   Free-standing

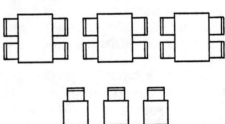

Close

Figure 8–2. Table Arrangements and Seating

Sizes of Tables
Tables can be any size which comfortably seats guests. Minimum comfortable sizes in a limited area are:

	Round	Square	Rectangular
2 persons	30″ dia.	24″ sides	—
4 persons	40″ dia.	24″ sides	48″ × 30″
6 persons	54″ dia.	—	48″ × 36″

Table height is 29 to 30 inches.

Service aisles should never be less than thirty-six inches from the back of one chair to the back of another.

Guest aisles should never be less than forty-eight inches wide when tables are on both sides. If a wall is on one side, it should be sixty inches.

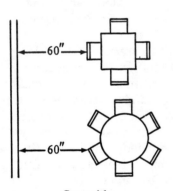

Guest aisle

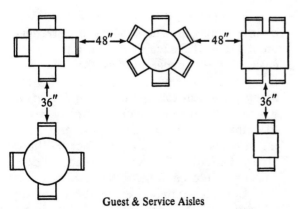

Guest & Service Aisles

Special Tables

Square tables are available with folding sides, which, when opened, make the table round. Extra aisle space must be provided when such tables are used.

Chair Allowances

In planning, allow eighteen inches from the edge of the table to the chair back for each chair. Allow eighteen inches for width of chair, twenty-four inches for an arm chair.

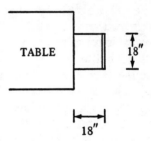

Estimating Capacity

$$\frac{\text{sq. ft. dining area}}{15 \text{ sq. ft.}}$$

Deduct such things as columns, service station, wall jogs, fireplaces, etc.

The above equation will be a rough estimate.

Making a Plan

To make a table plan, you will need:

1. A sketch of the perimeter of the dining area (to scale),
2. A list of items, other than chairs and tables, which will be in the room (e.g., service station, tray stands),
3. A scale ruler, a twelve inch ruler, and a compass,
4. A large sheet of paper to work from,
5. Some heavy paper (an old file folder is fine),
6. Details regarding chair measurements,
7. Scissors, pencils, eraser, glue, and tape.

Determine the location of the service station. Ideally, it should be located near the kitchen entrance and still be easily accessible to the dining area. When the location is decided on, draw it on the dining room sketch. Next, in pencil, draw in any other permanent furnishings you may have. The remaining area is available for tables and chairs.

Decide whether you will be using round tables, square, or a combination of both. Make up some scale models of tables, using the heavy paper for the models. The tables should be of the same scale as the dining room perimeter sketch. It is simpler to include the chairs in the table model than to make them separately.

Examples

To make round tables and chairs, simply make a circle with the correct scale diameter. Make another circle outside the first which is equivalent, in scale, to an eighteen inch chair. Cut out the larger circle and you have a model of a table surround by chairs.

To make square tables, make a square with the correct measurements. Extend the sides of the square in scale eighteen inches out. This will give you a model of a table with chairs on each side.

There is no precise way to determine beforehand exactly which size tables will fit. For this reason, you will need to make various size models. Two, or possibly three, of each size will suffice initially. More can be made of particular sizes after you have some idea of what is needed.

When the models are made, start laying out your plan. Do not forget the necessary aisles. Table arrangement is far from an exact science. If you have to give up an inch here and one there, you will probably still come out all right. Try not to make the aisles any less then the recommended minimum. It is not always necessary to have straight aisles between tables. Tables can be staggered, but be sure to have the correct distance behind chair backs.

You will most likely spend a good deal of time coming up with a satisfactory arrangement, but it will be worth the effort. It is much easier moving paper models than the real thing. In addition, you will know exactly how many seats you can get in the dining area, which, in turn, will tell you how many chairs to purchase, how many tables, and how much china and glassware to order. Without an exact count of the available seats, all purchasing would be done in the dark.

Consider purchasing an extra folding table or two. They can come in handy in an emergency. Also, you may want to consider having a round top that can be fitted on top of a square table. This can give you additional seating if needed.

The allowance for chairs is usually eighteen inches both in depth and length. If your chair has been selected, measure it for exact size. Armchairs are larger than those without arms. The arms should fit under the table when the chair is pushed forward.

Once the table and seating arrangement is completed, you will know exactly how many persons you will be able to serve at one time. This information is important to help you purchase the other furnishings necessary to complete the dining room.

The following list has been made up to include all the furnishings needed to complete a dining room (even those covered elsewhere).

Dining Room

Tables and chairs
Service area
Buffet stand or cabinet
Tray stands
Service cart or table cart
Storage area for clean linen
Reservation desk with telephone
Decorations (e.g., table lamps, extra furniture, pictures, curtains, wall sconces, chandeliers)
Table linen
Silver or stainless tableware
Chinaware
Glassware
Water pitchers (glass or metal)
Salt and pepper shakers
Butter dishes
Tea pots (glass or ceramic)

Sugar holders and cream pitchers
Individual salad bowls (if you use them)
Bread or roll baskets
Relish dishes or holders
Ash trays
Flower holders
Large salad bowl and utensils for tableside service
Cheese trays (if you use them)
Espresso pots (if you use them)
Salad dressing holders and oil and vinegar cruets
Ice bowl and tongs or small scoop
Pepper mill(s)
Special table coffee pots
Coffee warmers (electric) and coffee pots
Escargot dishes, forks and holders (if you use them)
Tableware holders or bins
Trays (various sizes and shapes)
Flambe dish, flambe liquid, and fuel for tableside service (if used)
Cup-Saver racks
Wine buckets (3) and stands
Candles and holders (if used)
Place mats, cloth or paper (if you use them)
Reservation book
Paper napkins (if you use them)
"Reserved" signs for tables
Telephone slips for reservations
Sponge mop for spills
Small broom and dust pan
Furniture polish and dust cloths
Register and checks, extra register rolls and ink pads, order pads
Special lighting in addition to regular lighting, if needed
Uniforms, aprons, jackets

Side towels

An extra jacket and ties for guests who come improperly dressed (if you require a certain dress)

Matches (for promotion, even if no one smokes)

Menus and wine lists

Service area and buffet stand are areas in which the service personnel are able to store tableware, dishes, glassware, linen, and condiments, so they do not have to run in and out of the kitchen. In a very small restaurant, there may not be room for such an area. In this case, have as much as possible in the dining room. This area should be shielded from the sight of the guests if possible, because there is a tendency for it to be untidy. If you use a good deal of ice, it would be worthwhile to make provision for this as well as the other items you need.

Tray stands should be placed in strategic locations throughout the dining room. There is nothing worse than coming out of the kitchen with a full tray and not having a place to set it down.

A *service or table cart* can only be used in a larger restaurant which has tableside service. If you are too small or do not have tableside service, do not bother with one.

A *reservation desk* is nice to have. Again, you may not have room for one. Any arrangement you can come up with will be fine.

Decorations do not have to be elaborate, just interesting. Your restaurant should be as attractive as possible. Poor atmosphere can really detract from your fine food.

The only *glassware* you must consider for the dining room is the water glass. All others are discussed in the beverage and wine chapter. The glass you choose should fit in with the other glassware. Try to make this an interesting piece, but not too elaborate. It is one of the first things noticed by the guests when they sit down.

Water pitchers should be as attractive as possible. Unfortunately, the commercial glass companies are not aware of this after all these years. You can find some nice silver or imitation pewter (or real pewter) pitchers. *Never* use plastic in a fine restaurant.

Salt and pepper shakers are another hard to find item when you want something different. Use only large holed tops. The small ones clog easily.

Butter dishes are nice to use on each table. Any small, low dish will suffice. If you use ice, be sure it is flaked, not cubed. Have a large butter bowl at the service station to save kitchen trips.

Tea pots should be interesting to look at. There are many to be found in retail stores. When choosing, be sure they are durable. Replace chipped pots and lids as soon as they are discovered.

Sugar holders and cream pitchers can usually be found in your china pattern. However, there are many possibilities in the retail stores. Most commercial ones look just that—commercial.

Individual salad bowls can be of wood if you like. However, the flat salad plate you have in your china is very acceptable.

If you want to use *baskets* for rolls or bread, there is nothing better than a wicker basket with a fresh napkin. Unfortunately, silver bread baskets are getting out of reach in cost.

Relish dishes or holders can be just about anything your imagination can dream up. Do not count on anything commercial; there just isn't anything imaginative available.

Use *ash trays* which are deep enough to adequately hold the lighted tip of the cigarette. Many a good tablecloth has been ruined because of burn holes. Ash trays do not have to be very large because they should be emptied or replaced frequently.

Flower holders are only necessary if you are using fresh flowers. A few fresh daisies or mums on a table can be quite pleasant. You may also want them elsewhere in the room. Do not use plastic flowers.

Small *espresso pots* are more useful than larger ones. Large pots are used infrequently and it is difficult to make a small amount of coffee in one. Once the coffee is brewed, the pot can be placed on the table on top of a small plate. Coffee may be poured into a full cup or a demi-tasse.

Salad dressing holders are necessary if you pass the salad dressings. If the salads are mixed with the dressing in the kitchen, you will not need the holders.

An *ice bowl* is necessary, because more ice may be needed in the water glass during the meal. It should be made of metal, glass, or china and be light in weight. Never pour warm water into a guest's glass without adding more ice.

Special table coffee pots are used to make coffee service more attractive. If you are happy with the usual glass coffee bowl, then use that.

Coffee warmers are just that—warmers. Don't expect to be able to brew coffee with one. They keep the coffee warm and are also helpful in keeping tea water hot. The temperature should never be allowed to reach the point where the liquid bubbles. This destroys the flavor of the coffee. If coffee remains on the warmer for more than fifteen or twenty minutes, it should be discarded. For most small restaurants, a two burner warmer is large enough.

Metal *escargot dishes* look the best. However, they are more expensive than ceramic ones. They do not break or chip and last for sometime so, the added cost may be justified. For individual service, a six hole dish is adequate. Buy real escargot forks. Do not try to get by with cocktail forks.

If you have about six *tableware holders*

between the dishroom and the dining room, this should be enough. When more silver or stainlessware is needed, just remove the old bin and replace it with a filled bin from the kitchen. Bins usually have four compartments, which is satisfactory.

Trays come in various sizes, shapes, and colors. They are made of metal or some form of plastic. Metal trays are quite noisy to use and look rather unsightly after they have been used for a while. Trays should be selected with care. There are many sizes to choose from, so select the ones that fit your purposes. Oval and rectangular trays are best for carrying entrees. When buying trays for this purpose, actually place the entree dishes on the tray to be sure to get the correct fit. Also, if you use plate covers, put these on over the plates before selecting the tray. If you do not, the tray may be too small. Be sure the trays have a cork or vinyl covering on the inside surface to prevent sliding. Round trays are used mostly for glasses and small items. The best sizes are eleven inch and fourteen inch. The most useful rectangular sizes are fourteen inch and eighteen inch. The best size oval tray is the one that fits your plates the best. When selecting colors, do not pick anything too light. Light colors always look soiled, even if they are not.

Cup-saver racks are rectangular plastic trays about 14" × 18" that hold twelve cups inverted. One tray can be placed on top of another. They save time, eliminate breakage, and reduce storage space. They can be filled in the kitchen and brought into the dining room with a minimum of effort and handling.

Wine buckets are no good without *stands*. A wine bucket should never be placed on the table. Consequently, without a stand there is no place to put the bucket. Do not use paper buckets. They do not last, look cheap and are hard to handle. Use metal or heavy, wood-grained plastic.

Candles should never be over ten inches

high, because they are impossible to see over or through. Save candle stubs for later use.

Placemats lend an informal touch. Usually, they are used at luncheon. Be sure the table tops are nice if placemats are used. Cloth mats look better but must be laundered. Paper mats are disposable. Whichever you use, be sure they are large enough to accommodate a glass, tableware, and an entree plate.

If you use *paper napkins* buy a good quality, soft, two or three ply napkin of ample size. Napkins come in various colors.

"Reserved" signs are made in metal or heavy paper. The metal ones last forever. Some restaurants prefer the paper ones because the guest's name can be written on them.

Telephone slips are a must so that messages are not missed. They can be used for reservations, as well as messages.

Uniforms are an essential part of a fine restaurant. They are discussed elsewhere.

Side towels should be provided for dining room personnel to be used in wiping up spills. If you do not provide towels, your expensive napkins will be used for this purpose. An inexpensive cloth towel can be purchased for this purpose. It should be a hard and fast rule that anyone using a napkin to clean up a spill (other than someone at the guest's table) will be charged for the napkin.

If you have a dress code, it is a good idea to have a few *neckties* and a *jacket* or two around for the guest who didn't know.

Requirements for Dining Room Chinaware, Tableware, and Glassware (Service for 50 persons)

Chinaware

Rim soup plates (if used)	3 dz.
Dinner plates	9 dz.
Salad and dessert plates (total)	15 dz.
Bread and butter plates	9 dz.
Cups	9 dz.
Saucers	9 dz.
Demi-tasses (if used), cup and saucers	3 dz.
Fruits (if used)	3 dz.
Service plates (if used)	5 dz.*
Tea pots	1 dz.*
Creamers	3 dz.
Sugar holders	3 dz.
Sauceboats (if used)	1 dz.*
Nappes, souffle, or ramekin desserts	6 dz.
Casseroles, oval (if used)	3 dz.
Casseroles, round (if used)	3 dz.

*Chinaware usually comes packed in three dozen lots. These items can be obtained in smaller quantities.

Tableware

Knives, dinner (serrated)	8 dz.
Knives, butter	8 dz.
Forks, dinner	8 dz.
Forks, salad and dessert (total)	12 dz.
Forks, cocktail (if used)	5 dz.
Spoons, tea	15 dz.
Spoons, bouillon (if used)	5 dz.
Spoons, iced tea	3 dz.
Spoons, dessert (can double for service)	3 dz.
Snail forks and tongs (if used)	1 dz. sets
Lobster crackers (if used)	1 dz.

Most tableware can be obtained in any quantity even though it is packed in three dozen lots.

Glassware

Water glass or goblet	9 dz.*
Special dessert (if used)**	9 dz.
Ash trays (if using glass)***	6 dz.

  *If stemware is used, order twelve dozen to allow for greater breakage.
 **Sometimes bar glassware may be used (e.g., stem champagne).
***Same ash tray can be used throughout restaurant.

Miscellaneous Items

Salt and pepper shakers (large openings)	1 set/table + extra
Water pitchers	6
Butter dishes (if used)	3 dz.
Salad bowls (if used)	6 dz.
Bread or roll baskets (if used)	3 dz.
Snail dishes (if used)	1 dz.
Pepper mills	2

Dining Room Linen Requirements

Purchasing table linens is one of the least troublesome tasks you will encounter in the restaurant business. All you need are table-cloths and napkins. To determine the amount to purchase, consider:

1. How many meals you will need the linens for. Will you be open for luncheon as well as dinner? How many days (and nights) will the restaurant be open? Are linens to be used at luncheon and dinner or only one of these meals each day?

2. How many times in a particular meal period will the tables turn over?

3. Besides table service, what other purpose will linens be used for?

4. How frequently will the laundry company deliver?

If you are open seven days a week, you will need more linen than if you are open five. Being open for luncheon and dinner will require more linen than only one meal will. The same is true if you use linens at two meals instead of just one. With a turnover of three times you must plan for more linen than with a turnover of only twice. On the other hand, some tables turn over more slowly than others (large tables turn over more slowly than deuces, for example), requiring less linen. If napkins are used as side cloths or there are extra side tables to be covered, you will need additional linens. Finally, if the laundry company delivers three or four times a week instead of two, linen turnover will be greater and less inventory will be needed.

Example

You expect to use linen at dinner only, six evenings a week. There are five tables of two, nine of four, and three of six for a total of sixty-four seats. You expect to turn the twos over three times in an evening and the other tables twice. The laundry will deliver clean linen on Tuesday, Thursday, and Saturday. You will be closed on Sunday. There are no extra uses for linen.

Worksheet

For each seating you will need:

5 small cloths
9 square cloths
3 large cloths
64 napkins

For each night you will need:

15 small cloths (5 × 3)
18 square cloths (9 × 2)
6 large cloths (3 × 2)
138 napkins (30 + 72 + 36)

If the laundry will be delivered every two days, you need to double the above amount. In addition, it is a good idea to have an extra day's linen on the shelf. Because there is no way to precisely predict how many guests you will have in an evening, it is a good practice to have an extra safety margin of 10 or 15 percent. Factor all this information into the above figures and you will have a good starting point from which to make your order.

Consider also other potential uses of linen in your establishment. It is better to over order slightly than to under order. Besides, business may be so good you will need those extra linens.

Suppose, after you get this all figured out, you find the cash outlay is more than you can afford? What do you do now? There are two alternatives: borrow the money if you can, or go to rental linens.

If you are looking for top quality and something other than the usual white or simple solid colors, do not expect to find it with a rental linen company. Unless you are extremely lucky, rented linen will be very unsatisfactory. If a local laundry will purchase the linen you would like and rent it to you, this could be a good deal. However, there are not many laundries that will do this and the cost may be prohibitive.

One distinct advantage to renting is the limited liability involved. Unless things would really get out of hand, you would not have to concern yourself with loss or damage to the linen.

Unfortunately, I cannot recommend renting over purchasing. The only control you have over the quality is to threaten to go to a new laundry. This works only as long as there are new laundries to go to. Even then, you cannot be sure a new laundry service will be any better.

Regardless of whether you purchase or rent linens, choose the best laundry possible. This is especially important if the linens are your own. Look for a company that does not use an excessive amount of chemicals in the wash process. Chemicals can substantially reduce the life of the linen. In addition, the proper ironing is extremely important. If a tablecloth is ironed incorrectly only a few times, it will be ruined. Both tablecloths and napkins must be ironed squarely, with ends meeting, or else they will become misshapen. When this happens, the cloths will not hang correctly and the napkins will not fold neatly.

A good laundry company will also add starch to the linen as it is needed. This becomes necessary as the linen loses its original firmness. If it is not added, the linens become limp and no longer enhance a dining room's appearance.

Because first impressions are so meaningful in a restaurant, table linens are of the utmost importance. The first things seen by the guests as they sit down are the glassware, tableware, and linen. The pleasant impact of sparkling glasses and tableware can be downgraded significantly if the linens are spotted, improperly ironed, or otherwise poorly presented.

Proper selection is important when purchasing linens. Do not purchase anything that is not specially made for commercial use. The simple home fabric will not hold up in a professional laundry. It was never meant to be washed two or three times a week, fifty-two weeks a year.

The fabric can be anything from the finest real linen to cotton to a synthetic. There are also combinations of these. Which you choose may be influenced to some degree by cost. Pure linen is the most expensive. Pure cotton is next. Mixtures of cotton and synthetics are even less expensive. Pure synthetics are generally the least expensive.

If you are looking for that firm, crisp look, stay with linen or cotton. If this look is not important, use a combination of cotton and synthetic or all synthetic. The latter two fabrics require very little, if any, ironing—an advantage if you are planning to launder the linens yourself.

There are a multitude of colors, designs, and patterns to choose from. The primary consideration should be the chinaware. Plain china goes well with either plain or patterned linen. The only thing you need look for is color coordination. Chinaware with a design can only be used effectively on top of plain linen. A white plate with maroon bands, for example, will look great on a plain or solid tablecloth. It will go completely unnoticed on a cloth with a checkered pattern.

Solid, deep colors, although attractive, tend to fade with wear. This could be a problem if the tablecloths were a different color than the napkins, for example, or the napkins faded differently. Keep this in mind when making the color selection.

In addition to the above problem, solid, deep colors tend to show any foreign materials deposited on them in the laundry or on the table. For these reasons, pastel shades and patterns or designs are the best choices.

The next consideration when purchasing linen is the proper size for each table. If all the tables are the same size, your job is easy. In most situations, this will not be the case. Each different size table will require a different size cloth. For this reason, it is a good idea to limit the number of table sizes.

Tablecloths can be square, rectangular, or round. Napkins are square. Round tables usually take square tablecloths. Round tablecloths are quite expensive because of the waste in cutting.

The most useful napkin is approximately 20″ × 20″ in size.

The most common sizes of stock tablecloths are:

45″ × 45″	45″ × 54″
54″ × 54″	54″ × 63″
63″ × 63″	63″ × 72″
72″ × 72″	
82″ × 82″	

Tablecloths, except rounds, which hang in an irregular pattern, should hang approximately twelve inches from the top of the table. However, they should not hang below the chair seat top or inconvenience the guest as he or she is seated. A thirty inch table will require a fifty-four inch cloth. A forty inch table will require a sixty-four inch cloth. Tablecloths may be specially made for rectangular tables if you cannot find the size you need in stock.

Banquet cloths are irregular sizes and shapes and must be specially chosen for your needs. Except for the head table (which hangs to the floor, in the front), banquet cloths have the same twelve inch drop as regular tables do. Buffet cloths hang to the floor.

When ordering linen, specify that it is to be preshrunk. Also, make sure that measurements reflect after hemming size. If they do not, the company should inform you of the actual size.

Linen should be stored on flat shelves that are deep enough to accommodate it without folding, bending, or crushing. The shelves should be labeled to save time when a cloth is needed. It is annoying to unfold the incorrect tablecloth when you are in a hurry to reset a table. Invariably, this cloth ends up unused in the soiled linen hamper, because a person did not want to take time to refold it.

Finally, decide if undercloths or underpads are to be used on the tables. The same cloths are used as both undercloths and top cloths. The top cloth is changed as each table is reset. The undercloth is never removed during the meal (unless it is inadvertently soiled). If an undercloth remains in good condition, it can be used over and over again. Of course, the use of undercloths will necessitate a larger linen supply.

Underpads are used in the same manner as cloths are. Underpads are made of foam rubber or a heavy fabric and are sized to exactly fit the table top.

Undercloths and pads reduce the noise of china and glassware, as it is placed on the table and provides a softer feeling to the table setting. In addition, they eliminate the starkness a bare table presents when it is without a table covering. In some restaurants, both a pad and a cloth are used.

When dining room tables are set with tablecloths, at no time should a bare table top be seen, regardless of how good a condition it is in.

Purchasing linens for a fifty-seat restaurant will cost, at the present time, between $2000 and $2500 on average. This is no small investment. Consequently, it is important that you instruct your employees in proper and careful handling. Here are a few ways to increase the life of the linens:

1. Store them properly.
2. Provide a hamper for soiled linens.
3. Never allow wet linen to be put in the hamper unless it is to be laundered within twenty-four hours.
4. Never throw wet linen in a corner somewhere and forget about it. Mildew develops and the stains cannot be removed.
5. Do not allow personnel to use napkins or tablecloths for wiping up spills. Stains

obtained this way frequently cannot be removed from the fabric.

6. Be sure all paper is removed from linen before it is placed in the hamper. When paper goes through the laundering process, it shreds. These bits sometimes adhere to the linen surface and look very unsightly.

When you send soiled linen to the laundry, have someone count it first. When doing this, you may discover tableware which has been accidently left in the tablecloth. This linen should be counted again when it is returned. This assures you that your linen is not getting lost and that you are being properly charged.

With proper care, an initial linen order should last two to three years, depending on the number of meals at which it is used. The higher figure would be for a restaurant that served dinner five or six nights a week. Length of use may vary somewhat, depending on the quality of the material.

Whether linen is purchased or rented, laundering is not an inexpensive item. Three ways you can cut the laundry expenses are:

1. Use place mats at luncheon. They can be paper (if you can find satisfactory ones) or fabric. Fabric placemats can be easily washed in a home washer.
2. Paper napkins can be used at luncheon. These should be no less than 16" × 16" and at least two-ply, preferably three-ply for a more pleasant effect.
3. Do not let the laundry fold the napkins. Doing it yourself can save from one to three cents per napkin.

Selecting your linens carefully and caring for them properly will pay off in appearance and added life.

The preceding lists and information regarding dining room furnishings will help you in purchasing the needed items. However, do not lose sight of the fact that every restaurant should have its own personality. Although the lists may guide you as to necessity and quantity, they cannot create an atmosphere or an impression. Only you can do this.

Public Area and Restrooms

Two other areas, which were briefly mentioned earlier, are the public areas and the rest rooms.

The public area is the area used as a waiting room or lounge. In very small restaurants, this may only consist of a coat rack and a chair or two. The following list includes all the items needed, not only in this area, but in the rest of the restaurant as well.

The items needed in the rest rooms are basic for either the men's or women's room. Both areas should be kept clean, neat, and in good repair.

Public Area

Clothes rack and hangers

Door mats, inside and outside (to protect carpet)

Emergency exit signs

Fire extinguishers, Type "A" (see Chapter Thirteen)

Cigarette urns (or the like), sand and strainer

Ash trays

Vacuum cleaner

Carpet sweeper (handy for quick clean-ups)

Dust mop

Broom

Dust pan, small broom (for minor accidents)

Water bucket and detergent

Window squeegee

Liquid cleaner for mirrors and windows, with spray bottle

Furniture polish and cloths

Dust cloths, cleaning cloths, sponges

Insect spray

Ice melting compound, snow shovel, scraper (in cold areas)

Emergency lighting

Restrooms

Plumbing: sink(s), water closet(s)

Metal stalls

Exhaust fan (separate switch from lights)

Lighting (overhead and/or side lights)

Entrance door(s)

Cigarette urn and/or ash trays

Refuse container

Soap or liquid soap dispenser and liquid soap

Cleaner for sinks, mirrors, counters, etc.

Bowl cleaner and mop or brush

Air freshener (not deodorizer)

Paper towels and dispenser

Toilet tissue and holder(s)

Tissues and dispenser box

Sanitary napkin bags

Mirror

Door signs to indicate men's and women's rooms

Clothes hooks (to hang jacket, pocketbook, or coat)

Attractive decorations

Washable floor covering and walls

Sinks and waterclosets come in any number of shapes, sizes, and colors. It should not be difficult to find what you need. Do not get into too elaborate colors which will hamper your decorating ideas in the future. Depending on the size of your restaurant, there should be two water closets in the women's room and one, plus a urinal, in the men's room. You would have to get very large to require anymore than this. Be sure to have water turnoffs for each piece of plumbing if you are redesigning or building new.

Metal stalls are only needed if you have more than one water closet. They are primarily for privacy. If your restroom can only accommodate one person at a time, there is no need for a stall.

An *exhaust fan* is a necessity. It should be on a separate switch from the lights. If not, it will remain on as long as the lights are on, which can be very expensive in terms of heating.

It is good to have at least one *overhead light* that is turned on at the entrance. If more *lighting* is needed, it can be in the form of overhead or side lights. Women prefer softer lighting than men do.

The door into the restroom should always swing in. This can prevent embarrassment, especially in the smaller rooms.

Ash trays are most desirable, but have a way of being broken or disappearing. For these reasons, and because there may not be room for them, use a *sand urn*. Be sure to keep the sand clean. This can be done with a small tea strainer to sift the sand.

Refuse containers should be as fire resistant as possible. More than once, lighted cigarettes have been thrown in with paper towels to cause a fire later on. For this reason, it should be mandatory to have these containers emptied at the end of each meal, especially at night.

Bowl cleaner should be used everyday in

the bowls and urinals. This is the only way to prevent odors. Deodorizers only mask odors, they do not stop them at the source.

Use a good grade *paper towel*. It is cheaper in the long run. Install the *towel cabinet* at elbow level, not at eye level. You will have fewer messy walls to clean up and the guest will appreciate it.

Mirrors should be placed over the sinks.

If restrooms are located in dead-end hallways (as they often are), the *women's room* should be first.

Clothes hooks are very helpful and should not be overlooked.

Restrooms should be immaculate at all times. You have probably heard the expression, "you can tell a restaurant by the condition of its restrooms." How true. Also, make the rooms as attractive as possible. A pleasant, waterproof wallpaper will cost a little more than paint but it will look a lot nicer and be easier to keep clean.

If employees use the restrooms because you have no other facilities, instruct them to help keep them tidy. Above all, tell them to be sure to wash their hands after using the restroom.

In order to be able to mop the *floors* each day, which must be done, they should be covered with a hard, non-porous surface. The least expensive is some sort of vinyl covering. This can be made of tiles or a solid piece. If possible, have ceramic tile walls installed from floor level to approximately four feet above it. This, again, makes cleaning a lot easier.

Service Staff

When choosing a staff consider:

1. The necessary jobs,
2. How many are needed and when,
3. Personal characteristics,
4. The restaurant's procedures,
5. Training,
6. Employee dress.

The jobs to be filled in any restaurant dining room are, with few exceptions, not related to its size. Every restaurant requires a room manager, waiters or waitresses, bus personnel, and bartenders. Large restaurants may employ a maitre d', service captains, and wine stewards because of their size. However, such positions are merely extensions of the basic staff.

The most important position in the room is the manager. This person may be called the host, hostess, or maitre d'. The name is not as important as the function. The manager will be responsible for greeting the guest, handling reservations, seating guests, distributing menus, supervising employees, taking orders (in some cases), opening and closing the room, scheduling, acting as a liaison between the kitchen and the dining room, and general guest satisfaction.

This position, if at all possible, should be filled by the owner. There is no one with a more genuine concern for the operation. This also presents the best opportunity the owner has to be on top of everything. Granted, it is difficult to be in the dining room, bar, and kitchen all at the same time, but the opportunity is there. If the owner is cooking, the opportunity to be in the dining room or bar is almost nonexistent.

If it is not possible for the owner to be in the dining room, then the manager must be hired with extreme care because of the enormous responsibilities.

The next positions to be filled are those of waiter, waitress, and bartender. Which you employ, male or female, depends more on availability than anything else. You want dependable people, regardless of their sex.

Bus personnel can also be either male or female. The work is not that difficult. What they are required to do will vary with the restaurant. Their primary duties are to clear and set tables, carry trays, keep the room supplied with china, glassware, etc. and generally assist the server.

In addition to a bus person, we had a modified position of coffee-boy or coffee-girl. The name was something we came up with. It didn't really limit their duties. This person was primarily responsible for water, butter, and rolls being on the table, both at the beginning of the meal and during it. In addition, they asked the guests if they wanted coffee or tea and were responsible for serving it. This extra service pleased the guest and lightened the work of the service person. We felt it important because it provided the extra little things which are often neglected in a busy restaurant.

By drawing up a tentative schedule, you will be able to determine how large a staff you need and when you will need it. This should be done long before you start hiring (see Chapter One). The basic requirements are:

1. A manager for each meal,
2. Approximately one waiter or waitress per twenty seats,
3. One busperson,
4. One coffeeperson (optional),
5. One bartender per approximately one hundred guests.

To make up a schedule, it is necessary to chart the days and/or nights the restaurant is open, the basic jobs to be filled, and the hours personnel are needed.

Illustration

The restaurant is open six nights (Monday to Saturday) from 6 P.M. to 9 P.M. on week nights; until 11 P.M. on Saturday. There are fifty seats.

SCHEDULE						
Position	Mon	Tue	Wed	Thur	Fri	Sat
Manager	x	x	x	x	x	x
Servers						
1	x	x	x	x	x	x
2	x	x	x	x	x	x
3	o	o	o	o	x	x
4	o	o	x	x	o	o
Busperson	o	o	o	o	x	x
Coffeeperson	x	x	x	x	x	x
Bartender	x	x	x	x	x	x

If the schedule in the figure were in actual use, the x's would be replaced by the actual hours the employee is scheduled to work.

On nights when the potential for heavy business is not likely, the staff can be cut back. This is noted in the chart (o). On these nights, the servers are cut back to two and the coffeeperson can do double duty on bussing if necessary.

Because you never really know how busy you will be in an evening, the tendency is to overstaff if you think there is any possibility of being busy. We had an arrangement which may be helpful to others.

To protect ourselves and to give our waitresses some advance notice, we kept a third waitress "on call" on the slow evenings. This meant, we would call her by 7 P.M. if we needed her that night. Many times, reservations came in late, so such a system worked well. The waitresses were able to get extra work and we did not have the problem of having to call all over town to find someone to work.

The final item to decide in scheduling

is whether the positions are to be filled by full-time, regular part-time, or fill-in part-time personnel. This is discussed in Chapter Four.

Dining room employees should have pleasant personalities because they are in direct contact with the guest. This is so important that I consider it the number one criterion for hiring this kind of employee. If a person does not know how to do a job, he or she can be shown and trained. If he or she has a negative attitude or unpleasant personality, you will have a difficult time trying to change it.

In addition to personality, dining room personnel should be satisfactory in other ways. They should be clean, neat, generally well groomed, and pleasing to look at.

Except for the bartender, past experience is not a crucial factor with dining room personnel. As a matter of fact, within reason, the less experience they have when you hire them, the better. Too much wrong experience can make a person more difficult to train. Basic skills however, are essential.

Once the staff size is decided (whether or not they are actually hired is not important) the restaurant procedures should be decided on. This is important because before the staff comes to work, training sessions are needed.

The first session (more if needed) should be devoted entirely to the food server. This is necessary so that servers are familiar with your special requirements. Do not just tell them what you expect, show them as well. Set up a table and provide everything necessary to complete your presentation. Make use of role playing. It relieves the tension and gives the employees a chance to get to know each other.

The next session should include the dining room employees, the bartender, and the kitchen preparation staff. This session should cover the general aims of the restaurant and be concentrated on the importance of coop-

eration between the individual departments. The chef, if you have one, should be given an opportunity to say how he or she wants to run the kitchen. If you are the chef, tell them how you will want to operate. If orders are not to get mixed up, such an explanation is essential.

This is an excellent time to explain the beverage and wine lists and the ordering procedures. In addition, this is the time to explain the pre-check system. Most employees are not familiar with it. A separate session may be scheduled at a later date for a more detailed explanation.

At all training sessions, substantial refreshments should be served after the session is completed. Again, this gives everyone (you included) a better opportunity to get to know one another.

The above procedures are necessary whether a new restaurant is started or one is acquired and operating. It might even be advantageous to close an existing operation down for a few days to retrain the employees.

Although the procedures mentioned may be considered formal training, the training does not end there. The dining room manager must be constantly alert to the way service personnel perform. It is a constant job of observing and correcting. If the manager is not effective in this regard, he (or she) is of little value to you.

Some method should be set up to train new employees as they join your organization. An abbreviated formal session and on the job training are the best means to accomplish this.

In general, guests should be treated in the following manner:

1. Greeted at the door, without being kept waiting,

2. Taken to their table or to the cocktail lounge (if so requested),

3. Have their cocktail order taken,

4. Have the menu placed in their hands (not simply dropped on table),

5. Be cheerfully greeted by service personnel,

6. Have their order taken quickly,

7. Have their order served quickly (unless otherwise requested),

8. Receive a final inquiry regarding further service,

9. Have the check presented,

10. Receive a friendly goodbye from all concerned.

The next subject, training, which has been stressed so often, is the key to a successful operation.

All new employees (and old ones, if you have inherited them from an existing restaurant) should be supplied with a pertinent job description before they start to work. Even though the dining room personnel will have had at least basic experience, they must be taught your method of operating. Once they have begun work, they should be supervised and reminded of the correct job method. Seldom does a new employee perform satisfactorily at first. For further discussion of this topic, see Chapter Four.

As mentioned earlier, first impressions go a long way in forming an opinion about a restaurant. If guests are turned off by the first people they see, they will more than likely be negatively influenced throughout the meal. If a favorable impression is to be created, it is necessary to have some uniformity of dress. This does not necessarily mean a formal uniform. Here are a few examples. For the waitress, a special jumper over a blouse and white shoes. For the waiter, a spe-

cial vest over a white shirt, a bow tie, black trousers, and black shoes. The busser may simply be dressed in a long sleeved white shirt, a bow tie, dark trousers or skirt and black shoes.

In the above examples, the jumper and vest would be chosen by the restaurant to provide uniformity. The remaining garments would be at the choice of the individual except where specific colors are prescribed.

To ensure absolute dress conformity, a restaurant can purchase uniforms or require the employee to purchase a certain style and color. The problem with you doing the purchasing is the unlimited expense involved. There is no certainty that each person you hire will fit the uniforms you have available. If they are of a different size, additional uniforms will have to be purchased for each new employee. Furthermore, if you purchase a uniform and the employee does not stay with you, you are left with still another uniform to store.

To help reduce the expense of purchasing uniforms, a number of cooperative plans can be worked out with employees. One such plan would be to have the employee pay a portion of the cost of the uniform. Another plan, which works well, is for you to pay for the purchase of one uniform for each employee after he or she has worked for six months. The employee would make the original purchase and you would reimburse him or her after the six month period. From then on, you would pay for the new replacement. The employee would have the option to purchase the uniform at a reduced rate when he or she leaves your employ. The theory behind this system is that if an employee stays six months, he or she will be a long time employee.

Uniforms can be purchased from local uniform shops and from national companies. There is usually a cash and/or a quantity discount available. Samples are available, from either source, in all styles and colors. A final selection should never be made without letting a few of the employees try the uniforms on. The well proportioned models found in catalogs are seldom found in restaurants.

Purchase uniforms that are easy to launder and maintain. In addition, be sure the material is proper for the temperature in which the employee will work. Colors and patterns should be colorfast so repeated washings do not produce fading to an appreciable degree.

If employees are allowed to wear their own clothes, they must be kept clean, pressed, and in good repair. Anything less will reflect badly on your operation. If you are interested in having a more formal guest-employee relationship, then uniforms should be worn. If you prefer a more casual manner, some other form of dress can be used. Whichever is chosen, the standards should be high.

Type of Service

It is important to establish the type of service to be used before you start your restaurant. There is no way to know the operation's personnel requirements unless this is determined beforehand. As a matter of fact, you cannot even decide on the menu to be used if the service requirements are not known.

First, you must decide whether table service, buffet service, or a combination of the two will be used. If table service is decided upon, it should then be designated as American, French, or Russian service. If buffet service is chosen, other considerations must be made.

Because buffets are becoming more and more popular, we will talk about them first.

Buffet Service

There is the somewhat erroneous opinion among operators that buffets are a means of making a great deal of money. With high volume, this may be true. However, a careful analysis should be made to determine if this is even partially true in your particular operation.

Consider the two main factors: raw food costs and labor costs.

It is true that dining room labor costs will be reduced with buffet service due to the reduction of the service staff. However, consider how much time will be spent in the kitchen preparing the buffet. An elaborate, interesting buffet could result in a good deal of extra work. Kitchen employees are more costly than dining room personnel. Thus, the money saved in the dining room may be offset by the increased payroll of the kitchen staff.

Consider also the food preparation for the buffet. A buffet, to be attractive, must offer a large variety, be plentiful, and present a fresh looking appearance. All the foregoing denote some degree of waste. Consequently, even if the guest were to eat less (per dollar) at a buffet, the waste factor could negate any savings you might realize on the amount consumed.

Finally, consider the cost of the special equipment needed to have a buffet. Attractive buffet settings are not inexpensive.

It is clear then that buffets may not be the money makers operators think they are. It is up to you to make a careful analysis of the costs involved before deciding on buffet service. If, after such an analysis, you determine the return is not great enough, you should forego the idea.

For those of you who decide to go ahead, I have listed below the items needed for buffet service. Where possible, I have indicated the amount of each item needed. In most cases, the amount will depend on the size of the buffet.

Items, such as chafing dish insets, can be interchanged with those used in the kitchen.

However, in practice, I have found this does not work well. Kitchen equipment does not get the tender loving care the buffet service should get. Consequently, it gets to look a little shabby. Buffet equipment should be stored carefully, away from everyday use. There is a big investment here. It deserves special care.

Buffet Equipment

Trays (at least 8)

Can be made of silver, pewter-like metal, glass, plastic, and stainless steel.

Have a variety of sizes and shapes. Round trays should be 13″–15″ diameter for most meats and cheeses. Other items may utilize smaller sizes. Rectangular trays of 18″ × 21″ are the most useful. You may need some smaller ones. Trays should never be so large they make the food on them look lost or unappetizing. Using a napkin on top of a tray can make even the most unsightly ones look good.

Chafing Dishes

Large dishes are 20″ × 12″. Small dishes are 10″ × 12″. In addition, there are round dishes of various sizes available. Inset pans can be 2½″ or 4″ deep. For most occasions, the 2½″ depth will be sufficient. Have at least one back-up pan for each pan on the table. Three back-ups would be better. Insets come in stainless steel or plastic.

Water pans are pans in which the insets fit. They hold the water which keeps the food hot. The size of this pan is determined by the size of the inset. It would be wise to purchase the deeper water pan (approx. 5″). It

can be used with either the 2½″ or the 4″ inset.

Covers are another item needed. They come in full or half sizes. The handles should be so constructed that they do not convey a great deal of heat when picked up. There should be a cover for every pan. Full size covers can be used over two half pans but two half covers are not efficient over a full size pan.

Heat can be provided by fuel or electricity. The problem with the electric dish is that a receptacle must be nearby or it cannot be used. Fuel type dishes are more versatile but are more expensive to operate. It is possible to get chafing dishes that utilize both electricity and fuel.

A petite marmite is a 6 or 8 quart metal or ceramic soup pot. In addition to being used for soups, it can be used for stews, creamed dishes, etc.

Platters

Platters are made of china, metal, glass, or plastic. They come in various sizes and shapes.

Bowls

Bowls come in various sizes and may be made of china, glass, plastic, or metal. Bowls are very helpful in adding contrasts to the buffet table. By intermingling different sizes and designs of bowls, an interesting table arrangement can be obtained. There should be at least one back-up bowl for each one on the table. Bowls may be on pedestals or sit flat on the table. Pedestal bowls give the added advantage of height. Sizes, such as 1½ quarts, 2½ quarts, and 4½ quarts, are useful for smaller presentations. The larger sizes, such as the 16 or 18 quart bowl, are useful for green salads and fruit.

Serving Utensils

Spoons

Tongs

Forks

Cake servers

Turners

Ladles

Linen

To make a buffet more attractive, one may use different colors, textures, materials. For example, pink linen could be used on Valentine's Day. In addition, it is possible to purchase skirts for the sides of tables. These not only provide interest but save laundry costs. They may be attached with clips, velcro or pinned. Skirts or cloths should hang to within two inches of the floor.

Miscellaneous Needs

Punch bowl and cups

Sneeze guards

Coffee urn

Cruets or decanters

Salad bar unit (ice or refrigerated)

Wedding cake knife (optional)

Flowers or other interesting centerpiece

Greens, such as fern between dishes and platters

Procedures in the Handling of Buffets

Use foods that do not dry out quickly over heat.

If you have someone carving, be prepared for the added labor cost.

Always have back-up food ready. If the service moves very fast, get one pan ready as the preceding one leaves the kitchen. Adjust according to the speed of serving.

Never dump food from one pan to another at the buffet. Simply remove the pan which is in the chafing dish and replace it with a fresh pan. Never remove the empty pan until the fresh pan is ready to be inserted. An empty, steaming chafing dish is not very attractive.

Always use clean napkins when transferring food from the kitchen to the buffet table.

Keep chafing dishes filled at all times. If business is slow, use smaller insets so that too much food is not kept out at one time.

Food should always be fresh. Some operators will not allow food to be kept in a room for more than twenty minutes before replacing it. By using smaller dishes, food can be replaced or refilled more frequently. The danger of contamination in a warm, smoky room can be very serious.

Do not allow spoons or other utensils to fall into the food. Tongs should not be allowed to rest atop the salads.

Keep an eye on the fuel containers. Replenish them as soon as they go out. Remember, they get *hot*. Be careful when removing them.

Gravy spills and other spots should be immediately wiped up. If the stain is unsightly, cover it with a napkin.

One person should be assigned to the buffet table to replenish food, china, etc. and to help the guests in any way possible. At a buffet dinner, the table is the most important aspect of the entire affair. If it is not kept 100 percent presentable, it indicates poor service.

The guest's table should be set with the needed tableware, linen, glassware, etc. If an item, such as a napkin, is to be left off the table, then it should be on the buffet.

When setting up the food arrangement, cold food is first, hot foot next, and, finally, desserts. If soup is served, it may be placed before the cold food or after it. Sometimes, desserts are served from a separate table. There should be plates for the salads (just in front of the salads) and dinner plates (next to the hot food). Soup cups should be in the immediate vicinity of the soup holder. If napkins and tableware are on the buffet table, they may be located after the hot food. This makes it easier for the guest to carry them. If pie or cake is served in its entirety, plates should be available for the slices (along with dessert forks).

When pans, platters, etc. are replaced, they should be replaced in the same location on the table, in the same manner in which they were removed. Be sure to replace the service utensil with a clean one.

Candles should never be used on a buffet table.

Tables do not have to be arranged in a straight line. For added interest they can be arranged in different shapes. Just be careful that the line is free flowing, easily accessible, and does not dead-end into a corner. Because the buffet is the focal point, try to locate it in the center of the room.

The use of special lighting, stands, flowers, greens, special linens, table skirts, and the like will enhance the buffet substantially. Specially decorated foods (e.g. hams, turkeys) and ice carvings always lend a special touch.

A buffet dinner (or luncheon) must be as beautiful and fresh looking as you can make it.

What Food Should Be Used. Do not attempt buffet service unless you can produce something which is different and of the highest quality. If you have the usual tossed salad, cole slaw, creamed chicken, barbecued spare ribs, jello and chocolate puddings, forget the whole idea. You will only attract those gluttons that want to fill their stomachs, regardless of how good it is. All you can do is lose money. Concentrate on high quality and items that are different. The cost will be more but the return will be greater.

How Much to Charge. Charge enough to cover all expenses, including everything mentioned earlier. If you cannot make the usual profit, a buffet is not worth doing. If the price must be so high you cannot attract customers, then you should not be featuring a buffet.

Frequency. Unless you are in a heavily populated area (large city), do not even consider having buffet service every night of the week. The attendance will be so light, you will get a great deal of waste (food and labor). To cut down the waste, you will make cuts in the buffet. When you cut down on the buffet, fewer people will come. You know what will happen next.

Buffets are most successful when they are something special. One restaurant, which had a buffet three nights a week, including Saturday night, had a mediocre response. They changed to having it only on Saturday nights. Now it is necessary to call weeks in advance for a reservation.

Light buffets, along with a menu, work well at luncheons. They appeal to those in a hurry and those who do not like to eat too much at lunch.

Service Staff. The first person required is a runner. This person's primary responsibility is to keep the table supplied with food. At not so busy times, he or she may also keep the table tidied up and replace used plates and tableware.

To save on labor, many restaurants eliminate this person and have someone from the kitchen do it. If the kitchen person is in usual work clothes (soiled), this practice is very detrimental to the presentation. If kitchen personnel are to be used, they must wear spotless clothing.

If you are quite busy and the runner cannot handle two jobs adequately, then an additional person (maybe more) should be stationed behind the table to assist the guests, keep the table neat, replace used plates and check the fuel under the chafing dishes.

A good server should be able to handle between twenty-five and thirty guests if the liquor and wine business is not too heavy. If it is, a cocktail server should be on the floor.

One busperson should be enough for the average small restaurant.

Service Procedures. The service procedure involves movement at the buffet table and the duties of the server at the guest's table.

Buffet serving lines traditionally move slowly. The more items on the table, the slower the movement. It is necessary to do whatever is possible to speed this movement. The obvious method is to reduce the number of items on the table. However, this defeats the purpose of a buffet and should be used only as a last resort.

There are two better solutions. The first is to have as many helpers behind the table as are needed. Assisting the guest with the food will make the line move faster. The second solution is to have more than one serving line. This can be accomplished by utilizing two separate buffets or by having a two-sided buffet table. The advantage of two serving lines is the ability to close one when it is no longer required.

Further modifications would be to have appetizers, salads, and desserts at separate tables, away from the main table.

The duties of the server are similar to those of regular table service. The basic differences are simpler service and the necessity of being alert to the need for removal and replacement of soiled china and tableware at the guest's table.

When the guest is seated, the cocktail order should be taken. Once cocktails are served, the wine list should be presented. This is different from regular service in that there is no choice of food and the meal begins as soon as the guest goes to the buffet table.

Once the first course is eaten, the guests will return to the buffet. While they are at the buffet, the soiled dishes and tableware they left behind should be removed. Water glasses should be refilled, necessary tableware should be replaced, and ash trays emptied. *Do not leave soiled tableware to be used again.* Replace it with clean pieces.

If the guest returns to the buffet again, the above procedure should be repeated.

When the guest returns to the buffet for dessert, the table should be cleared of everything but the water glass and teaspoon (just the same as in regular table service). In addition, if the beverage has not already been served, the order should be taken.

The server's duties at a buffet are easier in that he or she does not have to order and pickup food. However, he or she must be constantly alert to the guest's movements to and from the buffet table. This is necessary because of the added duty of picking up and replacing soiled dishes and tableware. In other aspects, the server's duties are much the same as they are in table service.

Table Service

By far the most common method of serving in restaurants is table service. Such service can range from outright disgraceful to absolutely elegant. The quality of service does not depend on the price one pays. Many expensive restaurants have poorly trained servers, while just as many lower priced restaurants have well trained personnel. It depends on management and how particular they are with their standards.

There are three types of service: American, French, and Russian. Except in the better restaurants, American service is the one used most frequently. In many restaurants, it may be only a fragment of its original self.

The basic difference between American and the other two types of service is that the food is portioned and put on plates in the kitchen. The waiter picks up the complete plate and serves it directly to the guest. With Russian service, the food is portioned and placed on large platters. It is then served by the waiter or waitress from this platter. In French service, the food is brought from the kitchen on platters and placed on warmers. The guest's plate is then portioned out at the waiter's station. Whereas the other two services require only one server, French service requires two.

For their convenience, many restaurants serve vegetables in side dishes, often called monkey dishes. Ostensibly, this system was invented to speed service from the kitchen. However, I suspect the real reason was the inability of the service and kitchen staffs to correctly match entrees with the vegetable choices. Whatever the origin, it is doubtless one of the biggest detriments to interesting food ever created. Vegetables are so colorful that, unless they are dripping in water, they can do nothing but enhance the appearance of the plate. It seems a mistake to put them off to the side. This is not truly American service.

Although the placement of the individual items on the table is different for each of the services, the items are basically the same. If fine china and glassware are used, the setting can be equally as attractive, regardless of the service used.

American service is mostly from the left (with beverages from the right), as is Russian. French service is predominately from the right.

Tray stands are a necessity for both American and Russian service. French service requires a cart equipped with rechaud dishes to keep the food and plates heated.

The advantages of the American style are the speed with which the service can be performed, the control of portion sizes, and the reduction of the need for highly skilled servers. French service, on the other hand, requires a high degree of skill, can result in wasted food, utilizes a great deal of labor, and is slower. Russian service fits somewhere in between and for this reason, it is more frequently found in today's finer restaurants.

Which of the services you choose is really up to you. If there is an abundance of labor available in your area and the waiters and waitresses can be trained to perform properly, you may want to consider French or Russian service. Unfortunately, there are few places in the United States in which such an abundance of labor is available. Consequently, you will probably find it necessary to use the American style of service. Although not as impressive as the French, it can be done very nicely by well trained personnel.

When American service is used, it is possible to garnish it with some ideas from the other styles. For example, a Chateaubriand for two is often found on menus today. Why not serve it Russian style? Casseroles are usually placed on the table for the guests to serve themselves. Wouldn't it be different to serve the casserole, along with the vegetables, from a side cart, similar to the manner in which it is done in French service? There are no limitations as to what can be done (except for the limitations of labor).

Whatever service or combination you choose, train your employees carefully. It will be noticed and appreciated.

Other Aspects of Service

When two people are talking about a restaurant, invariably the question, "how was the service?" is asked. The vast majority will answer with a vague, "very nice," "terrible," or "not bad." They really are not sure what they are relating to, but they are probably referring more to the speed of service than the quality of it. Most people in the United States are primarily interested in how fast they can eat. They have no idea what it is to enjoy a meal in leisurely fashion. Consequently, no discussion concerning service would be complete without considering a few of the things which make for faster service and will enhance the quality of the service as well.

Ways in which Servers Can Speed their Service

1. Check your tables for missing items before you begin.
2. Know and understand *everything* about the menu.
3. Have a system for taking orders and serving them.
4. Take orders carefully and accurately to avoid the wasted time and effort in correcting the mistake.
5. Keep service station filled with the items that may be needed. Refill before it is necessary.

6. Refrain from long conversations with guests.
7. Keep non-business conversation with fellow employees to a minimum.
8. Cooperate with other employees. Work as a team, not as individuals.
9. Present dessert menu before beverage is served. This gives guest time to look it over while you are getting beverage.
10. Present the check promptly. Also, pick it up for payment promptly.
11. Be well rested so you can be alert on the job.

Ways Servers Can Improve the Quality of their Service

1. Treat guests in a friendly, sincere, and interested manner.
2. Always check chairs for crumbs before a guest is seated.
3. Do not just take an order, sell the menu. Show an interest. Bigger checks result in bigger tips and a happy owner.
4. When you pick up your food in the kitchen, if it is not right, do not accept it.
5. Make every effort to serve cold food *cold* and hot food *hot*.
6. If it can be avoided, never reach across when serving. If you must, excuse yourself.
7. When food is served in a casserole, try to assist the guest in getting the food on his or her plate.
8. Learn to use a serving spoon and fork in case a guest needs assistance in serving. This is a particularly useful skill at a buffet.
9. Be alert to the needs of your guests. Do not make them ask for something—see it before they do.

10. The server who keeps water glasses filled and ash trays emptied will be remembered.
11. Pick up empty drink glasses as soon as possible. Do not let them stay on the table throughout the meal.
12. Serve wines using the proper procedures. This impresses the guest. Repour when the glass gets low. Do not think you job ends after the first glass is poured.
13. Stay in the dining room so you can be alert to the guest's needs.
14. Clear each cover completely before going on to the next.
15. Crumb the table after the entree dishes are cleared. This also makes a big impression.
16. Keep the tray stands empty of soiled dishes. Never scrape dishes in the dining room.
17. Keep beverages in the cup when serving, not in the saucer. If an accident happens, change the saucer.
18. Never assume on your own that a guest does not want a second drink, does not have time to see the dessert menu, or is not interested in an after-dinner drink.
19. Do not run in the dining room. It makes many guests nervous.
20. *Never* pick up glasses by placing your fingers inside the glass.
21. Keep your hands out of your hair and do not slouch.
22. Do not give a guest a bad time. If there is a problem, call the owner or manager.

The name of the game is satisfaction.

Next to the preparation of food, there is no more important element in a restaurant than the human factor. An employee who is well trained, informed, and considerate will have a lasting effect on anyone who eats in your restaurant.

Chapter Nine

The Menu: Your Best Seller

After food and service, the next most important element of a restaurant operation is the menu. There are many options to be considered before deciding upon a menu format. In the following discussion, we will treat:

1. Technical and structural details,
2. Type and size of menu,
3. Food,
4. Miscellaneous considerations.

The menu presents a list of your offerings to the guest in a descriptive, interesting, and stimulating manner. The menu is your calling card, introducing your products, and representing your image. A successful menu does not have to be fancy or elaborate.

Technical and Structural Details

Menus can be written on blackboards, printed, or presented orally. Blackboard menus are flexible, easy to prepare, and inexpensive. Unfortunately, they are not designed to do much in the way of selling. Oral menus are often difficult to follow and tend to intimidate the guest. Although more expensive to produce, the printed menu is the most satisfactory way to present your offerings.

If you find it necessary to use a blackboard or an oral presentation, consider the following information. A blackboard menu should be large enough to be easily seen from anywhere in the room. If the blackboard is hanging on a wall, place it so that it is easily seen. If this is not possible, either have more than one blackboard or bring the blackboard to the guest's table. The handwriting should be legible and the serviceperson should supplement the menu orally.

An oral menu should be relatively short, because it is difficult for guests to remember long lists of items. The recitation of the menu should be slow and distinct. If there is any doubt what an item is, the serviceperson should explain what the item contains and how it is prepared. The price of each item should be clearly stated. The tone of the recitation should never be bored or aloof, and the menu should be repeated if necessary

The Printed Menu

The structural elements of the printed menu are much the same as those of magazine or newspaper advertising. The layout, copy, typeface, size, and shape have to be considered.

You should not incur a large expense for menus until you are sure what you need. All your effort should be directed toward having a simple, effective, neat, and easily read and understood menu. You can do a lot with an attractive typeface, a colored stock, an unusual shape or size, and an effective layout. If you are inexperienced, it is worth the cost to obtain professional help in designing your menu.

Menus can be produced in a number of ways: printed on a letterpress, printed on an offset press, photocopied, mimeographed, or handwritten. Letterpress printing is the ultimate in quality, but it is expensive. Next in quality is offset printing, which is less expensive than letterpress. Photocopying is better than mimeographing but neither method produces the professional results of printing. Handwritten menus can be quite attractive. They are easy to produce, inexpensive, and informal. The writing must be legible.

Menus can be printed on paper, cards, or folders. Paper menus are usually insets in two-page folders. The inside of the folder may also be printed. The name of the restaurant should always be on the outside of the folder. Cards usually have a printed face and a blank back. Folders can be any number of pages, and copy can appear on the inside, outside, or on an inset. The stock should be fairly heavy. Folders can be simply folded, or

hinged, stapled, or tied. They are the most versatile and the most costly of all the types of menus. The cost of folders can be reduced by having the outside, which changes infrequently, printed in a large quantity and the inside printed as needed. For example, a thousand folders can be printed on the outside and a hundred printed on the inside each time they are needed. By doing this, the printing cost is reduced and you are able to make periodic changes when necessary.

It is never advisable to have a large quantity of menus printed at one time. The cost of printing is less, but when changes are necessary you have to discard the menus on hand and purchase new ones or make pencil corrections. Pencil corrections are almost as bad for your image as soiled menus.

A good layout and effective typography draw the reader's attention, but the selling is done by the copy. Menu copy should be large and clear enough to read. Spelling and grammar should be correct. Copy should be honest and accurate, and written with an eye to selling your food, without overembellishment.

Be consistent in your use of languages. English is the preferred language. If a foreign language is used, give explanations in English. Of course, there are certain sauces and dishes, such as Bordelaise, chasseur, coq au vin, Chateaubriand, and scampi, that should not be translated.

Selling with the Printed Menu

Some items always sell better than others, either because of quality, or because the guests are not stimulated to try new dishes. If the reason is quality you should speak to the kitchen staff. With a well written menu and an interested staff, even the items most frequently passed over in ordering, appetizers and desserts, should sell well.

Separate dessert menus are another

good merchandising technique. The service-person will find it easier to show the separate menu to the guest for dessert selection. By having a separate dessert menu or list, you can be sure the guest is aware of everything available. In addition, a bigger and more interesting dessert list can be used. Dessert selections should not be too lengthy. Better to have fewer, more delectable items than a large number of less appetizing ones.

If your restaurant is open for luncheon and dinner, two separate menus will be needed. If some items appear on both menus, be careful of the price structure. Guests may be annoyed to see the same item selling for more at dinner than at luncheon.

Clip-ons are often used to denote specials or specialties. They do effectively draw the attention of the reader to the special, but they are not as effective as oral selling. They tend to look sloppy and fall off the menu, and often catch on other menus in the stack. A better way to promote or sell an item might be to run a little contest among the service-people. The one who sells the most specials gets a bottle of wine, for example.

Table tents are another sales aid. These are usually more permanent than clip-ons. Because of this, they tend to get messy, folded, mutilated, written on, and pushed onto the floor. In addition, they detract from the table setting and are one more thing to move when tables are reset.

It is not unusual for guests to ask for menus to take with them. Because of this advertising potential, you should have your name, address, telephone number, and hours of operation printed on the menu.

Type and Size of Menu

Menus can be categorized as table d'hôte, (prix fixe), a la carte, special, cyclical, daily, set, or seasonal. With a table d'hôte menu, the price for the complete meal is fixed. With an a la carte menu each course is charged for separately. Some restaurants offer both types of menus.

The table d'hôte menu gives the restaurant a better chance to show its capabilities by balancing the menu. With an a la carte menu there is always a chance that the guest will choose combinations that do not mix well, which could reflect on the restaurant. Prix fixe menus appear more expensive than a la carte. In fact, however, a guest may end up spending far more for an a la carte meal. In general, an a la carte menu is more profitable for the house.

Be certain everything listed on your menu is available at all times. Do not put seasonal items on an a la carte menu unless you are changing the menu on a seasonal basis. Seasonal menus capitalize on food that is readily and cheaply available during particular times of the year.

Menus can be changed daily, remain the same (set), or may be cyclical. Daily menus are advantageous when your chef has an abundance of ideas. Set menus are used over a period of time. You should change at least a portion of the menu every three or four months, depending on the number and popularity of items and how many repeat customers you have. The less popular items can be removed and replaced with new items when a change is made. Specials can be used to supplement a set menu.

To set up a cyclical system, prepare a series of menus. Number and use them in order. After the last menu in the series is used, number one is repeated. Such menus can be changed daily or weekly.

Cycle menus have many advantages. Once they are made up, you can go for a long time without changing them because of the variety they offer. They are balanced in that the same items do not reappear. It is possible to advance order the necessary food. The printed menu can be reused each time that particular number reappears in the cycle.

Setting the cycle up the first time does involve a great deal of time and effort, but the time saved later on easily offsets this effort. Be careful to use an odd number of items or menus to prevent the same item from always appearing on the same day of the week.

You must decide the number of items to have on the menu taking the kitchen size, the available equipment, the size of the staff, type of menu, style of food, type of service, seating capacity, and operating hours into consideration. In addition, keep in mind that it is far better to have a few really great items on a menu than a number of poor ones and that the longer the menu the larger the inventory. Large inventories are not recommended for small restaurants.

Food, Philosophy, and the Menu

The three most important factors in food presentation are quality, taste, and eye appeal. If any one of these is missing, the others can be overshadowed. Before deciding what to serve, consider these questions:

What kind of food do you want in your restaurant? Will it be plain, down to earth, fancy, foreign, natural, ethnic?

Who will prepare it?

Is the preparer qualified to do what you expect of him or her?

Are the basics for your preparation available all year around?

Are you in an area in which it is possible to obtain deliveries of quality products throughout the year?

Can the menu be designed around your style of preparation?

Is there someone in your organization who really knows what the guest wants?

Is everyone dedicated to turning out the finest, not only through their own knowledge, but by researching and testing?

Are you prepared to accept criticism?

Not until all these questions can be answered satisfactorily, will you have food you can be proud of.

Many times, we do things to the best of our ability but unknowingly, our ability is not sufficient. We are successful by our own standards but the peak is really far above us. This is a frequent occurrence in restaurants. Not until we are sure our preparation is the epitome of its kind, can we consider ourselves really successful.

When a plate leaves your kitchen it should look like a picture. For this reason, vegetables should be served on the plate instead of in side dishes. Colorful vegetables should be used to enhance the appearance of the plate.

A la carte items may or may not include vegetables with the entree. If they are included, it has been my experience that guests do not really want to bother selecting vegetables. They are happy to accept whatever they are given, providing the vegetables are tasty and well prepared. If vegetables are not part of the entree price, then they must be listed on the menu. The server should mention them as well, in case the guest has overlooked them.

Although table d'hôte menus include vegetables, if a selection is offered, they too should be listed. Whether the menu is a la carte or table d'hôte, the selection should be limited to no more than five or six.

Salads also have great eye appeal. Because they are not included with the entree on most a la carte menus, they offer an excellent opportunity to boost the average check. Today, people are more conscious of what they eat and, as a result, are more apt to order a salad when the serviceperson suggests one. You should have several choices available. The green salad is still the number one seller and should be available with four or five different dressing choices, one of which should be a special house dressing. Such salads are best when the dressing is mixed in before serving it to the guest. This is also more convenient for the guest. Green salads must be very fresh and made up of at least three varieties of greens. Other popular salads are caesar salad and spinach salad. Gelatin, molded salads, and cole slaw are also popular with certain dishes. If your menu is table d'hôte, or the salad is included with the a la carte entree, you do not need anything more than a house salad. Other salads may be offered at an additional charge. Salad bars, which now appear so often, have no place in a fine restaurant.

Desserts should be so scrumptious that a guest cannot say no. A dessert tray is a wonderful visual aid for selling desserts. Also consider after dinner drinks, such as Irish coffee and brandy Alexanders, (made with ice cream) for the dessert list.

Adequate variety is important to any menu. It enables you to:

1. Make the menu more interesting,
2. Balance food categories and flavors,
3. Control waste.

The basic entree menu should contain beef, chicken, and seafood. At luncheon, this could be supplemented with an egg dish or a vegetarian item. At dinner, veal and pasta may be additional selections. Once the basic requirements are fulfilled, additional variety can be added with lamb, pork, or variety meats, or you may double or triple the basic entrees.

Take care to balance flavors, textures, colors, and nutrients. Balance strong flavored vegetables with milder ones. If only one vegetable is used, choose one that is acceptable to almost everyone. Attention should be given to the number of carbohydrates on the menu. Do not have such items as potatoes, rice, lima beans, and corn on the same menu, unless they are equally offset with non-carbohydrate foods.

Too much variety can be expensive in terms of food cost. It is always a challenge to give the guest variety without having slow moving items end up in the garbage pail.

An example of how a complete item can be utilized is illustrated with the purchase of a beef tenderloin for the dinner menu. After trimming, the center cuts can be used for filet mignons, the next cutting can be used for tournedos or slices and the remaining meat can be used in such dishes as Beef a la deutsch, Chinese beef and peppers, or stroganoff. The chain can be ground and used as hamburger. Similar versatility can be obtained from other meat cuts such as veal legs and pork tenderloins. Many variations can be obtained from chicken breasts which can be cut up or left whole.

Obtaining variety from a particular cut of meat enables you to utilize it efficiently, provide a more varied menu, and reduce your inventory.

The final consideration in determining the items to appear on the menu is the preparation equipment and its capabilities. If too much preparation is concentrated on one piece of equipment, you may find that piece of equipment is not large enough to handle the load. This can seriously affect service. End preparation is usually completed by broiling, baking, frying, or sauteing. Try to arrange your menu so that you use a number of forms of final preparation.

Miscellaneous Considerations and the Menu

Pricing

We discussed in Chapter Six the way to determine the selling price for each item. Now we must decide how to price the entire menu.

Proper menu pricing can be crucial to a new restaurant. Too high prices will keep people away. Too low prices make it difficult to make the profit so badly needed in a new operation. Initially, it is better to keep prices a shade on the low side. Later, as volume increases and you are satisfied you have things running the way you want them, prices can be increased to a realistic level.

Start out slowly, until you are sure your operation is running smoothly. When you are completely satisfied you are giving your guests the best you have to offer, push your prices up to where they should be. There is nothing wrong with high prices, if you give value.

Technical Considerations of Pricing. First, decide the price range within which you would like to keep the menu. If you would like the a la carte dinner menu between $6.00 and $13.00, for example, then only consider items which can be prepared within this range. To arrive at the amount to allot to raw food cost, use the formula in Chapter Six.

If you do not have a one price menu, then you should have a range of prices. One or two should be high, one low, and four or five in the middle. A menu with less variety than this may be too limited. Depending on your operation, prices may be listed with the most expensive first or the least expensive first. A more interesting and logical manner is to list by the ingredients in the entree.

Prices are usually written to the nearest quarter. The less expensive items are sometimes written to the nearest nickel or dime. When setting prices, remember that no menu item should ever be priced below your cost.

Luncheon prices should be lower than dinner prices only if the cost of food and labor is less. Food cost can be reduced by using smaller portions at lunch. Salaries may be reduced if the service is not as involved at lunch as at dinner. If costs cannot be reduced, comparable products will be priced the same at luncheon as they are at dinner.

When setting up prices, leave yourself a little leeway. Set them a bit higher the first time they are listed to protect yourself against later cost increases. When menus are changed frequently, this is not necessary.

Menu Analysis

Even with all the forethought and effort put into the compilation of a menu, there is no sure way to know how successful it will be. Consequently, you must have some method of measuring results. Menu analysis is not at all difficult. It requires a few minutes of time after each meal and a few minutes more at the end of the week. The results are tabulated (see Figure 9-1) and analyzed and conclusions are drawn.

Once the form is made up, the necessary information is obtained either from the cash register printout or directly from the guest checks. Insert the number of each item sold in the proper box and total the daily column. This gives you a daily count of the number of persons served. At the end of the week, total all columns across and enter the results in the last column. This column is then totaled

Item	M	T	W	Th	F	S	S	9/20 Total	%
Beef Bur.	7	6	8	7	9	1.8		55	20.8
Tournedos	3	3	4	2	4	9		25	(9.5)
Sirloin St.	2	1	3	5	3	6		20	(7.6)
Chicken Mon.	5	7	9	6	7	12		46	17.4
Chicken Poet.	1	2	3	2	3	6		17	(6.4)
Shrimp	5	6	8	7	10	17		53	20.1
Crab	7	5	6	7	9	14		48	18.2
Totals	46	44	62	41	67	98		264	

Figure 9–1.   *Sample Menu Analysis Form*

to give you the number of meals served during that week. To determine the percentage of each item that is served during the week, divide the total of each item by the weekly meal total. Place this percentage next to each item on the list. Once the week is completed, you can tell at a glance which items are the most popular and which are least popular. Compare percentages, rather than numbers, for an accurate analysis.

Menu analysis serves two functions. First, it shows you how popular each item is. If an item sinks below a certain level, it should be removed from the menu and a new item should be substituted. Second, menu analysis helps you determine the approximate amount of food to prepare. If, for example, lamb curry usually comprises 14 percent of the total number of meals served and you expect about 125 persons for dinner then prepare approximately eighteen portions for that night.

Menu analysis keeps guests interested, because the menu is constantly updated and it provides accurate information to help you curtail waste in food production.

Chapter Ten

Setting Up the Beverage Department

It has always been my contention that excellent food is the most important element of any fine restaurant. However, good drinks and an adequate wine list are indispensable in a well-rounded, profitable operation. Some people will not frequent restaurants in which drinks are not served, so you should attempt to have some type of bar and wine service.

Once you decide to have a bar, you must choose between a public bar or service bar. The problem many people face is a lack of space. If there is too little room for a public bar, you may have to be satisfied with a service bar.

A service bar can be located anywhere that is convenient for the service personnel. It may even be in the kitchen. The bartender usually does not serve the drinks. The waiter or waitress will perform this function. Use the same controls as you would for a bar in the dining room. Details for arranging such a bar setup will be the same as the public bar, except for possible space limitations. The bar-tender will have the same duties: mixing drinks and dispensing wines. There must be some means of locking up when the bar is not in operation.

A public bar is usually located near the entrance to the restaurant. There are ways of screening off this area if it is really necessary. Of course, it is also possible to have a separate lounge. This is certainly most desirable if room is available.

Your bar must be attractive and fit in with the general decor. The basic considerations are:

1. Bar and bar area must be neat and un-cluttered. This area is seen directly by the guest.
2. There should be adequate room for glass storage.
3. In addition to the regular bottle display, have enough storage for a few extra bottles. Have bulk storage elsewhere.

4. Have adequate refrigeration under the bar or behind the bar. Provide enough for beer and wine bottles, juices, and fruit. The minimum size would be twelve to fourteen cubic feet. It should have provision for adequate, adjustable shelving.

5. If you are washing glasses at the bar, have a small, three-compartment sink.

6. Provide a work area for the bartender. This should include an ice bin, room for a few bottles, a speed rack, cutting board, and a garnish holder.

7. If cash is taken at the bar, have space for the register.

8. Save a little space for the service people to write their checks and and pick up their orders.

9. If guests will be sitting at the bar, have comfortable bar stools with backs, if possible.

10. If there is to be a lounge, make it as warm and informal as possible. Guests should be able to feel relaxed. If the bartender is servicing the tables, make them accessible to the bar so he or she can get to them quickly and easily.

11. If more than one person will be working behind the bar at one time, allow extra room.

12. Mixes are usually stored on the floor. You may want to consider shelving or a closet.

13. It is preferable to have a hard floor behind the bar, because it is easier to keep clean.

14. Wine racks for the storage of wine can usually be both utilitarian and attractive. Do not hide them.

15. Have enough lighting behind the bar for the bartender to see, but not so much as to make the equipment noticeable.

Utensils and Small Equipment

Blender
Ice crusher
Cutting board
Set of brushes for glass washing
Swing away holder for sugar and fruit
Speed rail or rack
Cocktail shakers
Ice scoops (never use hands)
Serrated knife
Small water pitchers
Funnel
Bottle opener
Wine bottle opener
Hand lemon squeezer
Strainer
Long handled spoons
Teaspoons
Colored plastic stirrers
Bar picks
Line whiskey glasses for measuring
Bottle pourers, different colors
Towel holder and towels

Food and Liquor Supplies

Superfine (verifine) sugar
Lemons
Limes
Lemon juice
Lime juice, fresh and Rose's
Oranges
Martini olives
Tiny onions
Maraschino cherries
Tomato juice
Egg whites

Angostura bitters

Grenadine

Lea & Perrins Worcestershire Sauce

Tabasco

Pepper mill

Salt shaker (filled)

Snack food

Heavy cream or ice cream

Always have lots of fresh, pure ice. Never use leftover ice, because it melts too fast and can ruin a good drink. Ice should be made from the freshest water, kept away from offensive odors, and protected so it is not contaminated by foreign matter.

Glassware

Good quality glassware can make a good drink seem better. Thick or unattractive glassware does just the opposite. Try to have a completely matching line. An inventory of glassware should include:

Hi-ball

Rocks or old-fashioned

Sour

Cocktail

Beer—not heavy mugs—glasses should be thin

Champagne saucers for special drinks

Sherry (at least 4 oz.)

Cordial or pony

Brandy snifters, large and medium sizes

Any glass needed for your own special drinks.

Be sure all glasses are washed clean. They must be spotless and sparkling. Wash them in the dishmachine or by hand. If the water is the proper temperature and the cor-

rect detergent is used, you will never have to towel them. Beer glasses must be washed with a special detergent or the beer will not form a head when poured. There are no such problems with other drinks.

There should be plenty of room to store glasses. Setting one within another is unsanitary and can result in breakage. Hanging racks can be used for glass storage.

Liquor Supply—Basic Items

Bar Liquor. This is what you pour when a guest does not specify a brand name. Do not use junk but on the other hand, you do not need premium brands. No one reorders a bad drink. When mixing sours, for example, use a stronger flavored liquor so it can be tasted. For bar liquor, you need a scotch, bourbon, blend, gin, vodka, rum, brandy, and sweet and dry vermouth.

Premium Liquor. These are brand name liquors that people often request. I recommend keeping only the *very* popular brands, unless you have a good customer that drinks only a particular brand. After awhile, you will develop a feel for this. If you are keeping your bar brands low in price, then you will charge extra for premium brands. Do not try to substitute. Most people can tell the difference.

Cordials. For run-of-the-mill cordials such as creme de menthe, and creme de cocoa, the one to get is the one you think tastes the best. Price is not a determinant. For other items, such as Benedictine and Grand Marnier, there is no substitute.

Brandies. There are three general categories of brandies: 1) plain 2) fruit, and 3) Cognac. Plain brandy is used in mixed drinks. Fruit brandies are almost always used in mixing.

Cognacs are always sipped to appreciate their fine flavor. Stock your bar accordingly. Certainly the cognac should be of the finest, but the other brandies can be of lesser quality.

Wines. Good dry and sweet sherries are musts. Always have a good quality sweet and dry vermouth at the bar. It can be used for cockails like the martini and Manhattan and can be drunk on the rocks. To buy a poor quality vermouth to save money is a false economy.

Aperitifs. Generally, you can limit a small bar to Dubonnet (dark and light). Lillet is sometimes popular, as is Campari.

Beer. Carry two or three of the most popular and one or two imported brands. You may also want to carry an ale.

There should be a price list made up for liquor or beer. Such a list is just as important as a menu or wine list.

Inventory and Storage

It is always a good idea to keep as small an inventory as practical, but try not to keep an inventory so tight that you run out of an item often. The bartender should always have an adequate reserve stock. Bulk storage should be under lock and key. Each night when the bartender leaves, he should give you a list of what is needed for the next day. Fill the request from your storeroom. The storeroom should be dry and cool. You can probably keep the wine, beer, and soda in the same area. Some 2 × 4 uprights, some ½-inch mesh wire fencing, a door and some shelving will make quite a secure room at any location.

The important fact to remember is to keep your inventory at a workable level, no more. Money invested in inventory does not give you any return.

Bartender's Duties

The bartender's actions reflect the feelings of the owner. If the bartender is sloppy, grumpy, and disinterested, the guest feels the owner is as well. For this reason, it is necessary to set guidelines that must be followed.

1. Your appearance can be casual, if this is what is required, but it must always be neat. Barmen should be clean shaven (assuming they do not have beards). Hair should be no more than collar length. Barmen and women should be freshly bathed, free from odor, and wear no heavily scented perfumes or lotions. Barwomen should have their hair tied back if it is long. Uniforms should be fresh each day.
2. You should have a ready smile and a pleasant personality.
3. You are a salesperson. If the house has a specialty, recommend it.
4. Be on time.
5. Keep the bar area clean, neat, and tidy. In addition, keep it stocked properly. The bar should be kept dusted, as should bottles and anything else that adorns the bar. Is the liquor, beer, soda, and wine stock up to par? Are there ash trays on the bar and the tables or are they neatly stacked behind the bar keeping clean?
6. When you start your day, slice fruit, make your twists, fill your sugar container, fill the garnish containers, check your stock.
7. If the cash register is your responsibility, count the bank, check your change, make sure there is enough tape, etc.
8. Fill the ice bin.
9. When serving a guest be sure there is an ash tray and snack bowl, and a cock-

tail napkin under the drink. Do not forget to check back to see if something else may be desired.

10. Keep drinks fresh. Never use old garnishes. Always use a fresh glass for each round.

11. Fill the orders quickly, whether for the guest or for the service employee.

12. Do not make mistakes when filling orders. This is costly and embarrassing. Remember your orders by the glass and color of stirrer used. If you make a mistake, do not argue or make excuses, just correct it.

13. Keep the area as uncluttered as possible. Put things back when you are done with them. Clean up as much as possible after each order. Always clean out your shakers after each drink.

14. Make drinks with the same proportion of ingredients each time. Consistency will make your reputation. Measure each drink.

15. Stir drinks that should be stirred. Shake drinks that should be shaken.

16. Do not expect to know every drink a guest can come up with. Get a good recipe book. I recommend *Mr. Boston, Official Bartender's Guide*.

17. Use spotless glasses.

18. Always remember you work for the owner, not the guest. If you satisfy the owner, the guest will automatically be satisfied. If you have any suggestions, make them known. They may be helpful to everyone.

19. Speed is of the essence. Develop a system, so that you are able to fill orders quickly. Make it a point to know as much as you can about your job. This will make you more efficient and will have a definite effect on your tips.

How to Take and Serve an Order

1. Have a pencil and a decent size piece of paper. A small 3″ × 5″ pad is perfect.

2. Write all orders down. This acts as a double check in case you forget to charge a person. When the check is properly made out, throw the order sheet away.

3. To take an order use the same basic approach as you do when taking a food order.
   a. Greet the person.
   b. Get the order. I found the best approach was to say, "May I take your order?"
   c. Write the order. Be sure to write down all the details such as a twist of lemon, a dash of soda, etc. This is very important in having a satisfied guest.
   d. Be helpful. Sometimes a person needs a little help. Make suggestions.

4. Whether the bartender takes the order or the service person takes the order, the system is the same. Start with a certain person and go right around the group without skipping anyone. When you have the completed order, you start again with this person and serve the drinks in the correct order. People will be amazed at how you remember who gets which drink.

   Another system is to use identifying characteristics. There is always one thing that stands out about an individual. When you write the order, note this characteristic next to the drink the person ordered.

5. How do you tell one drink from another when they are all made and sitting on a tray? Purchase solid-colored, plastic

stir sticks. They come in a variety of colors. Designate a particular color for each category of whiskey. When the drink is mixed the correct colored stick is inserted in the drink and everyone knows what is going on. You may have to improvise once in awhile, but the system will prevent most problems.

6. Most places use cocktail napkins with drinks. If this is the case, place the napkin in front of the person and place the drink on top of it. (This is not necessary when serving at a table with a tablecloth.)

7. Check your table or bar for a clean ash tray and anything else that should be on it. Wait a few seconds to be sure all the drinks are satisfactory and then go on with your business.

8. Do not forget to check back when you see the drinks getting low. Too often, guests are just forgotten after they are served. Give your guests lots of attention. This is what they are paying for.

Mixing and Serving

Only good quality liquor should be used. The difference in cost between a bottle of poor whiskey and a bottle of good whiskey may be a dollar or so, which amounts to five to ten cents per drink. Establishing a reputation for good drinks is worth it.

With the fine quality frozen juices available today you would be foolish to squeeze your own. However, use only the most naturally flavored juice. Although, generally, the better juices will be higher priced, do not use price alone as a guide. Again, do not mix juice more than a day or so ahead. The flavor changes drastically as it gets older.

Adding an egg white to each thirty-ounce can of lemon juice will produce a nice, natural head on your sours. You may have to experiment to come up with the correct amount. If you mix by hand you will need more egg white than if you mix mechanically. Powdered mixes containing the egg white, along with the flavoring, are available. If fresh or frozen juices present a problem to you, powders should be considered.

Use fresh fruit each day for garnishing. Never cut up fruit to last for three or four days. If properly wrapped and stored, however, cut fruit will keep very nicely over one night.

Fresh fruit should be cut so the guests can squeeze it into their drinks if they like. Never cut it so thin it crumbles or so thick it looks bulky. Limes should be cut into eighths. Lemon twists should be cut about one half inch wide and about one and a half inches long. They should be cut from only the yellow skin. The white pith produces bitterness and off flavors. To do this, get a sharp knife. Starting at one end of the lemon, cut down toward the other end. You will end up with a strip about twice the length you need. Continue doing this around the entire lemon. Save the lemon for juice or for use in the kitchen. Both sliced fruit and twists can be kept very nicely if you cover them with a moistened cocktail napkin. This stops them from drying out. When storing overnight, leave the napkin on and tightly cover with plastic wrap.

Ingredients should be measured for two reasons: consistency of end product and cost control.

When I say measure, I do not mean the bartender should stand there and look like a druggist measuring a prescription. He or she should use reasonable care. The best way to ensure this is to buy the proper measuring devices. If the drink is to be an ounce and a half, purchase a shot glass that is one and five-eighths ounces to allow for a little space at the top to prevent spilling. There are also measured pourers and electronic devices. I find measured pourers too slow when you are rushed. The electronic devices are too expensive and impersonal for a small operator.

An example of measuring would be:

Whiskey Sour

1 jigger whiskey
½ jigger lemon juice
1 spoon sugar
½ scoop crushed ice

Drinks can be made in three basic ways:

1. Poured directly from the bottle,
2. Mixed,
3. Stirred.

The important point is that mixed drinks should be mixed and stirred drinks should be, just that, stirred. Too often, a cocktail such as a martini is stirred so much that it becomes a highball. It is so horribly diluted it has little recognizable flavor. In the case of drinks like sours which require shaking, I find an electric blender works well. Blenders are noisy, however, so yours must be located to minimize the disturbance.

Do not premix unless you know you will be using the premixed drinks within one day. Flavor and character deteriorate quickly as drinks get older. If you must premix for a large party, make less than you will need and finish up mixing to order.

Using the corrrect glass adds to the attractiveness of the drink. Certainly a brandy served in a large snifter is more attractive than one served in a shot glass. Garnish the drink well. Do not make it look gaudy, but do make it interesting.

Determining the Selling Price

It is essential that a drink, a bottle of wine, beer, or any other item, be sold at a price that will return you the profit you would like to receive. To calculate the selling price, first, decide on the size of drink you wish to serve. Divide the number of ounces in a bottle by the size of the drink.

$$\frac{32 \text{ oz.}}{1.5 \text{ oz.}} = 21.3 \text{ drinks/bottle}$$

For the sake of simplicity, we will say each 32 oz. bottle will contain 21 drinks.

Next, determine the cost of a particular whiskey. Assume it is $7.68 for a one quart bottle. Divide the cost of the bottle by the number of drinks in a bottle. This will give you the cost per drink.

$$\frac{\$7.68}{21 \text{ oz.}} = \$.3657$$

The formula for determining selling price is:

$$\frac{\text{Cost per Drink}}{\text{Liquor Cost Percentage}} = \text{Selling Price}$$

Round the selling price up to the nearest nickel.

If, on the other hand, you do not want to charge more than a certain price for a drink and you know what cost percentage you want, use this formula:

Required price × cost % = cost liquor should be

Example

You want to make a special house drink and want to keep the price at $1.50. You know you are operating on a 28 percent liquor percentage. How much should the drink cost to make?

$$1.50 \times 28\% = \$.42$$

Some operators charge the same price for all drinks in a certain category. The way we did it was to charge $1.25 for most cocktails. For liqueurs, which are generally more expensive, we charged $1.50. If, for instance, someone wanted a Brandy Alexander made with Courvoisier VSOP instead of our regular bar brandy, we charged an extra amount. We tried not to have too many special prices. This made ringing checks much simpler and, consequently, we had fewer mistakes.

At this point, you may be wondering what the liquor cost percentage is. The liquor cost percentage is based on $1.00 of sales. Whenever you are figuring percentages in the restaurant business, *sales* always represents 100 percent. This is more carefully explained in the chapter on financial analysis.

If $.28 of your sales dollar is what the liquor in a particular drink costs, then your cost percentage is 28 percent. What complicates the concept is that we are seldom dealing with such a figure as $1.00 or only one drink. Usually, we are dealing with more complicated figures such as:

Sales = $1,258.25
Liquor Cost = $ 352.75

What is our cost percentage?
By using the following formula, we can always come up with the answer:

$$\frac{\text{Cost}}{\text{Sales}} = \text{Cost Percentage}$$

Example

$$\frac{\$352.75}{\$1,258.25} = 28\%$$

Cost percentage is important, because it tells you how much out of every dollar you are spending for liquor. If your cost percentage is not what you think it should be, check some of these possibilities:

1. Purchase prices may be increasing and you have not been checking them,
2. The bartender may not be following the recipes or measuring the ingredients,
3. Your employees may be dishonest,
4. Could there be a flaw in your cash system? Is all the money received going into your cash deposit or someone else's?
5. Waste resulting from breakage or spilling may not have been taken into account.
6. Is the bartender inexperienced or not very careful? This can equal waste,
7. Out and out stealing.

Beverage Control

It is clear that you must have some means of control over your beverage department. Beverage control is only one aspect of the entire control system. It must ultimately be tied in with the controls on food, cash, and payroll.

Steps to a Complete Control System

1. Check prices and quantities of purchased items. This assures you that your cost/price calculations are correct. It also assures you that you have received what you paid for.
2. Immediately after it has been purchased, store the liquor properly. If someone did the purchasing and delivering for you, check as in step 1. Lock it up.

3. Issue liquor only by written requisition dated for future reference.

4. Let your bartender know she or he is responsible once the liquor has been turned over to her or him.

5. Assuming you have already determined the size of the drink and the selling price, keep an accurate record of sales for each meal or period of operation. This can only be done accurately with the aid of a register. Compare your sales with the amount of liquor used. This can be done on an educated guess basis or by utilizing the next step.

6. Take an inventory at least once a week. It can be done daily, if you suspect something is going on. The inventory can be taken by you or it can be taken by the bartender and you can spot check it. If you are suspicious, it is a good idea to mix these methods to check on honesty and accuracy.

7. Compute potential sales by multiplying the amount of each type of liquor sold by its selling price per drink. This should be very close to your actual sales. The sale of non-alcoholic drinks may throw this figure off slightly.

8. Figure your cost percentage. This should be less than a point in either direction from the percentage you have established. After a few such checks, if you find your cost percentage is in line, do it less frequently. Probably once a month will be sufficient. Don't announce the change beforehand however.

    Checking on a daily basis is very laborious and time consuming. I do not recommend it unless you suspect dishonesty. If you find dishonesty, be sure you have irrefutable proof.

Finding the Liquor Cost Percentage

Definitions

Purchases. In the case of a weekly or monthly inventory, the actual purchases you make from the dealer or store are considered purchases. These must be done during the period you are looking at. Do not add in any from the prior period or after the inventory was taken. Purchases, in this case, are related to your entire inventory of liquor. In the case of a daily inventory, purchases are what you add to the bar supply each day.

Credits. These would occur, for example, if a bottle was broken, *you* removed a bottle from inventory, or some liquor was used in cooking.

Closing Inventory. This is the inventory you (or the bartender) took. This figure should be in dollars and cents, not in number of drinks. Count the number of drinks left in each bottle and multiply it by the drink's cost. Some people like to count drinks by tenths. Some like to do it by quarters of the bottle. I prefer tenths because it is more accurate and it is easier to figure the cost (one tenth of $6.35 equals .63 or .64). Just do not mix up the two methods.

Opening Inventory. This is the same as the closing inventory for the previous period.

The Formulas

Purchases + Opening Inventory
− Closing Inventory − Credits
= Cost of Liquor Consumed

$$\frac{\text{Cost of Liquor Consumed}}{\text{Sales}} = \text{Cost Percentage}$$

Examples

Sales	$3,571.42	$142.85
Cost of Sales:		
Purchases	1,170.37	39.81
+ Opening Inv.	486.74	112.23
− Closing Inv.	(502.56)	(107.86)
− Credits	(4.82)	–
	$1,149.73	$ 44.18
Cost Percentage (Cost/Sales)	32.19%	30.92%

Wines

Wine sales are an excellent profitmaker for your restaurant because they require a minimum of labor to serve, inventories of the more popular wines can be turned over quickly, and wines require only minimal storage facilities.

Establishing and maintaining a good wine list will require a definite knowledge of wines by at least one person in the operation. An indepth study course in wines is essential, if you are to be at all knowledgeable. If this is not possible, the very least you should do is read about them as extensively as you can. Go to wine tastings if they are available. If not, purchase some wines and have your own tastings. There are a number of excellent books on wine available. Two very good ones are *Grossman's Guide to Wines and Spirits* by Harold J. Grossman and *Encyclopedia of Wines and Spirits* by Alexis Lichine.

Wines come under five general categories. They are appetizer, white and red table, dessert, and sparkling.

1. Appetizer wines are wines such as sherry, vermouth, Dubonnet, and Lillet. They are drunk before the meal. Some are dry and others are semi-dry. The alcoholic content is usually between 15 and 20 percent. Because of this, some monopoly states have special restrictions on the purchase and sale of these wines.

2. Red table wines are usually served with the meal. They come primarily from North America, France, Italy, or Spain.

3. White table wines are usually served with the meal. They come primarily from North America, France, Italy, Germany, or Spain.

4. Dessert wines are served either with or immediately after dessert. Some examples are Madeira, Porto, and sweet sherries. They also contain a high level of alcohol (about 20 percent) and may come under the same restrictions as the appetizer wines.

5. Sparkling wines may be served before, during, or after a meal. They come in varying degrees of dryness and for this reason they are quite versatile. Some examples are Champagne, sparkling burgundy, and Asti Spumanti.

Wine is still packaged in bottles, although there have been a few attempts with plastic. Some bottlers have eliminated the cork in favor of a screw top or plastic cork, but, by and large, wines are sealed with natural corks.

As a rule, you can tell the kind of wine

by the bottle. Certain wines use particular shape bottles. In addition, the color of the bottle can denote the type of wine. (See Figure 10–1.) For example, with French wines a dark bottle is used for red wines and a clear bottle is used for whites. Bordeaux are in one shape bottle and Burgundies are in another. In Germany, a brown bottle is used for a Rhine wine, while a green bottle is used for a Moselle.

Still wines are bottled in half bottles and bottles. The exact number of ounces can vary slightly depending on the wine. Sparkling wines usually come in splits, half bottles, bottles, and magnums.

With imported wines, the most important consideration in purchasing is the shipper. A reliable shipper will not put his name on a wine that is not of the best quality.

I can only present guidelines to aid you in the selection of wines for your list. Read your reference books and taste as many wines as possible to learn all you can. Check the local retail stores for an idea of what is popular at the moment. You will probably want a few of these on your list. Also, check some other restaurants in the area to see what they are carrying. Take note of their prices as well. This will give you some idea of how others price their wines.

Important Aspects of Selling Wine

1. Selection and wine list,
2. Pricing,
3. Storage,
4. Selling,
5. Presentation,
6. Glassware,
7. Opener and opening,
8. Service.

Figure 10–1.   Various Bottle Shapes and Tints (Art courtesy of Schieffelin & Co.)

Selection

It is not necessary to have an extensive wine list, but what you do have should be well chosen for quality and variety. A few wines from each category are sufficient. As your business grows, add to the list.

First, decide whether or not you want to restrict your list to American wines, imported wines, or a combination of both. Unless you have strong feelings for having only one or the other, a combination of both is by far the best. There are well liked wines in both groups. To eliminate one or the other would make some guests unhappy and also reduce sales. A satisfactory range of prices can be found among imported, as well as American wines. Although French wines are high, there are a number of good, sound regionals available at reasonable prices. In addition, there are wines such as a Muscadet, which are excellent values. Both Italian and German wines offer a nice price variety. There are many, quite passable, American wines at lower prices, in addition to the higher priced items. Furthermore, American wines come in large bottles and jugs, enabling you to carry a house wine, which can be sold by the glass at a lower price.

One purpose for carrying wine is to sell it for added income. It is better to sell a guest a half bottle at $3.50, than not sell to that guest at all. You should consider all the factors that encourage a guest to buy: price, bottle size, quality, and prestige name, before completing the wine list.

The following is suggested as a basic list. The French nomenclature is used in the most part. The American wines are inserted where they fit most appropriately. If you prefer, when making your list, they can be listed as a separate category.

For a list that combines American and imported wines, the following wines are suggested as a beginning.

Bordeaux—Red (St. Emilion, Medoc, one or two American)

—White (Graves, Sauterne, maybe one American)

Burgundy—Red (Beaujolais, Cote de Beaune, Chambertin, and one American)

—White (Chablis, Pouilly-Fuisse, one or two American.)

Rhone—(Chateauneuf du Pape)

Loire—(Muscadet, Vouvray, Pouilly Fume)

German—Rhine (Liebfraumilch)

—Moselle (Piesporter, Bernkastler)

Italian—(Valpolicella, Soave, Frascati, Verdicchio, maybe a good Chianti)

Rose—(Mateus, because it is one of the best sellers, also, one or two good American.)

Champagne—(One good import and two American, one very good, one less expensive.)

Sparkling Burgundy

In addition to these you may want to add a Chateau Latour or Chateau Margaux (Bordeaux), a Volnay, Nuits-St.-George or Pommard (red Burgundy), Macon, Meursault or Montrachet (white Burgundy), Bardolino (Italian), Tavel (rose), Asti Spumanti (sparkling), and other American wines.

Two or three months before you are ready to open, call the local distributors to see what is available. If you have some idea of what brands you want, have them bring samples. Better yet, ask them to set up a wine tasting. Most distributors are more than happy to do this because they would like you to carry their wines. When you have finished the tastings, decide which you would like on your list. It is a good idea to have others sampling the wine along with yourself to get a concensus. Never add a wine to your list without tasting it first.

Wine List

The two most important factors in selling wine are an informed salesperson and a neat, interesting wine list. Most wine companies will be only too happy to print a list for you at a nominal charge. Your obligation, of course, is to use some of their wines. Such an arrangement is beneficial to both parties. However, do not obligate yourself for wines you do not wish to carry. You would be better off paying full price for the lists elsewhere.

Wine lists can be simple. List the type of wine, the name or brand, the year, possibly the shipper, and the price. A short description of each wine's characteristics is not necessary, but does add a nice touch. If space is available, list each type of wine on a separate page. You can then provide a general description of the wine at the top or bottom of the page. Directly opposite the name of the wine, list the price. Note whether it is a full bottle or half bottle. (See Figure 10–2.)

Wine lists can be on cards, folded pages, or in book form. The book form is the most formal, but is preferred because you can replace a single page when a change is required. Such books are usually tied together with an attractive ribbon or string.

Wine lists need to be updated constantly. Never cross out or noticeably erase a price or a year. There are a number of satisfactory ways to make changes. First, you can have lists printed without the year or price and neatly write in the prices yourself. Second, you can have only the side of the list that does not contain changing information printed in large quantities. The other side can be printed as needed. Third, you can have only a small number of lists printed each time.

A method I have found very satisfactory is to use small, pre-gummed, peelable labels that match the color of the list. Type in the year or price and carefully affix the labels to your list in the appropriate place. For consistency, use the labels on the entire page.

You may wish to sell house wine by the glass or carafe. Carafes come in full or half sizes. You are able to sell this wine at a lower price, because it is purchased in bulk and poured into the glass or carafe at the bar by the bartender. Use a good quality wine and store it properly. At the present time, such companies as Gallo, Inglenook, and Paul Masson bottle excellent bulk wines.

There is a trend developing which I am not exactly in accord with. The intentions are good but the degree of customer satisfaction can be disastrous. I am speaking of the serving of fine imported (or American) wines by the glass, in the same manner as bulk wine.

Fine wines are very delicate. Once opened, they must be used or stored under optimum conditions. The chances of finding such conditions in most restaurants is remote, to say the least. Even then, within a day or so, the character of the wine will change considerably. Unless the bottle of wine is consumed very quickly, it is obvious the last glass will not be the same as the first. Other than the person who drinks the first glass(es), no one really benefits, least of all the operator.

Pricing

Pricing wines will probably be one of the easiest things you will do in the restaurant business. Once you set up the formula, the rest is simple. Look around at other restaurants

BORDEAUX RED

		BOTTLE $	HALF-BOTTLE $
CHATEAU TRIMOULET GRAND CRU St. Emilion	1967	7.50	
	1966		4.00
ST. EMILION Chauvenet	1967	6.50	3.50
CHATEAU LATOUR Haut Medoc	1964	24.00	
MEDOC Cantermerle Grand Cru	1967	14.00	
MEDOC Chauvenet	1967	6.50	
CABERNET SAUVIGNON Louis Martini	1968	6.00	

BORDEAUX RED WINES GENERALLY TERMED CLARET, OFFER
A VARIETY OF CHOICE SECOND TO NONE, FOR THEY RANGE
FROM LIGHT TO SUPERB FULLNESS OF BODY. THE CLASSI-
FIED GROWTHS ARE INCOMPARABLE IN DELICACY AND INDIV-
IDUAL CHARM. CLARETS ARE SPLENDID WITH ALL MEALS
WHERE MEAT OR FOWL IS SERVED.

Figure 10–2. A Page from a Wine List

and the retail stores that sell the most wines to get some idea of price levels. In addition to using a retail store as a price check, you can also determine the most popular wines by speaking to the operator. Prices charged in other restaurants are not necessarily the prices you should be using. However, they do serve as a guide.

You are in business to sell your products. This means you must price realistically. You can have the best wine list in town but if you are overpriced, few people will buy your wines. It is far better to price properly and sell as much as possible. We sold wine to 80 percent of our guests. Granted, this wasn't all due to pricing, but a great deal of it was.

The pricing formula I recommend is certainly not earth shattering, but it is effective.

Wines costing up to $5.00, mark up 2 times cost.

($3.75 cost = selling price $7.50)

Wines costing over $5.00, mark up by adding $5.00 to cost.

($6.50 cost = selling price $11.50).

This formula can be modified for very popular wines and sparkling wines. Generally speaking, you should be able to get an extra fifty cents to a dollar more for a wine that is very popular. Sparkling wines are generally ordered to celebrate a special occasion, such as a birthday or a wedding anniversary, so you can usually mark them up an additional dollar. Rounding off your determined price to the next highest quarter makes life a little easier for the service personnel.

A wine list that includes low, moderate, and higher priced wines in the most popular categories will help you make additional sales.

Storage

The ideal situation is to be able to buy the year's supply of white wines and, in a good year, more than that of red. You are then assured of a stable low price and you will only have to change your wine list once a year. Many times you are not able to get a vintage that can be used immediately, so you are forced to purchase ahead for the following years or put a wine that is too young on your list. This is a particular problem with very popular wines. You will have to decide whether it is wise to purchase wines that must be kept for a number of years until mature, or whether you are better off to purchase them at a later date. If you decide on the latter course of action, you should keep in mind that the price will have increased considerably and that the wine may no longer be available when you need it.

The three important factors to be considered in the storage of wines are temperature, light, and humidity. If you do not have the inclination, time, or money to build a special air conditioned wine room or enclosure, you will probably use the basement for storage. Because basements are dark, you won't have to worry about bright sunlight ruining the wine. If the temperature stays rather constant between 50° and 65° F, you are in business. Do not store wine in the same room as the heating or air conditioning system. Violent swings in temperature, even between the limits above, can really change the wine. High humidity can be damaging to wine labels and impart an odor to the cellar which can be picked up in the cork of the bottle and thus to the wine. However, a certain amount of humidity is desirable to keep corks moist.

You can build a satisfactory storage enclosure quite simply with wooden two-by-fours and some ½" or 1" wire mesh. The two-by-fours form the frame and the wire mesh becomes the walls. The open walls provide good ventilation and the two-by-fours help provide support for some shelving.

Wine bottles should be stored lying down to keep the corks from drying out. You could lay the wine cases on their sides and store the wines in them but cardboard wine boxes are not very durable and they cannot be stacked one on top of another. Wooden shelves are much more satisfactory. If the shelves are slanted slightly be sure to put an extra lip on the bottom so the bottles do not fall out. Flat shelves are quite satisfactory and are much simpler to make. To keep bottles from rolling, make a few wooden or cardboard wedges to place under the bottom bottles.

Unopened cases should be stored off the floor. Place the cases on two-by-fours to keep them dry. Be sure the cases are placed so the bottles are laying on their sides.

Keep an accurate running inventory of what you have in stock to make ordering easier and to keep track of which wines are moving the fastest. (See Figure 10–3.)

Generally, white wines and roses should be rotated carefully. Always be sure to use the oldest wines first. Red wines may or may not be rotated; it depends on the wine and whether or not you are "laying" it down. Beaujolais, for instance, would always be rotated.

Selling

Wine and after dinner drinks are two items that, as a rule, must be sold. People come to a restaurant to eat. Most of them will expect to have a drink. A small number will be planning to have a bottle of wine with dinner. Only a very few will expect to end the evening with a cordial. It is up to you to convince the ones having food and drink that they should have wine as well.

Examples of passive salesmanship are wine displays, wine lists on the table, table tents, and tables preset with wine glasses. Of the four, wine displays have the most merit *when* they are used in conjunction with a good wine selling program. Wine lists and table tents on the table are a lazy approach to suggesting wine. In addition, they get soiled and worn and they impede the resetting of tables. The worst one of the group is the presetting of the table with wine glasses. Consider that:

1. The glass may not be the correct one for the wine served.
2. It has to be removed if the guest does not order wine.
3. It has to be washed even if not used.
4. You are using subtle pressure in forcing someone to order wine.
5. Part of wine service is the showmanship. This is reduced when the glasses are on the table.
6. Most important, if the server does not ask the guest about wine, the glass looks silly on the table.

Really aggressive selling of any product turns people off completely. I think it is especially bad in a restaurant. A guest comes to relax, not to match wits with a waiter or waitress who is pushing aggressively.

For this reason, I developed a method for selling wine which does not offend the guest. Such a system not only produced a larger sales check but a larger tip for the serviceperson. Most importantly, the guest was happier because he received a little more attention than he expected.

Fall, 1968   WINE INVENTORY

RED BORDEAUX

Ch. Trimoulet	7.72	*(handwritten tally marks)*
Simmard St. Emilion	3.95	*(handwritten tally marks)*
St. Emilion, Johnston ½	—	*(handwritten tally marks)*
Chauvenet Medoc	2.70	*(handwritten tally marks)*
Ginestet	1.78	*(handwritten tally marks)*
Cantermerle		*(handwritten tally marks)*
Ch. Latour	26.58	*(handwritten tally marks)*
Martini, Cabernet Sauvignon	3.00	*(handwritten tally marks)*
Freemark " "	6.00	*(handwritten tally marks)*
Ch. Trimoulet ½	3.03 / 2.85	*(handwritten tally marks)*
Ch. Dissault	5.00	*(handwritten tally marks)*
Ch. Greysac	3.95	*(handwritten tally marks)*

WHITE BORDEAUX

Graves	2.00	*(handwritten tally marks)*
Wente Dry Semillon	2.20	*(handwritten tally marks)*
Ch. Oliver	3.50	

RED BURGUNDY

Beaujolais, LaChaize	3.50 / 3.25	*(handwritten tally marks)*
Beaujolais, " ½	1.90 / 1.82	*(handwritten tally marks)*
Cote de Beaune	3.20 / 4.00	*(handwritten tally marks)*
Latricieres-Chamber. '66		*(handwritten tally marks)*
" " '67	6.45	*(handwritten tally marks)*
Martini Pinot Noir	2.67	*(handwritten tally marks)*

WHITE BURGUNDY

Chablis, Bruck		*(handwritten tally marks)*
" " ½	2.90	*(handwritten tally marks)*
Chablis, H of B	5.12 / 4.24	*(handwritten tally marks)*
" " ½	2.68	*(handwritten tally marks)*
Pouilly Fuisse, Chauv.	6.10	*(handwritten tally marks)*
" " " ½	3.20	*(handwritten tally marks)*
Pouilly Fuisse, Sichel		*(handwritten tally marks)*
Pinot Chardonnay	6.00	*(handwritten tally marks)*

Figure 10–3. Wine Inventory Sheet

A Quick Course in Selling Wine

Would you refuse a pay increase of $5.00 to $10.00 a meal if it were offered to you? That's what you are doing when you don't suggest wine to your guests. Almost every bottle of wine sold will result in an extra tip of $1.00 or more . . . with very little effort on your part.

Follow the procedure outlined below and you will sell 75% of the people who are thinking about having wine, and 10 to 20% of those who weren't thinking about it. It is not a high pressure system, but a suggestion. It would take an extra 60 seconds of your time.

Wine Selling Procedure

1. Before taking the food order, be sure you have a wine list with you.
2. Take the order for food. Then . . .
3. Open up the wine list and say, "Would you like to see the wine list?" At the same time, place the wine list in front of the person who appears to be the host or hostess. It is essential that you say exactly the above and that you open the list and show it.
4. At this point, the guest will almost always take it and look at it. If they refuse, that's the end of it. If they accept the list, walk away to give them time to look it over carefully.
5. Return to the table and take the wine order. Be careful that you get the exact wine and bottle size ordered.
6. Go to the bar and pick up the proper bottle. It might be helpful to mention the color of the wine to speed its location.
7. Return to the table. Show the bottle of wine to the guest by holding the bottom of the bottle in the palm of the hand and the top of the bottle with the fingertips. Be sure the label is facing the customer.

No napkin is needed at this point. If the customer is happy, do the next step.

8. If the wine is a red wine, open it immediately and place it on the side table. If it is a white or rose wine, place the wine in an ice bucket. (If the wine was pre-chilled, place it on top of the ice.)
9. The cork must always be presented to the guest. As soon as the bottle is opened, place the cork in front of the guest just above the service plate. He or she will inspect it.
10. Get the wine glasses and place them to the right of the water glass. You are now finished until it is time to serve the wine.
11. When you serve your appetizer or soup, ask if they would like their wine then. If so, serve it. If not, it should be served *before* you bring in the entree . . . not after.
12. The proper procedure for pouring wine is:
    a. Pour a little in the glass of the person who ordered the wine. He or she will taste it.
    b. If the wine is approved, proceed to the person on the right and so on around the table, filling each glass about ⅔ full. (Never fill close to the top.)
    c. When pouring, it is a good idea to have a folded napkin in your other hand to catch the drip that sometimes falls from the end of the bottle.
    d. When you have finished pouring, give the bottle a half twist to prevent the drop from going on the tablecloth.
    e. Place the red wine bottle on the table in a convenient place. Place the white or rose wine bottle back in the bucket.
    f. The most important aspect of wine

selling is the service. *Do not forget to go back to the table and refill the glasses.*

This procedure applies to bottle sales. If you sell carafes, it is still a good idea to refill the wine glasses.

Most bottle sales will be at dinner. Therefore, you need not present the list at luncheon, but you should still suggest wine.

The actual opening of the wine bottle is done by the bartender. This may take time when he is busy mixing drinks. Opening the bottle is relatively simple.

a. Remove the foil around the top of the bottle by cutting it away with a knife, just at the small lip at top of bottle.
b. Wipe top of bottle with clean napkin.
c. Insert corkscrew with a few twists, being sure it is straight up and down. (This is extremely important).
d. When corkscrew has been properly started, twist in the rest of the screw part to the top of the cork.
e. You are now ready to pull the cork. How this is done depends on the type of the opener.

There is nothing offensive in this selling method. If the guest doesn't want the list, he will say so and nothing more is said. You have made the guest aware of one of your products in a subtle manner without being aggressive. You have eliminated the problems previously mentioned and increased your chances of a sale considerably.

Another aspect of selling wine, which cannot be overlooked, is having properly trained personnel. They must not only know how to serve wine, but must know what they are serving. The most important aspects of training are:

1. Memorization of the wine list, if possible. At the very least, they must know the color of every wine on the list. One of our waitresses had a good system. She always suggested the white, red, or rose she liked (and had tasted) when anyone asked her to recommend a wine. If a guest needed more information, she called me.
2. Set up wine tastings periodically so employees will have tasted every wine on your list (within reason).
3. Train them in selling and service according to the prescribed method I have outlined. Do not just hand them the instructions and expect them to do it. *Show them.*
4. Service people should be familiar with the proper glassware for each wine.
5. It is extremely important that salespeople know how to handle a bottle of wine (with reverence) from the presentation to the service.
6. Give instruction on the proper procedure for opening a bottle. Show them the correct method of using a corkscrew. Supply a corkscrew to each of them.

Incentives to sell are always helpful. The system we used was simple. We first estimated the maximum number of tables a salesperson would serve in an evening to be ten. We felt it was not unusual to sell wine to half this number. Arbitrarily, we said that if a service person sold more than six bottles in one evening, we would give a dollar for each one sold over six. In addition, the person selling the most bottles in the week got a five dollar prize. There was no differentiation between full or half bottles or as to the price of the wine. This system works well. If you use your own, be careful not to make it so easy that you lose money or so remunerative that the salespeople pressure the guests.

Selling any product can only be done well if you know the product. Train and instruct your people and they will be able to do a good job for you.

Presentation

The bottle should be clean and dry, with the label intact. It should be presented with the label facing the guest. Hold the bottle so it is resting in the palm of one hand and supported at the neck with the fingers of the other hand. Some will take it to look at it, others may not. This is a very important part of the service. It is better to have the guest accept or reject the bottle at this point before it is opened.

If all is well, the bottle is then opened (red wine) or placed in an ice bucket (white, rose, sparkling). The more popular whites and roses can be pre-chilled to save waiting time but the slower moving wines should not be. The wine bucket should only be half filled with ice. If the wine is pre-chilled, place it on top of the ice. If it has not been chilled, place it in the ice with a little water. A temperature of 40° to 50° F is an excellent temperature for drinking. The wine will take about twenty minutes to reach this temperature depending on the temperature beforehand, and the bottle size and thickness. Be sure to wipe the bottle dry when it is removed from the bucket.

Glassware

The wine glass should be both beautiful and functional. It should be beautiful to enhance the beauty of the wine and to draw the attention of others in the dining room who may also order wine. There are three basic wine glasses: 1) white, 2) red, and 3) sparkling. (See Figure 10–4.) There should be room in the glass to swirl the wine and develop its bou-

1. Champagne saucer
2. Champagne tulip
3. Traditional Rhine wine
4. All-purpose tulip
5. All-purpose wine taster's
6. White Burgundy and Bordeaux
7. Red Burgundy

Figure 10–4.   Basic Wine Glasses
(Art courtesy of Schieffelin & Co.)

quet. The glass should have a large bowl that is slightly tapered toward the top to concentrate the aromas. Wine glasses should always be clear and without coloring. Coloring hides the beauty of the wine.

It is not necessary for a restaurant to have a great number of different glasses. Two basic shapes are best. One glass can be used for still red, white, and rose wines and another, tulip shape glass, can be used for sparkling wines.

Opening the Bottle

The most important item in opening a bottle correctly is the opener. Openers range from the simple waiter's corkscrew to be the most exotic gas injecting type. (See Figure 10–5.) My preference, for speed and simplicity, is the waiter's corkscrew which consists of a screw, a knife blade or hook, and an anchor. The screw should be long enough to penetrate the cork completely, it should not have sharp edges, and the point should end in the center of the screw. All these things are important so that you do not break the cork as you extract it from the bottle.

The first step in opening the bottle is to cut the foil covering the cork. You will notice a small lip just below the top of the bottle. Press the knife blade against the side of the bottle at the top of this lip, and rotate it around the bottle. Hold the knife much the same way in which you would to peel a potato. The foil is removed in this manner so there is no possibility of the wine touching it when it is poured.

Next, take a clean napkin and wipe the top of the bottle. Gently insert the screw tip of the opener into the center of the cork. Make a few turns to get it started. Once started, turn it down until the tip has reached the bottom of the cork. This is usually when the spiral is completely covered by the cork. Be

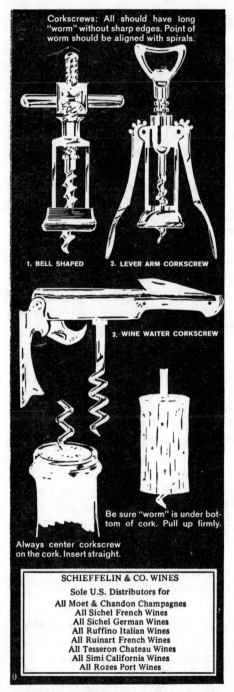

Figure 10–5.   Corkscrews
(Art courtesy of Schieffelin & Co.)

sure to keep the shaft completely perpendicular. Rest the end of the anchor on the top of the bottle. Now with upward pressure, and keeping the shaft exactly vertical, remove the cork. You will find that as you pull up, the anchor end will push downward. This gives you increased upward pressure and the cork will come out very quickly. Remove the cork from the opener and present it to the guest.

Hints for Opening A Wine Bottle

1. Always be sure the shaft is in a vertical position when pulling the cork. If it isn't, you may rip the cork (and leave half of it in the bottle) or you may not be able to obtain enough leverage to pull the cork completely out.
2. If you do not insert the screw deeply enough, the cork may break off, leaving a portion of the cork in the bottle. If this happens, carefully insert the screw back into the cork and ever so gently, pull.
3. If the corkscrew pulls out of a dry cork try reinserting the corkscrew back into the same hole and leaning it toward the side of the bottle. (This is what I told you not to do above). Sometimes, by getting the point under the end of the cork, you can force the cork out.
4. As a *last* resort, you can explain your misfortune to the guest. If she or he is agreeable, push the cork into the bottle and then carefully decant the wine. If you are so inclined, do not charge for the bottle. After all, you would have lost it anyway.
5. If you run into a stubborn cork, sometimes a sharp tap of the hand on the top of the opener (before pulling) will make it easier. If it is just a tight fit, the only thing that works is brute force.
6. As you get very good and fast, you may insert the screw too deeply, thereby having the sharp tip extend beyond the end of the cork. Sometimes, when you pull very quickly, you can gouge the skin between your thumb and forefinger with the tip. Be careful.
7. If you have trouble with the anchor slipping off the edge or holding the shaft in a vertical position, try wrapping your free hand near the top of the bottle. You can then hold the anchor in place and hold the bottle down at the same time.
8. It is *always* easier to pull the cork if the top of the bottle is lower than your elbow. You get much better leverage this way. Try to rest the bottle on something that is about thirty inches above the floor. Do not use your knee.

Opening a bottle of wine is really a very simple thing once you have mastered the technique. A waiter or waitress who does it well is a sight to behold.

Serving the Wine

We have now reached the final step in the selling of a bottle of wine . . . the serving.

The one question we haven't answered is, when to serve the wine? The wine is served whenever it is wanted. Some guests will like it in place of cocktails. Others will want it with the soup or appetizers. Still others will want it with the entree. The earlier it can be served, the better chance you have of selling another bottle (or ½ bottle). This is salesmanship. Remember, suggest, do not push.

Hold the bottle in your hand in such a way as not to obscure the label. In the other hand, have a clean napkin. Pour a small amount (two or three tablespoons full) into the glass of the person who ordered the wine. Let him or her taste it. They will indicate for you to proceed. Go to the next person on the right and so on around the table. If you must pour more glasses from a bottle than normal, tend to underpour. This way, you will not run out at the last person. Otherwise pour ½ to ⅔ full. Usually, you get about six glasses to a full bottle. As you finish pouring, give the bottle a twist as you lift it. This will eliminate that last drop going on the tablecloth. Touch the top of the bottle to the napkin to remove any wine that may be clinging there. This is the only use for the napkin. Do not wrap the bottle with it. When you have served everyone, place the bottle on the table (room temperature) or back on top of the ice. Repour when the glasses are low. This is all part of the service.

Wine service is an integral part of any fine restaurant. Whether it is simple or elaborate, it must be done correctly. This involves the selection, storage and pricing as well as the selling, presentation, and serving. Learn all you can about the wines of the world. Select the ones you think will be best for your restaurant. Train yourself and your people. Make your guests happy and increase your sales and profits.

Beer and Ale

Beer and ale can contribute to your profit picture. Aside from the cost of the product, there is only the expense of glassware and a small amount of labor. Beer and ale are easy and quick to serve and cannot be ruined by a bad bartender. Because guests are now drinking more of the higher priced beers and ales, expenses become a smaller portion of the selling price. Thus, the operator retains more on the profit side.

More and more people are beginning to realize what a fine accompaniment to certain foods beer is. It is particularly good with spicy foods, such as Indian curry, and robust and heavy foods, such as sirloin steaks.

Beer and ale are easy items to serve. There is no waiting for a drink to be mixed, nor is there any special ritual of service to be observed as there is with wine. All that is needed to serve beer or ale is a properly chilled glass. The glass is placed in front of the guest and the beverage is poured into it. When it is poured into the glass, a nice head should be formed. Be careful not to allow the beverage to run over the top of the glass or to make the head too high. When you are pouring, the bottle should not touch the glass. Always use a tray to carry the bottle and glass.

As with wine, beer and ale can be enjoyed most when drunk from a thin walled glass. Thick, heavy mugs not only detract from the enjoyment of beer and ale but also look out of place in a fine restaurant.

Do not place the glassware in the freezer to frost it. When the frost melts, the water runs into the beer and also makes the glass uncomfortable to hold. For similar reasons, glasses should not be run under cold water for cooling. There is nothing wrong, however, with chilling glasses in the refrigerator.

Be careful when washing the glassware that the detergent is designed to be used on beer and ale glasses. If it is not, beer and ale will not retain a head after pouring.

The temperature at which beer and ale are served is very important to the enjoyment of them. Ideally, the temperature should be 45° F for beer and 50° F for ale. Beer that is too cold will have little flavor. Keep a thermometer in the beer box, so the temperature can be checked periodically.

Bottled beer and ale are most popular in restaurants. Cans look commercial and certainly should not be a part of fine service. Throw-away bottles are preferred over returnables, because returnables tend to look shabby after they have been around for awhile.

A draft system is not recommended for a small restaurant. It is expensive to install, requires added space, and must be maintained. If draft beer is something you would like to have, consider mini-kegs that fit into a refrigerator.

Because beer and ale require expensive refrigeration space, which probably is limited, it is not wise to carry too large a variety. Five or six brands, in most cases, will be the limit. This can be divided among the most popular domestic and imported brands. If more space is available, by all means, stock whatever moves quickly. Because beer and ale are enjoyed more when fresh, you are better off stocking only the most popular brands to ensure fast turnover.

When space limitations are a factor, carry only premium brands and, maybe, a popular local beer. Most people are brand drinkers when it comes to beer, so a bar beer is not necessary.

The correct care and storage of both beer and ale are essential. Here are a few suggestions:

1. Try to keep a supply that lasts only two to three weeks. Beer and ale taste better when fresh.
2. Store cases in an area that has a relatively cool, constant temperature. Basements are ideal if the storage area is not near a furnace or too damp. Keep the storage away from direct sunlight.
3. Beer is best stored in the carton it comes in, which acts as an insulator.
4. Incorrect refrigeration or icing ruin beer and ale. Neither can tolerate changes in temperature very well. Repeated chilling and warming will eventually make beer and ale cloudy and change their flavor.
5. Be sure to sell the oldest beer and ale first. Sometimes bottles have a way of being pushed back and by-passed at the time of sale.

Beer and ale have a place in any operation. Service is simple and little extra space is required to stock them.

Chapter Eleven
Advertising

Unlike many other retail and service businesses, we, in the restaurant business, have the advantage that once our business is established, we can cut back on advertising and rely on word-of-mouth. Unfortunately, before word-of-mouth will work for you, you must establish your restaurant as one of the best. This is where formal advertising makes its contribution. Keep in mind, however, that word-of-mouth can also work against you.

There are three distinct phases in an advertising campaign. When you open, you use one phase. Once you are open and off to a good start you change your concept. Finally, after you are successful, a third approach is used. It is very important to set up your plan or campaign from the beginning so that you do not get sidetracked from your original goals.

Before we begin our discussion on advertising, I will give you a few definitions every businessperson should know.

Media The carriers or transmitters of your advertising, such as newspapers, radio, or televison, are called the media.

Copy The information you want to convey to your audience, when put in written form, is called the copy.

Layout The layout is a working drawing of the position in which you want to place the various elements (copy, illustrations) of your ad.

Logo A logo is your identifying symbol. It may be one of the most important elements of your advertising campaign, so a great deal of thought should go into its design.

Mat Papier mache mold into which type is cast.

Point A point is a unit of measurement used in typography. One inch is approximately equal to seventy-two points.

Agate line A unit of measurement used in newspaper work. An agate line is one column wide and approximately one-fourteenth of an inch deep.

You should not advertise without formulating an overall plan as to how much money will be spent and how it will be spent. The steps to follow in establishing a workable and practical plan are:

1. Decide on a budget.
2. Decide on the media to be used and the allotment of the budget to each.
3. Decide which media you will use initially, and which you will drop once you have passed the opening stage.
4. Determine what portion of the total budget will be devoted to opening advertising and what portion will go toward regular advertising.
5. Price each of the media and allot the proportionate share to the opening and regular programs.

The usual amount allotted to regular advertising expense is from 2 to 5 percent of projected sales. If you expect to do $50,000 in sales, you should allocate $1000 to $2500 for advertising. You may get tremendous response from your initial program and be able to cut these figures. On the other hand, you may get a poor response and the 5 percent may not be enough. Evaluate your program after six months. Do not be disappointed if the initial response is not what you expected. Continue your program, but re-examine it.

At the outset, in addition to the percentage of projected sales, you will have available whatever amount you set aside for advertising when you determined your opening expenses.

Once you start advertising, it is essential that you keep accurate records of the expenses involved. Copies of the ads should also be kept on file. As your popularity increases, you will be able to cut back on some of your advertising. In order to do this, you will have to know where you are getting the least results for your advertising dollar. From your records, you will also be able to determine if certain media costs have increased beyond your budget.

General Advertising Guidelines

1. Be honest. There is no faster way to alienate a new customer than to promise something you cannot produce.
2. Advertising can get new customers to your restaurant, but it cannot bring them back if your product is not first rate. Do not spend your money on advertising, if you have not perfected your product.
3. Frequency is more important than size in advertising. A number of small ads are more effective than one large one. A large, one-shot ad may impress the person seeing, reading, or hearing it, but what of all the others who missed it? In addition, you will be able to get frequency discounts from the media.
4. Study the advertising of others, especially restaurants of your calibre. Do not copy them, but do let them stimulate your creative ability.
5. Inject your personality and the personality of your restaurant into the adver-

tising. If you have a quiet and reserved place, show it in your ad. If yours is a fun place, reflect it in your ad.

6. Establish a central idea or theme for your advertising program. Follow it throughout. Again, you are creating an image. Use the same theme in all media. Give the theme a fair test. If you are sure it is not producing results, *then* consider changing.

7. Develop a logo and a slogan or phrase. Use them in all your advertising to give you an identity.

8. Take advantage of free advertising. Send press releases to the newspapers whenever anything important happens at your restaurant. Try to get the local newspaper, radio, or television company to do a story about you, one of your employees, or your restaurant. Visits by celebrities and important dinners are news. Well written news releases are often used when poor ones are not because newspapers do not want to take the time to rewrite items which are not significant.

9. Do not hesitate to use an advertising agency, if you can find one that will handle small accounts. The cost to you is very little, if anything. Agencies make most of their money from the media. They can save you a great deal of work, because advertising is their business. (See Figure 11–1.)

10. All advertising should contain your address, telephone number, and hours of operation. Also, tell them the days you are open if there is space or time. Depending on the media used, your name should be mentioned at least three times (beginning, middle and end). Don't forget to tell them what you do and how you do it. "A quiet, country inn dedi-

Figure 11–1.   *An ad prepared by William B. Kamp Co. for* Gourmet *magazine.*

cated to producing the finest international cuisine," is more descriptive than, "Gourmet Restaurant."

Using the Media

Newspapers

According to the National Restaurant Association, newspapers are used more than any other media for restaurant advertising. Newspapers can reach a large number of people at a minimum cost, can respond quickly to your needs, and require less preparation time than most other media.

To assemble a newspaper ad you must be concerned with:

1. copy (headline and body),
2. layout,
3. photographs or sketches.

The headline is particularly important if photos or sketches are not used in the ad, because it is the only means of drawing the attention of the reader to your ad. Look at a number of newspaper ads to see the different forms headlines take. It is not just the size of the type that makes an ad eye-catching. The words themselves are equally as important. Used in conjunction with photos and sketches, headlines can be even more effective.

The headline catches the eye, but the

copy catches the customer. Make the copy interesting and provocative. Describe your restaurant, the menu, the food, the service, and the atmosphere. Inundate the reader with good things. Make him want to act. Do not overembellish or exaggerate.

The layout is the relation of all the elements of the ad, including the headline(s), the copy and pictures. The layout of your ad must direct the reader's eye. This is called flow. Flow takes certain natural patterns, which are classified as Z (in which the eye reads from the top left and ends at the bottom right), C (in which the eye reads from the top right and ends at the bottom right), and S (in which the eye picks the upper right corner and meanders downward to the lower left corner). The headline, or some other immediate eye-catcher, placed at the beginning of the flow pattern will lead the eye into the copy naturally. Put your final message at the end of the flow pattern. Use your name or logo or maybe something like, "Call us for a reservation at. . . ." It is very important that the reader see a definite, readable pattern at first glance. Too many items fighting for attention confuse the mind and cause the reader to simply give up and go on to something more interesting.

Use white space to set off your ad. (See Figure 11–3.) A few choice words and/or a good sketch or picture on a large empty background can get more attention and results than a cluttered ad. When laying out your ad, remember that the optical center is not the center of the page. People look first at a point about one-third down the page and slightly to the right of center, so place something very important in this location. Of course, if you are using a flow pattern, this may not be of the same importance.

The style of type you use is also important. I prefer roman to italic. Vertically spelled words are hard to understand. Above all,

The Round Table

Main Street, Hanover

WE SPECIALIZE IN FLAMBE AT YOUR TABLE

FRENCH NIGHT
THURSDAY, OCT. 30th

BUFFET (All French) ● FRENCH MUSIC
Also HALLOWEEN PARTY
PRIZES FOR BEST COSTUMES

For Reservations Call 000-1234

Every Monday we serve Buffet
from 5 till closing — $9.95

HAPPY HOUR 3-6 PM — RAW BAR
PIANO BAR — REDUCED PRICES
Banquet Facilities up to 170 People.

OPEN DAILY TILL MIDNIGHT — SUN. 2 TILL 9 P.M.

NEW COLOR TV FOR YOUR FAVORITE SPORTS

P.S.   MAKE RESERVATIONS FOR YOUR
CHRISTMAS PARTY NOW

Figure 11–2. Example of a Newspaper Ad. This is a symmetrically balanced ad. The border is well done, and the name stands out clearly. But the ad as a whole is too cluttered with information. The address and telephone number are hidden and it is difficult to determine what kind of a restaurant it is. Ads of this nature should be clear and more limited in scope.

your typeface should be clear. If the letters are too small, they are difficult to read. In addition, small type does not always print clearly on newsprint. Use upper and lower case letters, not just capitals. (See Figure 11–4.)

Use the same typeface in all your ads. This will help make your ads distinctive and help create the image you are looking for. Consistency in your ads helps make them stand out.

Borders can be effective attention-getters. They cut down somewhat on the area available for copy, but this may be offset by

A perfect newspaper or magazine ad. It has everything . . . flow, white space, easy to read, informative and eye-catching.
Figure 11–3.

the fact that they set your ad apart from others on the page.

You should use a picture or sketch if space permits. A blurred or confusing photograph or sketch is of little value, and conveys a careless image. Glossy, black and white photos reproduce most successfully.

Using a picture or sketch will make the first appearance of the ad more expensive. This expense is reduced for each subsequent running of the same ad.

Keep single-column ads at least three inches long. Two-column ads should be at least two inches in length. Proportion becomes the dominant element when you get into large ads. A long, single-column ad will usually not be as effective as a two-column ad, half the length. (See Figure 11–5.)

Finally, after the layout and copy are completed and sent to the printer, get a *proof*. Be sure you get it on newsprint, so you will see it exactly as it will appear. This is extremely important, because ink tends to spread on newsprint, blurring type and illustrations. By looking at the proof, you will be able to determine if the ad will look as you expected. Do not be surprised at what you may see.

Now is the time to make any necessary changes.

Now that we have dealt with the mechanical and physical aspects of the advertisement, let us consider some of the other facets of newspaper advertising.

Logo, Slogan, Phrases. You must develop the best possible logo for your business. A logo is the ultimate eye-catcher and identifier. The key to the use of a good logo is repetition so that readers become familiar with it. The logo should be simple, descriptive, and eye-catching. Once you have a logo, you should use it whenever and wherever possible. It can be used on all promotional materials, including the menu, match covers, napkins, writing paper, and envelopes.

Some businesses adapt a slogan or phrase to be used along with the logo. I once managed a basement cafeteria. Our slogan was, "Where you step down to good food." I do not know how many came because of the phrase, but I can tell you people read it because they commented on it. To get some ideas look at magazines. Look especially at beer and liquor ads.

THE LEMON TREE

LANCASTER, PA.

Presents

AN IMAGINATIVE

THANKSGIVING DINNER

Served from Noon 'til 5 P.M.

Chesapeake Oyster Bisque   Fresh Mushroom Chowder
Coquille St. Jacques   Minted Fruit
Rock Cornish Game Hen, Bigarrade
Date-Nut Rice Stuffing
Duchess Potatoes
Honey Glazed Baby Onions & Belgium Carrots
Garden Peas & Baby Limas with Braized Celery
Mixed Greens, Lemon Tree
Hot Breads — Sweet Butter
Pecan-Cocoanut Pumpkin Tart   Cranberries Jubilee
Lemon Tree Sherbet, Cider Menthe Sauce
Salted Almonds   Fresh Fruit Basket
Beverage

$6.00 adults $4.00 children

RESERVATIONS ONLY 394-0441

This ad uses two different type-faces, one in the body of the ad, the other in the headings. In addition, there are four sizes of type used in the headings for emphasis. All are clear and easy to read. The border around the ad helps it to stand out on the page. Because there is plenty of white space, the ad does not appear to be crowded, yet, it contains a good deal of information. The layout has a somewhat informal balance, but is probably more of a balanced type. The optical center is focused on the words, "Thanksgiving Dinner," which is the main theme of the ad.
Figure 11–4.

Location. The most creative ad will have trouble getting results if it is not placed correctly in the right edition. The best location for a small ad is at the top of the page, preferably on the right side of the right-hand page or on the left side of the left-hand page. Results get progressively worse as you move toward the bottom of the page.

After placement on the page, the next consideration should be the page itself. In most newspapers, pages two and three are excellent locations. In addition, you might consider the women's, society, and wedding and engagement pages, and the sports or television and radio sections. Try to specify a definite section or page. In some cases, there

THE BUTTERNUT TREE

LUNCHEONS
Tue. thru Sat.
12 - 2 P.M.

DINNER
Friday & Saturday
6 - 9 P.M.

—

Closed week of
April 1st

—

"SOPHISTICATED DINING
IN A COUNTRY SETTING"

Woodstock, Vt.
457-1818

Figure 11–5.   A Single Column Ad.

Timing and Selection. It is important to pick a good day to advertise. Do not place ads prior to your busy days, because you may not be able to take new customers that call. It is far better to place them before your slow days. This way, you will have room for those who call and you will be filling the dining room as well.

Selection of the proper edition and day is also an important consideration. Advertise on a day that is not too crowded. Mondays, Tuesdays, and Fridays are usually the best in this regard. Wednesday and Thursday are usually sales days, so steer clear of them. There are so many pages and ads, your ad will be lost. This same premise holds true many times between an evening edition and a morning edition of the same newspaper.

Which Newspaper? Many small towns have only one newspaper. If this is the case, you have little choice where to advertise. However, you should also consider out of town newspapers. Many people are willing to travel for good food.

In larger cities, there is usually more than one newspaper and you can decide where to spend your advertising dollar. Select according to the people who read the paper. Facts about the readership can be obtained from the newspapers themselves. In one city I lived in, the morning newspaper was Democratic while the evening paper was Republican. Both had their particular readers. Differences such as this can determine who reads a certain newspaper and, consequently, your ads.

Rates. Rates are determined by circulation and area covered. Usually, the larger the circulation and area, the higher the rate. If you have a choice, analyze the readership and area makeup before deciding. All things being

is an extra charge for a guaranteed location. Usually, if you give two or three preferences, the newspaper will honor one of them without a charge. Stay clear of listings and so-called "Dining Guides." Although the rates may be cheaper, the results seldom justify the money spent.

equal, advertise in the paper with the larger circulation.

Rates are also determined by the number of lines contracted for, the particular day, frequency of insertion, zones (if available), color, special locations (as previously mentioned), and special sections.

Capitalize on a special event by running a special ad or two to promote it. Sometimes, the newspapers will pick this up as a very important event and run a feature article. You might also try to get the local newspaper to do a special article about you, your restaurant, or one of your employees. This could be additional free publicity. (See Figure 11–6.)

Advertising in newspapers is low in cost, can reach a great number of people, can be saved and re-read, and can be creative to some extent. Some disadvantages might be that newspapers can be read too quickly and your advertisement may be missed and there are bad days to advertise, your ad can be buried and not seen, and ads do not always reproduce well. All things considered, newspapers give you more for your advertising dollar than any other media. For this reason, they are most acceptable to the small restaurateur.

Radio

More than 95 percent of the homes in the United States have radios. The percentage is almost the same for car radios. Think of the potential market for your advertising.

Radio may be AM or FM or AM and FM combined. At present there are more AM stations available than FM stations. In addition, there are more radios equipped with only AM, than AM-FM. For this reason, AM reaches a large number of listeners. Newly

THE LEMON TREE — Lancaster (394-0441) 1766 Columbia Ave., via Rte. 30 west. For gracious dining while in Pennsylvania Dutch country, seek out this appealingly yellow-hued house. It harbors some extremely exciting dining, indeed, thanks to imaginative owner-hosts, the Chiffrillers. Their international menu runs the taste-tempting gamut from Polynesian chicken to garlic shrimp Lemon Tree. Perhaps a thick but refreshingly chilled blueberry soup and the combination appetizers (chicken livers rumayaki, stuffed mushrooms, quiche Lorraine) to put you in the properly adventuresome mood? You'll delight, as well, in the candlelit charm and hospitality of the Williamsburg-minded decor in each of the three nicely proportioned dining rooms. Separate cozy, carpeted cocktail lounge with service bar. Dinner only, from 5:30 to 10, a la carte entrees $3.25 to $5.95. Closed Sun. and Mon. Reservations advised.

Write-ups like these are free and can do a great deal for your image.
Cue Magazine, June 8, 1968
Figure 11–6.   Free Publicity.

manufactured radios are almost all equipped with FM receivers. If you want to reach a local audience, both AM and FM work well. However, if you desire distance, AM is the one to use. The exact distance each reaches is difficult to pin down, because there are so many influencing factors. Your local station can give you this data. Consider also, the following:

FM is usually static free; AM is not.

FM features stereo; at present, AM does not.

FM is usually more limited timewise than AM. Desirable time slots may be difficult to obtain.

The quality of programming is usually better on FM.

You'll find a more limited audience on FM but it may be more specialized.

Radio is expensive, but the expense

must be weighed against the benefits. Radio has two important advantages over the printed word. You can be more selective about your audience and you have the appeal of the spoken word. If you operated a quiet, sophisticated restaurant you would not advertise on a rock station, nor would you advertise late at night if you wanted to reach the housewife. An oral ad has a longer lasting initial impact than a written one. It has the potential to incite someone to react more quickly.

Radio advertising has some disadvantages. The biggest one is that it cannot be saved. Second is its brevity. Even one-minute commercials are short in comparison to ads in some other media.

When advertising on radio, first consider the group you wish to reach, then decide what it is you wish to sell, and finally, stimulate an action. Because you are limited in the time you have to present your message, you have to be sure to say the right things. First, tell the potential customers what you have to offer. Second, assure them you have what they are looking for. One way to determine a satisfactory approach is to make two lists. In one, list the items you think are important and exceptional about your restaurant. In the other, have two or three people make a list of what they think is important in a restaurant. Compare the lists and note the items that are repeated frequently. These will be the items you should consider in your advertising.

Be sure the name of the restaurant is mentioned at the beginning, middle, and end of each commercial. The address should be given, along with the telephone number. Try to mention the meals you serve (luncheon, or dinner, or both). Unless you have a long ad, there is no need to mention the days or hours you are open. Customers will find this information in other media, or they will ask when they call for a reservation. Once you have all

the necessary information together, give it to the radio station and let professionals make up the commercial for you.

Commercials are sold in "spots," from ten seconds to a number of minutes. A thirty-second spot would contain about seventy-five words. Rates are based on the time involved, the number of listeners, and the time slot. In addition, there are the usual discounts for frequency. The longer the ad, the more the cost. However, the cost does not increase proportionately with time. Certain times of the day are more effective for advertising than others. Because of demand, rates are higher for these periods. However, they may be worth it to you. Consult your local stations for their rates.

Suggestions for Radio

1. Never say yes to a commercial until you have heard it exactly as it will sound on the air.

2. Try to come up with a slogan or phrase that is interesting and provocative and that can be repeated in all your ads. It will help people think of you.

3. If you use music as a background, keep it low. You do not want to drown out the message. Music has a masking effect when it is too loud.

4. Keep your radio advertising simple. Do not crowd too much into a given amount of time. It will have to be spoken so quickly, it will be impossible to make an impression on the listener. He or she may not even be able to understand it. Say what has to be said, and eliminate clutter. Do not try to get more than one idea into a commercial.

Remember, a newspaper ad can be re-read. A radio commercial cannot be repeated (at that particular time). You *must get attention* from the first few words or the entire time will most likely be wasted. You *must keep* this attention by keeping your ad interesting. You get *results* only by telling the listener what to do next. (Call for a reservation, of course.)

Television

Television is frightfully expensive for the small operator. The question is whether or not you can afford it. I think with careful budgeting you can. It may be one of the media you will drop once you are successful enough to cut back on the advertising budget. However, it can be very effective in helping you get started.

The guidelines for writing television copy are much the same as those for radio copy. However, you now have the advantage of the spoken word *and* a picture to demonstrate or illustrate your product. It is important that both be interesting and stimulating. You are competing with all the other commercials airing in that time slot.

Once you decide what you want to say and show, consult with the television station for the makeup. If the station cannot do a satisfactory job for you, consult an agency. This is definitely a job for professionals. It is important to have an eye-catching and interesting ad. The viewer should have a strong desire to try your restaurant after she or he has seen your commercial. In a short spot, this is a very difficult feat. If your ad is longer, the task becomes easier.

As with radio, the proper timing is most important. A great commercial in the wrong time slot is a waste of money. The television people have all sorts of data to help you choose the time slot.

Television is no different than other media in one respect—the more you adver-

tise, the better. Many small ads are still better than one large one. During certain times of the year, many channels offer special rates for a number of short spots. In addition, you can take advantage of the regular frequency and volume discounts. There are times when channels have special promotions during which they offer special rates. Keep alert to all the possibilities to reduce your expenditures and to stretch the budget.

Magazines

If you really want to pinpoint your advertising audience use magazines. *Gourmet* magazine and *Bon Appetit* are two magazines that appeal to food enthusiasts. *New Yorker* magazine appeals to a certain strata of society. *Time* appeals to a broader readership, but it has its particular type of reader.

Magazines may be national, regional, or local. The rates will vary with circulation. Rate cards may be obtained from any of the periodicals. This card gives you complete information regarding rates, circulation, and deadlines. The usual frequency and quantity discounts apply.

The advantages of magazine advertising are the ability to pinpoint the reader, excellent reproduction of copy and photographs, and longer life. Another plus may be the prestige attached to advertising in certain magazines.

Most of the same guidelines apply to magazine advertising as newspaper advertising. Because it is a different media, there are some specialized guidelines to consider as well.

1. White space can be used more effectively in magazines, because of the better contrast between white and black (or color). Because of the excellent contrasts obtained, an ad consisting of copy alone can be quite effective.

2. Pictures can be reproduced with excellent clarity. Use them for attention-getters. Provide 8″ × 10″ glossy photos for reproduction, whenever possible. They have greater detail and can be easily reduced in size if necessary. Black and white reproduce better than color photographs.

3. Flow, layout, and design are just as important in magazines as they are in newspapers. Use your logo to best advantage.

4. Most of the previous recommendations made for newspaper advertising apply to magazines as well. The layout and copy makeup follow the same principles. The main difference is that you are dealing with a smaller page and must adjust accordingly.

5. Select your periodicals very carefully. If you pick the wrong one, you are wasting your advertising dollar.

Magazine advertising is a very important part of the advertising dollar. When properly placed, it can produce excellent results. Depending on the type of magazine you use, you may wish to advertise periodically instead of every issue, or you may wish to alternate between a small ad one month and a larger ad the next.

Yellow Pages

No matter how tight your advertising budget gets, *never* eliminate the telephone directory yellow page advertising. For the money, this is one of the best bargains you will get. I feel that nine out of ten persons will consult the yellow pages to find your location or telephone number. For this reason only, I want my name in the yellow pages. Simple, heavy, lettered lines are all that is needed for a good ad in this medium. Because this advertising is so inexpensive, I recommend a one-half to one inch ad to start out. If you wish to increase this later, you can do so. In addition to your name, in large letters, the ad should contain your address and your telephone number, and some information about the hours and days of operation and the type of restaurant yours is.

When writing copy for this form of advertising, keep it simple. Use your logo, if possible. Pictures and illustrations tend to clutter small ads, so do not use them unless you are sure they do not create the problems mentioned. Save the creativity for where it can really pay off.

You should also have the name of your restaurant in the white pages in bold type. It makes you easier to spot when someone is looking for your telephone number. Also, it may be seen when someone is looking for some other number.

Direct Mail

I have never felt very strongly about direct mail advertising for small restaurants. It takes a great deal of time and effort to compile an effective mailing list. There is so much junk mail thrown out everyday, there is no reason to assume your's will not meet the same fate. Add the cost of postage to the cost of printing, the envelope, and, perhaps, makeup costs and each piece becomes quite expensive. If you have to pay for a mailing list, you have an additional cost. Direct mail can be most effective if mailings are sent to people who have frequented your restaurant.

Direct mail is much like television. You must catch the eye as quickly as possible. Keep letters or flyers to one page. Try to get the message all on one side. If it's on the reverse, the sheet may never be turned over.

In addition, messages printed on two sides tend to look sloppy and confusing due to "show-through." If you can get your message on a postcard, you may find they can be very effective and as a bonus, they are quite inexpensive to produce.

Classified

Classified advertising may appear in the classified section, or, in some newspapers, on the front page. The latter may only be one quarter inch high, but it can be read by many. (See Figure 11–7.) Front page advertising is much more expensive than that which appears in other sections of the paper or periodical. Because of the great exposure, the cost is reduced, because you can use a smaller ad.

Classified advertising is very inexpensive. It reaches a certain market that may meet your needs. In setting up this kind of ad, all that is necessary is a bold headline or bold first words. The copy can be very simple, but try to make it as interesting as possible. White space helps make your ad stand out so use it if you can.

Signs and Billboards

Signs are either on location or on a highway or building. The on location type, in most

LUNCHEONS
Tuesday thru Saturday
Beginning Next Week

DINNERS
Friday and Saturday
a la carte from $4.75

BUTTERNUT TREE
Woodstock, Vermont

Figure 11–7. Classified Advertising in a small town newspaper.

cases, will be the sign at the front door. The highway or building signs can be located anywhere from a block away to many miles away.

Generally, signs are read quickly. Because of this, they should have a simple message, and the lettering should be large and eye-catching. Once the sign is designed it must be placed in an advantageous location. You want as many people as possible to see and read it. This may require leasing space from someone. In some cases, you may even buy a location.

When you sign a lease for your business, it is a good idea to include a section in the lease regarding the right to have a sign on the property. You will certainly want to hang a sign at your place of business. This is not just an inherent right you receive when you rent property. Have it spelled out in the lease. Also, it is a very good idea to check with the local government regarding the right to hang a sign. They will probably have some restriction in this regard. Once the lease is signed, it is too late to find out.

Usually, a simple message pertaining to the type of food you serve, whether or not you have alcoholic beverages, your address, the telephone number, and, if necessary, directions to your location are all that are necessary for a roadside or building sign. (See Figure 11–8.) This is about all a driver can assimilate while driving. On location signs can contain added information, if it is needed, because people are generally walking, or driving more slowly. However, even this sign should be kept as simple as possible for ease of reading.

Billboards and outdoor advertising are basically the same makeup as the smaller signs mentioned. However, you have a great deal more area to work with. This enables you to use sketches or line drawings, which would crowd a smaller sign. It is still important to keep your message simple, have large,

A two sided, outdoor sign facing the highway. Note the use of the logo, along with the name. The information was limited because of the speed in which it was read. Note the removable bottom portion. This information could be changed without changing the entire sign.

Figure 11–8.

heavy, readable letters, be eye-catching, and provide the best possible location. In most cases, you will not buy the sign or its location. You will lease it from a company specializing in this type of advertising. They will not only provide the sign and location, but can also provide the artwork and copywriting. You generally sign a lease for a specified period of time. The company will maintain the sign and periodically change the advertising message.

This is a very expensive form of adver-tising. Rates are based on location. The better the location, the higher the rates. Size is also a contributing factor. I would say, in most cases, outdoor advertising is beyond the reach of the small operator.

Other Methods

Your menu is an advertising instrument. Place one outside your doorway. Let the pas-serby know what you have. Sometimes, shops in the area will keep your menu as a service to their customers. You can also distribute them to local motels that do not have their own food service.

Book or box matches are another form of advertising. Well designed matchbooks or boxes are an inexpensive means of disseminating your name. An interesting book or box, an exciting color, and an interesting logo all contribute to an effective bit of advertising. Give the books or boxes away freely. We placed one at every place setting in the dining room, at the bar, on the cocktail tables, and at the exit. This is one of the few pieces of advertising that still produces results after it has been thrown away. Even laying in the street, it gives forth its message.

One gimmick we used to advantage was to donate matchbooks to charitable events. An example of this was the local hospital's annual bridge luncheon. Five hundred players took our matches home with them. Inexpensive advertising.

Public advertising is advertising in a club's program or the like. It is not advertising in any real sense, nor do you ever expect much success from it. However, in most communities you are more or less morally obligated to do a certain amount of it. By taking ads or sponsoring some charitable event, you fulfill this obligation.

Minor gifts may be considered more of a merchandising effort than advertising, but they bear mentioning. In my Lemon Tree restaurant, we gave away the best lemon drops you ever tasted. We gave wine openers to our good wine customers. Once we gave away the best city map you could find anywhere. Of course, our name was emblazoned on it. Think how long this stayed in the average household. One Christmas, we mailed a handwritten Christmas greeting and a lemon drop to our most valued customers.

Theatre program advertising is generally after-the-fact advertising. It is not looked at again after the show. A person sitting in a theatre has probably already eaten and reading about you on a full stomach, does not really help you much unless you serve late snacks.

The Campaign

The advertising campaign is an outline of how you will spend your advertising and promotional dollars. The items to be considered in undertaking this plan are as follows:

1. The restaurant name.
2. The restaurant logo.
3. Purpose of the campaign.
4. Who you wish to reach.
5. How much you have to spend.
6. The media to be used.
7. The theme of the campaign.
8. How long the campaign will last.
9. Promotional materials to be used (if any).
10. How will you measure results?

The Restaurant Name

The name of a restaurant is a direct indication of the restaurant's personality. Anyone can come up with a name like "Mary's Place" or the like. This does not do much for your image, however. Wouldn't something like "Mary's Cookery" sound a little more interesting and give an altogether different impression? We agonized for hours and hours trying to decide on the "right" name for our restaurants. I don't know how we ever came up with a name like The Lemon Tree for a Lancaster, Pennsylvania restaurant. We just liked the sound of it and felt it fit us. Our other restaurant, The Butternut Tree, was named after a tree indigenous to Vermont. In addition, we felt we could develop a nice logo with it. We discarded one name we liked very much, The Elegant Morel, because we could not come up with a suitable logo. So, the facilitation of a logo should also be a consideration.

The name may also denote the type of cooking you do. A name like The Wild Asparagus could denote a vegetarian menu. Le Cordon Bleu might indicate a French style. Words like inn, lounge, dining room, fireside, and rathskeller all convey a certain idea. Sometimes, not using any such words will convey a different image. You can tie in the name with a small phrase. The name we used, The Butternut Tree was tied in with the phrase, "Sophisticated Dining in a Country Setting." The two always appeared together.

The name should be you. It should give some indication of what you do. It must be adaptable to an interesting logo and pleasant and easy to say.

The Logo

It is absolutely essential to develop a good logo. The promotional value is immeasurable. It identifies *you*. The eye catches it and is drawn to it. Just thumb through a few magazines or newspapers and study the logos companies use. You will notice that companies use the same logos in all their advertisements, even if the ads are different. They never change. Repetition is one of the essentials of the proper use of the logo.

The logo can be a picture, drawing, a sketch, words, or a combination of these. Your name designed in a special manner can be very acceptable. The logo can be tied in with a phrase or some descriptive wording.

Be sure you develop a logo that can be used in any size. Many times, logos are de-

signed and you later find they do not reproduce well, because their small details become blurred or indistinguishable. This is one reason line drawings work better than photographs.

When designing your logo, always keep in mind the purpose it is to serve—*identification*. You want something you can be proud of. Something that will tell the world, "this is me."

The Purpose

A campaign is launched because you are trying to promote something. It may be the opening of the restaurant, an additional facility, a new concept in food or entertainment, or any number of ideas. Whatever the stimulus, you want the public to know about it.

Before any campaign is started, you must define what you wish to promote. Be very specific in this or your approach may be too broad and the desired results may not be attained. Write down the thoughts you have on the subject and combine them into a distinct idea or theme. Plan around this theme.

The Audience

Who you want to reach will depend somewhat on your advertising objective. If you are having a grand opening and want as many as possible to know, that is one thing. If you are changing the menu and want a specific group to know about it, that is something else.

This decision is most important because it will determine where to direct your advertising. In a small community you may not have many areas to direct advertising to. In a large city, you will.

The Budget

The budget is a key consideration. The determination of this amount has been thoroughly discussed under "The Budget" at the beginning of this chapter. However, at any given time, the amount available will have to be known so the budget is not exceeded. If you have spent the bulk of it earlier in the year and would like to embark on a large campaign at the end of the year, it is readily apparent you will not be able to do so (this is one reason why budgets are so helpful). If you have (or expect to) exceeded the budget, you should be aware that the money must come from somewhere. If, after serious consideration, you still feel you must exceed the budget because further spending is necessary, then by all means do it. Just be sure you know where the money is coming from.

A further consideration is the planning of your outlays over the year. If you spend it all in one campaign, where do you get the money for the remainder of the year? For many, this may seem like an unnecessary strategy, but believe me, this is just another reason for small restaurateurs failing.

The Media to Be Used

We have already discussed the media available to the small restaurant owner. It is up to you to decide which you want to use. This can only be determined after you have decided:

1. The extent of the campaign,
2. Who you wish to reach,
3. How much you have to spend.

When these three factors have been determined, it is an easy task to allocate the funds available among the media you deem the most effective.

In determining the media to be used, an influencing factor should be the nature of your program. For a one-shot deal, you may go all out, using many media. For a continuing program, you may wish to limit your choices to only one or two.

The Theme

The theme will depend on the advertising subject. If you are starting a new restaurant, for example, you will want to stress the menu, the atmosphere, prices, or, maybe, the wines. Again, this is your decision. Another example might be the addition of a cocktail lounge. You may want to promote special drinks, entertainment, happy hour, or the like. You may just want to promote a pleasant atmosphere, an interesting menu, and fine service. Whatever it is, jot down your ideas and formulate an approach.

Within a campaign you may want to promote a few ideas. An example of this would be four successive newspaper ads, each mentioning a different facet of the operation. Each ad could be tied in with radio spots. The entire campaign would then be centered around the four newspaper ads and the subject they contain. This would be considered one campaign. Later, it could be repeated exactly, changed somewhat, or an entirely new campaign could be formulated.

The important aspect is a central idea throughout. Too many different ideas tend to confuse people. It is better to run separate ads with different ideas, than to clutter one ad with all of them. Each ad would then develop its own idea; the entire campaign will then pull the ideas together and present an overall theme. (See Figure 11–9 which illustrates an ad campaign.)

Figure 11–9. An Ad Campaign.

Duration

The length of the campaign will be determined by the amount of money you have to spend and the time you feel is needed to do a successful job. It can always be shortened, if the response is better than expected. Be sure to allot enough time. It takes quite awhile to get the ball rolling. Generally, six weeks would be the very least. You will get much better results with one long campaign than you will with sporadic, short ones. It is im-

portant to have your name before the public long enough to be noticed.

Promotional Material

Listed below are a number of ideas that can be used as promotional material. It is essential that your name, address, and telephone number be on them whenever possible. Most of them can be used year round. They do not have to be limited to a promotion, but can be used at any time.

> The restaurant menu or a replica
> Coupon for an item on the menu
> Gift certificate
> Discounts
> Birthday cakes
> Matches (boxes or books)
> Pencils or pens
> Postcards or attractive name cards
> Candies
> Calendars or datebooks

Measuring Results

It is important to know if your campaign is getting results. Of course, the best way is to get the customer to tell you. This is not always easy. If you have the time you can ask new customers why they came. They will usually tell you they heard your ad on station WWWW or read about you in the *Daily*. Sometimes, they will say a friend sent them. When this happens, you know the word is getting around.

One gimmick you can use is a promise of a surprise, if the person seeing your ad brings it with them. This will give you a measureable result. Another method is the installation of a special telephone number for reservations. This number would only be used in the campaign ads. Calls received on this telephone would be a direct result of the campaign.

There are many sophisticated and expensive methods to measure the results of advertising. If you can afford them, by all means use them.

By following the suggestions I have outlined, I am sure you will be able to spend your advertising dollars well. I have tried to outline, in an understandable manner, what advertising is all about. As with any other expenditure, if you follow a careful plan in spending, you will not waste either your money or your time. In addition, the results will be gratifying. It is always nice to be able to sit back and say, "I did it myself."

Chapter Twelve

Energy and Cost Savings for Utilities, Heating, Ventilating, and Air Conditioning

For as long as I can remember, I have told my employees to turn off lights, close refrigerator doors quickly, and turn off the gas when not using it. This was always on the basis of saving money, not conservation. Today, many people feel conservation is just as important as cost savings. This gives you two reasons for being a skinflint when it comes to energy related savings.

A few interesting facts:

Save 1 kilowatt/hour/day of electricity and you save $15.00 a year.

Save 2 percent of your fuel bill for every one degree you set the thermostat back.

Save $30/year when you fix a faucet that leaks at the rate of 1 gallon/hour.

You can save money not only by cutting usage, but by eliminating waste as well. It is up to you, as an operator, to carefully analyze your operation and determine where consumption is too high. The money saved here directly affects the bottom line of the financial statement.

Bear in mind that the comfort of the guest is essential. Do not become overzealous in your efforts, if it means making your guests uncomfortable. Keeping the thermostat a few degrees warmer during the summer months, for example, may mean a direct cost saving, but if there is a loss of guests because of it, you really have not gained a thing.

There are a number of ways energy waste can be eliminated and its use controlled. The best procedure is to separate your restaurant operation into specific areas, such as refrigeration, heating, and lighting. Study each area and make the necessary improvements. Listed next are the most common considerations.

Potential Areas for Energy Savings and Conservation

Utility Bills

Billing for electricity, gas, and water is determined by means of a meter. Gas and water bills are usually very easy to compute and understand. You are charged for the amount directly recorded on the meter. However, electrical billings may be modified somewhat, depending on whether you are on a "demand" meter or straight kilowatt type. Most businesses are on the demand type.

Billings determined by demand can be reduced or increased by the user. Since demand is the result of a "peak" resulting from usage, the overall charge will be reduced if the peak is reduced.

Illustration

The average restaurant cook comes in to work in the morning and turns all the equipment on at one time—the ovens, the range tops, the grill, the steamer, etc. It does not seem important that some of these pieces will not be used until hours later. By doing this, he or she has set a demand peak for the period (probably, the highest of the day). Turning the equipment on only as needed would reduce the immediate load and, thereby, reduce the demand peak.

Peak usage determines your demand rate. It is important to keep the peak as low as possible. This can only be done by carefully watching your usage. Because the computation of demand charges will vary in all local-

ities, it would be a good idea to discuss this subject with the local electric company. They can also give you suggestions as to how you may reduce your bill each month.

Refrigeration

1. Keep doors open *only* as long as necessary.
2. Keep refrigeration coils free of ice and dust. Keep compressor coils free of dust and dirt.
3. Check gaskets, seals, and compressor belts periodically.
4. Check temperatures first thing every morning.
5. Allow hot foods to cool somewhat (covered) before refrigerating them.
6. Do not block compressors. They need air to operate efficiently.
7. Defrost freezers before ice buildup becomes too great (1/8").
8. Schedule periodic preventative maintenance, at least once a year.

Equipment and Cookware

1. Turn equipment on as needed. Only use warmup or pre-heat time when necessary.
2. Have oven thermostats, gas pilots, and flames adjusted periodically.
3. Do not keep oven doors open any longer than necessary. Every second open, results in a one degree drop in temperature.
4. Consider low temperature roasting for meats (250°F).
5. Items which can be cooked on either top of the range or in the oven (e.g. boeuf Bourguignon) will cook faster on top.

6. Turn off all equipment as soon as you are finished using it.

7. Use a steamer, instead of boiling water, for cooking. This saves water, electricity, and/or gas (and time).

8. A microwave oven will heat many items which are usually "finished" in a regular oven or salamandre. This saves electricity and time.

9. Meat thermometers help reduce cooking time.

10. Convection ovens are more economical to operate than regular ovens.

11. Pots should be flat on the bottom and fit tightly against cooking surfaces.

12. Use pot covers to reduce the amount of fuel needed to keep the product at proper temperature while cooking.

Water Use

1. Repair leaking faucets at first sign of leaking.

2. Insulate hot water pipes.

3. Heat water only as hot as it is needed (140° F).

4. Turn hot water heater down to 70° F when closing at night. Turn back up two hours before needed.

Dishmachine

1. Wash only full tray loads. It costs as much to run one cup through the machine as it does to run a full rack.

2. Fill machine tanks when needed, not ahead of time. This saves electricity or gas because the water does not have to be kept hot.

3. Run the machine for one long period, as opposed to many short periods.

4. Turn off booster heater units when machine is not being used (between meals and at closing).

5. Use manual pre-rinse just to rinse off heavy food particles, nothing more. This wastes water. Keep the water temperature at 100° F. Hotter water is not necessary.

6. The use of a cold water dishwasher can save as much as $600 in the cost of electricity, if a KWH cost $5.

Lighting

1. Turn off lights when not in use. This includes room lights, refrigerator lights (walk-in), and exhaust hood lights in kitchen.

2. Use automatic turn off devices on outside signs and lights. If needed, use on inside lights as well.

3. Use fluorescent lighting wherever possible to replace incandescent. Savings are almost 60 percent. Also, consider low energy light bulbs.

4. Keep fixtures clean. They reflect light better.

5. Use resistance type dimmer switches.

Heating, Ventilation, and Air Conditioning (HVAC)

1. Turn exhaust fans on only when needed. Turn them off as soon as the need for them is over. They not only remove air and fumes, but heat as well.

2. Have HVAC equipment, especially, thermostats, checked before using at the beginning of each season. Regular cleaning should be done monthly.

3. Turn off HVAC equipment when not in use and in unused areas.

4. Many times (in evenings), the outside

air is sufficiently cool to keep the restaurant interior cool. In such cases, turn cooling off and use outside air for cooling.

5. Whether cooling or heating, never use outside air unless it is necessary. It is far less expensive to heat or cool inside air because it has already been conditioned.

6. The use of an electronic air filter will remove smoke and dust particles from the air, making it cleaner and easier to heat or cool, because outside air does not have to be drawn in.

7. Set heat back to 55° F when closing for night. Turn air conditioning off completely.

8. Keep air filters clean in all parts of restaurant.

9. Open curtains, draperies, and blinds to let warm sun in and close them when you want to keep it out. Close them to keep heat in room during cold weather.

10. Insulate ductwork wherever necessary.

11. Keep outside doors closed Use automatic closers. Doors should fit tightly and be well weatherstripped. Storm windows and doors will reduce heating costs as much as 20 percent.

12. Keep records to determine your progress.

Although these recommendations may look overwhelming, you will find that 90 percent of them are simple maintenance and training. Maintenance is absolutely necessary and, certainly, training has top priority in any operation. Money saved here can go toward better things.

Kitchen

1. Are oven, range, broiler, fryer, and steamer off?
2. Is hood exhaust fan turned off?

3. Is heat lamp off?
4. Are refrigerators all tightly closed and locked?
5. Are water faucets off tightly?
6. Is icemaker door closed?
7. Is dishmachine off, drained, and cleaned? Is booster heater turned off?
8. Has hot water heater been turned down to 70° F?
9. Has garbage and trash been dumped?
10. Are all lights off?

Dining Room

1. Is heat turned down to 55° F?
2. Is air conditioning off?
3. Are coffee stoves turned off?
4. Are all tables cleared of food and soiled dishes?

Bar

1. Is everything locked up that should be?
2. Have garbage and trash been removed?
3. Are faucets off tightly?

Restrooms

1. Are lights and exhaust fans turned off?
2. Has trash container been emptied?
3. Are faucets off tightly? Are toilets running?

Items to be Checked at Closing Time

General

1. Have all windows and doors been checked? Closed and locked?
2. Is cash register drawer open?

Chapter Thirteen

Putting More Money in the Bank by Reducing Liability

Accident Prevention

In 1975, a respected food service magazine survey found the number of accidents in the food service industry was three times that of any other industry. Considering the lack of thought given to accident prevention and proper training in the average restaurant, this finding is not too difficult to understand.

Restaurants expose employees to cutting instruments, fire, steam, electricity, hot water, collision, slippery floors, and infection. Many owners and operators are unaware that such hazards exist or that they can be the cause of serious injuries.

An employee only slightly incapacitated, due to an injury, is certainly not capable of performing his or her work completely and properly. If he or she were more seriously injured, it might be days or weeks before a return to work. Injuries, therefore, are an inconvenience and expense to the operator.

Injuries occur for these reasons:

1. Lack of (or poor) training,
2. Carelessness,
3. Pressure.

New employees' training should include the care and use of all equipment and utensils in your kitchen. New employees tend to exaggerate their capabilities in order to impress you. It is your responsibility to observe their work and to correct them, if their methods are not right. An example of this would be the correct way in which to use a knife for chopping.

Demonstrating the proper use and pointing out the dangers of each piece of equipment and many of the utensils will make the employees more aware and safety conscious. It will, for instance, make them think twice before removing the cover from a steaming kettle, which may burn an arm if not removed correctly. This awareness is as important as the actual training, because safety must be a state of mind.

A helpful aid in accident prevention is the posting of proper procedures for handling dangerous equipment. A good illustration is the following instructions for the use and care of a slicing machine.

Always bear in mind when using this machine that it slices skin and bone, as well as the items you feed it.

How to Use Slicer

1. Place food to be sliced on cradle.
2. Set size of slice on gauge.
3. *Always* place holder in position so it is not necessary to use your hand for feeding food into blade.
4. Turn machine on.
5. Slice as fast as you are able, but never force the food against the blade enough to slow it. This could result in the food slipping and, possibly, in an injury to you.
6. When catching food as it falls, never allow hand to come in contact with blade.
7. When removing sliced food, turn machine off.
8. Turn off machine when slicing is completed. *Never* walk away from machine without turning it off.
9. Return blade setting to "0."

Cleaning Slicer

1. Be sure blade setting is at "0."
2. Wipe machine and blade with a clean, wet cloth which has been rinsed in detergent.
3. Clean slicer immediately after using, while food particles are easy to remove.

Major Cleaning (disassembly)

1. Remove plug from wall outlet.
2. Remove scrap drawer. Empty and wash.
3. Remove header around blade. Wash.
4. Wipe blade and other soiled areas. Be very cautious working around blade.
5. Replace header and scrap drawer.
6. Set blade at "0."
7. Plug in.
8. Turn slicer on briefly to be sure it is in working order.

This slicing machine is a dangerous weapon. Give it all your attention when using it.

Even when a person is properly trained, he or she may be careless. If, after a few warnings, the carelessness continues, it would be wise to give serious considerations to dismissing him or her. After all, you cannot be expected to watch over a person every minute of the working day. In addition, careless employees are not only a danger to themselves, but to others as well.

The final cause of accidents is pressure. We have all had to work under pressure at one time or another. When such a situation occurs, caution is sometimes thrown to the winds so a deadline can be met. This is when good training pays off. A well-trained person can instinctively do the right thing.

Ways to Minimize Accidents in the Kitchen Area

1. Proper training and familiarity with equipment and utensils.
2. Respect for the danger inherent in fire, steam, electricity, heat, and hot water.
3. Proper lighting. Not only does it make it easier to see, but it helps reduce fatigue as well.

4. Proper use of knives means they must:
   a. be kept sharp,
   b. be used properly,
   c. be kept clean,
   d. not be allowed to rest with the point or handle hanging over the edge of a table,
   e. not be played with,
   f. never be placed in a sink for washing (be cleaned and dried by the cook only),
   g. be avoided when they are falling,
   h. be kept flat, with sharp edge turned away from traffic, when left on a table top,
   i. be properly stored.
5. Use hot pads when removing items from a stove top, oven or broiler. Never use wet towels. Steam can be created and seriously burn you.
6. Keep area clean and neat. Wipe up after working. Clean up spills immediately. Keep floors clean and dry, so no one slips.
7. Instruct employees not to run and to look where they are going. This reduces the possibility of running into one another.
8. Wear proper clothing. Long sleeves protect arms from gas flames and steaming kettles. Aprons protect the wearer from splashes. Good shoes protect the feet from heavy objects and reduce fatigue.
9. Keep water away from hot fat.
10. Do not allow "horseplay" in the kitchen area.
11. Lift only what you can carry easily. Lift with your legs, not your back.
12. Do not block stairways with boxes, trash, etc.
13. Have employees report malfunctions of equipment at the first sign of trouble.
14. Store detergents, cleaning supplies, etc. so that they cannot come in contact with foodstuffs.
15. Have all electrical panel switches labeled.
16. Doors to and from dining room should be properly labeled and have a see through section at eye level.

The majority of injuries in restaurants are caused by *cuts*, *burns*, and *falls*.

When accidents happen, employees should be instructed to report them to you immediately. For your own protection, all accidents should be reported on the standard compensation form, regardless of how small they may be.

Constantly observe your employees, to be certain they are using correct, safe procedures. About once a month, check the equipment for problems. If you find any, have them repaired quickly.

Accidents are costly in terms of money, hours lost, and inconvenience (temporary replacements). The more you can do to reduce them, the happier you will be.

First Aid Treatment for Wounds and Burns

Wounds

Types

1. Incision (clean cut)
2. Abrasion (scrape)
3. Laceration (jagged cut)
4. Puncture (deep, little or no bleeding)

Treatment

1. Stop bleeding by:

a. Direct pressure. By pressing a sterile pad over the wound, until bleeding stops.
b. Elevation. In the case of an arm or leg, the limb should be held above the level of the heart.
c. Pressure point. If pressure point cannot be located, apply pressure to the vein or artery with your finger. For arterial bleeding, apply pressure between the heart and the wound. If from a vein, apply pressure near the wound on the side away from the heart. Hold pressure until bleeding stops; then apply pressure bandage (sterile pad).
d. Tourniquet. DO NOT USE A TOURNIQUET EXCEPT AS A LAST RESORT. If used, mark a "T" on the victim's forehead and get medical attention immediately.
2. Wash wound. When wounds are not bleeding badly, they should be washed with soap and water to reduce the possibility of infection. Infection is secondary to bleeding; bleeding must be stopped first. After washing, cover with a sterile bandage.
3. Make victim comfortable. If wound is serious, victim may be in state of shock. If so, he should be kept lying down, his feet should be raised, and he should be covered.

Precautions

1. Try not to contaminate wound with dirty hands or cloth.
2. Do not use an antiseptic of any kind.
3. Do not remove a bandage once it has been placed on wound. If it becomes saturated, place another one on top of it.

4. Puncture wounds always require medical attention.

Burns

Types

1. First degree (reddened skin)
2. Second degree (blisters develop)
3. Third degree (charring, in addition to above)

Treatment

1. First degree burns. Immerse in cold water. Medical opinion differs on the application of ice.
2. Second degree burn. Clean away anything that may be covering burn (e.g. clothing). If possible, immerse area in cold water (legs and arms), or else, cover with cold, wet dressing. Treat for shock.
3. Third degree burns. Cut away loose clothing. Do not attempt to remove it if it is adhering to the burn. Cover with layers of sterile, cold, wet dressings. Treat for shock. Get victim to hospital, as quickly as possible.

Never use ointments or fats (e.g., butter, lard) on any burn.

Fire Prevention and Protection

According to the latest information available, second to outright business failures, fire is the largest single cause of financial loss in the food service industry. Considering most fires are preventable, this is a sad commentary on the concern of owners and operators toward their main source of income—the physical plant. Such lack of concern probably stems from their: 1) ignorance of the devastation, financial loss, and inconveniences caused by fire; 2) attitude that "it can't happen to me;" 3) overconfidence in their ability to cope with a fire, if it should occur.

Prevention is eliminating the causes of fire. Protection is having the means to extinguish a fire should one occur. Both are essential in operating a safe restaurant.

Even if the fire company were located virtually next door and you were fully equipped for fighting a fire quickly, some damage would still occur. A certain amount of inconvenience and monetary loss will be incurred. The more severe the fire, the more severe the losses and inconveniences. For this reason, it makes more sense to prevent a fire than to fight one.

Fire Prevention

Consequences of a Fire

1. *Possible revenue loss.* The amount of closed down time will determine how serious a problem this will be. All fixed expenses continue, along with some variable ones. Income is necessary to fulfill your obligations.

2. *Possible loss of building and equipment.* Losing the building, or a large portion of it, could put you out of business permanently. Certainly, the amount of time needed for repairs will curtail your operation. Replacing equipment could take time. If it does, you may not be able to operate during the interim.

3. *Dining room or lounge loss.* If dining room or lounge furnishings are damaged or destroyed, operations will have to cease. Such damages can be the result of water and smoke, as well as fire.

4. *Employee loss.* In order to retain key employees for a prolonged period of time, you will have to pay them.

5. *Customer loss.* Will all the customers come back after you re-open? Usually not. How many you lose will depend on the amount of time you are shut down. This is where retentive advertising comes in.

6. *Financial loss.* Replacement costs are seldom the same as original costs. Even with full insurance coverage, there will be a portion of the loss which may not be covered. This will have to be made up from borrowing or future revenue. The expense of replacing damaged or lost equipment, furnishings, and inventories are examples of this type of loss. New working capital may have to be borrowed before insurance claims are settled in order to get repair and replacement work started.

7. *Loss of valuable architecture.* If your restaurant theme is based on a particular architecture, it may be difficult or impossible to replace it. For example, the woodwork in a house built in the early 1800s would be almost prohibitive in cost to replace.

8. *Inventories.* Inventories of food and liquor that are lost due to fire, water or smoke damage will have to be replaced. This may necessitate additional time to re-open.

9. *Immediate problems.* Even with a small fire, which is extinguished quickly and causes little damage, problems are created. There is the time utilized in fighting the fire, time needed to clean up, time wasted while everyone calms down and gets back into a productive groove. This is an expense seldom recovered on a fire insurance policy.

10. *Insurance premiums.* A costly fire could result in an increased cost of insurance.

11. *Injuries.* If proper procedures are not followed quickly when the fire is discovered, injuries to employees and guests could occur.

The logical approach to fire prevention is to determine where, when, and how fires begin. If we deal with these factors satisfactorily, the chances of a fire occurring are reduced dramatically.

Strangely enough, more fires begin after a restaurant is closed than when it is open. Most fires start in the kitchen, with the dining room, heating, and storage areas each running about equally for second place.

One could compile a long list of how fires start in restaurants. However, only the major categories will be discussed here. They are:

1. Ignition by person or nature,
2. Electrical causes,
3. Cooking,
4. Smoking,
5. Ducts.

Ignition by Person or Nature. Starting a fire intentionally is a crime (arson). Although this cannot be eliminated as a possibility, our concern is with careless practices. A few such practices are:

a. Dumping trays into a trash container when burning cigarettes are present. This practice occurs most frequently in the kitchen and bar areas.
b. The unintentional placing of a cigarette or match into a trash container when it is not completely extinguished. This is apt to happen in restrooms when ash trays or sand urns are not provided.
c. Unprotected candles can be knocked over, allowed to burn dangerously low or be placed too near flammable material.
d. The most prominent example of a natural fire is in garbage storage. Under proper conditions, garbage will create enough internal heat to ignite.

Electrical Causes. The primary culprit here is faulty wiring. Because of the heavy load placed on electrical circuits in restaurants, adequate wiring is essential. Old wiring should be replaced. Wiring that is not heavy enough to withstand the required load should also be replaced. If this is not possible, the wiring should be labeled as to its maximum use. Faulty wiring becomes heated when overloaded and can cause ignition of any flammable material with which it comes in contact. Such material may smoulder and go undetected during working hours. Later, when the restaurant is closed, it can be the catalyst for a disaster.

The use of proper fuses and breakers is also important in reducing overloads. If the fuse or breaker is too large, it will allow faulty equipment to operate, thus causing an overload and another potential for fire.

Cooking. Fires caused by cooking usually occur when someone is present. As a matter of fact, they are usually created by someone. Grease or fat fires are the most common. French fryers often ignite because they are heated to too high a temperature (the flash point). Such high temperatures are totally unnecessary for cooking. During sauteing, pan fats can be ignited in the pan or they can be spilled on the range top to be ignited. Accumulated grease buildups, due to improper sanitation practices, can also be ignited.

Faulty gas or electrical equipment can be the cause of kitchen or dining room fires. Faulty equipment should be serviced immediately to prevent potential problems.

Smoking. Smoking is not only hazardous to the health, it is hazardous to buildings, furnishings, and equipment as well. Employees should be given definite areas in which they are allowed to smoke. Such areas should be away from flammable materials.

You should have enough ash trays in the dining room and lounge so that there is no chance of a guest dropping a burning cigarette on the carpet or in the furniture. Employess should be instructed to check ash trays carefully before emptying them. All areas should be inspected after each meal and at closing for possible problems.

Ducts. If kitchen exhaust ducts are properly installed and the filters are kept clean, there is no reason for a duct fire to occur. Ducts are made of metal and cannot burn—accumulated grease can.

To protect against any possibility of fire in the ducts, an automatic extinguisher system should be installed.

When purchasing or leasing an existing restaurant, ductwork should be one of the first areas to be examined. A faulty duct installation, along with a malfunctioning extinguisher system or poorly installed filters, can result in a tremendous increase in your fire insurance rates. If any of these conditions exist in a restaurant being purchased, top priority should be given to correcting them. If you are leasing, the owner should make the repairs needed.

If you are building a new restaurant, or remodeling an existing one, consult with your insurer. He or she can provide National Fire Protection Association (NFPA) booklets which contain all the information needed for proper installation of ductwork and extinguisher systems.

Ductwork cleaning is usually performed by professionals, because special equipment is often needed. If you are fortunate enough to have a very simple and direct installation, you may be able to do this job yourself. If so, be sure to include cleaning fan blades as well as ducts. Check the condition of the motor and U-belt too.

Importance of Inventories

One of the major problems after a fire is the substantiation of a claim. It is in your best interest to have claims settled quickly, in order that reimbursement can be made as rapidly as possible.

The best way to prove what was actually lost in the fire is to have accurate and up-to-date inventories. Such inventories should contain the description and purchase price of each item along with the number of each.

Whenever possible, a photograph of the item(s) should be attached. Photographs of entire rooms can be made to document what is in them. A duplicate copy of the inventories and photographs should be kept off the premises, in a safe place. Sometimes, these are held by the insurance agent. Food, liquor, and perishable inventories may have to be estimated, because they can fluctuate daily.

Items to be Removed In Case of Fire

It is advisable to keep certain items available for immediate removal if a fire should occur. If possible, such items should be kept in a fireproof container, just in case you cannot get to them in time. These items are:

1. Cash,
2. Business books (ledgers, journals, payroll records, and checkbooks),
3. Inventory lists and photos,
4. Current invoices.

It is important that your staff be made aware of the problems a fire creates. Their cooperation is essential when it comes to prevention.

Fire Protection

We have discussed the advantages and requirements of a fire prevention program. Now, we must consider what can be done to control or extinguish a fire, if one occurs.

Because most restaurant fires occur after the restaurant is closed, it is logical to consider detection devices. Such devices can be tied in with a municipal or private service company, or they may merely sound an alarm on the premises. For the small operator, the former may be too expensive to install, even if it is the better system. However, the simpler system, if properly installed, can be quite effective.

For a fire to start, three elements must be present: heat, fuel, and oxygen. Take away any one of these, and a fire cannot burn. How quickly and at what intensity these elements combine will determine the seriousness of the fire. For example, grease spilled on top of a hot range will ignite quickly, because two of the elements, heat and fuel, present are in intense quantities. Another example is a smoldering cigarette in a linen hamper. A fire of this sort will require a great deal of time to reach the "flame stage," because the three elements are not present in very intense quantities.

Most restaurant fires that occur after closing are of the smoldering type. You must, therefore, concentrate on protecting the premises from this kind of fire. The most useful device to accomplish this is the smoke detector. Detectors are of two types: ionization and photoelectric.

The key to an early warning device, such as a smoke detector, is proper placement. The least expensive way to determine this is by consulting the local fire department. Generally, such devices are located at or near areas in which combustion can occur undetected (e.g., attics, basements, storerooms). Because such detectors may not sound an alarm loud enough to be heard, even when the restaurant is open, it is best to have them wired to a loud alarm. How and where this alarm is located should be discussed with the fire department representative.

There are a number of central systems available to the small operator. Such systems may be advantageous to your operation. Again, consult with the fire department for guidance in the selection.

If a fire should occur, and no one is present, the only hope for the small business is that the fire company arrives in time. Larger operations may have automatic sprinkler devices, security guards, or private alarm systems. Unfortunately, such aids may be prohibitive in cost for the small restaurateur.

Fires may be retarded, until the firefighters arrive, or extinguished by the use of chemical or water extinguishers. Such extinguishers may be in-place or portable in nature.

In-Place Extinguishers. The in-place extinguisher is usually located in the kitchen, over the cooking equipment, and in the exhaust system. The design and size will be determined by specific requirements for your particular kitchen set down by the state or the NFPA. The system goes off automatically when a particular temperature is reached. It can also be activated manually. The automatic feature gives you some degree of protection whether or not someone is present. This is especially important in the case of duct fires. The extinguisher contains a dry chemical, under pressure. When it is activated, the chemical is released. The spray nozzles from which the chemical is released are located in the ductwork, the hood, and over each piece of cooking equipment.

Along with an extinguisher installation, automatic fuel cutoffs should be installed. Such devices stop the flow of gas or electricity to the cooking equipment, thereby robbing it of one of the elements necessary to support combustion (fuel).

Classes of Fire

Fires are classified in three categories, A, B and C.

Class A fires are of paper, wood, and cloth. These are the ordinary materials found in restaurants.

Class B fires are of grease and flammable liquids. Such fires usually occur in kitchens.

Class C fires are electrical in nature. These fires occur most frequently in kitchen and mechanical areas.

Portable Extinguishers

Water: This extinguisher is filled with water, under pressure. It is effective *only* with Class A fires. It should never be used on a Class B or Class C fire.

Carbon Dioxide: This is a good all-around extinguisher. It is least effective on a Class A fire, because it is apt to spread the fire (due to its intense force). However, with care, it can be used. A CO_2 type is extremely effective on grease and flammable liquids. One of these extinguishers should be located in every kitchen. One distinct advantage to this extinguisher is that little cleanup is needed, since there is no residue or water.

Dry Chemical: This extinguisher is recommended for Class B and Class C fires. It contains the most effective vehicle for use on electrical fires, because it does not dissipate as CO_2 does. Most types are safe around foodstuffs. The best way to clean up the residue discharged from this extinguisher is with a vacuum cleaner.

Fight the fire by directing the flow from the extinguisher at the base of the fire and using a slow, side to side motion. Always have the extinguisher recharged as soon after use as possible. Hopefully, it will not be needed again but one never knows. In many communities, the fire department has facilities for recharging.

Purchase the proper size of extinguisher for your particular needs. This is one place it is not worth economizing. Better too large than too small.

Portable extinguishers should be installed where they are readily accessible, preferably near an entrance. Do not hide an extinguisher because it does not match the decorating scheme. Seconds lost in locating an extinguisher can mean the difference between getting the fire out and having it out of control.

Extinguishers should be inspected once a month. Check for pressure and tampering with the pin.

What to Do in Case of Fire

1. Sound the alarm or
2. Call the fire department. *The number must be located at the telephone.*
3. Clear the area of people.
4. If it can be done safely, an attempt should be made to extinguish the fire.

It is important that the fire department be called *immediately*. Do not be embarrassed to call because "it's only a small fire." You can always call back if you are able to extinguish the blaze before the fire trucks arrive.

There is no question that an extinguisher is the best means for extinguishing a fire. However, when one is not available, there is nothing wrong with a few pots of water or a hose being used. *Do not use water on grease or electrical fires.*

The old remedy of throwing salt or baking soda (not powder) on a fire is sometimes effective in putting out small ones.

If a fire is in an oven, keep the door closed. It may extingush itself as the oxygen and fuel are used up. Similarly, if the fire is in a pan, put a tight cover on top to extinguish it.

Training the Employee

Periodically, training demonstrations should be held to acquaint new employees with the use of fire protection equipment. In addition, they should be made aware of their responsibilities in the event of a fire.

Such training sessions should include:

1. The proper use of each type of extinguisher. Do not just demonstrate. Let each of them actually use one.
2. Their responsibilities toward guests, fellow employees, and themselves in the event of a fire. Stress the importance of remaining calm.
3. How to contact the fire department and the information that will be required. If an alarm is present, they should know how to set it off.
4. The location of all exits.

There should be at least one person available at all times who knows what to do in case of a fire. He or she should be capable of taking charge immediately if you are not present.

Fires may often be controlled and extinguished if discovered in time. However, this can only be accomplished if a knowledgeable person is available to use the equipment at hand. Such equipment must be of first quality and kept in proper operating condition at all times.

Security

Restaurant security is divided into two segments. One segment deals with protection against losses incurred through the acts of dishonest employees. The other part deals with dishonest acts by outsiders. The latter losses are classified as external; the other, as internal. Internal losses can be further broken down into direct and indirect.

Examples of direct, internal losses are the stealing of money, food, or liquor. Some indirect losses would be kickbacks, intentional overcharges, and falsification of work records.

Examples of external losses are:

1. Stealing of merchandise and furnishings by guests, outside company employees, or other persons.
2. Walking out on a meal or beverage check.
3. Presenting a bad check or credit card for payment of a bill.
4. Robbery, during or after operating hours.

Prevention of Internal Losses

Internal losses cannot go undetected if proper controls are utilized. Some losses may take longer to uncover, but they will show up. If control systems are faithfully adhered to, the crime will surface more quickly. Many times, however, control systems are instituted and not utilized, or they are maintained in such a careless and improper manner that they are almost useless.

Direct Losses. In Chapter Three a complete system for money handling was outlined. If the pre-check system is used properly, there can be no loss of cash without the knowledge of the owner. Once it is determined an employee has a habitual problem in this area, a warning or dismissal should follow. An immediate notation should be made on the employee's work record. Whether or not you prosecute will depend on the circumstances. Be careful of direct accusations, unless you have irrefutable proof.

Losses of food, liquor or other merchandise may take longer to detect than money losses. Unless you actually catch someone stealing an item, such losses will only come to light through suspicion. Such suspicions may come about from examinations of records or just a "feeling" something is amiss. Not until the records are carefully checked can you be sure. Even then, records can only verify a shortage, they cannot always tell you who is doing the stealing.

Inventories, if carefully taken and calculated, can be an enormous help in uncovering shortages. They act in the following ways:

1. An unusually high "usage" will show up immediately, indicating something abnormal. In most cases, heavy usage of a particular item will be quite legitimate and easily explained. When there does not seem to be an explanation, take action.

2. If no noticeable abnormality is perceived and the inventories are known to be correct, your cost percentages will be higher than normal. This, again, is a danger signal. Such a situation can only be the result of higher purchase costs (of which you should be aware), waste in preparation (perhaps, due to new personnel), or pilferage. The first two reasons will be readily apparent. If these are not the causes, then dishonesty probably is.

Here are a few of the ways dishonest employees can obtain your property:

1. Small items are placed beneath the person's clothes, in locations which can avoid detection. Very small items are simply placed in pockets or pocketbooks.

2. Items are placed in the trash hopper during working hours. After work, the employee salvages the loot and goes on his or her way.

3. Salable items are passed to friends and never charged for.

4. If an employee's car is parked nearby, it may not be too difficult for him to simply place an item in the car during working hours. Be suspicious of an employee who takes a lot of breaks during the day.

Employees sometimes work in pairs or groups. Such combinations can make detection more difficult.

Petty thievery is stealing by non-professionals. This type of person can be easily discouraged if you make it reasonably difficult for her or him to steal. The same methods will have little effect on the professional, who is interested in bigger things.

To make life more difficult for the petty thief:

1. Do not allow employees to bring packages into the work area. This way, there is no reason to bring one out.

2. Do not allow employees to take home dining room scraps or kitchen leftovers.

3. Keep all keys in your pocket or in a secure location.

4. Do not allow street clothes in the work area.

Indirect Losses. Indirect stealing differs from direct stealing in that money or merchandise is not obtained directly from the operation. Following are some illustrative cases:

An employee who falsifies his time by not recording the hours actually worked is obtaining money from you in an indirect manner.

An employee receiving kickbacks from a purveyor is obtaining compensation at your expense.

A service person purposely overcharging so he or she can pocket the difference is obtaining money using your good name.

Such practices can be eliminated through proper controls and constant, careful observation on your part.

Employees should never be allowed to record their own time. Someone in charge should do it. If you are large enough to afford a time clock, employees should be instructed not to ring anyone's time cards but their own.

If you suspect an employee is receiving kickbacks, do some investigating. Check the prices you are paying for certain items. Compare them with prices from other purveyors. If you find you are consistently paying higher prices, there is cause for concern. Check into the integrity of the dealer.

Kickbacks are unusual in a small restaurant, because the amount purchased is so small, the owner is almost always present, and the owner usually does the purchasing. As you grow in size and delegate more responsibility, kickbacks become more of a threat.

The most common areas for indirect thievery are in the dining room and bar. Again however, there can be no dishonesty in these areas if adequate controls are utilized. A two to three thousand dollar investment in electronic cash registers is all that is needed.

If you choose not to go electric, here are some of the more common schemes employees use:

1. By using duplicate, handwritten checks, a service person can present a higher priced check to the guest and a correctly priced check to the cashier. The guest pays the higher check (which is destroyed by the salesperson) while the waiter or waitress turns in the correctly priced check along with the proper amount of money. The difference is pocketed by the salesperson. A very difficult act to catch. Even more difficult, when the cashier and salesperson are working together. Such a practice can be accomplished with outside checks or the establishment's checks if the serial numbers are not kept track of.

2. A service person can write an incorrect, high price on the guest check, for any item. After the guest pays the check, the incorrect amount is erased and the correct amount inserted. The total is adjusted and the check is turned in for payment with the correct amount of money. This practice can be eliminated if erasures are not permitted. However, the checks must be examined after every meal.

3. Another time-proven method is the incorrect total. Some guest check forms do not use tinted paper in the area reserved for the total. Consequently, when a check is handwritten, a service person can make an "error" in addition (always on the high side) and later (after the guest pays), erase the error and write in the correct amount. The difference is then pocketed.

The above methods do not result in any direct loss to the restaurant owner. They are transactions between the service person and the guest. The guest loses and the service person gains. However, the ill will which can result if such acts are discovered by the guest will reflect on you and your restaurant.

Two other deceptions an employee may use are undercharges and freebies. Both hurt you directly.

Undercharges occur when the item is

incorrectly priced. This works most effectively when there is no written record of the price because then there is no way for the owner to determine if the item written on the check (by hand) is the same as the one served. Undercharges can occur as an honest mistake as well. This does not make them any less costly to you. Freebies are the ultimate undercharge. They are frequently found at the bar, as well as in the dining room. Without a control system, you will never catch them, unless you happen to be there when one takes place.

Finally, a tactic sometimes used is the selling of whiskey brought in by the bartender. The bottle is simply placed in with the restaurant stock and sold as such. The bartender can either keep a record of what is sold and reimburse him- or herself at the end of the evening or simply take the money for the entire bottle right away. Your liquor is never touched but you lose the sales money.

Unscrupulous employees can find any number of methods to capitalize on your ignorance, indifference, or neglect. Dishonesty among employees rates high among the reasons for restaurant failures. By spending extra money for an adequate control system and keeping your eyes open, you can increase your chances for success.

Most employees are honest, but you must still protect yourself from those who are not. Fortunately, the smaller the business, the less the opportunity for dishonesty.

Some other, less significant items, which in themselves are not large but can add up to sizeable expense if not regulated are:

Some restaurants allow their employees to borrow equipment, supplies, food, ice, etc., whenever they need it. This is a nice gesture, but often it is a privilege that is abused. The item may not be returned or it may be returned damaged.

For a small operator, this can be costly. The use of the telephone by employees should be restricted. Outgoing calls should only be allowed in an emergency. Toll calls should never be allowed without the owner's permission. Sometimes, when employees are not working, they will stop in to see a fellow employee or to just chat. This in itself should be discouraged because it is distracting to the working employee. However, the problem here is that many times they receive food and drinks without charge while on the premises. Another costly item.

Prevention of External Losses

External losses, those caused by persons other than employees, can be potentially more devastating than internal losses. Take, for instance, a burglary which happens at night, when no one is present; you can be virtually cleaned out by experienced thieves. It is necessary to protect yourself and your restaurant from such possibilities.

Protection from Burglary. Burglary, as spoken of here, is breaking into the premises, when no one is present, with the intent of stealing money and/or property.

Do not leave money on the premises at night. Deposit it in the night depository of your bank. It may take a few extra minutes each night, but it is worth it. Leave the cash drawers in the register open. This tells the thief there is nothing in them and saves damage to the register.

There is little you can do to protect furnishings and food, which are not locked up. Many local police departments provide a marking instrument that enables you to write an identifying number on valuable articles.

This is a deterrent when used in conjunction with window stickers advertising that such a system is being used.

Items which can be locked up should be locked with strong padlocks to make it very difficult for the thief to obtain your property. Use dead bolts, not ordinary snap locks, on all outside doors. Windows should have special locks. Ordinary latches are not sufficient. All the thief has to do is break the window and reach in to open or force the latch with a crowbar.

Leave some outside and inside lights on. Burglars do not like others see them work. Outside lights are most effective. Interior lights make it easier for the police patrol to look inside.

Small burglar alarm units may be attached to windows and doors. The one problem with these is that there may not be anyone around to hear them. Regardless, they will probably frighten the thief away.

An outside security firm can be employed. However, this is expensive for the small restaurateur.

Protection from Robbery. Robbery is stealing by violent means or by the threat of violence. The best advice is: do not resist. Your life is more valuable than the money. Do not argue with the thief. Observe as many details about the robber as possible, in order that a clear description can be given to the police. This may be difficult for you under such circumstances, but it will help the police apprehend the criminal.

Robberies are not a very common occurrence in restaurants. This is especially true during operating hours, because so many people are about.

Most robberies occur just after closing, when the money is being counted and few people are around. A few precautions which will help prevent a robbery are:

1. When the restaurant is nearly empty and ready to close, lock the doors. Always lock the doors once you are closed to new business.
2. Do not open the doors to anyone you do not know once you are locked up.
3. Do not count money where you can be observed through a window or door.
4. When leaving the building with the day's receipts, try to leave with at least one other person. This is especially important if you are walking to the bank. If driving, always check to see if you are being followed.
5. Have your key ready beforehand, when going to the night depository, so the money may be deposited as quickly as possible.

Walkouts. Walkouts in small restaurants are uncommon, due primarily to the limited number of tables each service person has. They can watch their guests more carefully. Walkouts are difficult to prevent because you do not expect them (small consolation, but true). Some restaurants absorb this loss, others, charge the salesperson.

Minimizing Bad Checks and Invalid Credit Cards. Checks can bounce if you do not get identification. Your main concern is verification that the person writing the check is the person who has the checking account. Always verify signatures and addresses.

When checks are returned to you because of insufficient funds, have the writer's bank attach the account of the defaulter. This assures you of payment, if and when enough money appears in the account to cover your check. If the amount is large enough, you may go to small claims court to recover it.

With all the safeguards built into the credit card procedure, there is no reason for losing money this way. Always check the signature on the card with the charge slip, the card's expiration date, and the delinquent card list. Call in, if the amount is over the maximum, or if you have any doubts whatever.

Guest pilferage. Ninety-nine percent (maybe more) of the people coming to your restaurant are not professional thieves. If any of them are, they are most likely coming to enjoy your fine food, not to steal from you. Guests sometimes "take" something on a whim or challenge but seldom is it done maliciously. Because food and liquor are usually guarded by the staff, the articles that disappear are usually the little knick-knacks or furnishings. It is next to impossible to guard against such stealing, short of nailing items down. Unless it is a serious problem, do not let it affect the way in which you furnish your restaurant. It may be judicious, nevertheless, not to have the more expensive decorations in too tempting a location.

Occasionally, someone's coat may disappear. In almost every case, it will be because someone took the wrong coat by mistake. If another coat of equal value is left, this is probably what happened. There may be times when a coat is actually stolen. If so, and you merely provided a coat rack, you are not responsible for reimbursing the guest as long as you have posted a sign saying, "not responsible. . . etc." If you provide a paid at-tendant to perform the function of caring for the garments, you are responsible for the loss.

Stealing by Outside Employees. Stealing by outside employees occurs when a delivery person helps her- or himself to your property. This situation can only be observed by careful scrutiny on the part of you or one of your employees. When it is discovered, it should be reported to the employee's company. If it is serious, you may want to report it to the police.

Vandalism. Because you never know when such acts will take place, there is not much you can do to protect the premises. Most acts of this nature occur after the restaurant is closed. Your best protection is outside lighting.

All the above losses can be covered by insurance. However, the more logical approach is prevention, whenever possible. Reimbursement from insurance only pays for replacement of the physical item, and not always completely. It does not take into account the inconvenience, embarrassment, emotional stress, and so forth, caused by the event.

Security is an important aspect of any operation. The losses outlined can happen to all operators, large or small. It is important for you to be familiar with the potential problems so you can deal with them when they appear.

Chapter Fourteen

Final Countdown

Even with careful attention to detail, there always seems to be something that is overlooked when a new operation is begun. Listed below are the items which are most frequently omitted or forgotten. Check this list a week or so before you are ready to open and again on opening day.

1. Does all the equipment function properly? Try each item a few times, to be sure. Check the kitchen oven, broiler, range top, exhaust fan, refrigeration, ice maker, etc. Check dining room equipment as well (e.g. coffee maker, coffee warmers). All plumbing fixtures and connections should be checked for leaks and malfunctions.

2. Is there an ample supply of hot water? Be sure the hot water heater works and is able to supply all the hot water that will be needed. This is especially important with electric heaters, because they have a slow recovery rate.

3. Has the fire extinguisher system over the cooking equipment been checked? Are there hand extinguishers where needed?

4. Do you have outside lighting? Is it on an automatic timer? If not, does someone know when to turn the lights on and off? Is your sign illuminated? It should be.

5. Is the telephone system installed and operating properly? Without it, it is impossible to receive reservations and inquiries. Does "Directory Assistance" have your telephone number listed?

6. Are the HVAC systems functioning properly? Do not wait until you need them to turn them on. Try them at least a week in advance of when they will be needed so there is time to get them repaired if need be.

7. If you have a parking lot, have the stripes been painted on the surface? Is it properly illuminated?

8. Have all final inspections been made? Do you have all the necessary permits to open (especially the one from the Health Department)?

9. If using a cash register system is the register working? Has everyone been trained to use it? Is there an adequate supply of guest checks, tapes, ribbons, etc.?

10. Have the kitchen detergents been purchased? Are the dispensers hooked up?

11. Have locks been installed in the new operation or changed in an existing one? Do *you* have all the keys? Are they on rings or just left laying around?

12. Are the windows washed?

13. Trash and garbage collector hired? Pickup days decided on?

14. Did all the things you ordered arrive? Check now. If you wait until the items are needed, it may be too late.

15. Are the menus and wine lists printed and on the premises?

16. Have glassware, chinaware, etc. been unpacked and washed?

17. Are the uniforms ready to go (altered, laundered, etc.)?

18. All the food is probably ordered for the menu, but did you remember the bread or rolls?

19. Are the liquor, soda, beer, and wine purchased? How about bar snacks (e.g. potato chips), have they been purchased? Do not forget containers to serve them in.

20. Is there a recipe book in the bar, along with the necessary utensils (knives, openers, cutting board, etc.)?

21. Are all the employees trained in their jobs? Have you checked to see if they all know when they are to arrive? Do this in ample time (a week or more before opening), so you will have time to look for replacements if some are needed.

22. Is there cash on hand for the petty cash fund?

23. Have you set up your accounts at the bank (both general and payroll)?

24. Are your credit sources established?

25. If using candles in the dining room and cocktail areas, are the candles and holders on the premises, ready to be used?

26. Are the restrooms furnished with soap, towels, toilet tissue, etc.?

27. Are ash trays available and placed in the proper locations? This item is frequently overlooked.

Index